The Complete CROCK POT COOKBOOK

FOR BEGINNERS AND ADVANCED USERS

ALEXA JACOB

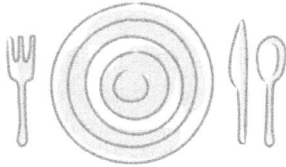

Copyright © 2020 by Alexa Jacob

All rights reserved. No part of this book may be reproduced in any form without permission in writing from the author

Disclaimer

No part of this works may be reproduced, distributed or transmitted in any form or by means, electronic or mechanical, including photocopying, recording or by any information storage and retrieval system express without written permissions from the author. This book is for motivating yourself. The views expressed are those of the author alone and should not be taken as expert instructions of commands. The reader is responsible for his or her own actions and decisions.

INTRODUCTION

Cooking time can sometimes be stressful for all of us. Busy schedules, cranky kids, and other challenges can test our patience when it comes to putting a good Recipes on the table. Well, I'm here to help you. I develop delicious recipes for homemade, family-friendly Crock pot Recipes, and in this book, I share my recipes with you.

In 2012, I was a stay-at-home mom with two small children. I'll never forget trying to make dinner with a kid (or two) hanging off my leg. I thought, "There has to be a better way!" Fortunately, I discovered the Crock Pot and fell in love with it.

The Crock Pot allowed me to get Recipes started in the middle of the morning while my kids were napping. In fact, I loved the freedom the Crock Pot slow cooker gave me so much that I decided to use it to cook dinner for 365 days straight and to write a blog to share the recipes with my readers. Writing the blog provided accountability, which helped me fulfill my goal, and I learned how to cook along the way! Now, many years later, my kids are involved in sports and other activities and they still keep me busy. They aren't hanging off my leg at five o'clock anymore, but they need me to drive them here and there or help with homework. Lucky for me, I still use the Crock Pot, and I love the support it provides to busy people. I truly appreciate how my family can eat when we're ready because the slow cooker is waiting for us on warm until we get home.

I've created over a thousand Crock Pot recipes over the past eight years. I have also discovered all sorts of handy tips and tricks for the Crock Pot that I will share with you in this book. I've also learned from my blog readers that they mostly want super simple and fast recipes they can get going in the morning.

I want to help you make delicious, highly nutritious food in the least amount of preparation time possible. I've kept my recipes short and sweet by limiting the primary ingredients to 5 items in each. Whether you are a working professional who is tired when you get home, a busy parent with a very hungry family, a college student who needs to study instead of cook, or an empty-nester working on your golf game, this book can help you. So let's get cooking!

CONTENTS

INTRODUCTION 3
WHAT IS A CROCK POT? 15
HOW DOES A CROCK POT WORK? 15
UNDERSTANDING YOUR CROCKPOT 15
BENEFITS OF USING A CROCKPOT 15
HOW TO USE THE CROCKPOT 16
TIPS AND TRICKS FOR USING THE CROCKPOT 16
SLOW COOKER OR CROCK-POT? 17
WHAT'S THE DIFFERENCE BETWEEN A CROCK POT AND A SLOW COOKER? 17
WHAT EACH FUNCTION MEANS 17
MEASUREMENT CONVERSION CHART 18

BREAKFAST RECIPES 21

1. Apple Granola Crumble 21
2. Banana and Coconut Milk Steel-Cut Oats 21
3. Coconut Cranberry Quinoa 21
4. Crockpot Breakfast Casserole 21
5. Grecian Egg Casserole 21
6. Spinach and Mozzarella Frittata 22
7. Frittata with Artichoke Hearts 22
8. Quinoa Energy Bars 22
9. Overnight Apple Oatmeal 22
10. Basic Overnight Quinoa and Oats 22
11. Crockpot Veggie Omelet 23
12. Enchilada Breakfast Casserole 23
13. White Chocolate Oatmeal 23
14. Bacon-Wrapped Hotdogs 23
15. Maple Brown Sugar Bacon 23
16. Scrambled Eggs in Ramekins 24
17. Bacon Hash Brown and Egg Casserole 24
18. Breakfast Sausage and Egg Casserole 24
19. Cheesy Bacon Hash Browns 24
20. Hodgepodge Omelet 24
21. Grandma's Apple Oatmeal 25
22. Chocolate Kid Friendly Oatmeal 25
23. Vanilla Blueberry Quinoa 25
24. Apple Orange Quinoa 25
25. Easy Yummy Breakfast Casserole 25
26. Restaurant Style Hash Browns 25
27. Creamy Coconut Oatmeal with Pumpkin Seeds 26
28. Vanilla Almond Steel Cut Oats 26
29. Yummy Winter Breakfast 26
30. Cheesy Hash brown Casserole 26
31. Thanksgiving Bacon Casserole 26
32. Amazing Spiced Omelette 27
33. Overnight Western Omelette 27
34. Vegetable and Ham Casserole 27
35. Creamy Oatmeal with Berries 28
36. Vegan Steel-Cut Oatmeal 28
37. Pumpkin Steel Cut Oats 28
38. Mouth Watering French Toast Casserole 28
39. Easy Sunday Beef Sandwiches 28
40. Lazy Man's Pizza 29
41. Chocolate French Toast with Honey and Bananas ... 29
42. Melt-In-Your-Mouth French Toast 29

43. Homemade Yogurt with Croissants 29
44. Cranberry Coconut Steel Cut Oatmeal 30
45. Overnight Oatmeal with Dried Fruits 30
46. Orange Poppy Seed Bread 30
47. Bacon and Veggie Quiche 30
48. Spiced Oatmeal with Nuts 31
49. Ham and Cheese Family Delight 31
50. Halloween Bread with Cranberries 31
51. Bread Pudding with Dried Figs 31
52. Spiced Apple Bread Pudding 32
53. Tater Tot Breakfast Casserole 32
54. Soft and Yummy Buttermilk Bread 32
55. Delicious Herb Bread 32
56. Cranberry-Raisin Bran Bread 32
57. Sloppy Joe-Style Burgers 33
58. Nutty Granola with Coconut Oil 33
59. Herbed Chili Cornbread 33
60. Caramel Flavoured Banana Bread 33
61. Pumpkin-Almond Bread 34
62. Cheesy Rosemary Bread 34
63. Vegetarian Sloppy Joes 34
64. Deluxe Beef Sandwiches 34
65. Best-ever Meat Sandwiches 34
66. BBQ Chicken Sandwiches 35
67. Saucy Pork Sandwiches 35
68. Summer Granola with Seeds 35
69. Easy-to-make Date Granola 35
70. Coconut Maple Granola 36
71. Pulled Pork Sandwiches 36
72. Winter Beef Sandwiches 36
73. Hearty Sausage Sandwiches 36
74. Country Smoked Sausages 36
75. Must-Eat Beef Tacos 37
76. Oatmeal with Prunes and Apricots 37
77. Muesli with Coconut and Peanuts 37
78. Cheese Steak Sandwiches 37
79. Beer Brats with Mushrooms and Onion 37
80. Yummy Sausage and Sauerkraut Sandwiches 38
81. Christmas Sausage Casserole 38
82. Overnight Sausage Casserole 38
83. Sunrise Pork Sandwiches 38
84. Beer Pulled Pork Sandwiches 39
85. Mom's Apple Crisp 39
86. Vegetarian Quinoa with Spinach 39
87. Easy Cheesy Quinoa with Veggies 39
88. Kale Frittata with Sausages 39
89. Delicious Weekend Frittata 40
90. Vegetarian Breakfast Delight 40
91. Protein Rich Bacon Frittata 40
92. Chili Mushroom Omelette 40
93. Banana Pecan Oatmeal 41
94. Hearty Oatmeal with Nuts 41
95. Tomato Artichoke Frittata 41
96. Sausage Mushroom Omelette Casserole 41
97. Pumpkin Pie Steel Cut Oats 41
98. Cocoa Steel Cut Oats 42
99. Nutty Pumpkin Oatmeal with Cranberries 42
100. Cocoa Oatmeal with Bananas 42
101. Cheese and Ham Quiche 42
102. Country Sausage and Cauliflower Breakfast 42
103. Broccoli Sausage Casserole 43
104. Winter Morning Sausage and Vegetables 43
105. Eggs Florentine with Oyster Mushroom 43
106. Cheese and Swiss chard Casserole 43
107. Nutty Banana Frittata 44
108. Yummy Spiced Pumpkin Frittata 44
109. Spiced Porridge for Busy Mornings 44
110. Family Mid-Winter Porridge 44
111. Amazing Apple Oatmeal with Prunes 45
112. Tropical Overnight Oatmeal 45
113. English Muffins with Tomato Topper 45
114. Southern Creamy Grits 45
115. Grandma's Grits with Parmesan cheese 45
116. Super Greens and Bacon Casserole 45
117. Delicious Wheat Berries 46
118. Multigrain Cereal Breakfast 46
119. Cereal with Fruit and Peanut Butter 46
120. Oatmeal with Fruits 46
121. Grandma's Rice Pudding 46
122. Orange Carrots with Nuts 47

123. Old-fashioned Fried Polenta ... 47
124. Famous Southwest Breakfast ... 47
125. Ham and Tater Tots Casserole ... 47
126. Beef and Potatoes Casserole ... 47
127. Pumpkin and Pecans Bread ... 48
128. Morning Butter Bread ... 48
129. Bread Pudding with Sauce ... 48
130. French Toast ... 48
131. Cheesy Eggs with Vegetables ... 48
132. Crockpot Spiced Omelet ... 49
133. Sunday Morning Risotto with Apples ... 49
134. Classic Banana Bread ... 49
135. Breakfast Fruit Casserole ... 49
136. Breakfast Vegetable Casserole ... 50
137. Creamy Vegetables and Cheese with Bread ... 50
138. Sunday Burger Sandwiches ... 50
139. The Best Chinese Pie Ever ... 50
140. Crispy Ham in Cola ... 50
141. Corn and Ham with Potatoes ... 51
142. Fruit and Cheese Breakfast ... 51
143. Beef Dip Sandwiches ... 51
144. Apple Cranberries Oats ... 51
145. Sausage Onion Pie ... 51
146. Sausage and Bacon Breakfast Casserole ... 52
147. Wake up Sausages and Squash Casserole ... 52
148. French-Italian Sandwiches ... 52
149. Hot Dogs with Chili Beans ... 52
150. Butternut Squash with Maple Syrup ... 53
151. Fruit Oatmeal with Almonds ... 53
152. Caramel and Nuts Biscuits ... 53
153. Eggs with Vegetables and Bacon ... 53
154. Wheat Berry with Apricots ... 53
155. Hot Dogs with Red Sauce ... 53
156. Cornmeal Pudding with Eggs ... 54
157. Oatmeal with Dates and Coconut ... 54
158. Crockpot Bread with Rosemary ... 54
159. Cheesy Spinach Quiche ... 54

MAIN MEAL RECIPES 55

160. Java Roast Beef ... 55
161. Garlic Apple Pork Roast ... 55
162. Crockpot Sweet Ham ... 55
163. Crockpot Carnitas Tacos ... 55
164. Pineapple Barbecue Pork Chops ... 55
165. Shredded Pork with Beans ... 56
166. Mexican Bubble Pizza ... 56
167. Tender Turkey Breasts ... 56
168. Crockpot Swiss Steak ... 56
169. Tex-Mex Beef ... 56
170. Maple Mustard Chicken ... 57
171. Brisket with Cranberry Gravy ... 57
172. Cherry Balsamic Pork Loin ... 57
173. Easy Chili Verde ... 57
174. Saucy Ranch Pork Chops ... 57
175. Barbecue Pulled Pork ... 58
176. Cranberry Pork Chops and Sweet Potatoes ... 58
177. Country Style Ribs ... 58
178. Carolina-Style BBQ Chicken ... 58
179. Slow Cooker Kalua Pig ... 58
180. Honey Baby Back Ribs ... 59
181. Pineapple Salsa Chicken ... 59
182. Simple Poached Salmon ... 59
183. Lemon Garlic Chicken ... 59
184. White Chicken Chili ... 59
185. Crockpot Italian Shredded Beef ... 59
186. Dr. Pepper Pulled Pork ... 60
187. Salsa Verde Chicken ... 60
188. Sweet and Spicy Cinnamon Meatballs ... 60
189. Easy BBQ Chicken and Cheese ... 60

LUNCH RECIPES 61

190. Spiced Turkey with Sauerkraut ... 61
191. Cranberry Turkey Breasts ... 61
192. Turkey with Onion-Garlic Sauce ... 61
193. Grandma's Cabbage with Beef ... 61
194. Delicious Beef Stroganoff ... 61
195. Country Corned Beef Brisket ... 62

196. Vegetable Pot Roast ... 62	236. Hot Chicken with Potatoes ... 70
197. Beef Roast with Root Vegetables ... 62	237. Chicken Paprikash with Noodles ... 70
198. Beef Steak with Mushroom Gravy ... 62	238. Orange Turkey Breasts ... 71
199. Juicy Pork with Apple Sauce ... 62	239. Teriyaki Chicken with Basmati Rice ... 71
200. Ham with Pineapple ... 63	240. Moist & Tender Chicken with Caramelized Onion ... 71
201. Cranberry Pork Roast with Sweet Potatoes ... 63	241. Curried Chicken with Almonds ... 71
202. Sausages with Sauerkraut and Beer ... 63	242. Amazing Chicken in Milk ... 72
203. Pork Steaks in Prune Sauce ... 63	243. Mom's Soft and Spicy Pork ... 72
204. Spicy Pork Roast with Vegetables ... 63	244. Asian-Style Pork ... 72
205. Country Pork Ribs with Ginger Sauce ... 64	245. Festive Glazed Pork ... 72
206. Pork Roast in Beer ... 64	246. Old-Fashioned Meatloaf ... 72
207. Piquant Chicken Chowder ... 64	247. Easy Zesty Meatloaf ... 72
208. Hot Chicken Chowder with Spinach ... 64	248. Poached Salmon with Onion ... 73
209. Shrimp Chowder with Avocado ... 64	249. Sunday Crab Supreme ... 73
210. Shrimp Chowder with Corn and Potato ... 65	250. Rich Tomato Shrimp Chowder ... 73
211. Saucy Pork Spare Ribs ... 65	251. Shrimp, Bean and Corn Chowder ... 73
212. Pork Ribs in Sweet Sauce ... 65	252. Summer Seafood Treat ... 74
213. Spicy Pork with Canadian Bacon ... 65	253. Lobster Chowder with Vegetables ... 74
214. Cream of Broccoli and Cauliflower Soup ... 65	254. Delicious Scallop and Potato Chowder ... 74
215. Family Broccoli-Spinach Soup ... 66	255. Italian-Style Seafood Chowder ... 74
216. Delicious Cream of Asparagus Soup ... 66	256. Salmon Chowder with Root Vegetables ... 75
217. Creamy Cauliflower Potato Chowder ... 66	257. Salmon with Corn and Roasted Pepper ... 75
218. Potato Cauliflower Bisque ... 66	258. Bermuda-Style Whitefish Chowder ... 75
219. Hot Cabbage Soup ... 67	259. Creamy Haddock Chowder ... 75
220. Sour Carrot Soup with Yogurt ... 67	260. Cod and Tomato Chowder ... 76
221. Dilled Celery Potato Soup ... 67	261. Cheesy Monkfish Chowder with Cauliflower ... 76
222. Cheesy Cream of Vegetable Soup ... 67	262. Hearty Flounder Chowder ... 76
223. Creamy Fennel Soup with Walnuts ... 68	263. Rich Seafood Soup with Bacon ... 76
224. Cream of Turnip Soup ... 68	264. Refreshing Fish Chowder with Eggs ... 77
225. Fragrant Garlic Soup with Bread ... 68	265. Spicy Sweet Potato Chili ... 77
226. Avocado and Potato Chowder ... 68	266. Chili with Turkey and Roasted Pepper ... 77
227. Cheesy Veggie Sausage Chowder ... 68	267. Black Bean Chili with Squash ... 77
228. Cold Weather Potato Chowder ... 69	268. Turkey and Cannellini Bean Chili ... 78
229. Hearty Bean Chowder ... 69	269. Easy Beef and Pork Chili ... 78
230. Great Northern Bean Soup ... 69	270. Italian-Style Chili ... 78
231. Potato Cauliflower Chowder ... 69	271. Family Favourite Chili ... 78
232. Mom's Chicken Chili ... 69	272. Easy Tenderloin Chili ... 79
233. Yummy Spicy Mushroom Chili ... 70	273. Yummy Tomato Bean Soup ... 79
234. Chicken and Potatoes with Gravy ... 70	274. Lamb Chili with Ham ... 79
235. Cheesy Saucy Chicken and Veggies ... 70	275. Creamy Vegetable Soup ... 79

276. Fall Brussels sprouts Soup ... 79
277. Vegetarian Creamed Corn Soup ... 80
278. Rich Potato Pistou Soup ... 80
279. Refreshing Roasted Red Pepper Soup ... 80
280. Old-Fashioned Beef Stew ... 80
281. Tangy Cucumber Soup ... 81
282. Easy Yummy Beef Stew ... 81
283. Hearty Chicken Stew ... 81
284. Sausage and Turkey Stew ... 81
285. Turkey and Kidney Bean Stew ... 82
286. Cod and Shrimp Stew ... 82
287. Summer Spiced Fish Stew ... 82
288. Soft and Creamy Chicken Breasts ... 82
289. Spiced Chicken with Couscous ... 83
290. Artichokes with Herbs and Lemon ... 83
291. Pork Chops with Squash in Sauce ... 83
292. Smokey Ground Beef and Beans ... 83
293. Crockpot Style Barbecue ... 83
294. Two-Bean and Beef Chili ... 84
295. Soft Beef with Bratwurst and Mushrooms ... 84
296. Easy Roast with Gravy ... 84
297. Vegetarian Split Pea Soup ... 84
298. Roast with Dill and Sour Cream ... 85
299. Mushrooms with Sour Cream ... 85
300. Vegetable Stew with Beans ... 85
301. Chip Beef Onion Soup ... 85
302. Pork Stew with Sweet Potatoes ... 85
303. Beans with White Bacon ... 86
304. Green Beans with Bacon ... 86
305. Bean and Kale Soup with Ham ... 86
306. Winter Beef Stew ... 86
307. Thick Potato Soup ... 86
308. Old-Fashioned Vegetable Soup ... 87
309. Vegetable Beef Soup ... 87
310. Chicken with Vegetables and Noodles ... 87
311. Beef and Rice Casserole ... 87
312. Chicken, Corn and Bean Chili ... 87
313. Soft Meat in Chili Sauce ... 88
314. Fluffy Vegetarian Pilaf ... 88
315. Veggie Chili with Almonds ... 88
316. Stuffed Peppers in Red Sauce ... 88
317. Turkey Breast with Bacon and Herbs ... 88
318. Thick Beef Stew with Kale ... 89
319. Tortilla Vegetable Soup ... 89
320. Tortilla Chili Pie ... 89
321. Tex-Mex Pork with Onions and Guacamole ... 89
322. Family Goulash with Macaroni ... 90
323. Soft Teriyaki Chicken ... 90
324. Teriyaki Pork Chops ... 90
325. Pork Chops and Squash with Rice ... 90
326. Swiss Steak with Potatoes ... 90
327. Creamy Chicken with Swiss Cheese ... 91
328. Old-Fashioned Roast ... 91
329. Pork in Sweet and Sour Sauce ... 91
330. Holiday Turkey Stew ... 91
331. Soup with Vegetables and Sausages ... 91
332. Creamy Cheesy Spinach with Herbs ... 92
333. Smoky Baby Potatoes in Sauce ... 92
334. Quick and Easy Spaghetti ... 92
335. Spaghetti Bolognese Authentic Recipe ... 92
336. Easy Salsa Chicken ... 92
337. Beef and Bacon Gravy with Noodles ... 93
338. Vegetarian Stew for All Seasons ... 93
339. Vegan Wheat Berry and Lentil Stew ... 93

DINNER RECIPES 93

340. Pork Shoulder with Noodles ... 93
341. Teriyaki Pork with Tortillas ... 94
342. Pork Chops with Creamy Sauce ... 94
343. Pork Chops with Apricot and Hoisin Sauce ... 94
344. Pork Chops with Honey and Mustard ... 94
345. Smoked Pork with Prunes ... 95
346. Sweet Orange Smoked Ham ... 95
347. Sherry Chicken with Mashed Potatoes ... 95
348. Kicked Up Chicken with Zucchini ... 95
349. Festive Cornish Hens ... 95
350. Salmon with Caper Sauce ... 96
351. Herbed Salmon Loaf with Sauce ... 96
352. Lazy Man Mac and Cheese ... 96
353. Mediterranean Chicken with Zucchini ... 96

354. Mediterranean Stuffed Spaghetti Squash 97
355. Everyday Tomato Casserole 97
356. Four Cheese Macaroni Casserole 97
357. Creamy Vegetable Noodle Casserole 97
358. Old-Fashioned Pasta Bolognese 97
359. Apple with Brats and Sauerkraut 98
360. Tender Chicken with Vegetables 98
361. Spiced Glazed Ham 98
362. Turkey Breasts with Pineapple 98
363. Pork Chops in Cherry Sauce 98
364. Chicken in Sweet and Spiced Sauce 99
365. Marinated Pork Roast with Pineapple 99
366. Chicken Sandwiches with Mushrooms 99
367. Pork Pockets Stuffed with Corn 99
368. Lasagna with Vegetable and Cheese 100
369. Ham Hocks with Kale 100
370. Chicken Drumsticks in Sweet and Sour Sauce 100
371. Family Red Chili 100
372. Turkey Chili with Kale 100
373. Piquant Chicken Sausage Chili 101
374. Pepperoni Hot Chili 101
375. Spaghetti with Beans and Asparagus 101
376. Easy Spicy Green Beans 101
377. Favorite Creamy Green Beans 102
378. Steak Roll Ups with Mushrooms 102
379. Favorite Hot Rouladen 102
380. Juicy Beef Short Ribs 102
381. Easy Italian-Style Meatloaf 102
382. Cheesy Everyday Meatloaf 103
383. Curried Peanut Meat Loaf 103
384. Mom's Spiced Mashed Beans 103
385. Kicked Up Cajun Jambalaya 103
386. Tangy Pork Roast 104
387. Hearty Stuffed Cabbage Leaves 104
388. Milk Braised Pork Loin 104
389. Mashed Potatoes with Carrots 104
390. Holiday Cooked Ham 104
391. Family Favourite Apple Butter 105
392. Italian-style Chicken with Broccoli 105
393. Chicken and Ham in Cheese-Tomato Sauce 105

394. Chicken Thighs with Sweet Potatoes 105
395. Korean Chicken with Potatoes 105
396. Beef Roast and Potatoes in Creamy Sauce 106
397. Meat and Beans Casserole 106
398. Spare Ribs in Spiced Sauce 106
399. Chicken Sandwiches with BBQ Sauce 106
400. Sandwiches with Ham and Pineapple Sauce 107
401. Summer BBQ Pork Ribs 107
402. Chicken Sandwiches with Root Beer Sauce 107
403. Saucy Chicken in Pretzel Buns 107
404. Smokey Beef Tacos 107
405. Saucy Sausages with Vegetables 108
406. Saucy Chicken Thighs with Vegetables 108
407. Bean and Quinoa Chili 108
408. Thai Chicken and Vegetables with Rice 108
409. Smoky Black Beans with Sausages 109
410. Easy and Light Veggies with Noodles 109
411. Saucy Beef with Mushrooms 109
412. Curried Pork with Apples and Onions 109
413. Old-Fashioned Macaroni and Cheese 109
414. Glazed Pork Roast 109
415. Bread with Raisins and Almonds 110
416. Baked Ham with Wine 110
417. Banana Almond Bread 110
418. Juicy BBQ Chicken 110
419. Meatballs in Spiced Sauce 110
420. Barley with Mushrooms 111
421. Mexican Traditional Enchiladas 111
422. Stuffed Chicken Breasts 111
423. Pasta with Tomato Sauce 111
424. Farfalle with Mushroom Sauce 111
425. Northern Italian Risi Bisi 112
426. Pecorino and Green Pea Risotto 112
427. Risotto with Zucchini and Yellow Squash 112
428. Egg Pie with Mushrooms 112
429. Aromatic Apple Risotto 112
430. Delicious Savory Soufflé 113
431. Spaghetti with Asparagus and Beans 113
432. Easy Yummy Green Beans 113
433. Vegan Mediterranean Treat 113

434. Hot Baked Beans	113
435. Baked and Herbed Cannellini Beans	114
436. Delicious Sweet-Spiced Beans	114
437. Easy Honey Beets with Raisins	114
438. Glazed Brussels Sprouts with Pearl Onions	114
439. Herbed Potato-Carrot Purée	115
440. Winter Cabbage with Bacon	115
441. Vegetarian Creamed Cabbage	115
442. Amazing Orange-Glazed Carrots	115
443. Mediterranean Creamy Cabbage	115
444. Orange-Glazed Sweet Potatoes	116
445. Delicious Family Corn Flan	116
446. Spicy Corn Pudding	116
447. Pork Shoulder with Hot Sauce	116
448. Leek and Garlic Custard	116
449. Stuffed Vidalia Onions	117
450. Fruit and Nut Candied Yams	117
451. Maple Honey Ribs	117
452. Yam Loaf for Winter Holidays	117
453. Squash and Sweet Potato Pudding	118
454. Rich and Creamy Potato Gratin	118
455. Creamy Potatoes with Smoked Ham	118
456. Creamed Root Vegetables	118
457. Mushroom and Zucchini Soufflé	118
458. Cheesy Spinach and Noodle Delight	119
459. Savory Bread Pudding	119
460. Corn and Potatoes with Shrimp	119
461. Rich and Healthy Summer Paella	119
462. Rabbit in Coconut Sauce	120
463. Vegetarian Potato and Eggplant Moussaka	120
464. Curried Chicken Thighs with Potatoes	120
465. Yummy Evening Pear Clafoutis	120
466. Evening Risotto with Apples	121
467. Cheese and Bread Casserole	121
468. French-Style Sandwiches	121
469. Bratwurst and Sauerkraut Pitas	121
470. Romantic Winter Dinner	122
471. Hot Pita Sandwiches	122
472. Turkey and Bacon Sandwiches	122
473. Kicked Up Pears with Cheese	122
474. Oatmeal with Veggies and Cheese	122
475. Creamy Polenta with Roasted Pepper	123
476. Garlicky Polenta with Yellow Onion	123
477. Rice Torta with Spinach and Cheese	123
478. Saucy Spicy Vegetables	123
479. Healthy Artichokes with Lemon Sauce	123

FAST SNACKS RECIPES 124

480. Party-Pleasing Fondue	124
481. Red Currant Jelly Meatballs	124
482. Jalapeño Corn and Cheese Dip	124
483. Saucy Tomato Meatballs	124
484. Turkey Meatballs with Paprika Sauce	125
485. Beer-Braised Meatballs	125
486. Saucy Cocktail Franks	125
487. Best Cocktail Sausages	125
488. Yummy Cereal Snack Mix	125
489. Easy Smoked Pecans	126
490. Easy Summer Snack	126
491. Cajun Nut Mix	126
492. Spiced Party Pecans	126
493. Cinnamon Vanilla Walnuts	126
494. Curried Mixed Nuts	126
495. Chili Honey Snack Mix	127
496. Easy Velveeta Dipping Sauce	127
497. Mexican-Style Appetizer	127
498. Old-Fashion Chicken Liver Pâté	127
499. Smoked Salmon Pâté	127
500. Vegetarian Lentil Pâté	127
501. Appetizer Meatballs with Barbecue Sauce	128
502. Hot Pineapple Chutney	128
503. Black Bean Dipping Sauce	128
504. Hot Corn Bean Dip	128
505. Vegetable-Rich Dipping Sauce	128
506. Eggplant Dip with Tahini and Cheese	129
507. Seafood Artichoke Dip	129
508. Delicious Cashew Snacks	129
509. Curried Honey Cashews	129
510. Party Pepper Almonds	129
511. Curried Party Mix	130

512. Spiced Soy Nuts and Pumpkin Seeds 130	552. Cheesy Crab Dipping Sauce 137
513. Crunchy Colourful Mix 130	553. Pepperoni Cheese Dip 138
514. Indian-Style Dipping Sauce 130	554. Rich-Tasting Prosciutto Spread 138
515. Party Favorite Artichoke Dip 130	555. Best Cocktail Meatballs 138
516. Artichoke Spinach Dip 131	556. Saucy Meat Appetizer 138
517. Cheese Pepperoni Dip 131	557. Chicken Pita Bites 138
518. Cereal Mix with Peanuts 131	558. Juicy Orange Chicken Wings 139
519. Crispy Hot Chicken Taquitos 131	559. Zesty Chicken Drumettes 139
520. Mom's Cocktail Party Mix 131	560. Kielbasa Bites with Tomato-Mustard Sauce 139
521. Candied Cashews and Walnuts 132	561. Amazing Country Bites 139
522. Sugar-Glazed Pine Nuts and Pecans 132	562. Sweet Hot Bites 139
523. Granola and Fruit Mix 132	563. Tangy Smoked Sausage 140
524. Kicked-Up Hot Party Mix 132	564. Cheesy Sausage Snack with Mini Pitas 140
525. Cereal and Nut Snack Mix 133	565. Tomato-Pepper Sausage Dip 140
526. Summer Pizza Dipping Sauce 133	566. Party Smoked Sausage Bites 140
527. Italian Style Cheese Dip 133	567. Summer Zesty Party Bites 140
528. Sauerkraut Beef Dip 133	568. Appetizer Saucy Franks 141
529. Warm Dried Beef Dip 133	569. Kielbasa Chipotle Dipping Sauce 141
530. Roasted Pepper and Garlic Dip 133	570. Hot and Tangy Appetizer Meatballs 141
531. Hot Cheese Bean Dip 134	571. Favorite Party Queso 141
532. Yummy Chili Dipping sauce 134	572. Yummy Super Bowl Dip 141
533. Three-Cheese Bean Appetizer 134	573. Mom's Crowd-Pleasing Dip 142
534. Mexican Queso Fundido 134	574. Yummy Game-Day Dip 142
535. Easy Seafood Dipping Sauce 134	575. Cheesy Artichoke Dip and Crackers 142
536. Delicious Salmon Dipping Sauce 134	576. Spiced Bacon Dip 142
537. Romantic Cheese Fondue 135	577. Apple Brown Betty 142
538. Honey Party Wings 135	578. Spiced Baked Apples 142
539. Pecans with Syrupy Coating 135	579. Saucy Cocktail Meatballs 143
540. Grandma's Blackberry Compote 135	580. Party Barbecued Meatballs 143
541. Favorite Pear Butter 135	581. Cheesy Party Dip 143
542. Hummus with Carrot Sticks 136	582. Easy Peanuts Snacks 143
543. Traditional Middle Eastern Spread 136	583. Chex Mix Snacks 143
544. Cream Cheese Vegetable Spread 136	584. Candied Cashews 144
545. Strawberry Fruit Dipping Sauce 136	585. Chicken Spread with Pita Bread 144
546. Sun-Dried Tomato Dip 136	586. Peanut Clusters 144
547. Squid and Scallop Dip 136	587. Veggie Sticks with Cheesy Bean Dip 144
548. Mediterranean Seafood Treat 137	588. Golden Stuffed Apples 144
549. Spiced Date Spread 137	589. Sweet and Sour Tofu Cubes 145
550. Amazing Autumn Spread 137	590. Easy Mini English Muffins 145
551. Nutty Beef Dipping Sauce 137	591. Onion Dip with Potato Chips 145

592. Tortilla Chips with Chili Cheese Dip 145
593. Chicken and Cheese Dip 145
594. Cheesy Spinach and Artichoke Dip 146
595. Beef and Bean Salsa Dip 146
596. Mushrooms Go-To Appetizer 146
597. Party Chicken and Yogurt Dip 146
598. Spiced Sweet Potatoes 146
599. Cereals and Nuts Mix 147
600. Bacon Wrapped Hot Dogs 147
601. Barbecued Pork Appetizer 147
602. Spiced Pecans for Movie Night 147
603. Easy Meatballs Appetizer 147
604. Crockpot Fondue with Bread Sticks 147
605. Cocktail Sausages in Mustard Sauce 148
606. Mini Chicken Sandwiches with Spicy Sauce 148
607. Pepper and Cheese Fondue 148
608. Italian Mushrooms Fondue 148
609. Orange Glazed Meatballs 148
610. Family Pork Sliders 148
611. BBQ Chicken Wings 149
612. Party Sticky Wings 149
613. Sausage Bites with Onion Sauce 149
614. Spiced Little Smokies 149
615. Sun-Dried Tomato Dip 149
616. Ground Meat and Olive Queso Dip 150
617. Mushroom Appetizer with Beer Sauce 150
618. Herbed Saucy Mushroom Appetizer 150

APPETIZER RECIPES   150

619. Cajun Spiced Pecans 150
620. Crockpot Asian Glazed Meatballs 150
621. Teriyaki Chicken Wings 151
622. Chili Cheese Taco Dip 151
623. Cocktail Kielbasa with Mustard Sauce 151
624. Chicken Enchilada Dip 151
625. Sweet and Spicy Mushrooms 151
626. Beer-Braised Chicken 152
627. Apricot Barbecue Wings 152
628. Sweet and Hot Nuts 152

SOUP RECIPES   152

629. Tomato Hamburger Soup 152
630. Home-Style Stew 153
631. Green Lentil Curry Stew 153
632. Creamy Cauliflower Soup 153
633. Crockpot Lazy Posole 153
634. Spicy Poblano And Corn Soup 153
635. Corn and Bacon Chowder 154
636. Sweet Potato, Leek, And Ham Soup 154
637. Southwest Chicken with White Bean Soup 154
638. Chicken Cabbage Soup 154

PASTA AND RICE RECIPES   154

639. Crockpot Cheddar Spirals 155
640. Easy Crockpot Two-Cheese Lasagna 155
641. One Pot Pasta with Chicken and Cheese ... 155
642. Chicken Alfredo Pasta 155
643. Chicken Spinach Pasta 155
644. Crockpot Cheesy Pesto Pasta 156
645. Chicken Parm Pasta 156
646. Butternut Squash and Chickpea Pasta 156
647. Butter Chicken Pasta 156
648. Cheesy Chicken Spaghetti 156

DESSERTS RECIPES   157

649. Slow Cooker Fruit Cobbler 157
650. Crockpot Banana Foster 157
651. Crockpot Rice Pudding 157
652. Warm Berry Compote 157
653. Crockpot Custard Dulce De Leche 157
654. Crockpot Peach Cobbler 158
655. Crockpot Applesauce 158
656. Crockpot Crème Brulee 158
657. Savory Sausages and Brussels Sprout Breakfast 158
658. Tropicana Coconut Cake 158

659. Super Keto Lemon Bars 159	699. Apricot Cobbler with Ice Cream 167
660. Chocolate Coated Nut Candies 159	700. Chocolate Raisin-Peanut Candy 168
661. Almond Fudge Brownies 159	701. Coconut Chocolate Brownies 168
662. Warm Collard greens and Kalamata Olive Salad 159	702. Kicked up Lemon Cake 168
663. Mediterranean Egg Muffins 159	703. Old-Fashioned Butterscotch Caramel Sauce 168
664. Crunchy Green Beans and Carrots Strips 160	704. Hot Chocolate Fondue 168
665. Creamed Spinach Puree with Parmesan 160	705. Amazing Coconut Rice Pudding 169
666. "Kapamas" Cauliflower 160	706. Rice Pudding with Whipped Cream 169
667. Savory Spinach and Bacon Chowder 160	707. Pudding with Cranberries and Bananas 169
668. Rabbit with Chorizo and Cinnamon 160	708. Rice Pudding with Candied Fruit 169
669. Creamy Lamb with Artichokes 161	709. Aromatic Pears and Apples 169
670. Crockpot Cinnamon Almonds 161	710. Berry Dump Cake with Ice Cream 170
671. Bread Pudding with Figs and Cherries 161	711. Ooey Gooey Chocolate Cake 170
672. Bread Pudding with Pecans and Fruits 161	712. Halloween Caramel Apples 170
673. Summer Peach Treat 161	713. Baker Days Zucchini Cake 170
674. Banana Butter Cake with Coconut and Almonds 162	714. Cocoa Cake with Coffee Glaze 170
675. Country Apple Cake with Walnuts 162	715. Sinfully Delicious Mocha Mousse Cake 171
676. Date Pudding Cake 162	716. Orange-Glazed Chocolate Cake 171
677. Grandma's Orange Coffee Cake 163	717. Chocolate Almond Pound Cake 171
678. Old-Fashioned Cheese Cake 163	718. Orange Rice Pudding with Raisins 172
679. Favorite Winter Compote 163	719. Peach Hazelnut Cobbler 172
680. Everyday Dried Fruit Compote 163	720. Amazing Fudge Pudding Cake 172
681. Carrot Cake with Hazelnuts and Golden Raisins 163	721. Warm Pudding-Style Cake 172
682. Ginger and Walnut Sponge Cake 164	722. Pear and Apple Oatmeal Pudding 172
683. Winter Gingerbread Cake 164	723. Rice Pudding with Prunes and Pistachios 173
684. Applesauce Genoise with Buttery Glaze 164	724. Pudding with Dried Cherries and Walnuts 173
685. Easy Chocolate Peanut Butter Cake 165	725. Easiest Tapioca Pudding 173
686. Delicious Apple Streusel Dessert 165	726. Spiced Challah Pudding 173
687. Holiday Pumpkin Pie Pudding 165	727. Luscious Chocolate Bread Pudding 173
688. Cocoa Cake with Vanilla Ice Cream 165	728. Pudding with Raisins and Walnuts 174
689. Easy Everyday Cherry Pie 166	729. Favourite Apple Brown Betty 174
690. Chocolate Candy with Almonds and Pecans 166	730. Easiest Orange-Vanilla Custard 174
691. Apple Sauce with Pecans 166	731. Apple-Carrot Pudding Cake 174
692. Family Apple Oatmeal Delight 166	732. Triple-Chocolate Pudding Cake 174
693. Bananas Foster with Vanilla Ice Cream 166	733. New York-Style Latte Cheesecake 175
694. Spiced Apples with Currants 166	734. Chocolate Pecan Cheesecake 175
695. Apple Walnut Cobbler 167	735. Cosy Winter Morning Apple Pudding 175
696. Cherry Cobbler with Custard 167	736. Orange Tapioca Pudding 175
697. Summer Peach Cake 167	737. Peanut Butter Pudding Cake 176
698. Country Honey-Sauced Pears 167	738. Rum Bananas Foster with Pecans 176

- 739. Coconut Bananas Foster ... 176
- 740. Amazing Rice Pudding with Cherries ... 176
- 741. White Chocolate and Strawberry Pie ... 177
- 742. Baked Stuffed Apples with Currants ... 177
- 743. Halloween Party Pie Pudding ... 177
- 744. Hot Blackberry Peach Cobbler ... 177
- 745. Vanilla Strawberry Cobbler ... 177
- 746. Winter Aromatic Fruit Compote ... 178
- 747. Brownies with Hazelnut Ice Cream ... 178
- 748. Easiest Banana Bread with Almonds ... 178
- 749. Sinfully Delicious Cherry Pear Compote ... 178
- 750. Apple and Almond Sweet Delight ... 178
- 751. Pear Homey Crumble ... 179
- 752. Vanilla-Orange Poached Pears ... 179
- 753. Apricot-Peach Crisp with Walnuts ... 179
- 754. Old-Fashioned Apple Butter ... 179
- 755. Ice Cream with Drunken Figs ... 179
- 756. Cocktail Party Prunes in Brandy ... 180
- 757. Vanilla Ice Cream with Steamy Fruit ... 180
- 758. Delicious Father's Day Dessert ... 180
- 759. Summer Fruit Treat ... 180
- 760. Bananas and Rhubarb in Aromatic Sauce ... 180
- 761. Spiced Caramel Popcorn ... 181
- 762. Chocolate and Sweet Potato Cake ... 181
- 763. Soft and Fudgy Chocolate-Coconut Cake ... 181
- 764. Avocado Cake with Dried Fruits ... 181
- 765. Apple-Lemon Pound Cake ... 181
- 766. Favorite Lemony Cheesecake ... 182
- 767. Apple and Coconut Crisp ... 182
- 768. Apple Compote with Cranberries ... 182
- 769. Apple Pudding with Dates ... 182
- 770. Fruit and Nuts Cheesecake ... 183
- 771. Candied Bananas with Coconut ... 183
- 772. Caramel and Nuts Cake ... 183
- 773. Caramel Rum Fondue ... 183
- 774. Old-fashioned Rice Pudding ... 183
- 775. Caramel Apples ... 184
- 776. Apple Dessert with Ice Cream ... 184
- 777. Homemade Apple Butter ... 184
- 778. Bread Pudding with Dates ... 184
- 779. Caramel Apples with Ice Cream ... 184
- 780. Easy Strawberry Cobbler ... 184
- 781. Creamy Lemon Cake ... 185
- 782. Tea Time Peach Butter ... 185
- 783. Cocoa Pudding Cake with Cream ... 185
- 784. Pumpkin Pie Pudding ... 185
- 785. Crock Pot Chocolate Treats ... 185
- 786. Crock Pot Peach Treats ... 186
- 787. Triple Chocolate Dessert ... 186
- 788. Cinnamon Raisin Biscuit ... 186
- 789. Mashed Peach Dessert ... 186
- 790. Blueberry Dump Cake ... 186
- 791. Creamy Caramel Pie ... 186
- 792. Rice Pudding With Coconut ... 187
- 793. Chocolate Cookies with Almonds ... 187
- 794. Rhubarb with Ginger and Orange ... 187
- 795. Chocolate Cake with Dried Fruits ... 187
- 796. Spiced Pears in Wine ... 187
- 797. Chocolate and Peach Bread Pudding ... 188
- 798. Rice Pudding with Raspberries ... 188
- 799. Rice Pudding with Blueberries and Almonds ... 188
- 800. Pears with Bittersweet Chocolate Syrup ... 188

WHAT IS A CROCK POT?

Crock-Pot is the original designer and manufacturer of the slow cooker – offering three types of slow cooker, each boasting their own unique features and benefits. Discover your skills and talents in the kitchen with our exceptional products at your side, and produce restaurant-quality meals for your friends and family with ease. Enhance the taste and texture of simple, low-cost ingredients with slow cooking, letting the flavors marry together over a matter of hours, without the need for stirring.

In today's world, time is of the essence. Emphasis is on things being done instantly and this includes our food. But crock pot takes the opposite approach. Instead of zapping the food like a microwave or squishing it together like a pressure cooker, the crock pot lets the food simmer for 4- 14 times longer than it would normally take. In short, a crock pot is the reverse of a pressure cooker.

Crock pot has a long and colorful history. Originally made out of clay and stone in prehistoric times and heated on the hearth, the crock pot was an invaluable tool for women who had to juggle a dozen domestic responsibilities at any given moment. It allowed food to be cooked with very low chance of burning. We use almost identical shapes and sizes as those crock pots of the old, except with modern materials and using electricity.

How does a Crock pot work?

After putting the food in, you pour some liquid (stock, wine, water) into the crock pot and turn it on. The crock pot will heat up to 80-90 °C, heating the liquid so it becomes steam, but not the super- heated kind like in pressure cookers. The steam will circulate inside the crock pot, evenly spreading heat over the food. After cooking for several hours (possibly longer if you used lower settings), the food is ready. Crock pots generally have a temperature probe inside, which determines when the food is cooked and automatically lowers the temperature to keep the food warm.

Understanding Your Crockpot

Also called a slow cooker, a crockpot is a countertop kitchen appliance that allows you to cook food at temperatures lower than the boiling point. As a result, the food is cooked longer so you can prepare food a few hours before you are ready to eat your meals.

Crockpots are not only used to make soups and stews but literally all types of foods including your favorite desserts. The crockpot has a heavy bottom made from a thick material with a heating element that cooks food at a temperature that ranges between 710C and 740C.

Benefits of Using a Crockpot

Crockpots are becoming very popular as more and more people want to take charge of their health and still eat healthy meals. But aside from convenience, there are so many benefits why you ought to use a crockpot when cooking food. Below are the benefits of why you ought to use a crockpot.

Cooks cheaper cuts of meat better than ordinary pots:

Meats that are cheaper cuts come with hard connective tissues. Although they create tastier dishes, they are tough to cook on the stovetop. But if you have a crockpot, cheaper meat cuts are cooked longer thus this method of cooking can bring out the best flavor of tougher meat cuts.

Consume less electricity:

A crockpot consumes less energy than stovetop cookers, so you can save more on your utility bills for a longer period of time.

Food does not burn:

The low-temperature setting that the food is cooked makes it safer to cook your food without the fear of burning it.

How to Use the Crockpot

Using a crockpot does not involve rocket science. In fact, it is so easy to use it that you can't go wrong with this kitchen device. Below are nifty tips on how to use the crockpot.

Fill the crockpot with ½ liquid. Using too much liquid requires a longer time to heat up the food thus you may need another hour or two to cook your food.

Place meat and root vegetable at the bottom of the pot as the food is submerged in the hot liquid. This will also allow the meat to soak up on the juices thus making it more delicious.

Trim off excess skin when cooking as this will cook the food quickly and might create smoke especially if the liquid used is too littles

The lid of the crockpot is made of glass so there is no need to lift the lid to check the food constantly. The thing is that whenever you lift the lid, you lose heat to cook your food and you may need to extend the cooking time to another half an hour.

Tips and Tricks for Using the Crockpot

The thing is that you can cook different types of food in a crockpot. But if you want to make delicious meals using your crockpot just like the pro, there are some tips and tricks that you need to take note of. Below are the things that you need to know when using a crockpot.

As much as possible, cook the meat in the skillet first to add that smoky flavor to it. But make sure that you drain some of the fats before cooking.

Add tender vegetables during the last minutes of the cooking time so that they do not get overcooked.

If the cooking time is long, add the dairy products like milk and cream last. Overcooking them often results in curdling.

When cooking seafood such as shrimps or squid, add them last because they might take on a rubbery texture.

SLOW COOKER OR CROCK-POT?

The term slow cooker is the generic name for an appliance that uses heating elements all around the insert, which bring food up to safe temperatures. Crock-Pot is the Rival corporation's registered trademark for its slow cookers. All Crock-Pots are slow cookers, but not all slow cookers are Crock-Pots. Other popular slow cooker brands include All-Clad, Cuisinart, and Hamilton Beach.

When you're shopping for a slow cooker, please keep in mind that there are appliances on the market referred to as slow cookers that have their heating element only on the bottom. Don't buy one of these to use for the recipes in this book. Appliances with heating elements only on the bottom heat food more slowly than those with heating elements all around the insert. Experts do not recommend cooking large cuts of meat in this type of slow cooker (although it works for soups and stews). So when purchasing your slow cooker, please make sure it is a true one with heating elements all around the insert.

What's the difference between a crock pot and a slow Cooker?

Crock pot is a subtype of slow cooker. On the outside, both crock pot and slow cookers look the same: heating segment, lid and pot. Crock pot was initially specialized for cooking beans, but over time it evolved into crock pot of today that can handle plenty of recipes. Originally being a brand name, crock pot eventually became a generic name for any kind of slow cooker. To be exact, crock pot today refers to any kind of slow cooker that has a ceramic pot inside the heating unit.

Both crock pot and slow cooker share a lot of similarities in design, such as being able to hold food in an airtight fashion inside the pot.

WHAT EACH FUNCTION MEANS

Crock Pot Express Pressure Cooker comes with a very comprehensive front that has display and functions you need to select before the cooker starts cooking your meal. Before you continue reading the recipes in this cookbook, it would be quite useful to learn what each function means.

- ↑ **Brown/Sauté** If you select this function, you will be able to cook your meal without the protective lid on the cooker. By pressing this function twice you have set the browning function; by pressing sauté and function and adjusting the button twice your cooker is ready for simmering.
- ↑ Keep the food **Warm/Cancel** – If you select this function you can cancel the previously selected function or simply turn off your Crock Pot Express.
- ↑ **Meat/Stew** – As the name says, this function is for cooking meat and stew. Adjusting the cooking time will set the cooker to cook the meat to the desired texture.
- ↑ **Poultry** – This is the function suitable for cooking chicken and turkey meat or any MEAT/STEW dish. You can set your desired pressure level as well as cooking time depending on your preferences or based on the requirements in the recipe you follow.
- ↑ **Rice/Risotto** – If you are cooking rice (any type of rice) set this function. The cooker will automatically cook your rice under low pressure; the time needed for the cooking will depend on the level of water you poured into the pot.
- ↑ **Steam** – Suitable for steaming vegetables or seafood, this function works better if you use it with the quick pressure releasing in order to avoid overcooking (which can happen if you let your Crock Pot Express release its pressure naturally).
- ↑ **Soup** – This is the function you need when cooking soups and broths. You can manually adjust the cooking time by clicking the 'Adjust' button (it all depends on how you want your soups, or based on your recipe).
- ↑ **Beans/Chili** - Crock Pot Express Pressure Cooker comes with this function that helps you prepare the best chili or beans. You can manually adjust the cooker from thirty to forty minutes, depending on how you prefer your chili or beans.

MEASUREMENT CONVERSION CHART

The charts below will help you to convert between different units of volume in US customary units.

Please note that US volume is not the same as in the UK and other countries, and many of the measurements are different depending on which country you are in.

It is very easy to get confused when dealing with US and UK units! The only good thing is that the metric units never change!

Every effort has been made to ensure that the Measurement Charts on this page are accurate.

VOLUME EQUIVALENTS (LIQUID)

US Standard	US Standard (ounces)	Metric (approximate)
2 tablespoons	1 fl. oz.	30 mL
¼ cup	2 fl. oz.	60 mL

½ cup	4 fl. oz.	120 mL
1 cup	8 fl. oz.	240 mL
1½ cups	12 fl. oz.	355 mL
2 cups or 1 pint	16 fl. oz.	475 mL
4 cups or 1 quart	32 fl. oz.	1 L
1 gallon	128 fl. oz.	4 L

VOLUME EQUIVALENTS (DRY)

US Standard	Metric (approximate)
⅛ teaspoon	0.5 mL
¼ teaspoon	1 mL
½ teaspoon	2 mL
¾ teaspoon	4 mL
1 teaspoon	5 mL
1 tablespoon	15 mL
¼ cup	59 mL
⅓ cup	79 mL
½ cup	118 mL
⅔ cup	156 mL
¾ cup	177 mL
1 cup	235 mL
2 cups or 1 pint	475 mL
3 cups	700 mL
4 cups or 1 quart	1 L

OVEN TEMPERATURES

Fahrenheit (F)	Celsius (C) (approximate)
250°F	120°C
300°F	150°C
325°F	165°C
350°F	180°C
375°F	190°C
400°F	200°C
425°F	220°C
450°F	230°C

WEIGHT EQUIVALENTS

US Standard	Metric (approximate)
½ ounce	15 g
1 ounce	30 g
2 ounces	60 g
4 ounces	115 g
8 ounces	225 g
12 ounces	340 g
16 ounces or 1 pound	455 g

BREAKFAST RECIPES

Apple Granola Crumble

Serves: 4 Preparation Time: 5 minutes Cooking Time: 3 hours

INGREDIENTS

- 2 Granny Smith apples, cored and sliced
- 1 cup granola cereal
- 1/8 cup maple syrup
- ¼ cup apple juice
- 1 teaspoon cinnamon

INSTRUCTIONS
- Place all ingredients in the crockpot. Give a good stir.
- Close the lid and cook on low for 3 hours.
- Once cooked, serve with a tablespoon of butter.
  - **Nutrition information: Calories per serving: 369; Carbohydrates: 56g; Protein: 5g; Fat:15 g; Fiber: 5g**

Banana and Coconut Milk Steel-Cut Oats

Serves: 7 Preparation Time: 5 minutes Cooking Time: 3 hours

INGREDIENTS

- 2 medium ripe bananas, sliced
- 2 cans coconut milk, unsweetened
- 1 cup steel cut oats
- 2 tablespoons brown sugar
- ½ teaspoon cinnamon

INSTRUCTIONS
- Place all ingredients in the crockpot. Add a dash of salt if needed.
- Give a good stir.
- Close the lid and cook on low for 3 hours.
- Once cooked, serve with a tablespoon of melted butter.
  - **Nutrition information: Calories per serving:101; Carbohydrates: 15.3g; Protein: 2.6g; Fat: 5.9g; Fiber:2.6g**

Coconut Cranberry Quinoa

Serves: 4 Preparation Time: 5 minutes Cooking Time: 2 hours

INGREDIENTS

- 3 cups coconut water
- 1 cup quinoa, uncooked and rinsed
- 3 teaspoons honey
- ¼ cup cranberries
- ½ cup coconut flakes

INSTRUCTIONS
- Place all ingredients in the crockpot.
- Add a dash of vanilla or cinnamon if desired. Give a good stir.
- Close the lid and cook on low for 2 hours.
  - **Nutrition information: Calories per serving: 246; Carbohydrates: 42g; Protein: 8g; Fat: 5g; Fiber: 5g**

Crockpot Breakfast Casserole

Serves: 4 Preparation Time: 10 minutes Cooking Time: 4 hours

INGREDIENTS

- 8eggs, beaten
- ¾ cup milk
- 2 bell peppers, julienned
- 1 head broccoli, cut into florets
- 6-ounce cheddar cheese

INSTRUCTIONS
- In a mixing bowl, combine the eggs and milk. Season with salt and pepper to taste.
- Pour the egg mixture into the crockpot and add in the bell pepper, broccoli, and cheddar cheese last.
- Close the lid and cook on low for 4 hours.
  - **Nutrition information: Calories per serving:320; Carbohydrates: 29.6g; Protein: 22g; Fat: 6.5g; Fiber: 5.3g**

Grecian Egg Casserole

Serves: 6 Preparation Time: 5 minutes Cooking Time: 4 hours

INGREDIENTS

- 12 eggs, beaten
- ½ cup milk
- ½ cup sun-dried tomatoes, soaked
- 1 cup baby Bella mushrooms, sliced
- ½ cup feta cheese

INSTRUCTIONS
- In a mixing bowl, combine the eggs and milk.
- Season with salt and pepper to taste or other seasonings that you want.
- Pour the egg mixture into the crockpot and add in the tomatoes, mushrooms, and feta cheese. Close the lid and cook on low for 4 hours.

Nutrition information: Calories per serving: 275; Carbohydrates: 6.99g; Protein: 21.2g; Fat: 17.75g; Fiber: 0.8g

Spinach and Mozzarella Frittata

Serves: 6 Preparation Time: 10 minutes Cooking Time: 4 hours

INGREDIENTS

- 6 eggs, beaten
- 2 tablespoons milk
- 1 cup baby spinach
- 1 cup mozzarella cheese
- 1 Roma tomatoes, diced

INSTRUCTIONS

- In a mixing bowl, combine the eggs and milk. Season with salt and pepper to taste.
- Pour the egg mixture into the crockpot and add the baby spinach, cheese, and tomatoes. Close the lid and cook on low for 4 hours.
- **Nutrition information: Calories per serving: 139; Carbohydrates: 4g; Protein: 12g; Fat: 8g; Fiber: 1g**

Frittata with Artichoke Hearts

Serves: 8 Preparation Time: 10 minutes Cooking Time: 4 hours

INGREDIENTS

- 8 eggs, beaten
- 1 can artichoke hearts, cut into small pieces
- 1 jar roasted red pepper, drained and chopped
- 4 ounces Feta cheese
- ¼ cup sliced green onions

INSTRUCTIONS

- Pour the egg mixture into the crockpot. Season with salt and pepper to taste.
- Stir into the eggs the artichoke hearts and red peppers. Add the feta cheese and sprinkle with green onions.
- Close the lid and cook on low for 4 hours.
- **Nutrition information: Calories per serving: 177; Carbohydrates: 3.8g; Protein: 11.7g; Fat:12.8g; Fiber: 1.1g**

Quinoa Energy Bars

Serves: 4 Preparation Time: 10 minutes Cooking Time: 8 hours

INGREDIENTS

- 2 cups quinoa flakes, rinsed
- ½ cup nuts of your choice
- ½ cup dried fruits of your choice
- ¼ cup butter, melted
- 1/3 cup maple syrup

INSTRUCTIONS

- In a mixing bowl, combine all ingredients.
- Compress the ingredients in a parchment-lined crockpot. Close the lid and cook on low for 8 hours.
- **Nutrition information: Calories per serving: 306; Carbohydrates: 39.9g; Protein: 7.3g; Fat: 13.9g; Fiber: 3.7g**

Overnight Apple Oatmeal

Serves: 4 Preparation Time: 5 minutes Cooking Time: 6 hours

INGREDIENTS

- 4 apples, peeled and diced
- ¾ cup brown sugar
- 2 cups old-fashioned oats
- 4 cups evaporated milk
- 1 tablespoon cinnamon

INSTRUCTIONS

- Stir in all ingredients in the crockpot.
- Close the lid and cook on low for 8 hours. Add in butter if desired.
- **Nutrition information: Calories per serving: 521; Carbohydrates:109.5 g; Protein: 16.4g; Fat: 11.6g; Fiber: 12.6g**

Basic Overnight Quinoa and Oats

Serves:8 Preparation Time: 5 minutes Cooking Time: 5 hours

INGREDIENTS

- 1 ½ cups steel-cut oats
- ½ cup quinoa
- 4 ½ cups evaporated milk
- 4 tablespoons maple syrup
- 1 teaspoon vanilla extract

INSTRUCTIONS

- Stir in all ingredients in the crockpot.
- Close the lid and cook on low for 7 hours. Top with your favorite topping.
- **Nutrition information: Calories per serving:194; Carbohydrates: 31.8g; Protein:8.9 g; Fat: 6.9g; Fiber: 3.5g**

Crockpot Veggie Omelet

⌀ Serves: 6 Preparation Time: 5 minutes Cooking Time: 6 hours

INGREDIENTS

- 6 eggs, beaten
- ½ cup milk
- 1 teaspoon seasoning of your choice (thyme or dried basil)
- 2 red and yellow bell peppers, julienned
- 1 cup broccoli florets

INSTRUCTIONS
- In a mixing bowl, combine the eggs, milk, and seasoning of your choice. Season with salt and pepper to taste.
- Pour the egg mixture into the crockpot. Add the vegetables on top.
- Close the lid and cook on low for 6 hours. Serve with cheese if desired.
- **Nutrition information: Calories per serving: 144; Carbohydrates: 2.3g; Protein: 9.4g; Fat: 10.7g; Fiber: 0.2g**

Enchilada Breakfast Casserole

⌀ Serves: 8 Preparation Time: 5 minutes Cooking Time: 10 hours

INGREDIENTS

- 6 eggs, beaten
- 1-pound ground beef
- 2 cans enchilada sauce
- 1 can condensed cream of onion soup
- 3 cups sharp cheddar cheese, grated

INSTRUCTIONS
- In a mixing bowl, beat the eggs and season with salt and pepper. Set aside. In a skillet, brown the beef for at least 5 minutes.
- Pour the beef in the crockpot and stir in the enchilada sauce and cream of onion soup. Stir in the eggs and place cheese on top.
- Close the lid and cook on low for 10 hours.
- **Nutrition information: Calories per serving: 320; Carbohydrates: 9.4g; Protein: 24.6g; Fat: 20.1g; Fiber: 1.2g**

White Chocolate Oatmeal

⌀ Serves: 6 Preparation Time: 5 minutes Cooking Time: 4 hours

INGREDIENTS

- 1 tablespoon white chocolate chips
- 1 cup water
- ½ cup oatmeal
- 1 tablespoon brown sugar
- 1 teaspoon cinnamon

INSTRUCTIONS
- Stir in all ingredients in the crockpot.
- Close the lid and cook on low for 4 hours. Top with your favorite topping.
- **Nutrition information: Calories per serving: 31; Carbohydrates: 5.4g; Protein: 0.5g; Fat: 0.9g; Fiber: 0.6g**

Bacon-Wrapped Hotdogs

⌀ Serves: 35 Preparation Time: 10 minutes Cooking Time: 8 hours

INGREDIENTS

- 1 package small hotdogs
- 1 package bacon
- 1 ½ cup brown sugar
- 4 tablespoons water
- Salt and pepper to taste

INSTRUCTIONS
- Wrap the individual hotdogs with bacon strips. Secure with a toothpick then place inside the crockpot.
- In a small mixing bowl, combine the sugar, water, salt, and pepper. Pour over the hotdogs.
- Close the lid and cook on low for 8 hours.
- **Nutrition information: Calories per serving: 120; Carbohydrates: 11.8g; Protein: 3.1g; Fat: 6.9g; Fiber: 0.1g**

Maple Brown Sugar Bacon

⌀ Serves: 6 Preparation Time: 5 minutes Cooking Time: 8 hours

INGREDIENTS

- 1-pound thick cut bacon
- ¼ cup pure maple syrup
- ¼ cup brown sugar
- 3 tablespoons water
- Salt and pepper to taste

INSTRUCTIONS
- Place the bacon slices in a mixing bowl and add the rest of the ingredients. Place inside the crockpot.
- Close the lid and cook on low for 8 hours or until the sauce is very sticky.
- **Nutrition information: Calories per serving: 306; Carbohydrates: 23.8g; Protein: 8.4g; Fat: 22.3g; Fiber: 2.1g**

Scrambled Eggs in Ramekins

Serves: 2 Preparation Time: 5 minutes Cooking Time: 4 hours

INGREDIENTS

- 2 eggs, beaten
- ¼ cup milk
- Salt and pepper
- ¼ cup cheddar cheese, grated
- ½ cup salsa

INSTRUCTIONS

✓ In a mixing bowl, mix the eggs and milk. Season with salt and pepper to taste. Place egg mixture in two ramekins. Sprinkle with cheddar cheese on top.
✓ Place the ramekins in the crockpot and pour water around it. Close the lid and cook on low for 4 hours.
✓ Serve with salsa.
- **Nutrition information: Calories per serving: ;243 Carbohydrates: 9.3g; Protein: 15.3g; Fat: 164g; Fiber: 1.6g**

Bacon Hash Brown and Egg Casserole

Serves: 7 Preparation Time: 10 minutes Cooking Time: 6 hours

INGREDIENTS

- 1 package hash brown potatoes, thawed
- 8 large eggs, beaten
- 1 can evaporated milk
- 2 cups sharp cheddar cheese, grated
- 1 package bacon, cooked until crispy

INSTRUCTIONS

✓ Place the hash brown potatoes in the crockpot.
✓ In a mixing bowl, mix the eggs and milk together. Season with salt and pepper to taste. Pour the egg mixture over the hash brown potatoes.
✓ Sprinkle with cheddar cheese. Sprinkle with bacon on top.
✓ Close the lid and cook on low for 6 hours.
- **Nutrition information: Calories per serving: 269; Carbohydrates: 13.8g; Protein: 13.6g; Fat: 17.5g; Fiber: 1.2g**

Breakfast Sausage and Egg Casserole

Serves: 8 Preparation Time: 10 minutes Cooking Time: 6 hours

INGREDIENTS

- 1-pound pork sausages, sliced
- 6 eggs, beaten
- ¾ cup milk
- 1 teaspoon dry mustard
- 1 ½ cups sharp cheddar cheese, grated

INSTRUCTIONS

✓ In a skillet heated over medium heat, sauté the pork sausages until the fat has rendered. Place in the crockpot.
✓ In a mixing bowl, combine the eggs and milk. Season with dry mustard, salt and pepper. Pour over the sausages.
✓ Sprinkle with cheese on top.
✓ Close the lid and cook on low for 6 hours.
- **Nutrition information: Calories per serving:293; Carbohydrates: 3.6g; Protein: 16.4g; Fat: 23.3g; Fiber: 0g**

Cheesy Bacon Hash Browns

Serves: 7 Preparation Time: 5 minutes Cooking Time: 3 hours

INGREDIENTS

- 1-pound hash browns, thawed
- 1 can cream of mushroom soup
- ¼ cup milk
- ½ pound sharp cheddar cheese, grated
- 10 slices of bacon, cook until crispy

INSTRUCTIONS

✓ Place the hash browns in the crockpot.
✓ Add the cream of mushroom soup and milk. Add the cheese on top.
✓ Close the lid and cook on low for 4 hours. Sprinkle with cheese on top.
- **Nutrition information: Calories per serving: 362; Carbohydrates: 14.6g; Protein: 14.5g; Fat: 27.4g; Fiber:1.5 g**

Hodgepodge Omelet

Serves: 2 Preparation Time: 5 minutes Cooking Time: 5 hours

INGREDIENTS

- 2 eggs, beaten
- ¼ cup milk
- 2 cooked turkey sausages, chopped
- 1 cup button mushrooms, chopped
- 1 red bell pepper, julienned

INSTRUCTIONS

✓ In a mixing bowl, combine the eggs and milk. Season with salt and pepper to taste. Place the egg mixture and stir in the sausages, mushrooms, and bell pepper.
✓ Close the lid and cook on low for 5 hours. Sprinkle with chopped green onions on top.

Nutrition information: Calories per serving: 332; Carbohydrates: 17.85g; Protein: 27.7g; Fat: 17.07g; Fiber: 1.2g

Grandma's Apple Oatmeal

(Ready in about 6 hours | Servings 8)

INGREDIENTS

- Margarine, melted
- 8 cups water
- 4 cups applesauce, unsweetened
- 1 1/2 cups steel cut oats
- 2 medium-sized apples, diced
- Grated nutmeg to taste
- Cardamom to taste
- Ground cinnamon to taste
- 2 tablespoons honey

DIRECTIONS
- ✓ Lightly grease your crock pot with margarine.
- ✓ Combine the rest of ingredients in a large mixing bowl. Pour this mixture into the crock pot.
- ✓ Cook on low heat setting at least 6 hours.

Chocolate Kid Friendly Oatmeal

(Ready in about 6 hours | Servings 10)

INGREDIENTS

- Non-stick cooking spray
- 10 cups water
- 6 bananas, mashed
- 2 tablespoons chia seeds
- 7-8 dried dates
- 2 cups steel-cut oats
- 1 teaspoon ground cinnamon
- 1/2 cup cocoa powder, unsweetened

DIRECTIONS
- ✓ Lightly oil a crock pot with cooking spray.
- ✓ Mix remaining ingredients in prepared crock pot.
- ✓ Cook on low heat setting approximately 6 hours.

Vanilla Blueberry Quinoa

(Ready in about 6 hours | Servings 6)

INGREDIENTS

- 4 cups vanilla flavoured almond milk
- 4 cups water
- 2 cups quinoa
- 2 cups blueberries
- 1/4 teaspoon grated nutmeg
- 1/4 teaspoon ground cinnamon
- 1/3 cup flax seeds
- 1/3 cup brown sugar

DIRECTIONS

- ✓ Stir all of the ingredients together in a crock pot.
- ✓ Cover with a lid; cook on Low for 8 hours or overnight.

Apple Orange Quinoa

(Ready in about 8 hours | Servings 6)

INGREDIENTS

- 2 cups water
- 1 cup quinoa
- 1 tablespoon fresh orange juice
- 2 cups apple juice
- 1 tablespoon chia seeds
- 1 teaspoon ground cinnamon
- 1/4 teaspoon grated nutmeg
- 1 cup raisins
- 1 teaspoon vanilla extract

DIRECTIONS
- ✓ Combine all ingredients together in your crock pot.
- ✓ Cover with a lid; cook on low heat setting 6 to 8 hours.

Easy Yummy Breakfast Casserole

(Ready in about 12 hours | Servings 8)

INGREDIENTS

- 1 (32-ounce) bag hash browns, frozen
- 2 carrots, thinly sliced
- 1 yellow onion, chopped
- 3 cloves garlic, minced
- 1 pound cooked ham
- 2 cups cheddar cheese, shredded
- 8 eggs
- 1 cup whole milk
- 1 teaspoon sea salt
- 1/4 teaspoon ground black pepper
- 1/4 teaspoon crushed red pepper

DIRECTIONS
- ✓ In a crock pot, alternate layers as follows: 1/2 of the hash browns, 1/2 of the carrots, 1/2 of the onions, 1/2 of the garlic, 1/2 of the cooked ham, and 1/2 of the cheddar cheese. Repeat one more time.
- ✓ In a mixing bowl, beat the eggs; then add remaining ingredients.
- ✓ Pour this mixture into the crockpot; cover; cook on low for 10 to 12 hours.

Restaurant Style Hash Browns

(Ready in about 8 hours | Servings 10)

INGREDIENTS

- 1 (32-ounce) bag hash brown potatoes
- 1 pound turkey bacon, cooked
- 1 jalapeño pepper, minced
- 3 cloves garlic, crushed
- 1 cup spring onions, diced

- 1 cup Cheddar cheese
- 1 cup whole milk
- 12 eggs
- 1 teaspoon salt
- 1/2 teaspoon ground black pepper
- 1 teaspoon dried thyme

DIRECTIONS
- In your crock pot, alternate layers as follows: 1/2 of hash browns, 1/2 of bacon, 1/2 of jalapeño pepper, 1/2 of garlic, 1/2 of onions, 1/2 of cheese.
- Next, add layers as follows: 1/2 of hash browns, 1/2 of bacon, 1/2 of jalapeño pepper, 1/2 of garlic, 1/2 of onions, 1/2 of cheese.
- In a mixing bowl, combine milk, egg, salt, black pepper, and thyme. Pour this mixture into the crock pot.
- Cook on low for 8 hours or overnight.

Creamy Coconut Oatmeal with Pumpkin Seeds

(Ready in about 8 hours | Servings 12)

INGREDIENTS
- 4 cups steel cut oatmeal
- 2 cans coconut milk
- 10 cups water
- 1/4 teaspoon cardamom
- 1/2 teaspoon ground cinnamon
- 1 teaspoon almond extract
- 3 tablespoons coconut sugar
- 1/2 cup coconut flakes, for garnish
- Pumpkin seeds for garnish

DIRECTIONS
- In your crock pot, place oatmeal, coconut milk, water, cardamom, cinnamon, almond extract, and coconut sugar.
- Turn to low and cook for about 8 hours, or until creamy.
- Garnish with coconut flakes and pumpkin seeds!

Vanilla Almond Steel Cut Oats

(Ready in about 8 hours | Servings 12)

INGREDIENTS
- 2 cups vanilla flavoured almond milk
- 2 cups steel cut oatmeal
- 8 cups water
- 1 teaspoon ground cinnamon
- 1/2 teaspoon grated nutmeg
- 1/4 teaspoon ground cloves
- 1 teaspoon vanilla extract
- 3 tablespoons maple syrup
- Raisins for garnish
- Chia seeds for garnish

DIRECTIONS
- In your crock pot, place almond milk, steel cut oatmeal, water, cinnamon, nutmeg, cloves, vanilla extract, and maple syrup.
- Set the crock pot to low and cook your oatmeal for about 8 hours.
- Garnish with raisins and chia seeds and enjoy!

Yummy Winter Breakfast

(Ready in about 8 hours | Servings 12)

INGREDIENTS
- Non-stick cooking spray
- 1 (26-ounce) package hash brown potatoes
- 2 cups sausages
- 2 cups Cheddar cheese, shredded
- 10 eggs
- 1 cup milk
- 1/2 teaspoon dried tarragon
- 1 tablespoon granulated garlic
- 1/4 teaspoon ground black pepper
- 1 teaspoon salt

DIRECTIONS
- Oil your crock pot with cooking spray. Place hash brown potatoes in the bottom of the crock pot.
- Heat a cast-iron skillet over medium-high flame. Then, cook sausage until they are browned, about 6 minutes. Then, spread cooked sausage over the hash brown potatoes.
- Place shredded cheese on top.
- In a large mixing bowl, beat the eggs with milk until frothy. Add spices and whisk to combine. Pour this mixture over the layers in the crock pot.
- Cook for 6 to 8 hours on low-heat setting. Serve hot!

Cheesy Hash brown Casserole

(Ready in about 8 hours | Servings 6)

INGREDIENTS
- 4 Bratwurst sausages, cooked
- 2 cups hash brown potatoes
- 1 cup sharp cheese, shredded
- 1 cup whole milk
- 4 large-sized eggs
- 1 tablespoon granulated garlic
- 1/4 teaspoon ground black pepper
- 1 teaspoon salt
- 1 teaspoon dry mustard

DIRECTIONS
- In a saucepan, cook the sausages until they are no longer pink. Place hash brown potatoes in a crock pot.
- Transform cooked sausages to the crock pot together with their grease. Lay sharp cheese on top.
- In a mixing bowl, combine the rest of ingredients. Pour this egg mixture into the crock pot.
- Cook on low for about 8 hours, or overnight. Serve with mustard and sour cream.

Thanksgiving Bacon Casserole

(Ready in about 10 hours | Servings 10)

INGREDIENTS

- 1 tablespoon olive oil
- 1 cup green onions, chopped
- 1 green bell pepper, thinly sliced
- 1 red bell pepper, thinly sliced
- 2 cloves garlic, minced
- 2 pounds hash brown potatoes, frozen and thawed
- 8 slices turkey bacon, cooked
- 1 1/2 cups Gouda, shredded
- 10 large-sized eggs
- 1 cup milk
- 1/4 teaspoon cayenne pepper
- 1 teaspoon sea salt
- 1/4 teaspoon ground black pepper
- 1 heaping tablespoon fresh parsley
- 1/4 cup chives

DIRECTIONS

- In a cast-iron skillet, heat olive oil over medium flame. Sauté green onions, bell peppers, and garlic until green onions are softened. Stir in hash brown potatoes and cook for 2 more minutes.
- Lay 1/2 of the onion-potato mixture in your crock pot; then, lay 1/2 of the
- cooked bacon and top with 1/2 of shredded Gouda cheese.
- Repeat layering in the same manner.
- Whisk eggs together with remaining ingredients; pour this egg mixture over cheese layer in the crock pot.
- Cook on low heat setting, 8 to 10 hours.

Amazing Spiced Omelette

(Ready in about 2 hours | Servings 4)

INGREDIENTS

- 6 eggs
- 1/2 cup whole milk
- 1 teaspoon sea salt
- 1/4 teaspoon freshly ground black pepper
- 1 teaspoon dried basil
- 1 teaspoon dried oregano
- 1 teaspoon dried thyme
- 1/4 teaspoon chili powder
- 1 small head of cauliflower, broken into florets
- 1 medium-sized red onion, chopped
- 1 garlic clove, minced
- 1 cup Cheddar cheese, shredded
- Chives for garnish
- Olives for garnish

DIRECTIONS

- Lightly oil the inside of your crock pot.
- In a mixing bowl or a measuring cup, whisk the eggs, milk, and spices. Mix until everything is well combined.
- Add cauliflower florets, onions and garlic to crock pot. Add the spiced egg mixture.
- Cover; then, cook on high approximately 2 hours, or until eggs are set.
- Scatter shredded cheese on top and place a lid; let stand until cheddar cheese is melted.
- Divide the omelette into wedges, garnish with chives and olives and serve.

Overnight Western Omelette

(Ready in about 12 hours | Servings 12)

INGREDIENTS

- 2 pounds hash brown potatoes
- 1 cup spinach
- 1 pound cooked ham, sliced
- 2 cloves garlic, minced
- 1 yellow onion, diced
- 1 red bell pepper, seeded and diced
- 1 cup Gouda cheese, shredded
- 10 eggs
- 1 ½ cup milk
- 1 teaspoon sea salt
- 1/4 teaspoon freshly ground black pepper
- 1/4 teaspoon chili powder

DIRECTIONS

- Lightly oil your crock pot with non-stick cooking spray.
- Alternate layers in your crock pot. Place 1/3 of the hash brown potatoes; place 1/3 of the spinach; then place 1/3 of cooked ham, 1/3 of garlic, 1/3 of the onion and 1/3 of bell pepper.
- Top with shredded Gouda cheese; repeat same layers two more times.
- In a large-sized bowl, mix together remaining ingredients. Pour in the crock pot.
- Cover with a lid; cook on low-heat setting for 10 to 12 hours. Serve with toasted bread and mustard.

Vegetable and Ham Casserole

(Ready in about 8 hours | Servings 4)

INGREDIENTS

- 1/4 cup extra-virgin olive oil
- 1 parsnip, peeled and chopped
- 1 turnip, peeled and chopped
- 2 cloves garlic, minced
- 1 cup ham, cooked and diced
- 3/4 cup whole milk
- 4 large-sized eggs
- 1/4 teaspoon turmeric
- 1/2 teaspoon rosemary
- 1/4 teaspoon dried thyme
- 1 tablespoon heaping fresh parsley
- Croutons for garnish

DIRECTIONS

- In your crock pot, combine together first four ingredients. Top with ham.
- In a bowl, whisk together milk, eggs, and spices. Pour over the vegetables and ham in the crock pot.
- Cook on low for 6 to 8 hours. Serve with croutons.

Creamy Oatmeal with Berries

(Ready in about 8 hours | Servings 4)

INGREDIENTS

- 1 cup oats
- 1/2 teaspoon allspice
- 2 cups water
- 1 cup coconut water
- 1 pinch of grated nutmeg
- 1 pinch of ground cinnamon
- 1 pinch of salt
- 1 cup half-and-half cream
- 1/4 cup brown sugar
- Berries of choice, for garnish

DIRECTIONS

- ✓ Simply put all ingredients together (except berries) into your crock pot, just before going to bed.
- ✓ Set the crock pot on low and cook overnight.
- ✓ Serve with your favourite berries or mixed berries and enjoy warm!

Vegan Steel-Cut Oatmeal

(Ready in about 3 hours | Servings 6)

INGREDIENTS

- 2 bananas, mashed
- 1 cup coconut water
- 4 cups water, divided
- 1 cup steel cut oats
- 1/4 cup dried figs
- 1/4 cup dried cranberries
- 1 teaspoon vanilla extract
- 1/2 teaspoon cardamom
- 1/2 teaspoon ground cinnamon
- Coconut sugar to taste

DIRECTIONS

- ✓ Purée bananas in your blender; then transfer mashed bananas to a crock pot.
- ✓ Add remaining ingredients.
- ✓ Cook on medium heat setting for 3 hours. Remember to stir every 30 minutes.
- ✓ Serve with additional fruit if desired and enjoy!

Pumpkin Steel Cut Oats

(Ready in about 6 hours | Servings 6)

INGREDIENTS

- Non-stick cooking spray
- 6 cups water
- 1 ½ cups steel-cut oats
- 1/2 cup brown sugar
- 1 (15-ounce) can pumpkin puree
- 1 teaspoon vanilla extract
- 1 teaspoon cardamom
- 1 tablespoon pumpkin pie spice
- 1 teaspoon ground cinnamon

DIRECTIONS

- ✓ Grease your crock pot with cooking spray.
- ✓ Place all of the ingredients.
- ✓ Cook on low for 6 hours. Divide among six serving bowls, sprinkle with pumpkin seeds and serve.

Mouth Watering French Toast Casserole

(Ready in about 5 hours | Servings 8)

INGREDIENTS

- 2 bread loaves, cut into bite-sized cubes
- 1 teaspoon lemon zest
- 6 large-sized eggs
- 1 ½ cups milk
- 1 teaspoon pure almond extract
- 1 cup half-and-half
- 1/4 teaspoon grated nutmeg
- 1/4 teaspoon ground cloves
- 1 teaspoon ground cinnamon
- 1 cup brown sugar
- 3 tablespoons butter, melted
- 2 cups slivered almonds

DIRECTIONS

- ✓ Grease a crock pot with non-stick spray or with a melted butter.
- ✓ Preheat the oven to 225 degrees F. Place prepared bread cubes on a cookie sheet and bake for about 30 minutes, or until the bread cubes are dried.
- ✓ Lay the bread cubes on the bottom of your crock pot.
- ✓ Mix together lemon zest, eggs, milk, almond extract, half-and-half, nutmeg, cloves, and cinnamon. Pour this mixture over the bread cubes in the crock pot.
- ✓ In a separate small-sized bowl, combine the brown sugar, butter, and almonds. Stir in your crock pot.
- ✓ Set crock pot to low; cover and cook approximately 5 hours.
- ✓ Serve with fruits and maple syrup if desired.

Easy Sunday Beef Sandwiches

(Ready in about 8 hours | Servings 6)

INGREDIENTS

- 1 jar of your favourite spaghetti sauce
- 3 pounds roast meat
- 2 bay leaves
- 5-6 peppercorns
- 1 cup beef stock
- Mustard for garnish
- Pickles for garnish

DIRECTIONS

- ✓ In your crock pot, place all of the ingredients. Cook on low for 8 hours.

- ✓ Remove bay leaves and peppercorns and ladle over English muffins.
- ✓ Serve with mustard and pickles and enjoy!

Lazy Man's Pizza

(Ready in about 4 hours | Servings 4)

INGREDIENTS

- 1 pound hamburger, browned and drained
- 1 pound noodles, cooked
- 2 cups mozzarella cheese, shredded
- 2 bell peppers, sliced
- 1 onion, chopped
- 1 teaspoon granulated garlic
- 1 can beef soup
- 1 cup mushrooms, sliced
- 2 jars pizza sauce
- 1/2 pound pepperoni, sliced

DIRECTIONS

- ✓ In your crock pot, alternate layers with the ingredients in the order given above.
- ✓ Cook for 4 hours on low; then serve.

Chocolate French Toast with Honey and Bananas

(Ready in about 2 hours | Servings 6)

INGREDIENTS

- 1 large-sized loaf bread, torn into cubes
- 2 cups low-fat milk
- 1/2 teaspoon cardamom
- 1/2 teaspoon ground cloves
- 1 teaspoon ground cinnamon
- 1 tablespoon hazelnut extract
- 5 large-sized eggs
- 2 heaping tablespoons chocolate cream, plus more for topping
- 1 tablespoon butter, unsalted
- 4 bananas, sliced
- 1 tablespoon honey

DIRECTIONS

- ✓ Put the bread cubes into your crock pot.
- ✓ In a large mixing bowl, combine, milk, spices, hazelnut extract, eggs, and chocolate cream. Whisk well to combine.
- ✓ Pour this mixture over the bread cubes in the crock pot to make sure the bread is well submerged.
- ✓ Cover the crock pot with a lid and cook on high approximately 2 hours.
- ✓ Heat a saucepan and add butter. Add bananas and honey to the hot butter and sauté 3 to 4 minutes, turning once.
- ✓ Divide chocolate French toast among six serving plates, add banana-honey mixture and enjoy with fat-free milk!

Melt-In-Your-Mouth French Toast

(Ready in about 5 hours | Servings 8)

INGREDIENTS

For the French Toast:

- 12-ounce loaf bread of choice
- 2 cups whole milk
- 3 eggs
- 1/2 cup brown sugar
- 1 tablespoon almond extract
- 1/4 teaspoon ground nutmeg
- 1/4 teaspoon allspice
- 1/4 teaspoon turmeric powder
- 1 teaspoon ground cinnamon
- 1 cup almonds, coarsely chopped
- 3 tablespoons unsalted butter, melted
- 2 bananas, sliced

For the Sauce:

- 1/2 cup brown sugar
- 1/2 cup half-and-half cream
- 1/2 cup butter
- 2 tablespoons corn syrup
- 1 teaspoon almond extract

DIRECTIONS

- ✓ Preheat the oven to 300 degrees F. Line a crock pot with disposable crockery liner.
- ✓ In a baking pan, place the bread cubes in a single layer. Bake for about 15 minutes or until the bread is golden. Then, replace bread cubes to prepared crock pot.
- ✓ In a large mixing bowl, whisk together whole milk, eggs, sugar, almond extract, nutmeg, allspice, turmeric, and cinnamon. Pour this spiced mixture over bread cubes in the crock pot. Press bread cubes down with a spoon to moisten them.
- ✓ In a small non-stick skillet, toast the almonds for a few minutes. Combine toasted almonds with melted butter. Pour this mixture over the ingredients in the crock pot.
- ✓ Cover, and then cook on low heat setting for about 5 hours. Remove crockery liner and set French toast aside.
- ✓ Next, prepare the sauce. In a medium-sized saucepan, over medium-high heat, cook the ingredients for the sauce. Bring to a boil, turn the heat to low and cook for 3 more minutes.
- ✓ You can cool prepared sauce to room temperature or set in a refrigerator. Pour the sauce over the French toast, top with banana slices and enjoy!

Homemade Yogurt with Croissants

(Ready in about 8 hours | Servings 16)

INGREDIENTS

- 1/2 gallon low-fat milk
- 1/2 cup milk powder
- 1/4 cup plain yogurt with active yogurt cultures, at room temperature
- 16 croissants of choice

DIRECTIONS
- In a saucepan, over medium heat, combine together milk and milk powder. Cook, stirring constantly, until an instant-read thermometer registers about 180 degrees F.
- Next, cool at room temperature
- In a bowl, combine together 1 cup of the warm milk mixture and the plain yogurt. Whisk until smooth. Next, slowly pour the milk-yogurt mixture into the saucepan, stirring constantly.
- Pour prepared mixture into canning jars and place them in a crock pot. Pour enough lukewarm water into the crock pot. Water need to reach just over halfway up sides of your filled jars.
- Cook on HIGH for 5 minutes. Then, allow to stand about 4 hours, until the mixture is thick. It's important to turn on your crock pot to high for 5 minutes, every hour.
- Chill the yogurt at least 4 hours or until yogurt is set. Store in the refrigerator and serve with your favourite croissants. Enjoy!

Cranberry Coconut Steel Cut Oatmeal

(Ready in about 6 hours | Servings 8)

INGREDIENTS
- 2 cups steel-cut oats
- 4 cups water
- 2 cups coconut water
- 1/2 cup almonds, chopped
- 1 tablespoon brown sugar
- 1/2 teaspoon ground cinnamon
- 1/2 teaspoon salt
- 1/4 cup dried cranberries
- 1/4 cup snipped apricots
- Shredded coconut for garnish

DIRECTIONS
- In a crock pot, combine together oats, water, coconut water, almonds, sugar, cinnamon, and salt. Cover; cook on low-heat setting approximately 6 hours.
- Top each serving with cranberries, apricots, and coconut and serve warm.

Overnight Oatmeal with Dried Fruits

(Ready in about 6 hours | Servings 8)

INGREDIENTS
- 2 cups steel cut oats
- 1 cup raisins
- 1 cup dried cherries
- 1 cup dried figs
- 8 cups water
- 1 cup half-and-half

DIRECTIONS
- Into a crock pot, put all of the ingredients.
- Set the crock pot to low heat and cover with a lid.
- Cook overnight or 8 to 9 hours.

Orange Poppy Seed Bread

(Ready in about 2 hours | Servings 12)

INGREDIENTS
- Non-stick cooking spray
- 1/4 cup poppy seeds
- 2 cups flour, all-purpose of choice
- 1 tablespoon baking soda
- 1 tablespoon honey
- 3/4 cup brown sugar
- 1/2 teaspoon kosher salt
- 3 large-sized eggs
- 1/2 cup canola oil
- 1/2 cup sour cream
- 1/4 cup whole milk
- 1 teaspoon orange zest
- 1/4 cup fresh orange juice
- 1 teaspoon vanilla extract

DIRECTIONS
- Coat a crock pot with non-stick cooking spray.
- In a bowl, stir together poppy seeds, flour, and baking soda, and set aside.
- In another bowl, combine together honey, sugar, salt, eggs, canola oil, sour cream, whole milk, orange zest, orange juice, and the 1 teaspoon of vanilla extract. Add this orange mixture to poppy seeds mixture. Stir to
- combine and place in the prepared crock pot.
- Cover and cook on high for about 2 hours.
- Cool completely before serving time and enjoy with freshly squeezed orange juice.

Bacon and Veggie Quiche

(Ready in about 5 hours | Servings 6)

INGREDIENTS
- Disposable slow cooker liner
- 4 slices bacon
- 1 tablespoon olive oil
- 1 red bell pepper, chopped
- 1 green bell pepper, chopped
- 2 cups mushrooms, chopped
- 1 cup spinach
- 1 ½ cups Swiss cheese, shredded
- 2 cups whole milk
- 8 large-sized eggs
- 1 teaspoon granulated garlic
- 1 tablespoon fresh basil
- 1 teaspoon fine sea salt
- 1/4 teaspoon cayenne pepper
- 1/4 teaspoon ground black pepper
- 1/2 cup biscuit mix

DIRECTIONS
- Line your crock pot with disposable slow cooker liner.
- In a saucepan, fry bacon slices until crisp; drain and crumble.

- ✓ In same saucepan, heat olive oil over medium-low heat. Sauté bell pepper
- ✓ and mushrooms until tender. Stir in spinach and Swiss cheese.
- ✓ In a mixing bowl, combine milk, eggs, granulated garlic, basil, salt, cayenne pepper, and black pepper. Add this mixture to mushroom mixture in the saucepan.
- ✓ Next, fold in biscuit mix. Replace prepared mixture from the saucepan to the crock pot. Scatter the crumbled bacon on top.
- ✓ Cover with a lid; cook on low-heat setting for 5 hours. Cool slightly before serving time, divide among serving plates and enjoy!

Spiced Oatmeal with Nuts

(Ready in about 8 hours | Servings 4)

INGREDIENTS

- 1 cup steel cut oats
- 1 tablespoon butter
- 1/4 teaspoon turmeric powder
- 1/2 teaspoon allspice
- 2 tablespoons maple syrup
- 1 cup dried figs
- 1 cup dried apricots
- 2 cups water
- 2 cups coconut water
- 1/2 cup half-and-half
- 1/2 teaspoon sea salt

DIRECTIONS

- ✓ Combine all ingredients in your crock pot.
- ✓ Cover the crock pot with a lid. Cook 8 hours on low or 4 hours on high-heat setting.
- ✓ Serve with chopped nuts of choice!

Ham and Cheese Family Delight

(Ready in about 4 hours | Servings 6)

INGREDIENTS

- Non-stick cooking spray
- 1 cup whole milk
- 2 cups light cream
- 4 eggs
- 1 red bell pepper, chopped
- 1 yellow bell pepper, chopped
- 1 onion, finely chopped
- 1 teaspoon dried basil
- 1/4 teaspoon turmeric powder
- 1 teaspoon dried thyme, crushed
- 1/2 cayenne pepper
- 1/4 teaspoon ground black pepper
- 6 cups toasted bread cubes
- 1 cup cooked ham, chopped
- 1/2 cup hard cheese, cubed
- 1/3 cup dried tomatoes

DIRECTIONS

- ✓ Lightly oil a crock pot with cooking spray.
- ✓ In a bowl, whisk together milk, light cream, and eggs. Stir in red bell pepper, yellow bell pepper, onion, basil, turmeric, thyme, cayenne pepper
- ✓ and ground black pepper.
- ✓ Next, add bread cubes, ham, cheese and tomatoes. Add the mixture to the crock pot.
- ✓ Cook on low heat setting for about 4 hours or until a toothpick (knife) inserted in centre comes out clean. Enjoy!

Halloween Bread with Cranberries

(Ready in about 2 hours | Servings 8)

INGREDIENTS

- Non-stick cooking spray
- 3/4 cup canned pumpkin
- 1/2 cup half-and-half
- 2 tablespoons sugar
- 1 teaspoon ground cinnamon
- 1/4 teaspoon cardamom
- 1/4 teaspoon allspice
- 2 cups all-purpose flour
- 1 teaspoon baking soda
- 1 teaspoon baking powder
- 1/2 teaspoon salt
- 1/4 cup unsalted butter, cubed
- 1/2 cup cranberries
- 1/2 cup maple syrup
- 2 tablespoons butter, melted
- 1/2 cup chopped walnuts, toasted

DIRECTIONS

- ✓ Grease your crock pot with non-stick cooking spray.
- ✓ In a mixing bowl, combine pumpkin with half-and-half, sugar and spices.
- ✓ In a large bowl, stir together the 2 cups of flour, the baking soda, baking powder, and salt. Next, cut in cold butter. Add pumpkin mixture to prepared flour mixture. Gently stir to combine.
- ✓ Fold cranberries into the batter.
- ✓ Spoon mixture into your crock pot. Pour maple syrup and melted butter over the batter. Then, scatter the walnuts over the top.
- ✓ Cook on high-heat setting for about 2 hours. Serve warm.

Bread Pudding with Dried Figs

(Ready in about 3 hours | Servings 6)

INGREDIENTS

- 8 cups bread cubes of choice
- 1/2 cup dried figs, chopped
- 4 medium-sized eggs
- 2 cups whole milk
- 1/4 cup butter, melted
- 1 teaspoon honey
- 1/4 cup brown sugar
- 1/4 teaspoon mint extract
- 1/4 teaspoon ground cinnamon

DIRECTIONS
- ✓ Put prepared bread cubes together with dried figs into a crock pot.
- ✓ In a large mixing bowl, whisk together eggs, milk, butter, honey, brown sugar, mint extract, and cinnamon. Pour this mixture into the crock pot. Toss to coat.
- ✓ Cook on low heat setting about 3 hours.

Spiced Apple Bread Pudding

(Ready in about 3 hours | Servings 8)

INGREDIENTS
- 4 medium-sized apples, cored and chopped
- 3 cups bread, cubed
- 3 large-sized eggs
- 3/4 cup packed brown sugar
- 1/4 teaspoon allspice
- 1/2 teaspoon ground cloves
- 1 teaspoon ground cinnamon
- 1 teaspoon nutmeg
- 2 (12 fluid ounce) cans evaporated milk

DIRECTIONS
- ✓ Lay apples and bread cubes in a crock pot.
- ✓ In a bowl, beat eggs until frothy. Stir in remaining ingredients and mix to combine.
- ✓ Pour prepared egg mixture over apples and bread in the crock pot.
- ✓ Cook on high heat setting for 4 hours or until custard forms.

Tater Tot Breakfast Casserole

(Ready in about 8 hours | Servings 8)

INGREDIENTS
- 1 (30-ounces) package tater tots
- 1 cup bacon
- 1 cup green onions, chopped
- 2 cups sharp cheese, shredded
- 12 eggs
- 1 cup whole milk
- 3 tablespoons all-purpose flour
- 1/4 teaspoon ground black pepper
- 1/4 teaspoon cayenne pepper
- 1 teaspoon kosher salt

DIRECTIONS
- ✓ In a greased crock pot, place 1/3 of the tater tots, then, 1/3 of the bacon, 1/3 of green onions and finally, add 1/3 of shredded cheeses. Repeat these layers two more times, ending with the cheese.
- ✓ In a large-sized bowl, whisk together the rest of ingredients; add to the crock pot.
- ✓ Cover the crock pot and set on low; then, cook 6 to 8 hours.

Soft and Yummy Buttermilk Bread

(Ready in about 3 hours | Servings 8)

INGREDIENTS
- 1 ½ cups all-purpose flour
- 1 teaspoon baking soda
- 1 teaspoon baking powder
- A pinch of salt
- 4 tablespoons butter, cut into pieces
- A pinch of grated nutmeg
- 3/4 cup buttermilk

DIRECTIONS
- ✓ In a large-sized mixing bowl, combine all-purpose flour, baking soda, baking powder, and salt; cut in butter until this mixture resembles small crumbs.
- ✓ Stir in grated nutmeg and buttermilk.
- ✓ Knead dough and then pat it into greased springform pan.
- ✓ Place on a rack; cover and cook on high for about 2 ½ hours. Serve with milk.

Delicious Herb Bread

(Ready in about 3 hours | Servings 8)

INGREDIENTS
- 1 ½ cups all-purpose flour
- 1 teaspoon baking powder
- 1 teaspoon baking soda
- 1 teaspoon dried dill weed
- 1 teaspoon ground black pepper
- 1 tablespoon dried chives
- A pinch of salt
- 4 tablespoons cold margarine, cut into pieces
- 3/4 cup buttermilk

DIRECTIONS
- ✓ In a mixing bowl, combine first seven ingredients. Then, cut in cold margarine until the mixture resembles small crumbs.
- ✓ Stir in buttermilk and replace the dough on the floured surface.
- ✓ Knead your dough for about 3 minutes.
- ✓ Place on a rack and bake on high for about 2 hours. Serve warm and enjoy with cheese.

Cranberry-Raisin Bran Bread

(Ready in about 3 hours | Servings 16)

INGREDIENTS
- 1/2 cup whole-wheat flour
- 1 ½ cups all-purpose flour
- 1 teaspoons baking powder
- 1 teaspoon baking soda
- 1 teaspoon pumpkin pie spice
- 1 teaspoon allspice
- 1/4 teaspoon grated nutmeg
- 1/2 teaspoon salt
- 1 ½ cups whole-bran cereal flakes
- 2 cups buttermilk
- 1/4 cup maple syrup
- 3 tablespoons butter, melted
- 2 eggs

- 1/2 cup dried cranberries, coarsely chopped
- 1/2 cup raisins, coarsely chopped
- 1/4 cup pecans, chopped
- 1⁄4 walnuts, chopped

DIRECTIONS
- ✓ In a large-sized mixing bowl, combine first nine ingredients until everything is well combined.
- ✓ Next, add buttermilk, maple syrup, butter, eggs; stir to combine.
- ✓ Gently fold in dried cranberries, raisins, pecans and walnuts.
- ✓ Pour prepared dough into greased and floured loaf pan.
- ✓ Bake on high for about 3 hours, or until a toothpick (or a knife) inserted in centre of your loaf comes out clean.
- ✓ Serve with fruit jam or honey!

Sloppy Joe-Style Burgers

(Ready in about 3 hours | Servings 12)

INGREDIENTS
- 2 pounds lean beef, ground
- 1 yellow onion, finely chopped
- 1 zucchini, chopped
- 1 yellow bell pepper, chopped
- 1 red bell pepper, chopped
- 1 cup button mushrooms, sliced
- 1/2 cup fried bacon, crumbled
- 1 teaspoon garlic powder
- 1/2 teaspoon chili powder
- 3/4 cup tomato paste
- 1 cup reduced-fat cheese, cubed
- 2 bay leaves
- 1 teaspoon sea salt
- 1/4 teaspoon ground black pepper
- 12 burger buns

DIRECTIONS
- ✓ In a large saucepan or a wok, over medium flame, cook ground beef with onion, zucchini and bell peppers. Cook until ground beef is browned.
- ✓ Add to the slow cooker and then stir in remaining ingredients (except buns).
- ✓ Cook on low for 2 to 3 hours. Serve on burger buns and add pickles if desired.

Nutty Granola with Coconut Oil

(Ready in about 2 hours 30 minutes | Servings 12)

INGREDIENTS
- Cooking spray
- 4 cups rolled oats, old fashioned
- 1 cup almonds, chopped
- 1/2 cup pecans, chopped
- 1/2 teaspoon allspice
- 1 teaspoon cinnamon
- A pinch of salt
- 1/2 cup maple syrup
- 1/2 cup coconut oil, melted
- 1/4 cup brown sugar
- 1 teaspoon pure almond extract

DIRECTIONS
- ✓ Oil your crock pot with cooking spray. Add the rolled oats and reserve.
- ✓ Add the almonds and pecans.
- ✓ In a mixing bowl, whisk together remaining ingredients.
- ✓ Pour this mixture over the oats and nuts in the crock pot.
- ✓ Cook approximately 2 hours on low, stirring every 30 minutes.
- ✓ Spread prepared granola out on a sheet of aluminium foil and let it cool.

Herbed Chili Cornbread

(Ready in about 2 hours | Servings 8)

INGREDIENTS
- 3/4 cup all-purpose flour
- 1⁄4 cup cornmeal
- 1 tablespoon sugar
- 1 teaspoon baking soda
- 1 teaspoon baking powder
- 1 teaspoon dried basil
- 1 teaspoon ground cumin
- 1⁄2 teaspoon dried oregano
- 1/2 teaspoon salt
- 1 large-sized egg, beaten
- 1/2 cup buttermilk
- 1/4 poblano pepper, cooked and minced
- 1/4 cup whole kernel corn

DIRECTIONS
- ✓ Combine first ten ingredients in a large-sized mixing bowl.
- ✓ Stir in buttermilk, poblano and corn and. Stir well to combine.
- ✓ Transfer the dough to greased and floured baking pan.
- ✓ Next, place this baking pan on a rack in your crock pot. Cover; cook on high-heat setting approximately 2 hours.
- ✓ Allow to cool for about 10 minutes before serving time.

Caramel Flavoured Banana Bread

(Ready in about 2 hours | Servings 8)

INGREDIENTS
- 4 tablespoons butter, melted
- 1⁄4 cup applesauce
- 2 medium-sized eggs
- 1 tablespoon water
- 1 tablespoon milk
- 3/4 cup brown sugar
- 3 ripe bananas, mashed
- 1 ¾ cups all-purpose flour
- 1 teaspoon baking powder
- 1 teaspoon baking soda
- 1⁄4 teaspoon salt
- 1⁄4 cup almonds, coarsely chopped

DIRECTIONS

- In a bowl, beat butter, applesauce, eggs, water, milk, and brown sugar until creamy and uniform.
- Add mashed bananas, flour, baking powder, baking soda, and salt. Stir in almonds.
- Pour batter into suitable loaf pan.
- Cook on high for about 3 hours until a toothpick (or knife) inserted in centre of your banana bread comes out clean.
- Remove banana bread from loaf pan and cool to room temperature.

Pumpkin-Almond Bread

(Ready in about 3 hours 30 minutes | Servings 16)

INGREDIENTS

- 1 cup pumpkin, canned
- 4 tablespoons margarine, melted
- 1/2 cup granulated sugar
- 2 medium-sized eggs, beaten
- 1/2 cup milk
- 2 cups all-purpose flour
- 1 teaspoon baking powder
- 1 teaspoon baking soda
- 1/4 teaspoon grated nutmeg
- 1 teaspoon pumpkin pie spice
- A pinch of salt
- 1/2 cup almonds, toasted and chopped

DIRECTIONS

- In a large-sized bowl, combine pumpkin with margarine and sugar until well blended; stir in eggs and milk.
- Add flour, baking powder, baking soda, nutmeg, pumpkin pie spice, and salt; mix in chopped almonds.
- Spoon batter into loaf pan and place in your crock pot. Cook on high about 3 ½ hours.
- Allow your pumpkin bread to cool on a wire rack. Serve with honey and enjoy!

Cheesy Rosemary Bread

(Ready in about 2 hours | Servings 8)

INGREDIENTS

- 6 tablespoons butter, room temperature
- 1 cup grated Parmesan cheese
- 1 tablespoon fresh rosemary
- 1 medium-sized loaf bread

DIRECTIONS

- Combine butter, Parmesan cheese and fresh rosemary and mix until everything is well blended.
- Cut loaf bread into 8 slices. Spread both sides of bread slices with rosemary-cheese mixture.
- Wrap bread slices in an aluminium foil.
- Place in your crock pot and cook on low-heat setting for 2 hours. Uncover and allow to cool for about 5 minutes.

Vegetarian Sloppy Joes

(Ready in about 3 hours | Servings 8)

INGREDIENTS

- 1 cup mushrooms, thinly sliced
- 1 cup onion, chopped
- 1 red bell pepper, chopped
- 1/4 poblano pepper, minced
- 2 teaspoons minced garlic
- 1 cup tomato catsup
- 1 teaspoon celery seeds
- 1 ½ cup water
- 1/4 cup sugar
- 1 teaspoon kosher salt
- 1/4 ground black pepper
- 8 whole-wheat hamburger buns

DIRECTIONS

- Combine mushrooms, onions, bell pepper, poblano pepper, garlic, catsup, celery seeds, water, and sugar.
- Cover your crock pot with a lid and cook Sloppy Joes on high 2 to 3 hours. Season with salt and pepper.
- Serve in buns with your favourite salad.

Deluxe Beef Sandwiches

(Ready in about 3 hours | Servings 12)

INGREDIENTS

- 2 pounds lean ground beef
- 1 red bell pepper, chopped
- 1 green bell pepper, chopped
- 1 yellow onion, chopped
- 1 cup mushrooms, thinly sliced
- 2 cloves garlic, minced
- 1/2 cup fried turkey bacon, crumbled
- 3/4 cup tomato paste
- 1 tablespoon tomato catsup
- 2 tablespoons dry red wine
- 1 cup processed cheese, cubed
- Salt and pepper, to taste
- 12 sandwich buns, toasted

DIRECTIONS

- Heat a large skillet over medium heat; cook ground beef, bell peppers and onion until meat is browned and onion is translucent. Replace to the crock pot.
- Add remaining ingredients, except sandwich buns; cook on low-heat setting for about 3 hours.
- Serve on sandwich buns, garnish with mustard and salad and enjoy.

Best-ever Meat Sandwiches

(Ready in about 3 hours | Servings 12)

INGREDIENTS

- 1 pound mixed beef and pork, ground
- 3/4 cup spring onions, chopped
- 1 clove garlic, minced
- 1 cup tomatoes, diced and drained
- 1 tablespoon Worcestershire sauce

- 1/4 cup packed light brown sugar
- 1 tablespoon mustard
- 1 heaping tablespoon cilantro
- 1 heaping tablespoon fresh parsley
- 1 teaspoon sea salt
- 1/4 teaspoon ground black pepper
- 1/4 teaspoon red pepper, crushed
- 12 sandwich rolls, toasted

DIRECTIONS
- In a wide and deep saucepan, over medium-low flame, cook mixed meat, spring onion, and garlic; crumble with a fork; add to the crock pot.
- Add the rest of ingredients, except sandwich rolls; cook on high 2 to 3 hours.
- Arrange sandwiches with rolls and serve with some extra ketchup and mustard.

BBQ Chicken Sandwiches

(Ready in about 8 hours | Servings 8)

INGREDIENTS
- 1 pound chicken breasts, boneless and skinless
- 1/2 cup chicken stock
- 1/4 cup BBQ sauce
- 1/4 cup water
- 1 cup catsup
- 2 tablespoons white dry wine
- 1/3 cup yellow mustard
- 1 teaspoon tarragon
- 1 celery stalk, chopped
- 1 large-sized carrot, chopped
- 2 tablespoons brown sugar
- 1/2 cup chopped onion
- 1 clove garlic, minced
- Salt and pepper, to taste
- 8 hamburger buns

DIRECTIONS
- In your crock pot, combine all of the ingredients, except hamburger buns.
- Cover with a lid and cook on low 6 to 8 hours, or overnight. Next, shred cooked chicken, adjust seasoning and serve with buns.

Saucy Pork Sandwiches

(Ready in about 8 hours | Servings 12)

INGREDIENTS

For the Sandwiches:
- 1 pork loin roast, boneless
- 1 teaspoon garlic powder
- 1 teaspoon onion powder
- 1/4 teaspoon ground black pepper
- Sea salt to taste
- 1/2 cup water
- 12 sandwich buns

For the Sauce:
- 1 cup reduced-fat mayonnaise
- 1 clove garlic, minced
- 2 tablespoons lemon juice

DIRECTIONS
- Rub pork loin with garlic powder, onion powder, ground black pepper and salt to taste. Pour in water. Place in a crock pot and cook on low-heat setting overnight, or about 8 hours.
- Remove pork from the crock pot and shred it.
- Mix all ingredients for the sauce.
- Spoon cooked pork onto bottoms of sandwich buns. Then spoon prepared sauce and place top of the buns. Enjoy!

Summer Granola with Seeds

(Ready in about 2 hours | Servings 16)

INGREDIENTS
- 6 cups oats, old-fashioned
- 1 cup pumpkin seeds
- 1 cup sunflower kernels
- 1/2 teaspoon kosher salt
- 2 tablespoons orange juice
- 1/2 cup canola oil
- 1 cup maple syrup
- 1/2 cup dried figs, chopped
- 1 cup dried pineapple, chopped

DIRECTIONS
- In a crock pot, combine together oats, pumpkin seeds, sunflower kernels, and salt.
- In a small-sized bowl, whisk orange juice, oil and maple syrup until mixture is blended. Stir this mixture into oat mixture.
- Cook, covered, on high-heat setting for about 2 hours, stirring every 20 minutes.
- Remove from the heat and let granola cool. Add dried figs and pineapple and stir well to combine.
- Place prepared granola on a baking sheets, spreading evenly. Cool completely before storing.

Easy-to-make Date Granola

(Ready in about 3 hours | Servings 6)

INGREDIENTS
- 1/4 cup honey
- 6 tablespoons applesauce
- 1/4 teaspoon cardamom
- 1/4 teaspoon grated nutmeg
- 1/4 teaspoon ground cloves
- 1 teaspoon ground cinnamon
- A pinch of salt
- 1 teaspoon vanilla extract
- 1/2 teaspoon maple extract
- 1 tablespoon hemp seeds
- 3 cups rolled oats
- 1 cup walnuts, toasted and chopped
- 1 cup Medjool dates, pitted and chopped

DIRECTIONS
- ✓ Put honey, applesauce, cardamom, nutmeg, cloves, cinnamon, salt, vanilla extract and maple extracts into your crock pot. Add hemp seeds and stir well to combine.
- ✓ Stir in rolled oats and walnuts. Stir to combine.
- ✓ Cook on high for 3 hours, venting the lid slightly. Stir occasionally. Allow to cool slightly and then add chopped dates.
- ✓ Pour your granola onto a baking sheet and allow to cool completely before serving in the airtight containers.

Coconut Maple Granola

(Ready in about 3 hours | Servings 6)

INGREDIENTS
- 1/4 cup maple syrup
- 2 tablespoons canola oil
- 1 cup hulled sunflower seeds
- 2 tablespoons chia seeds
- 1/4 teaspoon ground cloves
- 1 teaspoon ground cinnamon
- A pinch of salt
- 1 teaspoon pure vanilla extract
- 1 cup coconut flakes
- 3 cups rolled oats
- 1 cup slivered almonds
- 1 cup dried cherries, chopped

DIRECTIONS
- ✓ Combine maple syrup, canola oil, sunflower seeds, chia seeds, ground cloves, cinnamon, salt, vanilla extract, coconut flakes and rolled oats in a crock pot.
- ✓ Cook approximately 3 hours, stirring occasionally. Allow granola to cool for about 15 minutes; add almonds and dried cherries. Stir until everything is well incorporated.
- ✓ Spread onto a baking sheet in order to cool completely.

Pulled Pork Sandwiches

(Ready in about 3 hours | Servings 12)

INGREDIENTS
- 1 pork loin roast, boneless
- 1 teaspoon curry powder
- 1 teaspoon cayenne pepper
- 1/2 teaspoon grated ginger
- 1 cup beef broth
- Salt to taste
- 1/4 teaspoon black pepper
- 1 bay leaf
- 48 bread slices

DIRECTIONS
- ✓ Rub pork loin roast with curry powder and cayenne pepper.
- ✓ Place seasoned pork in your crock pot; add grated ginger and beef broth. Add salt, black pepper and bay leaf.
- ✓ Cook on low for about 3 hours. Cut cooked pork into thin shreds. Taste and adjust the seasonings.
- ✓ Make sandwiches spooning meat with sauce into each bread slice.

Winter Beef Sandwiches

(Ready in about 8 hours | Servings 12)

INGREDIENTS
- 1 medium-sized beef chuck roast, boneless
- 1/2 teaspoon sea salt
- 1/4 teaspoon black pepper
- 1 teaspoon dried basil
- 1 tablespoon fresh sage
- 2 cups beef broth
- 1 cup dry red wine
- 1 clove garlic, minced
- 7-8 peppercorns
- 12 sandwich rolls
- Sauerkraut for garnish
- Chillies for garnish

DIRECTIONS
- ✓ Season beef chuck roast with sea salt and black pepper and lay in a crock pot.
- ✓ Add basil, sage, beef broth, wine, garlic, and peppercorns. Cover and cook on low approximately 8 hours, or overnight.
- ✓ Serve cooked beef on sandwich rolls with sauerkraut and chillies.

Hearty Sausage Sandwiches

(Ready in about 6 hours | Servings 6)

INGREDIENTS
- 8 links fresh sausages
- 1 cup beef broth
- 4 cups spaghetti sauce
- 1 chili pepper, minced
- 1 red bell pepper, sliced
- 1 green bell pepper, sliced
- 1 cup spring onions, chopped
- 1 heaping tablespoon fresh parsley
- 1 heaping tablespoon fresh cilantro
- 6 cocktail buns, split lengthwise

DIRECTIONS
- ✓ In a crock pot, place the sausage links, beef broth, spaghetti sauce, chili pepper, bell peppers and spring onions. Add parsley and cilantro. Stir to combine.
- ✓ Cover with a lid; cook on Low for 6 hours. Serve on cocktail rolls and enjoy!

Country Smoked Sausages

(Ready in about 6 hours | Servings 6)

INGREDIENTS
- 1 tablespoon extra-virgin olive oil
- 6 green onions, sliced
- 1 yellow bell pepper, sliced
- 1 red bell pepper, sliced

- 4 garlic cloves, smashed
- 2 pounds smoked sausage
- 1 (28-ounce) can tomatoes, diced
- 1 teaspoon salt
- 1/2 teaspoon ground black pepper
- 1/2 teaspoon red pepper flakes, crushed
- Mustard for garnish

DIRECTIONS
- In a large skillet, heat olive oil over medium flame. Sauté onions, bell peppers, garlic and sausages until vegetables are tender and sausages are lightly browned. Transfer to the crock pot.
- Add tomatoes, salt, black pepper and red pepper.
- Cook on low approximately 6 hours. Serve with your favourite mustard.

Must-Eat Beef Tacos

(Ready in about 8 hours | Servings 6)

INGREDIENTS
- 1 ½ pounds beef chuck roast, boneless
- 1 large-sized red onion, sliced
- 1 cup beef stock
- 1 (16-ounce) jar taco sauce
- 12 taco shells
- 2 cucumbers, thinly sliced
- 2 ripe tomatoes, sliced

DIRECTIONS
- Lay beef chuck roast and sliced onion in a crock pot. Pour in beef stock and taco sauce.
- Cook on LOW for 8 hours or overnight.
- In the morning, cut beef into shreds.
- Fill taco shells with shredded beef; add cucumber and tomato and serve!

Oatmeal with Prunes and Apricots

(Ready in about 8 hours | Servings 4)

INGREDIENTS
- 1 cup steel cut oats
- 4 ½ cups water
- 1/2 teaspoon grated ginger
- 1/2 teaspoon allspice
- 1/2 teaspoon ground cinnamon
- 1/2 teaspoon salt
- 3 tablespoons butter
- 1/2 cup prunes
- 1/2 cup dried apricots
- Maple syrup, to taste

DIRECTIONS
- Put all ingredients into a crock pot.
- Cover and cook on low-heat setting approximately 8 hours.
- Serve with milk and some extra fruit if desired.

Muesli with Coconut and Peanuts

(Ready in about 2 hours | Servings 12)

INGREDIENTS
- 4 cups rolled oats
- 4 cups water
- 1 teaspoon allspice
- 1/4 teaspoon turmeric
- 1 cup wheat germ
- 1 cup baking natural bran
- 1/2 cup shredded coconut, unsweetened
- 1/2 cup brown sugar
- 4 tablespoons butter, melted
- 1 teaspoon almond extract
- 2 tablespoons pumpkin seeds
- Peanuts for garnish

DIRECTIONS
- Add all of the ingredients, except peanuts, to your crock pot.
- Cover with a lid; cook on high-heat setting approximately 2 hours, stirring twice. Divide among 12 serving bowls, scatter chopped peanuts on top and serve!

Cheese Steak Sandwiches

(Ready in about 8 hours | Servings 8)

INGREDIENTS
- 1 pound round steak, thinly sliced
- 1 cup onions, sliced
- 1 green bell pepper, sliced
- 1 cup beef stock
- 1 clove garlic, minced
- 2 tablespoon red dry wine
- 1 tablespoon Worcestershire sauce
- 1 teaspoon celery seeds
- 1/2 teaspoon salt
- 1/4 teaspoon ground black pepper
- 8 hamburger buns
- 1 cup mozzarella cheese, shredded

DIRECTIONS
- Combine all of the ingredients, except buns and cheese, in your crock pot.
- Cover and cook on low 6 to 8 hours.
- Make sandwiches with buns, prepared meat mixture and cheese. Serve warm and enjoy!

Beer Brats with Mushrooms and Onion

(Ready in about 8 hours | Servings 8)

INGREDIENTS
- 8 fresh bratwurst
- 2 (12-ounce) 3 bottles beer
- 1 cup mushrooms, sliced

- 2-3 cloves garlic, minced
- 1 red onion, sliced
- 1 red bell pepper, sliced
- 1 teaspoon sea salt
- 1/4 teaspoon ground black pepper
- 1 teaspoon minced poblano pepper
- 8 hot dog buns

DIRECTIONS
- Combine all ingredients, except buns, in a crock pot.
- Cook, covered, on low 6 to 8 hours.
- Serve cooked bratwurst and veggies in buns. Add mustard, catsup and sour cream if desired.

Yummy Sausage and Sauerkraut Sandwiches

(Ready in about 8 hours | Servings 6)

INGREDIENTS
- 6 fresh sausages of choice
- 1 medium-sized onion, chopped
- 1 cup sauerkraut
- 1 small-sized apple, peeled, cored and thinly sliced
- 1 teaspoon caraway seeds
- 1/2 cup chicken broth
- Salt to taste
- 1/2 teaspoon ground black pepper
- 6 hot dog buns
- Catsup for garnish
- Mustard for garnish

DIRECTIONS
- Lay sausages in a crock pot. Then place onion, sauerkraut, apple, caraway seeds, chicken broth, salt and black pepper.
- Cook, covered, on low 6 to 8 hours.
- Make sandwiches with buns and serve with catsup and mustard.

Christmas Sausage Casserole

(Ready in about 8 hours | Servings 8)

INGREDIENTS
- Non-stick cooking spray butter flavour
- 1 (26-ounce) package frozen hash brown potatoes, thawed
- 1 zucchini, thinly sliced
- 1 cup whole milk
- 10 eggs, beaten
- 1 teaspoon sea salt
- 1/4 teaspoon crushed red pepper flakes
- 1/4 teaspoon ground black pepper
- 1 teaspoon caraway seeds
- 1 tablespoon ground mustard
- 2 cups sausages
- 2 cups Cheddar cheese, shredded

DIRECTIONS
- Grease a crock pot with non-stick cooking spray. Spread hash browns to cover the bottom of the crock pot. Then lay zucchini slices.
- In a medium-sized bowl, whisk milk, eggs, salt, red pepper, black pepper, caraway seeds, and ground mustard.
- Heat a cast-iron skillet over medium flame. Next, cook the sausages until they are browned and crumbly, about 6 minutes; discard grease.
- Lay sausage on zucchini layer, then spread Cheddar cheese. Pour egg-milk mixture over cheese layer.
- Cook on low for 6 to 8 hours. Serve warm with some extra mustard.

Overnight Sausage Casserole

(Ready in about 8 hours | Servings 12)

INGREDIENTS
- 1 ½ cups spicy sausage
- 1 red onion, chopped
- 2 garlic cloves, smashed
- 1 sweet bell pepper, thinly sliced
- 1 jalapeño pepper
- 1/4 cup fresh parsley
- 1 heaping tablespoon fresh cilantro
- 1 (30-ounce) package hash brown potatoes, shredded and thawed
- 1 1/2 cups sharp cheese, shredded
- 1 cup milk
- 12 eggs
- 1 teaspoon dry mustard
- 1 teaspoon celery seeds
- 1/2 teaspoon salt
- 1/8 teaspoon pepper
- 1/4 teaspoon cayenne pepper

DIRECTIONS
- In a non-stick medium skillet, over medium flame, cook sausage; drain and set aside.
- In a medium-sized bowl, combine onions, garlic, sweet bell pepper,
- jalapeño pepper, parsley and cilantro. Stir well to combine.
- Alternate layers. Lay 1/3 of the hash browns, sausage, onion mixture and cheese into the crock pot. In the same way, repeat layers twice.
- In a separate bowl, beat the rest of ingredients. Pour this mixture into the crock pot by spreading equally.
- Cover and cook on low approximately 8 hours or overnight. Serve warm.

Sunrise Pork Sandwiches

(Ready in about 8 hours | Servings 12)

INGREDIENTS
- 1 medium-sized pork butt roast
- 1/4 teaspoon black pepper
- 1/4 teaspoon crushed red pepper flakes
- 1 teaspoon sea salt

- 1 teaspoon dried thyme
- 1 tablespoon liquid smoke flavouring
- 12 pretzel buns

DIRECTIONS
- Pierce pork with a carving fork for better slow-cooking.
- Season with spices and then spread liquid smoke over pork butt roast.
- Lay pork roast into a crock pot.
- Cover and cook on Low for 8 to 10 hours, turning once or twice.
- Shred cooked pork roast, adding drippings to moisten. Make sandwiches with pretzel buns and enjoy!

Beer Pulled Pork Sandwiches

(Ready in about 10 hours | Servings 16)

INGREDIENTS
- 1 medium-sized pork butt roast
- 1 large-sized onion, chopped
- 3 cloves garlic, smashed
- 2 carrots, thinly sliced
- 1/2 teaspoon ground black pepper
- 1/2 teaspoon cayenne pepper
- 1 teaspoon sea salt
- 1 teaspoon ground black pepper
- 1 teaspoon cumin powder
- 1 (12 fluid ounce) can beer
- 1 cup barbeque sauce

DIRECTIONS
- Pierce pork with a carving fork.
- Put all of the ingredients, except barbeque sauce, into a crock pot.
- Set crock pot to high; cook for 1 hour. Then reduce the heat to low and cook 6 to 8 hours longer.
- Shred the cooked pork and return it to the crock pot. Add barbeque sauce and cook an additional 1 hour.
- Serve on your favourite hamburger buns and enjoy!

Mom's Apple Crisp

(Ready in about 3 hours | Servings 6)

INGREDIENTS
- 2/3 cup old-fashioned oats
- 2/3 cup brown sugar, packed
- 2/3 cup all-purpose flour
- 1 teaspoon allspice
- 1 teaspoon cinnamon
- 1/2 cup butter
- 5-6 tart apples, cored and sliced

DIRECTIONS
- In a medium-sized mixing bowl, combine together first six ingredients. Mix until everything is well blended.
- Place sliced apples in your crock pot.
- Sprinkle oat mixture over apples in the crock pot.
- Cover the crock pot with three paper towels. Set the crock pot to high and cook for about 3 hours.

Vegetarian Quinoa with Spinach

(Ready in about 3 hours | Servings 4)

INGREDIENTS
- 2 tablespoons olive oil
- 3/4 cup spring onions, chopped
- 1 cup spinach
- 2 garlic cloves, minced
- 1 cup quinoa, rinsed
- 2 ½ cups vegetable broth
- 1 cup water
- 1 tablespoon fresh basil
- 1 tablespoon fresh cilantro
- 1/4 teaspoon ground black pepper
- Salt to taste
- 1/3 cup Parmesan cheese

DIRECTIONS
- In a saucepan, heat olive oil over medium-high flame. Sauté spring onions, spinach and garlic until tender and fragrant. Transfer to a crock pot.
- Add remaining ingredients, except the cheese, and cover with a lid.
- Cook on LOW for about 3 hours.
- Stir in Parmesan cheese, taste and adjust the seasonings; serve!

Easy Cheesy Quinoa with Veggies

(Ready in about 3 hours | Servings 4)

INGREDIENTS
- 2 tablespoons margarine, melted
- 1 medium-sized onion, chopped
- 1 garlic clove, minced
- 1 cup button mushrooms, sliced
- 1 sweet red bell pepper
- 1 cup quinoa, rinsed
- 2 cups vegetable broth
- 1 ½ cup water
- 1 heaping tablespoon fresh parsley
- 1 heaping tablespoon fresh cilantro
- 1/4 teaspoon crushed red pepper flakes
- A pinch of ground black pepper
- Salt to taste
- 1/3 cup Parmesan cheese

DIRECTIONS
- In a medium-sized skillet, heat margarine over medium heat.
- Sauté onions, garlic, mushrooms and red bell pepper in hot margarine for about 6 minutes or until just tender. Replace to a crock pot.
- Add the rest of ingredients, except Parmesan cheese; set the crock pot to low and cook for about 3 hours.
- Add Parmesan cheese and enjoy warm!

Kale Frittata with Sausages

(Ready in about 3 hours | Servings 6)

INGREDIENTS

- Non-stick cooking spray
- 3/4 cup kale
- 1 sweet red bell pepper, sliced
- 1 sweet green pepper, sliced
- 1 medium-sized red onion, sliced
- 8 eggs, beaten
- 1/2 teaspoon ground black pepper
- 1 teaspoon salt
- 1 1/3 cup sausages

DIRECTIONS

- ✓ Combine all ingredients in a well-greased crock pot.
- ✓ Set the crock pot to low and cook until frittata is set or about 3 hours.
- ✓ You can reheat this frittata in microwave for 60 seconds.

Delicious Weekend Frittata

⌛ **(Ready in about 3 hours | Servings 6)**

INGREDIENTS

- Non-stick cooking spray
- 1 1/3 cup cooked ham
- 1 red bell pepper, sliced
- 1 sweet green bell pepper, sliced
- 1 spring onions, sliced
- 8 eggs, beaten
- 1 tablespoon basil
- 1 heaping tablespoon fresh cilantro
- 1 tablespoon fresh parsley
- 1 teaspoon salt
- 1/4 teaspoon ground black pepper
- 1/4 teaspoon cayenne pepper
- A few drops of tabasco sauce

DIRECTIONS

- ✓ Grease a crock pot with non-stick cooking spray. Combine all ingredients in the crock pot.
- ✓ Set the crock pot to low and cook your frittata approximately 3 hours.
- ✓ Divide among six serving plates and sprinkle with chopped chives, if desired; garnish with sour cream and serve!

Vegetarian Breakfast Delight

⌛ **(Ready in about 4 hours | Servings 4)**

INGREDIENTS

- 2 tablespoons canola oil
- 1 cup scallions, chopped
- 1 garlic clove, minced
- 2 medium-sized carrots, thinly sliced
- 1 celery stalk, chopped
- 1 cup quinoa, rinsed
- 2 cups vegetable stock
- 1 ½ cup water
- 1 tablespoon fresh cilantro
- A pinch of ground black pepper
- 1/4 teaspoon dried thyme
- 1/4 teaspoon dried dill weed
- Salt to taste
- 1/3 cup Parmesan cheese

DIRECTIONS

- ✓ In a medium-sized skillet, heat canola oil over medium heat.
- ✓ Sauté scallions, garlic, carrots and celery for about 5 minutes, or until the vegetables are just tender. Transfer the vegetables to a crock pot.
- ✓ Add quinoa, vegetable stock, water, cilantro, black pepper, dried thyme, dill weed and salt to taste.
- ✓ Cover and cook on LOW approximately 4 hours.
- ✓ Scatter Parmesan on top and serve warm!

Protein Rich Bacon Frittata

⌛ **(Ready in about 4 hours | Servings 6)**

INGREDIENTS

- Non-stick cooking spray
- 1 cup scallions, sliced
- 1 1/3 cup bacon
- 1 cup mushrooms, sliced
- 1 poblano pepper, minced
- 10 eggs, beaten
- 1 heaping tablespoon fresh cilantro
- 1 teaspoon salt
- 1/4 teaspoon ground black pepper
- 1/4 teaspoon crushed red pepper flakes

DIRECTIONS

- ✓ Combine all of the ingredients in greased crock pot.
- ✓ Next, set your crock pot to low; cover and cook the frittata 3 to 4 hours.
- ✓ Cut into six wedges, garnish with mustard and serve!

Chili Mushroom Omelette

⌛ **(Ready in about 4 hours | Servings 4)**

INGREDIENTS

- Non-stick cooking spray
- 1 green onions, sliced
- 2 cloves garlic, minced
- 2 cups mushrooms, sliced
- 1 chilli pepper, minced
- 2 ripe tomatoes, sliced
- 8 eggs, beaten
- 1 tablespoon fresh cilantro
- 1 teaspoon salt
- 1/4 teaspoon ground black pepper
- 1/4 teaspoon cayenne pepper

DIRECTIONS

- ✓ In your crock pot, place all of the ingredients.
- ✓ Cover with a lid; cook on low 3 to 4 hours.
- ✓ Cut into wedges and serve warm with sour cream and catsup.

Banana Pecan Oatmeal

(Ready in about 8 hours | Servings 4)

INGREDIENTS

- 2 cups water
- 2 ripe bananas
- 1 cup steel-cut oats
- 1/4 cup pecans, coarsely chopped
- 2 cups soy milk
- 1/2 teaspoon cinnamon
- 1 teaspoon pure almond extract
- A pinch of salt
- Honey to taste

DIRECTIONS

- ✓ Pour water into your crock pot. Use an oven safe bowl (glass casserole dish works here) and place it inside your crock pot.
- ✓ Mash the bananas with a fork or blend them in a blender. Transfer to the oven safe bowl.
- ✓ Add remaining ingredients to the bowl.
- ✓ Cook on low overnight or for 8 hours.
- ✓ Stir well before serving and add toppings of choice. Enjoy!

Hearty Oatmeal with Nuts

(Ready in about 8 hours | Servings 4)

INGREDIENTS

- 1 large-sized ripe banana
- 1 cup steel-cut oats
- 1/4 cup walnuts, coarsely chopped
- 2 tablespoons chia seeds
- 1 tablespoon hemp seeds
- 2 cups milk
- 1/4 teaspoon grated nutmeg
- 1/2 teaspoon cardamom
- 1/2 teaspoon cinnamon
- 1 teaspoon pure vanilla extract
- 2 cups water
- Maple syrup for garnish
- Fresh fruits for garnish

DIRECTIONS

- ✓ Mash banana with a fork. Add mashed banana to an oven proof dish. Stir in remaining ingredients.
- ✓ Pour water into a crock pot.
- ✓ Place the oven proof dish inside the crock pot. Cook on low heat setting overnight or for 8 hours. Top with maple syrup and fresh fruit.

Tomato Artichoke Frittata

(Ready in about 2 hours | Servings 4)

INGREDIENTS

- Non-stick cooking spray
- 6 large-sized eggs, beaten
- 1 cup chopped artichoke hearts
- 1 medium-sized tomato, chopped
- 1 red bell pepper, chopped
- 1 teaspoon onion powder
- 1 teaspoon garlic powder
- 1/4 teaspoon ground black pepper
- 1/4 teaspoon cayenne pepper
- 1/4 cup Swiss cheese, grated

DIRECTIONS

- ✓ Coat a crock pot with cooking spray.
- ✓ Add all of the ingredients to the crock pot.
- ✓ Cover with a lid and cook on low-heat setting for about 2 hours.
- ✓ Sprinkle with cheese; let stand for a few minutes until the cheese is melted.

Sausage Mushroom Omelette Casserole

(Ready in about 3 hours | Servings 4)

INGREDIENTS

- 1 pound chicken breast sausage, sliced
- 1 cup scallions, chopped
- 1 cup mushrooms, sliced
- 4 medium-sized eggs
- 1 cup whole milk
- 1 teaspoon sea salt
- 1/4 teaspoon ground black pepper
- 1/2 teaspoon dry mustard
- 1/2 teaspoon granulated garlic
- 1/2 cup Swiss cheese, grated

DIRECTIONS

- ✓ Arrange sausage in a crock pot. Then, place scallions and mushrooms over the sausages.
- ✓ In a mixing bowl, whisk together eggs, milk, and spices. Whisk to combine.
- ✓ Cook on low-heat setting about 3 hours. Then spread cheese on top and allow to melt.
- ✓ Serve warm with mayonnaise and mustard.

Pumpkin Pie Steel Cut Oats

(Ready in about 8 hours | Servings 4)

INGREDIENTS

- 1 cup steel-cut oats
- 3 cups water
- 1/4 teaspoon ground cinnamon
- 1 cup pumpkin purée
- 1 teaspoon vanilla extract
- A pinch of salt
- 1 tablespoon pumpkin pie spice
- 1/2 cup maple syrup

DIRECTIONS

- ✓ Combine all ingredients in your crock pot.
- ✓ Cover and cook on low overnight or for 8 hours.

✓ Serve warm with raisins or dates, if desired!

Cocoa Steel Cut Oats

(Ready in about 8 hours | Servings 4)

INGREDIENTS

- 3 ½ cups water
- 1 cup steel-cut oats
- 1/4 teaspoon grated nutmeg
- 1/2 teaspoon ground cinnamon
- 3 tablespoons cocoa powder, unsweetened
- A pinch of salt
- 1/2 teaspoon pure vanilla extract
- 1/2 teaspoon pure hazelnut extract

DIRECTIONS

✓ Add all of the ingredients to your crock pot.
✓ Cook on low heat settings overnight or for 8 hours.
✓ Stir before serving and add natural sweetener, if desired.

Nutty Pumpkin Oatmeal with Cranberries

(Ready in about 9 hours | Servings 4)

INGREDIENTS

- 1 cup steel-cut oats
- 3 cups water
- 1 cup whole milk
- A pinch of salt
- 1 tablespoon pumpkin pie spice
- 1/2 teaspoon cardamom
- 1/4 cup pumpkin purée
- 2 tablespoons honey
- 1/2 cup dried cranberries
- 1/2 cup almonds, coarsely chopped

DIRECTIONS

✓ In a crock pot, place steel-cut oats, water, milk, salt, pumpkin pie spice, cardamom pumpkin purée, and honey.
✓ Cook overnight or 8 to 9 hours.
✓ Divide among serving bowls; sprinkle with dried cranberries and almonds; serve.

Cocoa Oatmeal with Bananas

(Ready in about 8 hours | Servings 4)

INGREDIENTS

- 3 cups water
- 1 cup milk
- 1 cup steel-cut oats
- 1/2 teaspoon ground cinnamon
- 1 banana, mashed
- 4 tablespoons cocoa powder, unsweetened
- 1/2 teaspoon pure vanilla extract
- 1 banana, sliced
- Chopped pecans for garnish

DIRECTIONS

✓ Pour water and milk into a crock pot. Then place steel-cut oats, cinnamon, mashed banana, cocoa powder, and vanilla.
✓ Set your crock pot to low and cook overnight or for 8 hours.
✓ Stir before serving time; divide among serving bowls; garnish with banana and pecans and enjoy.

Cheese and Ham Quiche

(Ready in about 2 hours | Servings 4)

INGREDIENTS

- Butter flavour non-stick cooking spray
- 4 slices of whole-wheat bread, toasted
- 2 cups sharp cheese, grated
- 1/2 pound ham, cooked and cut into bite-sized cubes
- 6 large-sized eggs
- 1/2 teaspoon Dijon mustard
- 1 cup heavy cream
- 1/4 teaspoon turmeric powder
- 1 tablespoon fresh parsley, coarsely chopped
- 1/2 teaspoon sea salt
- 1/4 teaspoon crushed red pepper
- 1/4 teaspoon freshly ground black pepper

DIRECTIONS

✓ Generously grease the inside of a crock pot with non-stick cooking spray.
✓ Grease each slice of toasted bread with non-stick cooking spray; tear greased bread into pieces; arrange in the crock pot.
✓ Spread 1/2 of the sharp cheese over the toast, and then place the cooked ham pieces over the cheese; top with the remaining cheese.
✓ In a medium-sized mixing bowl or a measuring cup, beat the eggs together with the rest of ingredients; pour this mixture into the crock pot.
✓ Cover and cook on high-heat setting for 2 hours. Serve warm with mayonnaise or sour cream, if desired.

Country Sausage and Cauliflower Breakfast

(Ready in about 6 hours | Servings 8)

INGREDIENTS

- 1 pound sausage
- Non-stick spray
- 1 cup condensed cream of potato soup
- 1 cup whole milk
- 1 teaspoon dry mustard
- Salt to taste
- 1/2 teaspoon freshly ground black pepper
- 1 tablespoon fresh basil or 1 teaspoon dried basil
- 1 (28-ounce) package frozen hash browns, thawed
- 1 cup cauliflower, broken into florets
- 1 cup carrots, sliced
- 1/2 cup Cheddar cheese, shredded

DIRECTIONS
- In a cast-iron skillet, brown the sausage; cut into bite-sized chunks.
- Coat the inside of the crock pot with non-stick spray. Add all ingredients, except Cheddar cheese; gently stir to combine.
- Cover with a lid and cook for about 6 hours on low. Scatter Cheddar cheese on top. Let sit for 30 minutes before serving.

Broccoli Sausage Casserole

(Ready in about 6 hours | Servings 6)

INGREDIENTS
- 2 tablespoons olive oil
- 3/4 pound sausage
- 1 cup beef broth
- 1 cup milk
- 1 teaspoon dry mustard
- 1/4 teaspoon cayenne pepper
- 1/2 teaspoon black pepper
- 2 pounds frozen hash browns, thawed
- 1 cup broccoli, broken into florets
- 1 cup carrots, sliced
- 1/2 cup Cheddar cheese, shredded

DIRECTIONS
- Coat the inside of the crock pot with olive oil.
- In a medium-sized saucepan, over medium-high heat, cook the sausages until they are no longer pink or about 10 minutes. Transfer the sausage to the greased crock pot.
- Add in broth, milk, mustard, cayenne pepper, black pepper, hash browns, broccoli and carrot. Cook on low for 6 hours.
- Next, top with shredded cheese and allow to melt.
- Serve warm with your favourite mayonnaise and some extra mustard.

Winter Morning Sausage and Vegetables

(Ready in about 6 hours | Servings 6)

INGREDIENTS
- Non-stick spray
- 3/4 pound highly-spiced sausage
- 1 large-sized onion
- 1 sweet green bell pepper
- 1 sweet red bell pepper, chopped
- 1 cup whole milk
- 1 cup vegetable or beef broth
- 1/2 teaspoon chili powder
- 1/2 teaspoon black pepper
- Sea salt to taste
- 2 pounds frozen hash browns, thawed
- 1/2 cup Cheddar cheese, shredded

DIRECTIONS
- Oil the inside of your crock pot with non-stick spray.
- In a medium-sized skillet, cook the sausage about 10 minutes, until it's browned. Replace to the crock pot.
- Stir in remaining ingredients, except Cheddar cheese.
- Set the crock pot to low and cook about 6 hours.
- Scatter Cheddar cheese on top. Serve warm!

Eggs Florentine with Oyster Mushroom

(Ready in about 2 hours | Servings 4)

INGREDIENTS
- Non-stick spray
- 2 cups Monterey Jack cheese, shredded
- 1 cup Swiss chard
- 1 cup oyster mushroom, sliced
- 2-3 garlic cloves, smashed
- 1 small onion, peeled and diced
- 5 large-sized eggs
- 1 cup light cream
- Salt to taste
- 1/4 teaspoon ground black pepper

DIRECTIONS
- Treat the inside of the crock pot with non-stick spray. Spread 1 cup of the Monterey Jack cheese over the bottom of the crock pot.
- Then lay the spinach on top of the cheese.
- Next, add the oyster mushroom in a layer. Top the mushroom layer with the garlic and onion.
- In a measuring cup or a mixing bowl, beat the eggs with remaining ingredients. Pour this mixture over the layers in the crock pot.
- Top with the remaining 1 cup of cheese.
- Set your crock pot to high, cover with a lid and cook for 2 hours.

Cheese and Swiss chard Casserole

(Ready in about 4 hours | Servings 4)

INGREDIENTS
- Butter flavour non-stick cooking spray
- 4 large-sized eggs
- 1 cup cottage cheese
- 3 tablespoons all-purpose flour
- 1 tablespoon fresh cilantro
- 1/2 teaspoon sea salt
- 1/4 teaspoon freshly ground black pepper
- 1/2 teaspoon dried thyme
- 1/2 teaspoon baking soda
- 2 tablespoons butter, melted
- 1 cup sharp cheese, grated
- 1 cup scallions, finely chopped
- 1 cup Swiss chard

DIRECTIONS
- Coat a heatproof casserole dish with cooking spray. Pour 2 cups of water into the crock pot.
- Add the eggs and whisk them until frothy. Next, stir in the cottage cheese.

- ✓ Add the flour, cilantro, sea salt, black pepper, thyme, baking soda, and butter. Mix well until everything is well incorporated.
- ✓ Next, stir in remaining ingredients; adjust the seasonings.
- ✓ Place the heatproof casserole dish onto the cooking rack in the crock pot; cover with a suitable lid and cook on low-heat setting approximately 4 hours.
- ✓ Let cool to room temperature before serving time and enjoy!

Nutty Banana Frittata

(Ready in about 18 hours | Servings 6)

INGREDIENTS

- 1 tablespoon canola oil
- 1 loaf bread, cut into cubes
- 1 cup cream cheese
- 2 ripe bananas
- 1 cup almonds, coarsely chopped
- 10 large eggs
- 1/4 cup maple syrup
- 1 cup half-and-half
- A pinch of salt

DIRECTIONS

- ✓ Grease the inside of your crock pot with canola oil.
- ✓ Place 1/2 of bread cubes in the bottom of the crock pot. Then, evenly spread 1/2 of the cream cheese.
- ✓ Arrange the slices of 1 banana over the cream cheese. Then scatter 1/2 of the chopped almonds.
- ✓ Repeat the layers one more time.
- ✓ In a mixing bowl or a measuring cup, whisk the eggs together with maple syrup, half-and-half and salt; pour over the layers in the crock pot.
- ✓ Set in a refrigerator at least 12 hours. After that, cover and cook on low for 6 hours. Serve with some extra bananas if desired.

Yummy Spiced Pumpkin Frittata

(Ready in about 6 hours | Servings 6)

INGREDIENTS

- 2 tablespoons coconut oil, melted
- 1 loaf bread, cut into small cubes
- 1 cup cream cheese
- 1 cup pumpkin, shredded
- 2 bananas, sliced
- 1 cup walnuts, coarsely chopped
- 8 eggs
- 1 cup half-and-half
- 2 tablespoons raw honey
- 1/2 teaspoon ground cinnamon
- 1/4 teaspoon grated cardamom
- 1/2 teaspoon allspice
- 1 teaspoon of pumpkin spice
- Powdered sugar for garnish

DIRECTIONS

- ✓ Coat the inside of a crock pot with coconut oil.
- ✓ Place 1/2 of bread in the crock pot. Then, place 1/2 of the cream cheese.
- ✓ Next, evenly spread 1/2 of shredded pumpkin. Lay the slices of 1 banana over the pumpkin. Scatter 1/2 of the chopped walnuts over the bananas.
- ✓ Repeat the layers one more time.
- ✓ In a medium-sized mixing bowl, whisk the eggs with the rest of ingredients, except powdered sugar. Pour this mixture over the layers in your crock pot.
- ✓ Cook covered for 6 hours on low-heat setting. Dust your frittata with powdered sugar and serve!

Spiced Porridge for Busy Mornings

(Ready in about 8 hours | Servings 8)

INGREDIENTS

- 2 cups steel-cut oats
- 6 cups water
- 2 cups milk
- 1 tablespoon pure orange juice
- 1 cup dried apricots, chopped
- 1 cup dates, chopped
- 1 cup raisins, chopped
- 1/2 teaspoon ginger
- 1 teaspoon ground cinnamon
- 1/8 teaspoon cloves
- 1/4 cup maple syrup
- 1/2 vanilla bean

DIRECTIONS

- ✓ Combine all of the ingredients in a crock pot.
- ✓ Set the crock pot to low and leave overnight.
- ✓ In the morning, stir prepared porridge, scraping the sides and bottom. Serve with jam or leftover eggnog, if desired.

Family Mid-Winter Porridge

(Ready in about 9 hours | Servings 8)

INGREDIENTS

- 7 cups water
- 2 cups steel-cut Irish oats
- 1 teaspoon lemon zest
- 1 cup raisins
- 1 cup dried cranberries
- 1 cup dried cherries
- 1 tablespoon shredded coconut
- 1/2 teaspoon ginger
- 1 teaspoon allspice
- 1/8 teaspoon grated nutmeg
- 1/4 cup honey
- 1/2 vanilla bean

DIRECTIONS

- ✓ Place all ingredients in a crock pot; set crock pot to low.
- ✓ Cook overnight or 8 to 9 hours.
- ✓ Tomorrow, stir the porridge and divide among eight serving bowls. Serve with a dollop of whipped cream and roasted nuts, if desired.

Amazing Apple Oatmeal with Prunes

(Ready in about 7 hours | Servings 8)

INGREDIENTS

- 2 cups steel-cut oats
- 1 cup apple juice
- 5 cups water
- 1/2 cup dried apples
- 1/4 cup dried cranberries
- 1/4 cup prunes
- 1/4 cup maple syrup
- 1 teaspoon allspice
- A pinch of salt

DIRECTIONS
- Add all ingredients to a crock pot.
- Set a crock pot to low; cook the oatmeal for about 7 hours.
- Serve warm topped with heavy cream if desired.

Tropical Overnight Oatmeal

(Ready in about 8 hours | Servings 8)

INGREDIENTS

- 2 cups steel-cut Irish oats
- 4 cups water
- 1 cup apple juice
- 1 tablespoon fresh orange juice
- 1/2 cup dried papaya
- 1/2 cup dried pineapple
- 1/4 cup dried mango
- 1/4 cup maple syrup
- 2 tablespoon coconut flakes
- A pinch of salt

DIRECTIONS
- Combine all of the ingredients in your crock pot.
- Cover with a suitable lid; leave the oatmeal overnight or 7 to 8 hours.
- Serve with milk or a dollop of whipped cream. Enjoy!

English Muffins with Tomato Topper

(Ready in about 2 hours | Servings 12)

INGREDIENTS

- 2 tablespoons vegetable oil
- 2 large-sized red onions, chopped
- 1 (28-ounce) can crushed tomatoes
- 1 tablespoon Worcester sauce
- 1 teaspoon lemon zest
- 1 tablespoon fresh cilantro
- 1 tablespoon fresh basil, chopped
- 1 teaspoon sea salt
- 1/4 teaspoon ground black pepper
- 1 cup mozzarella cheese
- 12 English muffins

DIRECTIONS
- In a medium-sized heavy skillet, heat vegetable oil over medium-high heat. Reduce the heat and then add onions. Sauté red onions until they are tender and translucent.
- Transfer to the crock pot. Add in tomatoes and Worcester sauce. Cook covered on high for 1 hour or until the mixture begins to bubble around the edges.
- Add remaining ingredients, except English muffins, and cook 1 hour longer. Serve warm with toasted English muffins.

Southern Creamy Grits

(Ready in about 8 hours | Servings 12)

INGREDIENTS

- 1 ½ cups stone-ground grits
- 1 tablespoon butter
- 1/4 teaspoon turmeric powder
- 4 cups vegetable broth
- 1/2 teaspoon ground black pepper
- 1/2 teaspoon fine sea salt
- 1/2 cup sharp cheese, shredded

DIRECTIONS
- Combine all of the ingredients, except cheese, in your crock pot.
- Cook on low-heat setting for 8 hours or overnight.
- Add cheese to the prepared grits and enjoy. You can serve with eggs and bacon, if desired.

Grandma's Grits with Parmesan cheese

(Ready in about 9 hours | Servings 8)

INGREDIENTS

- 2 cups stone-ground grits
- 1 tablespoon butter
- 1 teaspoons salt
- 1/2 teaspoon black pepper
- 1/2 teaspoon white pepper
- 1/4 cup heavy cream
- 1/2 cup freshly grated Parmesan cheese

DIRECTIONS
- Add all ingredients, except heavy cream and Parmesan cheese, to your crock pot.
- Cook on low 8 to 9 hours.
- In the morning, stir in heavy cream and Parmesan cheese; serve with your favourite topping and enjoy!

Super Greens and Bacon Casserole

(Ready in about 2 hours | Servings 6)

INGREDIENTS

- 1 cup low-fat sharp cheese, shredded
- 1 cup leafy greens (such as spinach, kale, Swiss chard)
- 1/2 cup bacon, sliced

- 3 slices of bread, cubed
- 1 cup mushrooms, sliced
- 6 eggs
- 1/4 teaspoon black pepper
- 1/4 teaspoon cayenne pepper
- 1/2 teaspoon kosher salt
- 1 cup evaporated milk
- 1 cup vegetable broth
- 1 medium-sized onion

DIRECTIONS
- Spread half of the cheese on the bottom of the crock pot. Top with a layer of leafy greens. Next, lay 1/2 of the bacon.
- Add the bread cubes and then place the mushrooms.
- Add the remaining bacon and top with the remaining cheese.
- In a measuring cup or a mixing bowl, combine the rest of ingredients. Pour this mixture into the crock pot.
- Cook for 2 hours on high-heat setting. Divide among six serving plates
- and enjoy!

Delicious Wheat Berries

(Ready in about 10 hours | Servings 6)

INGREDIENTS
- 1 ½ cups wheat berries
- 4 cups water
- 1/2 cup dried cranberries
- 1/2 vanilla bean
- Brown sugar for garnish

DIRECTIONS
- In a crock pot, place wheat berries, water, dried cranberries, and vanilla bean.
- Stir to combine and cook for 8 to 10 hours.
- Stir before serving, sprinkle with sugar and enjoy!

Multigrain Cereal Breakfast

(Ready in about 8 hours | Servings 6)

INGREDIENTS
- 1/2 cup long-grain rice
- 1/2 cup wheat berries
- 1 cup rolled oats
- 1/2 teaspoon kosher salt
- 4 cups water
- Butter for garnish

DIRECTIONS
- Put rice, wheat berries, rolled oats, salt and water into a crock pot.
- Cook, covered approximately 8 hours.
- Stir before serving, add butter and enjoy!

Cereal with Fruit and Peanut Butter

(Ready in about 8 hours | Servings 6)

INGREDIENTS
- 1/2 cup wheat berries
- 1 cup Irish-style oats
- 1/2 cup basmati rice
- 1/4 cup brown sugar
- 1/4 teaspoon ground cinnamon
- 4 cups water
- 1 cup dried fruit of choice
- Peanut butter for garnish

DIRECTIONS
- Place wheat berries, oats, basmati rice, sugar, cinnamon and water in your crock pot; stir to combine.
- Cook for about 8 hours.
- Divide among six serving bowls; garnish with dried fruit and peanut butter and serve.

Oatmeal with Fruits

(Ready in about 8 hours | Servings 4)

INGREDIENTS
- Butter to grease crock pot
- 2 cups milk
- 1/4 cup brown sugar
- 1 tablespoon butter, melted
- 1/4 teaspoon salt
- 1/2 teaspoon cinnamon
- 1 cup rolled oats
- 1 ripe peach, chopped
- 1/2 cup dried apricots, chopped
- 1/2 cup chopped walnuts
- Milk (optional)

DIRECTIONS
- Butter the inside of the crock pot.
- Combine together milk, sugar, butter, salt, cinnamon, rolled oats, peach, and apricots in the crock pot. Cover the crock pot, set to low and cook overnight.
- In the morning, divide oatmeal among serving plates. Scatter the chopped walnuts and serve warm with milk.

Grandma's Rice Pudding

(Ready in about 6 hours | Servings 4)

INGREDIENTS
- 2 ½ cups cooked rice
- 1 ½ cups scalded milk
- 2/3 cup brown sugar
- 2 tablespoons butter, soften
- 1 tablespoon almond extract
- 1 teaspoon nutmeg, grated
- 3 eggs, beaten
- 1 cup raisins
- Cinnamon for garnish

DIRECTIONS

- Combine together cooked rice, milk, sugar, butter, almond extract, grated nutmeg, and beaten eggs. Stir to combine all ingredients.
- Pour this mixture into a crock pot.
- Cover and cook on low setting for 4 to 6 hours. Remove prepared pudding from the crock pot, sprinkle raisins, garnish with cinnamon and serve warm.

Orange Carrots with Nuts

(Ready in about 3 hours | Servings 6)

INGREDIENTS

- 3 cups carrots, sliced into matchsticks
- 2 cups water
- 1/2 teaspoon salt
- 3 tablespoons butter
- 3 tablespoons orange marmalade
- 2 tablespoons lemon juice
- 2 tablespoons almonds, chopped

DIRECTIONS

- Place carrots, water, and salt in a crock pot. Cook covered on high 2 to 3 hours.
- Drain the carrots well. Add butter, orange marmalade, lemon juice, and almonds.
- Cover the crock pot and set on high. Cook for 30 minutes.

Old-fashioned Fried Polenta

(Ready in about 9 hours | Servings 10)

INGREDIENTS

- 3 tablespoons butter, melted
- 1/4 teaspoon cayenne pepper
- 6 cups hot water
- 2 cups cornmeal
- 2 teaspoons salt
- Red pepper flakes for garnish

DIRECTIONS

- Grease the crock pot with 1 tablespoon of the butter.
- Set the crock pot to low, and add the remaining butter, cayenne pepper, water, cornmeal, and salt. Mix well, cover and cook for 6 to 9 hours.
- Fry the cooked polenta in a cast-iron skillet until it is well browned. Divide among serving plates, sprinkle with pepper flakes and serve warm.

Famous Southwest Breakfast

(Ready in about 8 hours | Servings 12)

INGREDIENTS

- 1 tablespoon olive oil
- 1 lb. bulk sausage, cooked
- 2 scallions, finely chopped
- 1 red bell pepper, chopped
- 4 ounces green chilies, chopped
- 2 ½ cups semi-hard cheese, shredded
- 18 eggs
- sour cream for garnish
- fresh parsley for garnish, chopped

DIRECTIONS

- Oil inside of a crock pot. Place the ingredients in this order: sausage, scallions, peppers, chilies, and cheese.
- Repeat this process until all ingredients are used.
- Whisk eggs until they are well combined. Pour it over prepared mixture.
- Cover and cook on low setting for 7 to 8 hours.
- Garnish with sour cream, sprinkle fresh parsley and serve warm.

Ham and Tater Tots Casserole

(Ready in about 10 hours | Servings 6)

INGREDIENTS

- 1 pound frozen tater tots
- 1/2 pound ham, sliced
- 1 white onion
- 1 red bell pepper, diced
- 3/4 cup Cheddar cheese, shredded
- 6 eggs
- 1/2 cup milk
- 1/4 teaspoon black pepper

DIRECTIONS

- Place the ingredients in the following order: tater tots, ham, onions, red bell pepper, and cheese. Repeat this process until all ingredients have been used.
- In a mixing bowl, whisk eggs with milk. Season with salt and black pepper.
- Pour egg-milk mixture over mixture in the crock pot. Set the crock pot on low, cover it and cook for 10 to 12 hours.

Beef and Potatoes Casserole

(Ready in about 10 hours | Servings 8)

INGREDIENTS

- 10 eggs
- 1/2 cup milk
- 1 teaspoon olive oil
- 1 onion, sliced
- 1 teaspoon salt
- 1/4 teaspoon black pepper
- 1 pound ground beef
- 1 teaspoon garlic, minced
- 1 red hot pepper, minced
- 5 large potatoes, sliced thin
- 1 ½ cup grated Mexican cheese blend
- liquid smoke to taste

DIRECTIONS

- Whisk the eggs with milk.
- Heat olive oil in a large cast-iron skillet over medium-high heat. Sauté the onions until tender. Season with salt and pepper.

- Add ground beef, garlic and red hot pepper. Add a few drops of liquid smoke to taste.
- In a greased crock pot, layer the ingredients in the following order: potatoes, beef, onion, and cheese. Repeat process until all ingredients have
- been used.
- Pour egg-milk mixture over mixture in the crock pot. Set the crock pot on low and cook for 8 to 10 hours.

Pumpkin and Pecans Bread

(Ready in about 3 hours | Servings 8)

INGREDIENTS

- 1/2 cup canola oil
- 1 cup sugar
- 2 eggs, beaten
- 1 cup pumpkin, canned
- 1 ½ cup all-purpose flour
- 1/2 teaspoon salt
- 1/2 teaspoon cinnamon
- 1 teaspoon baking powder
- 1 cup pecans, chopped

DIRECTIONS

- Blend canola oil and sugar. Stir in eggs and pumpkin. Combine together flour, salt, cinnamon, baking powder, and pecans. Prepare a greased and floured coffee can.
- Transfer batter in the coffee can. Place the coffee can in the crock pot.
- Cover top of the can with paper towels and put a lid.
- Bake on high setting 2 to 3 hours. If the toothpick comes out clean, the bread is done.
- Let it cool on a wire rack. Serve warm or at room temperature with a milk.

Morning Butter Bread

(Ready in about 4 hours | Servings 8)

INGREDIENTS

- 1 ½ cups fine pastry flour
- 1 teaspoon baking soda
- 1/2 teaspoon baking powder
- 1/2 teaspoon salt
- 1 teaspoon Allspice
- 1 cup canned pumpkin
- 1 cup brown sugar
- 1/2 cup buttermilk
- 1 egg, beaten
- 1 teaspoon vanilla extract
- 2 tablespoons butter, softened
- 1 cup almonds, chopped

DIRECTIONS

- Put a metal rack in your crock pot. Prepare greased and floured a 6 cup mold.
- Blend flour, baking soda, baking powder, salt, Allspice, pumpkin, sugar, buttermilk, egg, vanilla, and butter. Beat until all ingredients are well blended.
- Stir in almonds. Place batter into prepared cup mold. Cover cup mold with foil and place on the metal rack. Then add 2 cups hot water in the
- crock pot.
- Bake on high setting for 3 to 4 hours. Serve warm, or at room temperature or cool.

Bread Pudding with Sauce

(Ready in about 5 hours | Servings 4)

INGREDIENTS

- 8 slices bread of choice, cubed
- 4 eggs
- 2 cups whole milk
- 1/2 cup sugar
- 1/4 cup margarine, melted
- 1/4 cup raisins
- 1 teaspoon Allspice
- Sauce:
- 2 tablespoons margarine
- 2 tablespoons all-purpose flour
- 1 cup water
- 3/4 cup sugar

DIRECTIONS

- Oil a crock pot and place bread in it. Beat eggs with milk. Add sugar, margarine, raisins and Allspice.
- To make the pudding: Pour this mixture over bread cubes and stir to combine. Cover the crock pot and cook this mixture on high for 1 hour. Reserve.
- Decrease heat to low and cook for another 3 to 4 hours.
- To make the sauce: melt margarine in a wide skillet. Add flour and stir
- until smooth. Carefully add water and sugar.
- Continue cooking, stirring occasionally, until the sauce is thickened.
- Transfer prepared pudding on the serving plates, spoon the sauce onto each plate and serve.

French Toast

(Ready in about 8 hours | Servings 6)

INGREDIENTS

- 1/2 bread of choice
- 6 eggs
- 2 cup skim milk
- 1 teaspoon Allspice
- 1 tablespoon sugar

DIRECTIONS

- Cut a bread loaf into thin slices and place them in a crock pot.
- Combine together eggs, milk, Allspice, and sugar. Mix well to combine. Pour this mixture over bread.
- Set the crock pot to low and cook French toast overnight.

Cheesy Eggs with Vegetables

(Ready in about 8 hours | Servings 6)

INGREDIENTS

- 2 tablespoons canola oil
- 1 red bell pepper, seeded and sliced
- 1 yellow bell pepper, seeded and sliced
- 1 cup mushrooms, sliced
- 2 - 3 scallions, finely chopped
- 12 eggs
- 1/2 cup half and half
- 1 bag frozen hash brown potatoes, thawed
- 1 cup cheddar cheese, shredded
- 1 teaspoon salt
- 1/2 teaspoon black pepper
- 1 teaspoon basil

DIRECTIONS

✓ Heat canola oil in a wide saucepan. Sauté scallions and peppers until tender. Reserve.
✓ Whisk eggs with half and half. Combine together egg mixture, scallions-peppers mixture, mushrooms, hash browns, and cheese in a crock pot. Season with salt, pepper and basil, and stir gently to combine.
✓ Set the crock pot on low and cook overnight.

Crockpot Spiced Omelet

⌀ **(Ready in about 8 hours | Servings 12)**

INGREDIENTS

- Butter or oil for crock pot
- 1 (32-ounce) bag frozen hash brown potatoes, thawed
- 1 lb. ham, sliced into small chunks
- 1 large onion, sliced into small rings
- 1/2 cup carrots, chopped
- 3/4 lb. Cheddar cheese, grated
- 12 eggs
- 1 cup whole milk
- 1 teaspoon salt
- 1/4 freshly ground black pepper
- 1/2 teaspoon dried thyme
- 1/2 teaspoon dried oregano
- Red pepper flakes for garnish (optional)

DIRECTIONS

✓ Butter the inside of your crock pot. Place a half of prepared ingredients from the bottom to top, in this order: Potatoes, ham, onions, carrots, and cheese. Repeat the same process once again.
✓ Beat the eggs with whole milk. Add salt, black pepper, thyme, and oregano. Pour this mixture over layered mixture in the crock pot.
✓ Set the crock pot on low and cook omelet for 7 to 8 hours, or overnight.
✓ Divide cooked omelet among serving plates, sprinkle red pepper flakes and serve warm.

Sunday Morning Risotto with Apples

⌀ **(Ready in about 5 hours | Servings 4)**

INGREDIENTS

- 1/4 cup butter
- 3 apples, sliced into very small pieces
- 1 ½ cups rice
- 1 teaspoon Allspice
- 1/4 teaspoon cloves
- 1 tender salt
- 1/4 cup sugar
- 3 cups apple juice
- 1 cup half and half

DIRECTIONS

✓ Set the crock pot to high. Then add the butter and cook until it is melted.
✓ Add apples and the rice to the butter, and stir gently to combine well. Add Allspice and cloves.
✓ Season with salt, and stir in the sugar. Stir in the apple juice and half and half.
✓ Cover the crock pot and cook the risotto for 3 to 5 hours.

Classic Banana Bread

⌀ **(Ready in about 6 hours | Servings 8)**

INGREDIENTS

- 1 ¾ cup pastry flour
- 2 teaspoon baking powder
- 1/2 teaspoon salt
- 1/3 cup shortening
- 2/3 cup sugar
- 2 eggs
- 1/ ½ cup ripe banana
- 1/2 cup almonds, coarsely chopped

DIRECTIONS

✓ Sift flour, baking powder and salt. Blend shortening with an electric beater until tender. Gradually, stir in sugar.
✓ Beat eggs with a fork. Mash the bananas well. Combine with the flour mixture and the mashed bananas.
✓ Fold in almonds. Butter a baking dish. Place the batter into the baking dish and transfer to a rack in a crock pot. Cover, but prop the lid open with a toothpick, for example.
✓ Cook on high for 5 to 6 hours.
✓ Let cool on a metal rack for a few minutes and serve.

Breakfast Fruit Casserole

⌀ **(Ready in about 9 hours | Servings 4)**

INGREDIENTS

- 4 apples, peeled, cored and sliced
- 1/4 cup honey
- 1 teaspoon cinnamon
- 1/2 teaspoon grated nutmeg
- 2 tablespoons butter, softened
- 2 cups granola cereals

DIRECTIONS

✓ Combine together apples, honey, cinnamon, nutmeg, butter and cereals.
✓ Cook covered on low for 8 to 9 hours, or overnight. Serve warm.

Breakfast Vegetable Casserole

☒ **(Ready in about 12 hours | Servings 4)**

INGREDIENTS

- 1 (32-ounces) package of frozen potatoes
- 1 lb. bacon cut into pieces, fried and drained
- 1/2 cup onions, sliced
- 3/4 lbs. hard cheese (e.g. cheddar)
- 1 dozen eggs
- 1 cup milk
- 1/2 teaspoon dry mustard
- 1 teaspoon salt
- 1/2 teaspoon freshly ground black pepper
- Red pepper flakes for garnish

DIRECTIONS

- ✓ Prepare all ingredients. Slice bacon into thin slices and fry them on a non-stick saucepan. Slice the onions into the rings. Slice the cheese into bite-sized pieces.
- ✓ Place the ingredients in the crock pot, in the following order: the potatoes, bacon, onions, and cheese. Beat the eggs and mix with milk and mustard. Season with salt and black pepper. Mix to combine well.
- ✓ Pour the mixture over the casserole dish. Cook on low for 10 to 12 hours. Sprinkle red pepper flakes and serve warm.

Creamy Vegetables and Cheese with Bread

☒ **(Ready in about 2 hours | Servings 4)**

INGREDIENTS

- 1 1/2 cup cheddar cheese, grated
- 1 (9-ounces) package frozen spinach, thawed
- 1 cup bread, cubed
- 1 cup fresh mushrooms, thinly sliced
- 1/2 cup onions, sliced into thin rings
- 6 eggs
- 1 ½ cups skim milk
- 1/2 cup heavy cream
- 1 teaspoon salt
- 1/2 teaspoon black pepper
- 1 teaspoon basil

DIRECTIONS

- ✓ Lightly oil the slow cooker. Place a half of the cheddar cheese, and then add spinach, bread, mushrooms and onions.
- ✓ Beat the eggs, and beat in milk, cream, salt, pepper and basil until all ingredients are combined.
- ✓ Pour the egg-milk mixture over the cheese-spinach mixture. Top with the remaining half of cheese.
- ✓ Cook covered on high for 2 hours.

Sunday Burger Sandwiches

☒ **(Ready in about 7 hours | Servings 8)**

INGREDIENTS

- 1½ lbs. lean ground meet
- 1 (8-ounces) package pasteurized process cheese spread, shredded
- 2 tablespoons whole milk
- 1 red bell pepper, diced
- 4 spring onions, finely chopped
- 3 cloves garlic, minced
- 1 teaspoon salt
- 1/4 teaspoon black pepper
- 1/2 teaspoon cayenne pepper
- 8 sandwich American-style burger buns
- Lettuce leaves for garnish

DIRECTIONS

- ✓ Cook ground meat in a wide saucepan until it is well browned.
- ✓ Place cooked ground meat in a crock pot, and add pasteurized process cheese spread, milk, bell pepper, onions and garlic. Season with salt, pepper and cayenne pepper. Stir to combine.
- ✓ Cover and cook on low for 6 to 7 hours.
- ✓ Divide prepared meat mixture among burger buns, garnish with lettuce and serve immediately.

The Best Chinese Pie Ever

☒ **(Ready in about 9 hours | Servings 6)**

INGREDIENTS

- 1 large red onion, finely sliced
- 1 pound lean ground beef
- 2 red bell peppers, sliced
- 5 large potatoes, diced
- 2 tablespoons canola oil
- 2 (15-ounces) cans whole kernel corn
- 1 teaspoon salt
- 1/2 teaspoon black pepper

DIRECTIONS

- ✓ Heat a wide cast-iron skillet and sauté the onion until translucent or for 5 minutes.
- ✓ Stir in ground beef and bell peppers, and cook for 4 to 5 minutes more. Drain well, and place this mixture in the crock pot.
- ✓ Toss potatoes with canola oil and add to the crock pot. Then stir in the corn. Season with salt and black pepper. Cover and cook on low for 7 to 9 hours.

Crispy Ham in Cola

☒ **(Ready in about 8 hours | Servings 10)**

INGREDIENTS

- 2 tablespoon brown sugar
- 1 heaping tablespoon molasses
- 1 teaspoon Dijon mustard
- 1/4 cup cola
- 4 pound pre-cooked ham

DIRECTIONS

- ✓ Combine brown sugar, molasses and Dijon mustard. Add 1/8 cup of cola and make a paste with a smooth texture.
- ✓ Score prepared ham with shallow virgules in a diamond form. Add sugar-mustard mixture.
- ✓ Layer ham in the crock pot and stir in remaining 1/8 cup of cola. Cook covered on high setting for about 1 hour. Reduce the heat to low and cook for 6 to 7 hours.

Corn and Ham with Potatoes

(Ready in about 8 hours | Servings 4)

INGREDIENTS

- 5 potatoes, peeled and diced
- 1 ½ cups cooked ham, diced
- 1 (15-ounce) can kernel corn, drained
- 2 teaspoons instant onion, minced
- 1 (11-ounce) can cheese soup
- 1/2 cup whole milk
- 3 tablespoons whole white wheat flour
- Black pepper to taste

DIRECTIONS

- ✓ In a slow cooker, place potatoes, ham, kernel corn, and instant onion. Mix well to combine.
- ✓ In a mixing bowl, whisk cheese soup and milk. Then add flour and mix until the mixture is smooth.
- ✓ Pour soup-flour mixture over potato-ham mixture.
- ✓ Add black pepper to taste and mix carefully. Cover and cook on low setting for 8 hours. Serve warm.

Fruit and Cheese Breakfast

(Ready in about 1 hour 30 minutes | Servings 4)

INGREDIENTS

- 3 apples, peeled and cored
- 1 large can pineapple chunks with their own juice
- 1 cup Colby cheese, shredded
- 3/4 cup sugar
- 1/3 cup flour
- 1/3 cup butter (melted)
- 1/3 cup pineapple juice
- Raisins to garnish

DIRECTIONS

- ✓ Slice the apples into bite-sized cubes. Layer 1/2 of the apples and pineapple, and add a half of the dry ingredients (sugar and flour). Add also a half of the cheese.
- ✓ Repeat this again with one more layer.
- ✓ Combine butter and pineapple juice. Pour it over prepared layers.
- ✓ Preheat the oven to 350 degrees F. Bake your meal in an uncovered baking dish for about 30 minutes. Transfer it in the crock pot, and cook for 1 hour on high setting. Sprinkle raisins and serve.

Beef Dip Sandwiches

(Ready in about 12 hours | Servings 12)

INGREDIENTS

- 1 beef roast
- 1/2 cup tamari sauce
- 3 cloves garlic
- 1 beef bouillon cube
- 2 bay leaves
- 4 peppercorns
- 1 teaspoon dried rosemary
- 1 teaspoon fine sea salt
- 1/2 teaspoon red pepper
- Baguette of choice

DIRECTIONS

- ✓ Place beef roast in a crock pot. Mix together tamari sauce, garlic, bouillon cube, bay leaves, peppercorns, rosemary, salt and red pepper. Mix to combine.
- ✓ Pour in water to coat beef roast.
- ✓ Cover and cook over low setting 10 to 12 hours, or overnight.
- ✓ Cut the meat and make the sandwiches with slices of the baguette. Serve warm.

Apple Cranberries Oats

(Ready in about 8 hours | Servings 6)

INGREDIENTS

- 1 cup regular oats
- 3 ½ cups water
- 1 apple, peeled, cored and diced
- 1/2 cup dried cranberries
- 2 tablespoons butter, softened
- 1 tablespoon cinnamon
- 2 tablespoons sugar
- 2 tablespoon molasses

DIRECTIONS

- ✓ Place the oats, water, apple, cranberries, butter, cinnamon, sugar, and molasses into a crock pot. Mix to combine.
- ✓ Cover, set to low, and cook for 8 hours, or overnight. Sprinkle the cranberries on top and serve warm.

Sausage Onion Pie

(Ready in about 8 hours | Servings 4)

INGREDIENTS

- 1 teaspoon extra-virgin olive oil
- 8 eggs, beaten
- 1 yam, shredded
- 1 pound pork sausage, sliced
- 1 onion, diced
- 1 teaspoon garlic powder
- 1 tablespoon dried basil
- 1 sea salt
- 1/2 teaspoon black pepper

DIRECTIONS

- ✓ Oil a crock pot with olive oil.
- ✓ Cut the yum into small cubes.

- Add beaten eggs, sausages, onion and garlic powder. Season with basil, salt and black pepper. Stir to combine.
- Cook on low setting for 8 hours, or overnight.
- Remove from the crock pot, divide among serving plates and serve warm.

Sausage and Bacon Breakfast Casserole

(Ready in about 8 hours | Servings 8)

INGREDIENTS

- Non-stick cooking spray for greasing the crock pot
- 1/2 lb. bulk sausage, thinly sliced
- 6 ounces bacon, sliced into thin and small strips
- 1 onion, diced
- 1 lb. sweet potatoes, peeled and grated
- 2 orange bell peppers, seeded and diced
- 16 eggs, whipped
- 1/2 cup whole milk
- 1/4 cup almond milk
- 1 teaspoon salt
- 1 teaspoon dry mustard
- 1/4 teaspoon freshly ground black pepper
- Parsley for garnish

DIRECTIONS

- Generously spray a crock pot.
- Heat a wide saucepan over medium-high heat. Sauté the sausage and bacon for 10 minutes, or until the bacon is crispy, the sausage is browned and the onion is translucent and very tender.
- Place the sweet potatoes in the crock pot. Add the cooked sausage-onion mixture and stir in the bell peppers.
- Whisk together the eggs, milk and almond milk, then add salt, mustard, and pepper. Pour over the mixture in the crock pot.
- Cover and cook on low for 6 to 8 hours, or overnight. Transfer to a serving platter, sprinkle the parsley and serve warm.

Wake up Sausages and Squash Casserole

(Ready in about 10 hours | Servings 6)

INGREDIENTS

- 1 lb. chorizo sausage
- 1 yellow onion, sliced
- 12 eggs
- 1 cup almond milk
- 1 small butternut squash
- Butter for greasing the crock pot
- Fresh chopped parsley for garnish

DIRECTIONS

- Preheat a cast-iron skillet and cook the chorizo sausage for about 10 minutes. Add the onion and cook just until the onion is tender and translucent.
- Whisk together eggs and almond milk.
- Peel, discard the seeds and chop butternut squash.
- Butter the crock pot and place the squash, the sausage-onion mixture, and then stir in the egg-milk mixture.
- Set the crock pot on low and cook casserole for 8 to 10 hours, or overnight. In the morning, divide casserole among serving plates, sprinkle parsley and serve warm.

French-Italian Sandwiches

(Ready in about 10 hours | Servings 8)

INGREDIENTS

- 4 lbs. rump roast
- 1 package dry French au jus mix
- 1 package dry Italian dressing mix
- 1 (10.5-ounces) can beef broth
- 1 ½ cups water
- 1 medium yellow onion, sliced
- buns of your choice
- Cheese of choice for garnish
- Butter lettuce leaves for garnish
- Sea salt to taste

DIRECTIONS

- Place rump roast in a crock pot. Whisk French mix, Italian mix, beef broth and water and stir to combine. Pour this mixture over roast.
- Cook on low setting for 8 to 10 hours, or cook overnight. Remove roast and place onion in the crock pot, cook on high until the onion begins to soften. Reserve onion and sauce from the crock pot for serving.
- Slice cooked roast into very thin pieces.
- To make the sandwiches: Pile slices of the roast on buns with onions and layer the cheese of choice.
- Preheat oven to 350 degrees F. Bake the sandwiches for 10 minutes.
- Remove from the oven, garnish with lettuce leaves and season with sea salt to taste. Serve with additional sauce from the crock pot.

Hot Dogs with Chili Beans

(Ready in about 4 hours | Servings 5)

INGREDIENTS

- 1 (15-ounces) can of chili beans
- 1 (6-ounces) can tomato paste
- 1 large yellow bell pepper
- 1/4 cup scallions, finely chopped
- 1 teaspoon Dijon mustard
- 1 teaspoon kosher salt
- 1/3 teaspoon chili powder
- 10 frankfurters
- 10 frankfurter buns

DIRECTIONS

- Combine together chili beans, tomato paste, yellow pepper, scallions, mustard, salt, and chili powder.
- Cover and cook on low for 3 to 4 hours.

- ✓ In a deep saucepan, bring water to a boil. Place frankfurters into water and cook for about 5 minutes.
- ✓ Divide frankfurters among prepared buns. Spread chili mixture among buns and serve.

Butternut Squash with Maple Syrup

(Ready in about 5 hours | Servings 6)

INGREDIENTS

- 3 tablespoons butter, melted
- 1 butternut squash, peeled, seeded and cubed
- 1/2 cup maple syrup
- Juice of one fresh lemon
- 1 teaspoon pumpkin pie spice
- A dash of cinnamon

DIRECTIONS

- ✓ Set a crock pot on high. Grease the crock pot with the melted butter.
- ✓ Add cubed squash, maple syrup, lemon juice, pumpkin pie spice, and a dash of cinnamon.
- ✓ Cook on high for 4 to 5 hours. Mix well to combine all ingredients before serving.

Fruit Oatmeal with Almonds

(Ready in about 8 hours | Servings 4)

INGREDIENTS

- 2 cups milk
- 1/4 cup brown sugar
- 1 teaspoon almond extract
- 1 tablespoon butter, softened
- 1/3 teaspoon cinnamon
- 1 cup rolled oats
- 1 cup apple, thinly sliced
- 1/2 cup raisins
- 1/2 cup almonds, chopped

DIRECTIONS

- ✓ Grease the inside of a crock pot to prevent sticking.
- ✓ Combine together milk, sugar, almond extract, butter, cinnamon, oats, apple, and raisins. Stir to combine.
- ✓ Set the crock pot on low, and cook the oatmeal overnight, or for 8 hours. Scatter chopped almonds and serve warm.

Caramel and Nuts Biscuits

(Ready in about 2 hours | Servings 4)

INGREDIENTS

- Non-stick spray
- 6 to 8 biscuits
- 4 tablespoons butter, softened
- 1/2 cup brown sugar
- Chopped and toasted walnuts for garnish

DIRECTIONS

- ✓ Oil a crock pot with non-stick cooking spray.
- ✓ Place the biscuits on the bottom of the crock pot.
- ✓ In a wide cast-iron skillet, heat and melt butter with brown sugar. Cook until the mixture is well melted and combined.
- ✓ Pour this mixture over the biscuits. Cover, set crock pot on high, and cook
- ✓ 1 hour to 1 hour 30 minutes.
- ✓ Preheat oven to 350 degrees F.
- ✓ Grease a baking pan with non-stick cooking spray. Transfer your dish in the pan and bake for 20 minutes.
- ✓ Scatter chopped and toasted walnuts, divide the biscuits among serving plates and serve.

Eggs with Vegetables and Bacon

(Ready in about 8 hours | Servings 10)

INGREDIENTS

- 1 (32-ounce) bag frozen potatoes
- 1 lb. cooked bacon, slice into thin strips
- 1 white onion, diced
- 3/4 lb. hard cheese, shredded
- 12 eggs
- 1 cup milk
- 1/2 teaspoon dry mustard
- 1 teaspoon salt
- 1/4 teaspoon freshly ground black pepper
- 1 teaspoon dried basil

DIRECTIONS

- ✓ Place the ingredients in a crock pot in the following order, from the bottom to top: 1/2 of the potatoes, 1/2 of the cooked bacon, 1/2 of the onions and 1/2 of the cheese.
- ✓ Whisk the eggs, milk, dry mustard, salt, black pepper and basil. Pour this mixture over the vegetable-bacon-cheese mixture.
- ✓ Set the crock pot on low and cook for 10 to 12 hours.

Wheat Berry with Apricots

(Ready in about 9 hours | Servings 4)

INGREDIENTS

- 1 cup wheat berries, rinsed & drained
- 2 cups apple juice
- 1/2 cup apricots, sliced
- 1/4 cup cranberries
- 1/2 teaspoon Allspice
- 1/4 teaspoon clove
- 1/4 teaspoon cardamom

DIRECTIONS

- ✓ Place berries, apple juice, apricots, cranberries, Allspice, clove and cardamom in the crock pot.
- ✓ Cook on low overnight. Divide among serving plates and serve.

Hot Dogs with Red Sauce

(Ready in about 8 hours | Servings 4)

INGREDIENTS

- 2 lb. can baked beans
- 1/4 teaspoon garlic powder
- 1/4 cup tomato sauce
- 2 tablespoons sugar
- 1 white onion, diced
- 2 tablespoons molasses
- 1/4 cup barbeque sauce
- 1 lb. hot dogs, sliced
- 4 hot dog buns
- Mustard for garnish

DIRECTIONS
- ✓ Combine together beans, garlic powder, tomato, sugar, onion, molasses, barbeque sauce, and hot dogs.
- ✓ Cover and cook on low setting for 8 hours, or overnight.
- ✓ Serve with the hot dog buns and mustard.

Cornmeal Pudding with Eggs

⌀ **(Ready in about 2 hours | Servings 4)**

INGREDIENTS
- 1 cup yellow cornmeal
- 1/4 cup molasses
- 1/4 cup sugar
- 1/4 cup butter
- 1/4 teaspoon salt
- 1/4 teaspoon baking powder
- 2 eggs
- 6 cup hot milk

DIRECTIONS
- ✓ Combine yellow cornmeal, molasses, sugar, butter, salt, baking powder and eggs with 3 cups of milk in a deep and wide saucepan.
- ✓ Mix to combine and simmer for a few minutes.
- ✓ Pour in the remaining 3 cups of the milk. Place the mixture in the crock pot and cook for 2 hours.

Oatmeal with Dates and Coconut

⌀ **(Ready in about 9 hours | Servings 6)**

INGREDIENTS
- 1 tablespoon butter, melted
- 2 cup milk
- 1/4 cup brown sugar
- 1/2 teaspoon salt
- 1/2 teaspoon cinnamon
- 1/4 teaspoon nutmeg, grated
- 1 cup quick-cooking oats
- 1 apple, cut into very small chunks
- 1/2 cup dates, chopped
- 1/2 cup walnuts, chopped
- 2 tablespoons coconut flakes

DIRECTIONS
- ✓ Grease the inside of a crock pot with 1 tablespoon butter.
- ✓ Place milk, sugar, salt, cinnamon, nutmeg, oats, apples, dates, and walnuts and mix well to combine all ingredients.
- ✓ Cover the crock pot, set on low and cook the oatmeal overnight.
- ✓ In the morning, divide oatmeal among serving plates, sprinkle coconut flakes and serve warm.

Crockpot Bread with Rosemary

⌀ **(Ready in about 3 hours 30 minutes | Servings 12)**

INGREDIENTS
- 1 package dry active yeast
- 1¼ cups warm water
- 1 teaspoon honey
- 1 teaspoon salt
- 4 tablespoons fresh rosemary, chopped
- 2 tablespoons flax seeds, ground
- 4 tablespoons olive oil
- 3 ½ cups all-purpose flour

DIRECTIONS
- ✓ Combine together the water, yeast, and honey. Allow to stand for 10 to 15 minutes in a warm place, until the mixture is bubbly.
- ✓ Stir in salt, rosemary, flax seeds, 3 tablespoons of olive oil, and the flour. Add yeast mixture and stir well until all ingredients are combined.
- ✓ Let the dough sit in the warm, draft-free place for 1 hour.
- ✓ Knead the dough on a floured surface and let it rest for another 30 minutes.
- ✓ Turn the crock pot to high setting. Line the crock pot with parchment paper.
- ✓ Transfer the dough to the crock pot, coat it with paper towels and place lid on top.
- ✓ Cook the bread for 2 hours.
- ✓ To get the crunchy crust: Transfer your bread to the baking pan and bake in broiler for about 5 minutes.
- ✓ Drizzle the remaining 1 tablespoon of olive oil and let it cool on a wire rack before serving.
- ✓

Cheesy Spinach Quiche

⌀ **(Ready in about 3 hours | Servings 6)**

INGREDIENTS
- Non-stick cooking spray
- 4 eggs
- 1/2 cup sharp cheese, shredded
- 3/4 cup baby spinach
- 2-3 cloves garlic, minced
- 1/4 cup green onion, chopped
- 1/2 teaspoon sea salt
- 1/2 teaspoon black pepper
- 1/2 teaspoon cayenne pepper
- 1 ½ cups evaporated milk
- 2 slices whole grain bread, cubed

DIRECTIONS
- ✓ Lightly grease your crock pot with cooking spray.

- In a medium-sized mixing bowl, combine the eggs, cheese, spinach, garlic, onion, salt, black pepper, cayenne pepper and evaporated milk. Stir until everything is well incorporated.
- Arrange the bread cubes on the bottom of the crock pot. Pour the egg-cheese mixture over the bread cubes.
- Cover with a lid; cook for about 3 hours on high. Serve warm.

MAIN MEAL RECIPES

Java Roast Beef

Serves: 6 Preparation Time: 5 minutes Cooking Time: 12 hours

INGREDIENTS

- 1 boneless beef chuck roast
- 1 ½ cups strong coffee
- 5 cloves of garlic, crushed
- 1 ½ teaspoon salt
- ¾ teaspoon pepper

INSTRUCTIONS
- Place all ingredients in a mixing bowl. Gently give the beef a massage.
- Place in the crockpot – beef and all.
- Close the lid and cook on low for 12 hours.
  - **Nutrition information: Calories per serving: 192; Carbohydrates: 1.36g; Protein: 27.39g; Fat: 8.62g; Fiber: 0.1g**

Garlic Apple Pork Roast

Serves: 12 Preparation Time: 5 minutes Cooking Time: 10 hours

INGREDIENTS

- 3 ½ pounds boneless pork loin roast
- 1 jar apple jelly
- ½ cup water
- 2 ½ teaspoon minced garlic
- 1 ½ teaspoon salt

INSTRUCTIONS
- Place all ingredients in a mixing bowl. Place all ingredients in the crockpot.
- Close the lid and cook on low for 10 hours.
  - **Nutrition information: Calories per serving: 236; Carbohydrates: 19g; Protein: 26g; Fat:6 g; Fiber: 0g**

Crockpot Sweet Ham

Serves: 12 Preparation Time: 5 minutes Cooking Time: 6 hours

INGREDIENTS

- ½ cup brown sugar, packed
- 1 teaspoon ground mustard
- 2 tablespoons cola
- 1 teaspoon ground mustard
- 5 pounds cooked boneless ham

INSTRUCTIONS
- Place all ingredients in a mixing bowl.
- Place all ingredients in the crockpot. Close the lid and cook on low for 6 hours.
  - **Nutrition information: Calories per serving: 230; Carbohydrates: 11.6g; Protein: 32.1g; Fat: 6.6g; Fiber: 0g**

Crockpot Carnitas Tacos

Serves: 10 Preparation Time: 5 minutes Cooking Time: 10 hours

INGREDIENTS

- 3 pounds pork shoulder, trimmed from excess fat
- 1 envelope taco seasoning
- 1 can diced tomatoes and green chilies, undrained
- 2 cups Monterey Jack cheese, grated
- 1 cup sour cream

INSTRUCTIONS
- Cut the roast into thick slices and place in the crockpot. Season with taco seasoning and mix until well combined. Add the tomatoes and green chilies. Mix.
- Sprinkle with cheese on top.
- Close the lid and cook on low for 10 hours. Garnish with sour cream on top.
- Serve with corn tortillas.
  - **Nutrition information: Calories per serving: 414; Carbohydrates: 30g; Protein: 28g; Fat: 20g; Fiber: 10.5g**

Pineapple Barbecue Pork Chops

Serves: 4 Preparation Time: 5 minutes Cooking Time: 9 hours

INGREDIENTS

- 1 can crushed pineapples, undrained
- 1 cup honey barbecue sauce
- 1/3 cup onion, chopped
- 2 tablespoons chili sauce
- 4 bone-in pork chops

INSTRUCTIONS
- ✓ Place all ingredients in a mixing bowl.
- ✓ Place all ingredients in the crockpot. Close the lid and cook on low for 9 hours.
  - Nutrition information: Calories per serving: 257; Carbohydrates: 41g; Protein: 9g; Fat: 5g; Fiber: 1g

Shredded Pork with Beans

Serves: 10 Preparation Time: 5 minutes Cooking Time: 8 hours

INGREDIENTS
- 3 pounds pork tenderloin, cut into large chunks
- 2 cans black beans, drained
- 1 jar picante sauce
- 1 teaspoon oregano
- Salt and pepper to taste

INSTRUCTIONS
- ✓ Place all ingredients in a mixing bowl.
- ✓ Place all ingredients in the crockpot. Close the lid and cook on low for 8 hours. Serve with rice if desired.
  - Nutrition information: Calories per serving: 207; Carbohydrates: 14g; Protein: 26g; Fat: 4g; Fiber: 3g

Mexican Bubble Pizza

Serves: 7 Preparation Time: 10 minutes Cooking Time: 10 hours

INGREDIENTS
- 1 ½ pounds ground beef
- 1 can condensed tomato soup
- 1 envelope taco seasoning
- 1 tube buttermilk biscuits
- 2 cups cheddar cheese, grated

INSTRUCTIONS
- ✓ Heat skillet over medium-high heat and brown the ground beef for a few minutes. Place in the crockpot.
- ✓ Add the tomato soup and taco seasoning. Season with salt and pepper to taste. Place the buttermilk biscuits on top and sprinkle with cheddar cheese.
- ✓ Close the lid and cook on low for 10 hours.
  - Nutrition information: Calories per serving: 643; Carbohydrates: 46g; Protein: 35g; Fat: 35g; Fiber: 2g

Tender Turkey Breasts

Serves: 12 Preparation Time: 5 minutes Cooking Time: 8 hours

INGREDIENTS
- 6 pounds turkey breasts, bone-in
- ½ cup water
- 1 tablespoon brown sugar
- 4 cloves of garlic, minced
- 4 sprigs rosemary

INSTRUCTIONS
- ✓ Place all ingredients in a mixing bowl.
- ✓ Place all ingredients in the crockpot. Close the lid and cook on low for 8 hours.
  - Nutrition information: Calories per serving: 318; Carbohydrates: 2g; Protein: 47g; Fat: 12g; Fiber: 0.5g

Crockpot Swiss Steak

Serves: 6 Preparation Time: 5 minutes Cooking Time: 9 hours

INGREDIENTS
- 1 ½ pounds beef round steak, cut into 6 pieces
- 1 onion, chopped
- 1 rib of celery, chopped
- 2 cans tomato sauce
- Salt and pepper to taste

INSTRUCTIONS
- ✓ Place all ingredients in the crockpot. Give a good stir.
- ✓ Close the lid and cook on low for 9 hours.
  - Nutrition information: Calories per serving: 171; Carbohydrates: 6g; Protein: 27g; Fat: 4g; Fiber: 1g

Tex-Mex Beef

Serves: 9 Preparation Time: 5 minutes Cooking Time: 12 hours

INGREDIENTS
- 3 pounds boneless beef chuck roast
- 1 envelope chili seasoning
- ½ cup barbecue sauce
- 8 onions, quartered
- 8 slices cheddar cheese

INSTRUCTIONS
- ✓ Place all ingredients in the crockpot except for the cheddar cheese. Close the lid and cook on low for 12 hours.

- Once cooked, shred the meat with two forks. Serve in buns and top with sliced cheese.
  - **Nutrition information: Calories per serving: 573; Carbohydrates: 29g; Protein: 47g; Fat: 29g; Fiber: 2g**

Maple Mustard Chicken

Serves: 6 Preparation Time: 5 minutes Cooking Time: 7 hours

INGREDIENTS

- 6 boneless chicken breasts, skin removed
- ½ cup maple syrup
- 1/3 cup stone-ground mustard
- 2 tablespoons warm water
- Salt and pepper to taste

INSTRUCTIONS

- Place all ingredients in the crockpot. Give a good stir.
- Close the lid and cook on low for 7 hours.
  - **Nutrition information: Calories per serving: 430; Carbohydrates: 21.7g; Protein: 55.6g; Fat: 12.5g; Fiber: 1.3g**

Brisket with Cranberry Gravy

Serves: 9 Preparation Time: 5 minutes Cooking Time: 12 hours

INGREDIENTS

- 2 ½ pound beef brisket
- 1 can cranberry sauce
- 1 can tomato sauce
- ½ cup onion, chopped
- 1 tablespoon prepared mustard

INSTRUCTIONS

- Place all ingredients in the crockpot. Give a good stir.
- Close the lid and cook on low for 12 hours.
  - **Nutrition information: Calories per serving: 262; Carbohydrates: 21g; Protein:30 g; Fat: 6g; Fiber: 1g**

Cherry Balsamic Pork Loin

Serves: 10 Preparation Time: 5 minutes Cooking Time: 10 hours

INGREDIENTS

- 4 pounds pork loin roast, bone removed
- ¾ cup cherry preserves
- ½ cup dried cherries
- 1/3 cup balsamic vinegar
- ¼ cup packed brown sugar

INSTRUCTIONS

- Heat the skillet over medium heat and sear all sides of the pork loin roast. Transfer to the crockpot.
- Place all ingredients in the crockpot. Season with salt and pepper.
- Give a good stir.
- Close the lid and cook on low for 10 hours.
  - **Nutrition information: Calories per serving:359; Carbohydrates: 34g; Protein:33 g; Fat:10g; Fiber: 0.7g**

Easy Chili Verde

Serves: 12 Preparation Time: 5 minutes Cooking Time: 10 hours

INGREDIENTS

- 4 pounds pork shoulder roast, cut into 1-inch thick
- 3 cans green enchilada sauce
- 1 cup salsa Verde
- 1 can chopped green chilies
- ½ cup sour cream

INSTRUCTIONS

- Place all ingredients in the crockpot except for the sour cream. Give a good stir.
- Close the lid and cook on low for 10 hours. Garnish with sour cream on top.
  - **Nutrition information: Calories per serving: 287; Carbohydrates: 5g; Protein: 27g; Fat: 17g; Fiber: 0.7g**

Saucy Ranch Pork Chops

Serves: 6 Preparation Time: 5 minutes Cooking Time: 9 hours

INGREDIENTS

- 6 pork loin chops
- 2 cans condensed cream of chicken soup
- 1 cup milk
- 1 envelope ranch salad dressing
- Salt and pepper to taste

INSTRUCTIONS

- Sear the pork loin chops on a hot skillet for at least 3 minutes on all sides. Place all ingredients in the crockpot.
- Give a good stir.
- Close the lid and cook on low for 9 hours.
  - **Nutrition information: Calories per serving: 451; Carbohydrates:10.5 g; Protein: 44.4g; Fat: 24.8g; Fiber: 0.3g**

Barbecue Pulled Pork

Serves: 4 Preparation Time: 5 minutes Cooking Time: 12 hours

INGREDIENTS

- 1 ½ pounds pork loin fillet
- 1 can Dr. Pepper's cola
- 1 bottle barbecue sauce
- 1 bay leaf
- Salt and pepper to taste

INSTRUCTIONS
- Place all ingredients in the crockpot. Give a good stir.
- Close the lid and cook on low for 12 hours. Use two forks to shred the meat.
- Serve on a sandwich.
- **Nutrition information: Calories per serving: 348; Carbohydrates: 43g; Protein: 25g; Fat: 8g; Fiber: 2g**

Cranberry Pork Chops and Sweet Potatoes

Serves: 6 Preparation Time: 10 minutes Cooking Time: 12 hours

INGREDIENTS

- 6 pork chops
- 1 2/3 cups applesauce
- 3 pounds sweet potatoes
- 1 can cranberry sauce
- ¼ cup packed brown sugar

INSTRUCTIONS
- Season the pork chops with salt and pepper to taste.
- Place in a skillet heated over high flame and sear on all sides. Place in the crockpot and pour the rest of the ingredients.
- Add water if the consistency is too thick. Close the lid and cook on low for 12 hours.
- **Nutrition information: Calories per serving: 649; Carbohydrates: 101g; Protein: 31g; Fat: 14g; Fiber: 9g**

Country Style Ribs

Serves: 6 Preparation Time: 5 minutes Cooking Time: 10 hours

INGREDIENTS

- 1 ½ cups ketchup
- ½ cup packed brown sugar
- ½ cup white vinegar
- ½ teaspoon liquid smoke
- 2 pounds pork ribs

INSTRUCTIONS
- Place all ingredients in the crockpot. Season with salt and pepper to taste. Give a good stir to combine everything.
- Close the lid and cook on low for 12 hours or until the meat falls off the bones.
- **Nutrition information: Calories per serving: 346; Carbohydrates: 34.6g; Protein: 32.1g; Fat: 8.7g; Fiber: 0.2g**

Carolina-Style BBQ Chicken

Serves: 5 Preparation Time: 5 minutes Cooking Time: 8 hours

INGREDIENTS

- 1 cup white vinegar
- ¼ cup sugar
- 1 ½ pounds boneless chicken breasts
- 1 tablespoon chicken bullion
- 1 teaspoon red pepper flakes, crushed

INSTRUCTIONS
- Place all ingredients in the crockpot. Season with salt and pepper to taste.
- Give a good stir to combine everything. Close the lid and cook on low for 8 hours.
- **Nutrition information: Calories per serving: 134; Carbohydrates: 3g; Protein: 23g; Fat: 3g; Fiber: 0g**

Slow Cooker Kalua Pig

Serves: 8 Preparation Time: 5 minutes Cooking Time: 12 hours

INGREDIENTS

- 5 pounds Boston butt roast
- 1 ½ tablespoons salt
- 1 teaspoon pepper
- 5 cloves of garlic, minced
- 3 slices of bacon, fried until crispy

INSTRUCTIONS
- Place all ingredients in the crockpot. Give a good stir to combine everything.
- Close the lid and cook on low for 12 hours or until the meat falls off the bones.
- **Nutrition information: Calories per serving: 534; Carbohydrates: 0.8g; Protein: 48.5g; Fat: 36g; Fiber: 0.1g**

Honey Baby Back Ribs

⌀ Serves: 9 Preparation Time: 5 minutes Cooking Time: 12 hours

INGREDIENTS

- 2 ½ pounds baby back ribs
- 1 ¼ teaspoon smoked paprika
- Salt and pepper to taste
- 3 tablespoon Hoisin sauce
- ¼ cup honey

INSTRUCTIONS
- ✓ Place a parchment paper in the crockpot. Place all ingredients in the crockpot.
- ✓ Massage the baby back ribs.
- ✓ Place the ingredients in the crockpot. Close the lid and cook on low for 12 hours.
    - **Nutrition information: Calories per serving: 322; Carbohydrates: 11.4g; Protein: 25.1g; Fat: 20.1g; Fiber: 0.4g**

Pineapple Salsa Chicken

⌀ Serves: 6 Preparation Time: 5 minutes Cooking Time: 7 hours

INGREDIENTS

- 2 pounds chicken breasts, bones, and skin removed
- 1 jar tomato salsa
- 1 can pineapple chunks, juice included
- 3 zucchinis, sliced
- Salt and pepper to taste

INSTRUCTIONS
- ✓ Place all ingredients in the crockpot. Give a good stir to combine everything.
- ✓ Close the lid and cook on low for 12 hours or until the meat falls off the bones.
    - **Nutrition information: Calories per serving: 170; Carbohydrates: 16g; Protein: 24g; Fat: 3g; Fiber: 1g**

Simple Poached Salmon

⌀ Serves: 4 Preparation Time: 5 minutes Cooking Time: 6 hours

INGREDIENTS

- ½ cup dry white wine
- 1 onion, sliced
- 1 lemon slice
- 1 sprig dill
- 4 salmon fillets

INSTRUCTIONS
- ✓ Place all ingredients in the crockpot. Give a good stir to combine everything.
- ✓ Close the lid and cook on low for 6 hours or until the meat falls off the bones.
    - **Nutrition information: Calories per serving: 216; Carbohydrates: 1.3 g; Protein: 26.4g; Fat: 11.1g; Fiber: 0.1 g**

Lemon Garlic Chicken

⌀ Serves: 6 Preparation Time: 5 minutes Cooking Time: 10 hours

INGREDIENTS

- 4 lemons, sliced
- 3 cloves of garlic, minced
- 2-pound rotisserie chicken
- 1 sprig of fresh rosemary
- Salt and pepper to taste

INSTRUCTIONS
- ✓ Place a parchment paper in the crockpot. Place all ingredients in the crockpot.
- ✓ Massage the chicken and arrange the orange slices on top. Close the lid and cook on low for 10 hours.
    - **Nutrition information: Calories per serving: 456; Carbohydrates: 5.4g; Protein: 66.4g; Fat: 19.3g; Fiber: 0.4g**

White Chicken Chili

⌀ Serves: 9 Preparation Time: 5 minutes Cooking Time: 3 hours

INGREDIENTS

- 6 cups chicken stock
- 4 cups cooked chicken, shredded
- 2 cans Great Northern beans, drained
- 2 cups salsa Verde
- 2 teaspoons ground cumin

INSTRUCTIONS
- ✓ Place all ingredients in the crockpot. Season with salt and pepper to taste.
- ✓ Give a good stir to combine everything. Close the lid and cook on low for 3 hours.
    - **Nutrition information: Calories per serving: 443; Carbohydrates: 34.6g; Protein: 23.7g; Fat: 23.1g; Fiber: 1.1g**

Crockpot Italian Shredded Beef

⌀ Serves: 6 Preparation Time: 5 minutes Cooking Time: 14 hours

INGREDIENTS

- 3 pounds chuck roast, trimmed from excess fat and cut into chunks
- 1 packet Italian salad dressing mix
- 8 ounces pepperoncini pepper slices
- 1 can beef broth
- Salt and pepper to taste

INSTRUCTIONS
✓ Place all ingredients in the crockpot. Give a good stir to combine everything.
✓ Close the lid and cook on low for 12 hours.
✓ Once cooked, take the beef out and shred using two forks. Return the meat to the crockpot and cook for another 2 hours.
  ⏱ **Nutrition information: Calories per serving: 455; Carbohydrates: 6.6g; Protein: 61.5g; Fat: 20.5g; Fiber: 0.7g**

Dr. Pepper Pulled Pork

Serves: 9 Preparation Time: 5 minutes Cooking Time: 12 hours

INGREDIENTS

- 3 pounds pork loin roast
- 1 packet pork rub seasoning
- 1 12-ounce can Dr. Pepper
- ½ cup commercial BBQ sauce
- 1 bay leaf

INSTRUCTIONS
✓ Place all ingredients in the crockpot. Season with salt and pepper to taste. Give a good stir to combine everything.
✓ Close the lid and cook on low for 12 hours.
✓ Once cooked, take the pork out and shred using two forks. Serve with the sauce.
  ⏱ **Nutrition information: Calories per serving: 310; Carbohydrates: 4.6g; Protein: 40.9g; Fat: 13.4g; Fiber: 0.8g**

Salsa Verde Chicken

Serves: 6 Preparation Time: 5 minutes Cooking Time: 6

INGREDIENTS

- 6 chicken breasts, skin and bones removed
- 2 cups salsa Verde
- 1 bottle of beer
- 2 teaspoons cumin
- 1 jalapeno, chopped

INSTRUCTIONS
✓ Place all ingredients in the crockpot. Season with salt and pepper to taste.
✓ Give a good stir to combine everything. Close the lid and cook on low for 3 hours.
  ⏱ **Nutrition information: Calories per serving: 557; Carbohydrates: 7.5g; Protein: 61.1g; Fat: 27.6g; Fiber: 1.5g**

Sweet and Spicy Cinnamon Meatballs

Serves: 8 Preparation Time: 5 minutes Cooking Time: 6 hours

INGREDIENTS

- 2 pounds frozen meatballs
- 2 cups dried berries (cranberries or cherries)
- 1 ½ cups apple juice
- 1 teaspoon cinnamon
- Salt and pepper

INSTRUCTIONS
✓ Place all ingredients in the crockpot. Give a good stir to combine everything.
✓ Close the lid and cook on low for 6 hours.
  ⏱ **Nutrition information: Calories per serving: 474; Carbohydrates: 38.5g; Protein: 17.9g; Fat: 28.6g; Fiber: 4g**

Easy BBQ Chicken and Cheese

Serves: 4 Preparation Time: Cooking Time: 6 hours

INGREDIENTS

- 1-pound chicken tenders, boneless
- 1 cup commercial BBQ sauce
- 1 teaspoon liquid smoke
- 1 cup mozzarella cheese, grated
- ½ pound bacon, fried and crumbled

INSTRUCTIONS
✓ Place the chicken tenders, BBQ sauce and liquid smoke in the crockpot. Season with salt and pepper to taste.
✓ Give a good stir to combine everything. Close the lid and cook on low for 4 hours.
✓ Open the lid and give a good stir. Sprinkle with mozzarella cheese and bacon bits on top. Close the lid and continue cooking for another 2 hours.
  ⏱ **Nutrition information: Calories per serving: 520; Carbohydrates: 28.8g; Protein: 34.6g; Fat: 31/5g; Fiber: 3.2g**

✓

LUNCH RECIPES

Spiced Turkey with Sauerkraut

(Ready in about 8 hours | Servings 6)

INGREDIENTS

- 1 pound carrots, thinly sliced
- 1 stalk celery, finely chopped
- 1 cup leeks, chopped
- 2 cloves garlic, peeled and minced
- 1 large-sized turkey breast, boneless
- 2 pounds sauerkraut, rinsed and drained
- 6 medium-sized red potatoes, washed and pierced
- 2 cups beer
- 1/2 teaspoon dried sage
- 1/2 teaspoon dried rosemary
- Salt to taste
- 1/2 teaspoon ground black pepper

DIRECTIONS
- In a crock pot, arrange all of the ingredients.
- Set the crock pot to low; cook covered about 8 hours.
- Then, taste for seasoning and adjust if necessary; serve.

Cranberry Turkey Breasts

(Ready in about 8 hours | Servings 8)

INGREDIENTS

- Butter flavor cooking spray
- 1 teaspoon chicken bouillon concentrate
- 2 cups whole cranberry sauce
- 1/4 teaspoon water
- 1 medium-sized boneless turkey breast, quartered

DIRECTIONS
- Coat the crock pot with butter flavor cooking spray. Add the rest of ingredients; stir to combine.
- Cover and cook on low for 8 hours or cook on high for 4 hours. Serve with sour cream.

Turkey with Onion-Garlic Sauce

(Ready in about 8 hours | Servings 8)

INGREDIENTS

- 5 large-sized red onions, thinly sliced
- 4 cloves garlic, minced
- 1/4 cup dry white wine
- 1/2 teaspoon sea salt
- 1/4 teaspoon ground black pepper
- 1/4 teaspoon cayenne pepper
- 4 large-sized turkey thighs, skinless

DIRECTIONS
- Lay onions and garlic into the bottom of your crock pot. Pour in wine and sprinkle with salt, black pepper and cayenne pepper.
- Add turkey thighs. Cover; cook on low heat setting approximately 8 hours.
- Remove the turkey thighs from the crock pot. Clean flesh from turkey bones.
- Uncover the crock pot and continue cooking until the liquid has evaporated. Stir occasionally.
- Return the turkey to the crock pot. Next, nestle the turkey into the mixture in the crock pot. Serve.

Grandma's Cabbage with Beef

(Ready in about 4 hours | Servings 4)

INGREDIENTS

- 1 pound cooked beef, cut into bite-sized chunks
- 1 medium onion, peeled and diced
- 1 cup cabbage, chopped
- 2 medium-sized potatoes, diced
- 2 carrots, peeled and thinly sliced
- 1 stalk celery, chopped
- 1 clove garlic, peeled and minced
- 2 cups beef broth
- 2 cups canned tomatoes, diced
- Salt, to taste
- 1/4 teaspoon ground black pepper

DIRECTIONS
- Arrange all ingredients in a crock pot; stir to combine.
- Set the crock pot on high and cook for 1 hour. Then, turn heat to low and cook for 3 to 4 hours.
- Taste and adjust the seasonings; serve warm.

Delicious Beef Stroganoff

(Ready in about 4 hours 30 minutes | Servings 4)

INGREDIENTS

- 1 pound cooked beef, shredded
- 1/2 cup sliced mushrooms, drained
- 1 onion, chopped
- 2-3 cloves garlic, minced
- 1/2 cup beef broth
- 1 cup cream of mushroom soup
- 2 tablespoons dry white wine
- 1 cup cream cheese
- 1 bay leaf
- 1/2 teaspoon dried sage
- 1/2 teaspoon dried rosemary

DIRECTIONS

- Place all ingredients, except cream cheese, in your crock pot. Cover and cook on low heat setting for 4 hours.
- Then, cut the cream cheese into small chunks; add to the crock pot. Cover and cook on low for 1/2 hour longer or until the cheese is melted
- Serve over your favorite egg noodles.

Country Corned Beef Brisket

(Ready in about 8 hours 45 minutes | Servings 12)

INGREDIENTS

- 4 pounds corned beef brisket
- 2 cloves garlic, peeled and minced
- 2 onions, chopped
- 1 cup water
- 1 bay leaf
- 1/2 cup beef stock
- 1 tablespoon paprika
- 1/2 teaspoon freshly grated nutmeg
- 1/2 teaspoon white pepper
- A few drops of liquid smoke

DIRECTIONS

- Remove any excess fat from the beef brisket. Transfer the beef brisket to the crock pot.
- Add remaining ingredients; cover and cook for 8 hours.
- Preheat the oven to 350 degrees F. Place the beef brisket on a roasting pan; roast for 45 minutes.
- Serve over scalloped potatoes, if desired.

Vegetable Pot Roast

(Ready in about 8 hours | Servings 6)

INGREDIENTS

- 1 pound carrots
- 3 medium-sized potatoes, quartered
- 2 cloves garlic, peeled and minced
- 2 stalks of celery, diced
- 1 sweet red bell pepper, seeded and diced
- 1 large-sized onion, chopped
- 3 pounds chuck roast, boneless
- 1 teaspoon broth concentrate
- 1/2 teaspoon black pepper
- 1 cup water
- 1 cup tomato juice
- 1 tablespoon soy sauce

DIRECTIONS

- Arrange the vegetables in your crock pot.
- Cut the chuck roast into serving-sized portions. Place the pieces of roast on top of the vegetables.
- In a mixing bowl, combine together broth concentrate, black pepper, water, tomato juice and soy sauce. Whisk to combine. Add this liquid mixture to the crock pot.
- Cover and cook on low approximately 8 hours.

Beef Roast with Root Vegetables

(Ready in about 8 hours | Servings 12)

INGREDIENTS

- 4 russet potatoes, quartered
- 1 cup water
- 4 parsnips, quartered
- 3 rutabagas, quartered
- 1 onion, sliced
- 1/2 cup leeks, sliced
- 7 cloves garlic, sliced
- 4 pounds lean top round beef roast
- 1 beef bouillon concentrate
- 1 teaspoon smoked paprika
- 1/2 teaspoon freshly ground black pepper

DIRECTIONS

- Simply place all ingredients in your crock pot.
- Set the crock pot to low and cook for 8 hours.
- Slice the beef into serving-sized portions and serve with vegetables. Garnish with mustard if desired.

Beef Steak with Mushroom Gravy

(Ready in about 8 hours | Servings 12)

INGREDIENTS

- 2 medium onions, peeled and sliced
- 2 pounds beef round steak, boneless
- 3 cups mushrooms, sliced
- 1 cup turnips, sliced
- 1 (12-ounce) jar beef gravy
- 1 (1-ounce) envelope dry mushroom gravy mix

DIRECTIONS

- Lay the onions on the bottom of the crock pot.
- Trim fat from the beef round steak; then cut the beef into eight pieces.
- Place the beef on top of the onions, and then place the mushrooms over it. Top with sliced turnips.
- Mix together beef gravy and mushroom gravy mix.
- Add this gravy mixture to the crock pot; cover and cook on low for 8 hours. Serve over mashed potatoes if desired.

Juicy Pork with Apple Sauce

(Ready in about 6 hours | Servings 8)

INGREDIENTS

- 1/4 cup light brown sugar
- 1/4 cup Dijon mustard
- 1/2 teaspoon ground black pepper
- 4 pounds pork loin, fat removed
- 1/2 cup dry red wine
- 4 cups applesauce, unsweetened
- 1/2 cup scallions, chopped

DIRECTIONS

- In a small-sized bowl or a measuring cup, combine together sugar, mustard, and black pepper. Mix well to combine.
- Rub mustard mixture into the pork loin.
- Place the pork loin in the crock pot; add red wine, applesauce and scallions; cover with a lid.
- Cook on low for 6 hours. Serve with some extra mustard.

Ham with Pineapple

(Ready in about 6 hours | Servings 6)

INGREDIENTS

- 2 pounds ham steak
- 1 pound canned pineapple tidbits, drained, reserve 2 tablespoons of the juice.
- 1 cup leeks, chopped
- 2 cloves garlic, minced
- 3 large-sized potatoes, diced
- 1/2 cup orange marmalade
- 1/4 teaspoon paprika
- 1/4 teaspoon ground black pepper
- 1/2 teaspoon dried basil

DIRECTIONS

- Cut the ham into bite-sized pieces. Transfer to the crock pot.
- Add the rest of ingredients; stir to combine.
- Cover and cook on low for 6 hours.

Cranberry Pork Roast with Sweet Potatoes

(Ready in about 6 hours | Servings 6)

INGREDIENTS

- 3 pounds pork butt roast
- 2 cups canned cranberries
- 1 medium onion, peeled and diced
- 1/2 cup orange juice
- 2 tablespoons apple cider vinegar
- 1/2 teaspoon five-spice powder
- Sea salt to taste
- 1/2 teaspoon ground black pepper
- 3 large-sized sweet potatoes, peeled and quartered

DIRECTIONS

- Place the pork in a crock pot.
- In a measuring cup, mix together the cranberries, onion, orange juice, apple cider vinegar, five-spice powder, salt and black pepper; mix to combine.
- Pour cranberry mixture over pork butt roast in the crock pot. Arrange the potatoes around the pork.
- Cover and cook on low for about 6 hours.
- Transfer to a serving platter and enjoy!

Sausages with Sauerkraut and Beer

(Ready in about 3 hours 30 minutes | Servings 8)

INGREDIENTS

- 8 precooked sausages
- 2 large-sized onions, sliced
- 2 pounds sauerkraut, rinsed and drained
- 1 (12-ounce) bottle of beer

DIRECTIONS

- Add the sausages and onions to a crock pot. Cook on high for 30 minutes.
- Add the sauerkraut and beer; cover and cook on low for 3 hours.
- Serve with mustard if desired.

Pork Steaks in Prune Sauce

(Ready in about 6 hours | Servings 6)

INGREDIENTS

- 12 prunes, pitted
- 3 pounds pork steaks, boneless
- 4 medium-sized apples, cored, and quartered
- 3/4 cup apple juice
- 3/4 cup heavy cream
- 1 teaspoon sea salt
- 1/4 teaspoon freshly ground pepper
- 1 tablespoon butter

DIRECTIONS

- Add all ingredients to the crock pot. Cover and cook on low for 6 hours or until the meat pulls apart easily.
- Serve over mashed potatoes.

Spicy Pork Roast with Vegetables

(Ready in about 6 hours | Servings 4)

INGREDIENTS

- 1 tablespoon canola oil
- 1 large-sized onion, sliced
- 1 celery stalk, chopped
- 1 large-sized carrot, peeled and finely diced
- 1 jalapeño pepper, seeded and minced
- 1 teaspoon garlic powder
- Salt, to taste
- 1/2 teaspoon five-spice powder
- 1/4 teaspoon freshly ground black pepper
- 1/2 teaspoon dried oregano
- 1/2 teaspoon dried basil
- 1 (3-pound) pork shoulder or butt roast
- 1 cup vegetable broth

DIRECTIONS

- Add the canola oil to the cast-iron skillet. Heat canola oil over medium-high heat and then add vegetables. Sauté the vegetables until they are just tender or about 15 minutes.
- In a mixing bowl, combine garlic powder, salt, five-spice powder, black pepper, oregano, and basil; stir to mix.
- Rub this spice mixture into the meat. Add the pork roast to the crock pot; pour in vegetable broth. Cover and cook on low for 6 hours.

✓ Shred the pork with two forks. Ladle the sauce over the pork and serve warm.

Country Pork Ribs with Ginger Sauce

(Ready in about 8 hours | Servings 6)

INGREDIENTS

- 4 pounds country pork ribs
- 1 ¼ cup tomato ketchup
- 2 tablespoons rice vinegar
- 2 tablespoons tamari sauce
- 1/4 teaspoon allspice
- 1 large onion, peeled and diced
- 1 clove garlic, peeled and minced
- 2 teaspoons grated ginger
- 1/4 teaspoon red pepper flakes, crushed

DIRECTIONS
✓ Cut the pork ribs into individual serving-size portions.
✓ Broil the ribs for 5 minutes on each side or until they are fragrant and browned.
✓ To make the sauce: in a crock pot, combine tomato ketchup, rice vinegar, tamari sauce, allspice, onion, garlic, ginger and red pepper.
✓ Place the pork ribs in the crock pot, coating the ribs with the sauce.
✓ Cover and cook on low for 8 hours or until the ribs are tender.

Pork Roast in Beer

(Ready in about 6 hours | Servings 4)

INGREDIENTS

- 1 medium-sized pork sirloin
- 2 sweet onions, peeled and sliced
- 4 large-sized potatoes, quartered
- 2 cups carrots
- 1 envelope dry onion soup mix
- 1 (12-ounce) bottle of beer
- 5-6 peppercorns

DIRECTIONS
✓ Place the pork sirloin in your crock pot. Arrange onions, potatoes and carrots around the meat.
✓ Sprinkle with the soup mix. Pour in beer; then add peppercorns.
✓ Cover and cook on low for 6 hours. Divide among four serving plates and serve warm.

Piquant Chicken Chowder

(Ready in about 8 hours | Servings 8)

INGREDIENTS

- 1 quart chicken stock
- 1 pound chicken breast, boneless skinless, cut into cubes
- 3 cups whole kernel corn
- 1/2 cup chopped onion, finely chopped
- 2 cloves garlic, minced
- 1 green bell pepper, thinly sliced
- 1 teaspoon jalapeño chili, minced
- 1/2 teaspoon dried thyme leaves
- 1 teaspoon dried rosemary
- Salt to taste
- 1/4 teaspoon black pepper, ground
- 1 cup 2% reduced-fat milk
- 2 tablespoons cornstarch

DIRECTIONS
✓ Combine all ingredients, except milk and cornstarch, in a crock pot; cover and cook on low approximately 8 hours.
✓ Turn heat to high, stir in combined milk and cornstarch, and cook an additional 5 minutes, stirring constantly.
✓ Adjust the seasonings and serve with your favorite garlic croutons.

Hot Chicken Chowder with Spinach

(Ready in about 5 hours | Servings 4)

INGREDIENTS

- 1 cup chicken broth
- 1 ½ cup canned tomatoes, diced
- 1 ½ cup garbanzo beans, rinsed and drained
- 12 ounces chicken breast, boneless, skinless and cubed
- 1 medium-sized sweet onion, chopped
- 2 sweet potatoes, diced
- 2 cups packed spinach
- Salt to taste
- 1/4 teaspoon black pepper
- 1/2 teaspoon chili powder

DIRECTIONS
✓ Combine all ingredients, except spinach, in the crock pot; cover and cook on high for about 5 hours,
✓ Stir in spinach; adjust the seasonings.
✓ Divide among soup bowls and serve.

Shrimp Chowder with Avocado

(Ready in about 5 hours | Servings 4)

INGREDIENTS

- 2 cups water
- 1 envelope dry onion soup mix
- 1 red onion, chopped
- 1 plum tomato, chopped
- 3/4 teaspoon five-spice powder
- 1/8 teaspoon celery seeds
- 1/2 cup long-grain rice
- 1 ½ cups shrimp, peeled and halved crosswise
- 1 avocado, cubed
- Juice of 1 fresh lime
- Salt to taste
- 1/2 teaspoon paprika
- 1/2 teaspoon ground black pepper

DIRECTIONS

- In a crock pot, combine water, onion soup mix, onion, tomato, five-spice powder and celery seeds; cover and cook on high 5 hours.
- Add long-grain rice during last 2 hours of cooking time; add shrimp during last 20 minutes.
- Stir in the rest of ingredients. Ladle soup into bowls and serve hot.

Shrimp Chowder with Corn and Potato

(Ready in about 5 hours | Servings 4)

INGREDIENTS

- 2 cups whole kernel corn
- 1 cup water
- 2 cups chicken broth
- 1 can (8 ounces) tomato sauce
- 1 large-sized sweet onion, chopped
- 2 cloves garlic, minced
- 3 medium-sized Yukon potatoes, diced
- 1 sweet red bell pepper, sliced
- 1/4 cup dry sherry, optional
- 3/4 teaspoon five-spice powder
- 1/4 teaspoon dry mustard
- 1/4 teaspoon ground caraway seeds
- A few drops Tabasco sauce
- 1/2 cup whole milk
- 1 ½ cups shrimp, peeled and deveined
- Salt to taste
- Black pepper to taste

DIRECTIONS
- Combine all of the ingredients, except shrimp and milk, in your crock pot.
- Cover and cook on high for about 5 hours, adding milk and shrimp during last 20 minutes.
- Ladle into four soup bowls and enjoy.

Saucy Pork Spare Ribs

(Ready in about 8 hours | Servings 8)

INGREDIENTS

- 4 pounds lean pork spare ribs
- 1 red bell pepper, sliced
- 1 cup scallions, chopped
- 1/2 cup garlic-chili sauce
- 2 tablespoons brown sugar
- 1/4 cup rice vinegar
- 1 tablespoon dry red wine

DIRECTIONS
- Place pork spare ribs in your crock pot. Arrange slices of bell pepper around the pork ribs.
- In a mixing bowl, combine together remaining ingredients; whisk well to combine.
- Pour this mixture over the ribs. Cook covered for 8 hours.
- Place pork spare ribs on a serving platter. Pour the sauce into a small serving bowl; drain off fat. Serve.

Pork Ribs in Sweet Sauce

(Ready in about 8 hours | Servings 4)

INGREDIENTS

- 3 pounds pork ribs
- 1 medium-size onion, diced
- 3 cloves garlic, minced
- 1/2 cup maple syrup
- 2 tablespoons tamari sauce
- 3/4 teaspoon five-spice powder
- 1/2 teaspoon ground ginger
- 1/4 teaspoon paprika
- 1/2 teaspoon dried rosemary
- Sea salt to taste
- 1/4 teaspoon freshly ground black pepper

DIRECTIONS
- Arrange the pork ribs and onion in the bottom of the crock pot.
- Next, add remaining ingredients.
- Cover and cook on low for 8 hours or until the pork is tender enough to pull away from the bone.

Spicy Pork with Canadian Bacon

(Ready in about 6 hours | Servings 4)

INGREDIENTS

- 2 slices of Canadian bacon
- 1 pound pork shoulder, boneless and fat removed
- 1 cup leeks, chopped
- 2 cloves garlic, minced
- 1 cup chicken broth
- 2 cups canned tomatoes, diced
- 1 ½ cups canned beans, rinsed and drained
- 2 stalks celery, thinly sliced
- 3/4 teaspoon Italian seasoning blend
- 1/2 teaspoon dried thyme
- Salt to taste
- Freshly ground black pepper to taste

DIRECTIONS
- Cut the bacon into small-sized pieces. Then, fry the bacon in a nonstick skillet over medium-high heat; fry for 2 minutes or until bacon starts to render its fat. Transfer to your crock pot.
- Add the rest of ingredients
- Cover and cook on low for 6 hours or until the pork shoulder is tender.

Cream of Broccoli and Cauliflower Soup

(Ready in about 4 hours | Servings 6)

INGREDIENTS

- 1 cup water
- 2 cups reduced-sodium chicken broth
- 1 pound cauliflower, broken into florets
- 1 pound broccoli, broken into florets
- 1 yellow onion, finely chopped
- 3 cloves garlic, minced
- 1 heaping tablespoon fresh basil
- 1 heaping tablespoon fresh parsley
- 1/2 cup 2% reduced-fat milk
- Salt to taste
- 1/4 teaspoon white pepper
- 1/4 teaspoon black pepper
- Croutons of choice

DIRECTIONS
- Place water, broth, cauliflower, broccoli, onion, garlic, basil and parsley in your crock pot.
- Cook on high 3 to 4 hours.
- Transfer the soup to the food processor; add milk and spices and blend until uniform and smooth. Taste and adjust the seasonings; serve with croutons.

Family Broccoli-Spinach Soup

(Ready in about 4 hours | Servings 6)

INGREDIENTS

- 2 cups water
- 2 cups reduced-sodium vegetable broth
- 1 pound broccoli, broken into florets
- 1 cup green onions, chopped
- 3 cloves garlic, minced
- 1 heaping tablespoon fresh cilantro
- 1 heaping tablespoon fresh parsley
- 2 cups spinach
- Salt to taste
- 1/4 teaspoon black pepper

DIRECTIONS
- Combine together water, vegetable broth, broccoli, green onions, garlic, cilantro and parsley in a crock pot.
- Cook on high 3 hours. Add spinach and spices and cook for 20 minutes longer.
- Pour the soup into the food processor; process until smooth.
- Serve chilled or at room temperature. Garnish with a dollop of sour cream and enjoy!

Delicious Cream of Asparagus Soup

(Ready in about 4 hours | Servings 6)

INGREDIENTS

- 2 cups vegetable stock
- 1 cups water
- 2 pounds asparagus, reserving the tips for garnish
- 1 onion, finely chopped
- 1 teaspoon lemon zest
- 2 cloves garlic, minced
- 1 teaspoon dried marjoram
- 1 heaping tablespoon fresh parsley
- 1/2 cup whole milk
- 1/4 teaspoon white pepper
- Salt to taste

DIRECTIONS
- Place stock, water, asparagus, onion, lemon zest, garlic, marjoram and parsley in a crock pot.
- Cook on high-heat setting for 3 to 4 hours.
- Meanwhile, steam asparagus tips until crisp-tender.
- Pour the soup into a food processor; add milk, salt and white pepper and blend until smooth.
- Garnish with steamed asparagus tips and serve at room temperature. You can also set your soup in a refrigerator and garnish it chilled.

Creamy Cauliflower Potato Chowder

(Ready in about 4 hours | Servings 6)

INGREDIENTS

- 3 cups stock
- 1 cup carrot, chopped
- 3 ½ cups potatoes, diced
- 3 cups cauliflower, chopped
- 4 small-sized leeks, white parts only, chopped
- 1 cup milk
- 2 tablespoons cornstarch
- 1 teaspoon dried basil
- Salt to taste
- Black pepper to taste

DIRECTIONS
- Combine first five ingredients in a crock pot; set the crock pot to high and
- 3 to 4 hours.
- Stir in remaining ingredients and cook 2 to 3 minutes longer or until thickened.
- Blend the soup in a food processor or a blender until desired consistency is reached.
- Adjust the seasonings and serve with sour cream.

Potato Cauliflower Bisque

(Ready in about 5 hours | Servings 6)

INGREDIENTS

- 3 cups chicken broth
- 1 stalk celery, chopped
- 1 large-sized carrot, chopped
- 1/2 large head cauliflower, coarsely chopped
- 1 ½ cups potatoes, chopped
- 1 cup shallots, chopped
- 1 tablespoon dried basil
- 1 teaspoon dried thyme
- 1/2 teaspoon sea salt
- 1/4 teaspoon black pepper
- 1 cup milk

DIRECTIONS

- ✓ Combine all ingredients, except milk, in a crock pot; cover with a lid and set the crock pot to high
- ✓ Cook for 4 to 5 hours.
- ✓ Pour bisque into a food processor or a blender together with milk. Mix until smooth.
- ✓ Adjust the seasonings; sprinkle with chopped fresh parsley and serve at room temperature or chilled.

Hot Cabbage Soup

(Ready in about 4 hours | Servings 8)

INGREDIENTS

- 3 cups cabbage, shredded green
- 2 quarts reduced-fat beef broth
- 1 celery stalk, chopped
- 1 large-sized carrot, chopped
- 1 sweet red bell pepper, sliced
- 1 sweet yellow bell pepper, chopped
- 1 large-sized onion, chopped
- 1 clove garlic, minced
- 1 tablespoon vegetable oil
- 1 teaspoon ginger, minced
- 2 tablespoons soy sauce
- A few drops of tabasco sauce
- 1 tablespoon brown sugar
- 2 tablespoons cornstarch

DIRECTIONS
- ✓ Combine cabbage, broth, vegetables, oil and ginger in a crock pot; cover and cook on high-heat setting for 3 to 4 hours.
- ✓ Stir in combined remaining ingredients and cook 5 more minutes. Serve warm and enjoy.

Sour Carrot Soup with Yogurt

(Ready in about 4 hours | Servings 6)

INGREDIENTS

- 3 cups reduced-sodium chicken broth
- 2 cups canned tomatoes, undrained and diced
- 1 pound carrots, thickly sliced
- 1 cup leeks, chopped
- 2 cloves garlic, minced
- 1 teaspoon dried dill weed
- 1 tablespoon apple cider vinegar
- Salt to taste
- 1/4 teaspoon white pepper
- 1/4 teaspoon ground black pepper
- Plain yogurt for garnish

DIRECTIONS
- ✓ Combine first six ingredients in your crock pot; cover with a suitable lid and cook on high 3 to 4 hours.
- ✓ Next, mix soup in a food processor until smooth; add the rest of ingredients, except the yogurt, and stir well to combine.
- ✓ Stir before serving; garnish with a dollop of yogurt.

Dilled Celery Potato Soup

(Ready in about 4 hours | Servings 6)

INGREDIENTS

- 2 cups canned tomatoes, undrained and diced
- 3 cups vegetable broth
- 1/2 pound celery, chopped
- 1/2 pound potatoes, peeled and diced
- 1 cup scallions, finely chopped
- 1 ½ teaspoon dried dill weed
- 1 tablespoon lemon juice
- Salt to taste
- 1/4 teaspoon white pepper
- 1/4 teaspoon ground black pepper
- Plain yogurt for garnish

DIRECTIONS
- ✓ Combine tomatoes, broth, celery, potato, scallions and dill weed in your crock pot; cover, set the crock pot to high and cook approximately 4 hours.
- ✓ Then, purée prepared soup in a blender or a food processor until smooth;
- ✓ Add combined remaining ingredients, except the yogurt; stir well until everything is well combined.
- ✓ Garnish with a dollop of yogurt and serve chilled or at room temperature.

Cheesy Cream of Vegetable Soup

(Ready in about 4 hours | Servings 6)

INGREDIENTS

- 1 small head cauliflower
- 1 medium-sized carrot, chopped
- 3 ½ chicken broth
- 2 large-sized Idaho potato, peeled, cubed
- 1/2 cup leeks, chopped
- 2 cloves garlic, minced
- 1 tablespoon soy sauce
- 1/2 cup 2% reduced-fat milk
- 3/4 cup reduced-fat Cheddar cheese, shredded
- 1/4 teaspoon ground nutmeg
- Salt to taste
- Ground black pepper to taste
- Chopped chives, as garnish

DIRECTIONS
- ✓ Combine first six ingredients in a crock pot; cook on high-heat setting 3 to 4 hours.
- ✓ Purée 1/2 of prepared soup in a blender or a food processor until smooth and creamy; return to the crock pot.
- ✓ Stir in combined soy sauce and milk, and continue cooking, stirring 2 to 3 minutes. Stir well to combine. Add Cheddar cheese, nutmeg, salt and black pepper to taste.
- ✓ Divide among six serving bowls, sprinkle with chopped chives and serve!

Creamy Fennel Soup with Walnuts

(Ready in about 4 hours | Servings 6)

INGREDIENTS

- 3 ½ chicken broth
- 1 ½ cups fennel bulbs
- 1/2 cup celery, chopped
- 1 medium-sized carrot, chopped
- 2 large-sized Idaho potato, peeled, cubed
- 1/2 cup scallions, chopped
- 2 cloves garlic, minced
- 1 tablespoon soy sauce
- 1 tablespoon apple cider vinegar
- 1/2 cup 2% reduced-fat milk
- Salt to taste
- Ground black pepper to taste
- Chopped toasted walnuts, as garnish

DIRECTIONS

- In a crock pot, combine first seven ingredients. Cook on high approximately 4 hours.
- Place prepared soup in a food processor and blend until a smooth consistency is reached.
- Add remaining ingredients, except chopped walnuts, and continue cooking 5 more minutes.
- Divide among serving bowls; scatter walnuts on top and serve.

Cream of Turnip Soup

(Ready in about 4 hours | Servings 6)

INGREDIENTS

- 3 ½ vegetable stock
- 1 ½ cups turnips, chopped
- 2 medium-sized carrots, chopped
- 1 large-sized potato, peeled, cubed
- 1/2 cup onions, chopped
- 2 cloves garlic, minced
- 1 tablespoon tamari sauce
- 1/2 cup whole milk
- 1/4 teaspoon ground white pepper
- 1 teaspoon dried thyme
- Salt to taste
- Ground black pepper to taste
- 3/4 cup reduced-fat Swiss cheese, shredded
- Toasted bread cubes, as garnish

DIRECTIONS

- Pour vegetable stock into a crock pot. Add turnips, carrots, potato, onions, and garlic. Set the crock pot to high; cook for about 4 hours.
- Pour the soup into a food processor and blend until your desired consistency is reached.
- Return to the crock pot; add tamari sauce, milk, white pepper, thyme, salt,
- and black pepper. Cook an additional 5 minutes.
- Top with Swiss cheese. Garnish with toasted bread cubes and serve.

Fragrant Garlic Soup with Bread

(Ready in about 4 hours | Servings 4)

INGREDIENTS

- 8 cloves garlic, minced
- 1 quart vegetable stock
- 1/2 teaspoon dried oregano leaves
- 1/2 teaspoon celery seeds
- Salt to taste
- Black pepper to taste
- 2 tablespoons olive oil
- 4 slices of bread
- Chopped chives, as garnish

DIRECTIONS

- Combine garlic, vegetable stock, dried oregano leaves and celery seeds in a crock pot; cover and cook on high 4 hours.
- Season with salt and black pepper.
- In a heavy skillet, heat olive oil over medium heat. Fry the slices of bread,
- 2 to 3 minutes on each side, until golden.
- Place slices of bread in soup bowls; ladle garlic soup over them and sprinkle with chopped chives. Enjoy!

Avocado and Potato Chowder

(Ready in about 5 hours | Servings 4)

INGREDIENTS

- 1 ½ cups chicken broth
- 3 cups potatoes, peeled and diced
- 1 cup corn kernels
- 1 cup smoked turkey breast, cubed
- 1 teaspoon dried thyme leaves
- Juice of 1 fresh lime
- 1 cup avocado, cubed
- 1 teaspoon sea salt
- 1/2 ground black pepper

DIRECTIONS

- Combine chicken broth, potatoes, corn kernels, turkey breasts and thyme in a crock pot.
- Cover and cook on high 4 to 5 hours.
- Stir in lime, avocado, salt and black pepper. Serve.

Cheesy Veggie Sausage Chowder

(Ready in about 5 hours | Servings 6)

INGREDIENTS

- 1 cup smoked sausage, sliced
- 2 cups reduced-sodium beef broth
- 2 ½ cups cream-style corn
- 1 onion, chopped
- 1 ½ cups plum tomatoes, diced
- 1 sweet red bell pepper, chopped
- 2 cups whole milk

- 2 tablespoons cornstarch
- 3/4 cup Swiss cheese
- Salt to taste
- 1/4 teaspoon black pepper
- 1/4 teaspoon cayenne pepper

DIRECTIONS
- Combine first six ingredients in your crock pot; cover with a lid.
- Cook on high approximately 5 hours.
- Add milk and cornstarch, stirring about 3 minutes.
- Add in Swiss cheese; season with salt, black pepper and cayenne pepper; serve.

Cold Weather Potato Chowder

(Ready in about 5 hours | Servings 4)

INGREDIENTS
- 2 cups potatoes, cubed
- 2 cups kernel corn
- 1 medium onion, chopped
- 1 cup water
- 1 cup chicken broth
- 1/2 cup celery, sliced
- 1 teaspoon dried basil leaves
- 1/2 teaspoon dried dill weed
- 1 ½ cups milk
- Salt to taste
- 1/4 teaspoon white pepper

DIRECTIONS
- Combine potatoes, corn, onion, water, broth, celery, basil and dill weed in a crock pot.
- Cover and cook on high 4 to 5 hours.
- Stir in remaining ingredients and serve warm or at room temperature.

Hearty Bean Chowder

(Ready in about 6 hours | Servings 8)

INGREDIENTS
- 2 cups water
- 2 cups beef broth
- 15 ½ ounces canned beans, rinsed and drained
- 1 sweet red bell pepper
- 1 bay leaf
- 2 large sized onions, chopped
- 2 cloves garlic, minced
- 1/2 teaspoon chili powder
- 1/4 cup dry sherry
- Salt and ground black pepper, to taste
- Blue cheese for garnish

DIRECTIONS
- In a crock pot, place water, beef broth, canned beans, red bell pepper, bay leaf, onion, garlic, and chili powder.
- Cook covered on high-heat setting for 5 to 6 hours
- Add dry sherry during last 15 minutes; season with salt and pepper, taste and adjust the seasonings.
- Serve with blue cheese and enjoy!

Great Northern Bean Soup

(Ready in about 6 hours | Servings 8)

INGREDIENTS
- 2 cups chicken broth
- 2 cups water
- 2 cups Great Northern beans, rinsed and drained
- 1 large-sized carrot, slices
- 2 cups leeks, finely chopped
- 2-3 garlic cloves, minced
- 1 teaspoon dried basil
- 1 teaspoon dried thyme
- 1 teaspoon celery seeds
- 1 tablespoon apple cider vinegar
- 1/2 teaspoon salt
- 1/2 teaspoon ground black pepper

DIRECTIONS
- In a crock pot, combine chicken broth, water, beans, carrot, leeks, garlic, basil, thyme and celery seeds.
- Cover with a lid; cook on high 5 to 6 hours, adding apple cider vinegar during last 15 minutes. Add salt and ground black pepper; serve warm.

Potato Cauliflower Chowder

(Ready in about 4 hours | Servings 6)

INGREDIENTS
- 3 cups reduced-sodium chicken broth
- 3 ½ cups potatoes, peeled and cubed
- 1 cup scallions, chopped
- 1/2 head cauliflower
- 1/2 cup celery, thinly sliced
- 1/4–1/2 teaspoon celery seeds
- 1 cup whole milk
- 2 tablespoons cornstarch
- Salt and white pepper, to taste
- 1/4 teaspoon red pepper flakes, crushed
- Ground nutmeg, as garnish

DIRECTIONS
- Combine all ingredients, except whole milk, cornstarch, salt, white pepper, red pepper and nutmeg, in a crock pot.
- Cover and cook on high approximately 4 hours.
- Stir in combined remaining ingredients, except nutmeg, during last 20 minutes.
- Divide among six soup bowls; serve sprinkled with ground nutmeg!

Mom's Chicken Chili

(Ready in about 8 hours | Servings 6)

INGREDIENTS
- 1 pound chicken breast, boneless and skinless

- 1 cup leeks, finely chopped
- 2 plum tomatoes, diced
- 1 can (15-ounce) beans, rinsed and drained
- 2 cloves garlic, minced
- 1 teaspoon chili powder
- 1/2 teaspoon allspice
- 1 strip orange zest
- Salt and black pepper, to taste
- Chopped fresh parsley, as garnish
- Chopped coriander leaves, as garnish

DIRECTIONS
- Cut the chicken into small chunks.
- In your crock pot, combine all ingredients, except parsley and coriander.
- Cover and cook on low for about 8 hours.
- Serve over rice. Sprinkle with parsley and coriander. Enjoy!

Yummy Spicy Mushroom Chili

(Ready in about 8 hours | Servings 6)

INGREDIENTS
- 1 pound chicken breast, cubed
- 2 cups reduced-sodium chicken broth
- 1 cup water
- 2 cups canned kidney beans, rinsed and drained
- 2 large-sized red onions
- 1 sweet red bell pepper, chopped
- 1 cup mushrooms, sliced
- 1 teaspoon gingerroot, minced
- 1 teaspoon jalapeño chili, minced
- 1 teaspoon ground cumin
- 2 bay leaves
- 1/2 teaspoon sea salt
- 1/2 teaspoon ground black pepper
- 1/2 teaspoon cayenne pepper

DIRECTIONS
- Add all of the ingredients to a crock pot.
- Then, cook covered on low-heat setting for 6 to 8 hours.
- Taste, adjust the seasonings and serve.

Chicken and Potatoes with Gravy

(Ready in about 6 hours | Servings 4)

INGREDIENTS
- 3/4 cup chicken breasts, boneless and skinless
- 4 medium-sized potatoes, peeled and diced
- 1 medium-sized yellow onion, sliced
- 1 ½ cup cream of mushroom
- 1 ½ cup cream of chicken soup
- 1/4 teaspoon white pepper
- 1/4 teaspoon black pepper

DIRECTIONS
- Arrange all ingredients in your crock pot.
- Cover and cook on low for about 6 hours or until the meat is cooked through.
- Serve with a dollop of sour cream and your favorite tossed salad.

Cheesy Saucy Chicken and Veggies

(Ready in about 6 hours | Servings 4)

INGREDIENTS
- 2 cups chicken stock
- 4 medium-sized chicken breasts, boneless, skinless
- 1 pound green beans
- 1 sweet red bell peppers
- 1 onion, cut into wedges
- 3 medium-sized potatoes, peeled and diced
- 3 cloves garlic, minced
- 1/2 teaspoon dried marjoram
- 1/4 teaspoon freshly ground black pepper
- 1/2 cup cream cheese, cut into cubes
- 1 teaspoon Dijon mustard
- 2 tablespoons balsamic vinegar

DIRECTIONS
- Simply arrange all ingredients, except cheese, mustard and balsamic vinegar, in a crock pot.
- Cover and cook on low for 5 to 6 hours.
- Remove chicken and veggies from the crock pot and keep them warm.
- To make the sauce, add the cheese, mustard and vinegar to the broth in the crock pot. Stir until everything is well incorporated and cheese is melted.
- Divide the chicken and vegetables among four soup bowls.
- Ladle the sauce over the chicken and veggies. Serve warm.

Hot Chicken with Potatoes

(Ready in about 5 hours | Servings 4)

INGREDIENTS
- Non-stick cooking spray
- 1/2 cup potatoes
- 1 cup leftover cooked chicken, cubed
- 2 bay leaves
- 3-4 peppercorns
- 2 cups chicken stock
- 2 cups water
- 2 tablespoons dry white wine
- Ground black pepper, to taste
- 1 teaspoon chili powder

DIRECTIONS
- Coat your crock pot with non-stick spray.
- Place all ingredients in the greased crock pot.
- Cover and cook on low for 5 hours.

Chicken Paprikash with Noodles

(Ready in about 8 hours | Servings 8)

INGREDIENTS

- 2 tablespoons olive oil
- 1 large-sized onion, peeled and diced
- 2 cloves garlic, minced
- 3 pounds chicken thighs, boneless and skinless
- 2 bay leaves
- 1 teaspoon sea salt
- 1/2 teaspoon ground black pepper, to taste
- 1 tablespoon paprika
- 1/2 cup chicken broth
- 1/4 cup dry white wine
- 1 cup cream cheese
- Egg noodles, cooked

DIRECTIONS
- In a heavy skillet, heat olive oil over medium heat. Sauté onions and garlic until just tender.
- Cut the chicken thighs into small pieces. Add the chicken to the skillet, and stir fry for 5 to 6 minutes. Replace to the crock pot.
- Add in bay leaves, sea salt, black pepper, paprika, chicken broth and white wine; cover and cook on low approximately 8 hours.
- Stir in cream cheese and serve over cooked noodles.

Orange Turkey Breasts

(Ready in about 8 hours | Servings 8)

INGREDIENTS
- Non-stick cooking spray
- 3 pounds turkey breasts, boneless and skinless
- 1 medium-sized onion, chopped
- 1/2 cup orange juice
- 1 tablespoon orange marmalade
- 1 tablespoon balsamic vinegar
- 1 tablespoon Worcestershire sauce
- 1 teaspoon mustard
- 1/2 teaspoon kosher salt
- 1/4 teaspoon ground black pepper

DIRECTIONS
- Treat your crock pot with non-stick cooking spray. Cut the turkey into small pieces. Transfer to the crock pot and add onion.
- In a measuring cup or a mixing bowl, combine together the orange juice, marmalade, balsamic vinegar, Worcestershire sauce, mustard, salt and black pepper. Pour into the crock pot.
- Cover with a lid; cook on low approximately 8 hours.
- Serve over scalloped potatoes.

Teriyaki Chicken with Basmati Rice

(Ready in about 8 hours | Servings 8)

INGREDIENTS
- 2 pounds chicken, boneless and cut into strips
- 1 cup green peas
- 1 sweet red bell pepper, chopped
- 1 sweet yellow pepper, chopped
- 1 cup scallions
- 1/2 cup chicken stock
- 1 cup teriyaki sauce
- Sea salt to taste
- 1/4 teaspoon ground black pepper

DIRECTIONS
- Add all ingredients to the crock pot. Stir to combine.
- Cover and cook on low for about 6 hours.
- Serve over basmati rice.

Moist & Tender Chicken with Caramelized Onion

(Ready in about 6 hours | Servings 4)

INGREDIENTS
- 2 tablespoons butter
- 1 large-sized onion, chopped
- 1 teaspoon sugar
- 2 cloves garlic, minced
- 1 tablespoons curry powder
- 1 cup water
- 3/4 teaspoon chicken bouillon concentrate
- 8 chicken thighs, skinless
- Cooked long-grain white rice, as garnish

DIRECTIONS
- In a small-sized skillet, melt the butter over medium heat. Add onions and cook for 10 minutes, stirring occasionally.
- Then, turn the heat to medium-high; add sugar and cook an additional 10 minutes or until the onions become golden brown. Transfer to the crock pot.
- Add remaining ingredients, except cooked rice; cook covered for about 6 hours.
- Divide among four serving plates and serve over long-grain white rice.

Curried Chicken with Almonds

(Ready in about 6 hours | Servings 4)

INGREDIENTS
- 1 tablespoon olive oil
- 1 cup leeks, chopped
- 2 cloves garlic, minced
- 1 ½ tablespoons curry powder
- 1 cup almond milk
- 1/2 cup water
- 8 chicken thighs, skinless
- 1 1/2 cups celery, sliced diagonally
- 1 cup slivered almonds, toasted

DIRECTIONS
- In a heavy skillet, heat olive oil; sauté leeks until just tender. Transfer to the crock pot.
- Add the rest of ingredients, except slivered almonds.
- Cover with a suitable lid and cook for about 6 hours.
- Scatter the toasted almonds on top and serve warm!

Amazing Chicken in Milk

⏱ **(Ready in about 8 hours | Servings 4)**

INGREDIENTS

- Nonstick cooking spray
- 1 cup chicken soup
- 1 green bell pepper, sliced
- 1 red bell pepper, sliced
- 1 carrot, thinly sliced
- 1/2 cup milk
- 1 cup chicken breasts, boneless and skinless
- 1 ½ cups water

DIRECTIONS

✓ Coat a crock pot with nonstick spray.
✓ Add the rest of ingredients.
✓ Cover with a lid; set the crock pot to low and cook for 8 hours.

Mom's Soft and Spicy Pork

⏱ **(Ready in about 6 hours | Servings 4)**

INGREDIENTS

- 1 teaspoon olive oil
- 3 pounds pork loin
- 1 cup spring onions, chopped
- 4 cloves garlic, minced
- 1 cups water
- 1/2 cups dry red wine
- 1 envelope dry onion soup mix
- 1/4 cup orange juice
- 1 tablespoon ground cumin
- 1 teaspoon ground cayenne pepper

DIRECTIONS

✓ Heat the oil in a heavy skillet. Then, cook the pork 1 to 2 minutes on each side. Transfer to the crock pot.
✓ Next, pour the remaining ingredients over the pork. Cover with a lid and cook on low for 6 hours.
✓ Serve over mashed potatoes.

Asian-Style Pork

⏱ **(Ready in about 9 hours | Servings 6)**

INGREDIENTS

- 2 pounds boneless pork loin
- 1/4 cup dry white wine
- 4 cloves garlic
- 1 cup water
- 1 teaspoon honey
- 3/4 teaspoon five-spice powder
- 2 tablespoons dark soy sauce
- 3 whole star anise
- Salt to taste

DIRECTIONS

✓ Heat a nonstick skillet over medium-high flame. Quickly cook the pork on both side. Transfer to the crock pot.
✓ Add the rest of ingredients. Gently stir to coat the pork. Cook on low for 8 to 9 hours.
✓ Discard the star anise and serve warm.

Festive Glazed Pork

⏱ **(Ready in about 8 hours | Servings 4)**

INGREDIENTS

- 1/4 cup dried cherries
- 2/3 cup water
- 2 tablespoons dry white wine
- 1/4 teaspoon ground black pepper
- 1/4 teaspoon salt
- 1/8 teaspoon ground nutmeg
- 1¼ pounds pork loin

DIRECTIONS

✓ In a small-sized bowl or a measuring cup, whisk the dried cherries, water, wine, pepper, salt, and nutmeg.
✓ Place the pork loin in a crock pot. Next, pour the glaze over the meat.
✓ Cook on low for 8 hours. Serve warm.

Old-Fashioned Meatloaf

⏱ **(Ready in about 7 hours | Servings 8)**

INGREDIENTS

- 2 pounds mixed ground beef and pork
- 1 egg
- 1 cup beef stock
- Salt to taste
- 1/2 teaspoon black pepper
- 2 cups crushed seasoned croutons
- 1 ½ cups tomato sauce
- 2 tablespoons Worcestershire sauce
- 1 tablespoon balsamic vinegar

DIRECTIONS

✓ In a large-sized bowl, combine together ground meat, egg, beef stock, salt, black pepper, and croutons. Mix well to combine; then, form into a loaf.
✓ Lay the meatloaf into the crock pot.
✓ In a separate mixing bowl, whisk the tomato sauce, Worcestershire sauce and balsamic vinegar. Pour this mixture over the meatloaf.
✓ Cover and cook on low heat setting for 7 hours.

Easy Zesty Meatloaf

⏱ **(Ready in about 8 hours | Servings 8)**

INGREDIENTS

- 1 ½ pound lean ground beef and lean ground pork, mixed
- 1 teaspoon salt
- 1/4 teaspoon cayenne pepper

- Ground black pepper to taste
- 1 onion, finely chopped
- 1 stalk celery, finely chopped
- 2 medium-sized carrots, grated
- 1 large-sized egg
- 1 cup tomato paste
- 1/2 cup quick-cooking oatmeal
- 1/2 cup crackers, crumbled
- Non-stick cooking spray
- 1/3 cup tomato ketchup
- 1 tablespoon mustard

DIRECTIONS
- ✓ In a large-sized mixing bowl, place together meat, salt, cayenne pepper, black pepper, onion, celery, carrots, egg, tomato paste, oatmeal and crumbled crackers. Mix well to combine. Form the meatloaf and set aside.
- ✓ Treat the crock pot with non-stick cooking spray. Place the meatloaf in the crock pot.
- ✓ In another bowl, mix together tomato ketchup and mustard; spread this mixture over the top of the meatloaf.
- ✓ Cover and cook on low for 7 to 8 hours, until the meatloaf is cooked through.
- ✓ Allow the meatloaf to stand for 30 minutes before slicing and serving.

Poached Salmon with Onion

(Ready in about 1 hour | Servings 4)

INGREDIENTS
- 2 tablespoons butter, melted
- 1 small-sized onion, thinly sliced
- 1 cup water
- 1/2 cup chicken broth
- 4 (6-ounce) salmon fillets
- 1 tablespoon fresh lemon juice
- 1 sprig fresh dill
- Sea salt, to taste
- Ground black pepper to taste
- 1 lemon, quartered, as garnish

DIRECTIONS
- ✓ Grease the inside of the crock pot with the butter.
- ✓ Place the onion slices in the crock pot; pour in water and chicken broth. Set the crock pot on high and cook for about 30 minutes.
- ✓ Place the salmon fillets on cooked onion. Add in lemon juice and fresh dill. Cover and cook on high 30 minutes longer, until the salmon is opaque. Season with salt and black pepper.
- ✓ Garnish with lemon and enjoy!

Sunday Crab Supreme

(Ready in about 2 hours 30 minutes | Servings 8)

INGREDIENTS
- 2 cups sour cream
- 2 cups mayonnaise
- 1/4 cup dry sherry

- 2 tablespoons fresh lemon juice
- 1/4 cup fresh cilantro, minced
- 2 heaping tablespoons parsley, minced
- 2 pounds crabmeat
- 1/2 teaspoon dried basil
- 1 teaspoon dried rosemary
- Salt to taste
- Ground black pepper, to taste

DIRECTIONS
- ✓ Put first four ingredients into your crock pot. Whisk to mix; cook on low heat setting for 2 hours.
- ✓ Add in remaining ingredients. Cover and cook on low until the crabmeat is heated through or about 30 minutes.
- ✓ Serve with boiled potatoes, if desired.

Rich Tomato Shrimp Chowder

(Ready in about 5 hours | Servings 6)

INGREDIENTS
- 3 cups whole kernel corn
- 1 cup tomato juice
- 2 cups chicken broth
- 1 cup clam juice
- 2 large-sized red potatoes, peeled and diced
- 1 cup red onion, chopped
- 1 green bell pepper, chopped
- 2 cloves garlic, minced
- 1/4 cup dry sherry, optional
- 1 teaspoon dried basil
- 1/2 teaspoon dried oregano
- 1/4 teaspoon chili powder
- Salt to taste
- 1/2 teaspoon ground black pepper
- 1 ½ cups cooked halved shrimp, peeled and deveined
- 1/2 cup whole milk

DIRECTIONS
- ✓ Place all ingredients in your crock pot, except shrimp and milk.
- ✓ Cover with a suitable lid and cook on high 4 to 5 hours, adding shrimp and milk during last 15 minutes of cooking time.
- ✓ Adjust seasonings according to your tastes and serve.

Shrimp, Bean and Corn Chowder

(Ready in about 4 hours | Servings 8)

INGREDIENTS
- 1 ½ cups chicken broth
- 2 cups corn
- 2 cans (15 ½ ounces) Great Northern beans, rinsed and drained
- 1/4 cup scallions, chopped
- 1/4 teaspoon caraway seeds, ground
- 1/4 teaspoon dry mustard
- 1 cup 2% reduced-fat milk
- 2 tablespoons cornstarch
- Salt to taste

- 1/2 teaspoon red pepper flakes, crushed
- 1/2 teaspoon dried rosemary
- 1 ½ pounds shrimp, peeled and deveined

DIRECTIONS
- In your crock pot, combine broth, corn, beans, scallions, caraway seeds and mustard.
- Cook on high approximately 4 hours.
- In a medium-sized mixing bowl, whisk together milk, cornstarch, salt, red pepper and rosemary.
- Add the milk mixture and the shrimp to the crock pot during last 20 minutes of cooking time.
- Garnish with lemon wedges and sprinkle with some extra red pepper
- flakes, if desired. Enjoy!

Summer Seafood Treat

(Ready in about 4 hours | Servings 8)

INGREDIENTS
- 1 cup fish stock
- 1/2 cup water
- 1 ½ cup tomatoes, undrained and diced
- 2 large-sized Yukon gold potatoes, diced
- 1 cup spring onions, chopped
- 1 teaspoon garlic powder
- 1/2 teaspoon onion powder
- 1/2 teaspoon dried thyme
- 1 teaspoon dried tarragon leaves
- 1/2 teaspoon cayenne pepper
- 1 cup lobster tail, cooked and cut into small pieces
- 1/2 cup small shrimp, peeled and deveined
- 1 cup whole milk
- Salt to taste
- Black pepper to taste
- Paprika to taste
- Fresh cilantro, as garnish

DIRECTIONS
- Pour fish stock and water into your crock pot. Then, add tomatoes, potatoes, onion powder, garlic powder, thyme, tarragon and cayenne
- pepper.
- Next, cover and cook on low 4 hours.
- Add remaining ingredients, except cilantro, during last 10 minutes of cooking time.
- Sprinkle with chopped fresh cilantro and enjoy your summer chowder!

Lobster Chowder with Vegetables

(Ready in about 4 hours | Servings 8)

INGREDIENTS
- 1/2 cup water
- 1 cup clam juice
- 1/2 cup plum tomatoes, diced
- 1/2 cup tomato juice
- 1 large-sized carrot, chopped
- 1 celery stalk, chopped
- 1 cup spring onions, chopped
- 1 teaspoon garlic powder
- 1/2 teaspoon Italian seasoning mix
- 1/4 teaspoon Ancho Chile, ground
- 1 teaspoon dried tarragon leaves
- 1 cup lobster meat, cooked and cut into small pieces
- 1/2 cup small shrimp, peeled and deveined
- 1 cup whole milk
- Salt to taste
- Black pepper to taste
- Fresh parsley, as garnish
- Lemon wedges, as garnish

DIRECTIONS
- Combine water, clam juice, tomatoes, tomato juice, carrot, celery, spring
- onions, garlic powder, Italian seasoning mix, Ancho Chile and tarragon leaves in a crock pot.
- Set the crock pot to low and cook your chowder for about 4 hours.
- Add remaining ingredients, except parsley and lemon wedges; cook 10 minutes longer.
- Serve garnished with fresh parsley and lemon wedges.

Delicious Scallop and Potato Chowder

(Ready in about 4 hours | Servings 4)

INGREDIENTS
- 1 cup clam juice
- 1/2 cup water
- 1⁄2 cup dry white wine
- 2 large-sized red potatoes, peeled and cubed
- 1 clove garlic, minced
- 1 pound bay scallops
- 1⁄2 cup milk (2% reduced-fat)
- 1/2 teaspoon cumin
- Salt to taste
- Red pepper flakes, as garnish

DIRECTIONS
- Put first five ingredients into a crock pot; then, cover and cook on high 3 to 4 hours.
- Process this mixture in a blender until smooth and creamy; return to the crock pot.
- Stir in the rest of ingredients, except red pepper flakes. Cover and cook on high until scallops are cooked through or about 10 minutes.
- Divide among soup bowls, sprinkle with red pepper flakes and serve warm.

Italian-Style Seafood Chowder

(Ready in about 4 hours | Servings 8)

INGREDIENTS
- 1 cup tomatoes, diced
- ½ cup fresh tomato juice
- 1 cup fish stock

- 2 medium-sized potatoes, diced
- 1/2 cup sweet red bell pepper, chopped
- 1 yellow onion, chopped
- 1/2 cup dry white wine
- 1 teaspoon dried Italian seasoning
- 1 cup haddock, cubed
- 1/2 cup bay scallops
- 1 teaspoon hot pepper sauce
- Salt, to taste
- Black pepper, to taste
- Sour cream, as garnish

DIRECTIONS
- Combine tomatoes with tomato juice, fish stock, potatoes, bell pepper, onion, white wine, and Italian seasonings.
- Cover and cook on high about 4 hours, adding haddock and bay scallops during last 20 minutes of cooking time.
- Stir in the sauce, salt, and black pepper. Serve with a dollop of sour cream.

Salmon Chowder with Root Vegetables

(Ready in about 6 hours | Servings 4)

INGREDIENTS
- 3 cups potatoes, peeled and cubed
- 2 medium-sized carrot, thinly sliced
- 1/2 cup scallions, chopped
- 1 cup turnips, chopped
- 1/2 cup rutabaga
- 1 cup water
- 2 cups clam juice
- 1/2 teaspoon dry mustard
- 1/2 teaspoon dried marjoram leaves
- 1 teaspoon celery seeds
- 1 pound salmon steaks, cut into bite-sized chunks
- 1 cup milk
- 2 tablespoons cornstarch
- Salt, to taste
- Black pepper, to taste

DIRECTIONS
- In a crock pot, combine potatoes, carrots, scallions, turnips, rutabaga, water, clam juice, dry mustard, marjoram, and celery seeds.
- Cover and cook on high 6 hours.
- Purée chowder in a food processor or a blender until smooth and uniform;
- return to the crock pot. Stir in salmon and cook an additional 15 minutes.
- Next, stir in combined milk and cornstarch, stirring frequently about 3 minutes. Season with salt and black pepper. Enjoy!

Salmon with Corn and Roasted Pepper

(Ready in about 5 hours | Servings 4)

INGREDIENTS
- 1 cup reduced-sodium chicken broth
- 1 cup whole kernel corn
- 1 cup chickpea
- 2 medium potatoes, peeled and cubed
- 1 roasted red pepper, chopped
- 1 roasted yellow pepper, chopped
- 2 teaspoons minced garlic
- 1/2 teaspoon Ancho Chile, ground
- 1/2 teaspoon Fenugreek Seed, ground
- 1 teaspoon cumin seeds
- 1 teaspoon dried oregano leaves
- 1 ½ cup salmon steaks, cubed
- Salt, to taste
- White pepper, to taste

DIRECTIONS
- Combine all ingredients, except salmon, salt, and white pepper, in a crock pot; cover and cook on high 4 to 5 hours
- Next, add salmon during last 15 minutes of cooking time. Season with salt and white pepper.

Bermuda-Style Whitefish Chowder

(Ready in about 8 hours | Servings 6)

INGREDIENTS
- 2 cups clam juice
- 1 cup water
- 1/4 cup dry white wine
- 1 ½ cups plum tomatoes, undrained and chopped
- 1/3 cup tomato paste
- 2 cloves garlic, smashed
- 1 cup onion, finely chopped
- 1 celery, chopped
- 1 parsnip, chopped
- 2 small smoked pork hocks
- 2 ½ teaspoons soy sauce
- 2 bay leaves
- 1 teaspoon dried marjoram leaves
- 1/2 teaspoon curry powder
- 1/2 teaspoon grated ginger
- 1 pound whitefish fillet, cubed
- Salt, to taste
- White pepper, to taste
- Avocado slices, as garnish

DIRECTIONS
- Combine all ingredients, except fish, salt, pepper and avocado, in your crock pot.
- Cover and cook on low approximately 8 hours, adding whitefish fillets during last 20 minutes of cooking.
- Discard pork, season with salt and white pepper; serve garnished with slices of avocado.

Creamy Haddock Chowder

(Ready in about 8 hours | Servings 6)

INGREDIENTS

- 2 cups water
- 1 cup chicken stock
- 1/4 cup dry white wine
- 1 tablespoon apple cider vinegar
- 2 tablespoons tomato ketchup
- 3 medium-sized tomatoes, chopped
- 1 cup shallots, finely chopped
- 1 carrot, chopped
- 1 parsnip, chopped
- 2 ½ teaspoons Worcester sauce
- 1 teaspoon rubbed sage
- 1 teaspoon dried parsley flakes
- 1/2 teaspoon ground nutmeg
- 1 pound haddock fillet, cut into bite-sized chunks
- Salt, to taste
- White pepper, to taste

DIRECTIONS
- Combine all of the ingredients, except fish fillets, salt, and white pepper, in a crock pot.
- Cook, covered, about 8 hours, adding fish during last 15 minutes.
- Season to taste with salt and white pepper.

Cod and Tomato Chowder

(Ready in about 8 hours | Servings 6)

INGREDIENTS

- 3 cups fish stock
- 1/4 cup dry white wine
- 1 cup tomato paste
- 1 cup spring onions, chopped
- 1 Yukon gold potato, diced
- 1 carrot, chopped
- 1 parsnip, chopped
- 1 tablespoon tamari sauce
- 1 teaspoon rubbed sage
- 1 teaspoon dried parsley flakes
- 1/4 teaspoon ground Mace, optional
- 1 pound cod fillet, cut into bite-sized pieces
- Salt, to taste
- Cayenne pepper, to taste
- Fresh parsley, to taste

DIRECTIONS
- Combine all of the ingredients, except cod fillets, salt, cayenne pepper and parsley, in your crock pot.
- Cook, covered, 7 to 8 hours. Add cod fillets, salt, cayenne pepper and fresh parsley; continue cooking 15 more minutes. Serve warm.

Cheesy Monkfish Chowder with Cauliflower

(Ready in about 8 hours | Servings 4)

INGREDIENTS

- 1 can (14 ounces) reduced-sodium chicken broth
- 1 pound Yukon potatoes, peeled and cubed
- 1/2 cup green onions, chopped
- 1 large-sized carrot, chopped
- 1/2 head cauliflower, broken into florets
- 1 pound monkfish, cubed
- Salt, to taste
- Crushed red pepper flakes, to taste
- 3/4 teaspoon hot pepper sauce
- 1/2 cup reduced-fat Cheddar cheese, shredded

DIRECTIONS
- Arrange first five ingredients in your crock pot. Set the crock pot to low; cook about 8 hours.
- Next, process cooked mixture in a food processor until your desired consistency is reached; return to the crock pot.
- Add remaining ingredients, except the hot sauce and cheese; continue cooking on low heat setting for 15 minutes longer.
- Add the hot pepper sauce and cheese; allow to sit until Cheddar cheese is melted. Serve warm or at room temperature.

Hearty Flounder Chowder

(Ready in about 6 hours | Servings 4)

INGREDIENTS

- 2 cups clam juice
- 3 medium-sized potatoes, cubed peeled
- 1 cup broccoli florets
- 1 cup green beans
- 1 cup leeks, chopped
- 1 carrot, chopped
- 1 rib celery, chopped
- 1 garlic clove, smashed
- 1/2 teaspoon dried marjoram leaves
- 1/4 teaspoon Mace, ground
- 1/4 teaspoon dry mustard
- 2 cups whole milk
- 8 ounces flounder fillets, skinless and cubed
- 4 ounces crabmeat
- Celery salt to taste
- 1/4 teaspoon white pepper

DIRECTIONS
- In a crock pot, place clam juice, potatoes, broccoli, green beans, leeks, carrot, celery, garlic, marjoram, mace, and dry mustard.
- Set the crock pot to low and then cook approximately 6 hours.
- Add milk and continue cooking for 30 minutes longer. Increase heat to high; add flounder fillets, crabmeat, celery salt and white pepper during last
- minutes of cooking time.
- Divide among soup bowls and serve with croutons, if desired.

Rich Seafood Soup with Bacon

(Ready in about 5 hours | Servings 4)

INGREDIENTS

- 1 ½ cups clam juice
- 1/4 cup dry cherry wine

- 4 large-sized Yukon gold potatoes, peeled and cubed
- 1 large-sized sweet onion, chopped
- 1 rib celery, chopped
- 1 rutabaga, chopped
- 1 cup 2% reduced-fat milk
- 1 pound halibut, cubed
- A few drops of Tabasco sauce
- 3/4 teaspoon rubbed sage
- 1 teaspoon dried parsley flakes
- Salt, to taste
- Paprika to taste
- 2 slices of cooked bacon, crumbled

DIRECTIONS

- First of all, put first six ingredients into your crock pot.
- Next, cook on high 4 to 5 hours. Replace prepared soup to a blender or a food processor; add in milk and blend until everything is well combined; return to the crock pot.
- Add remaining ingredients, except crumbled bacon. Continue cooking an
- additional 15 minutes.
- Divide the soup among four serving bowls, scatter the bacon on top and enjoy!

Refreshing Fish Chowder with Eggs

(Ready in about 8 hours | Servings 6)

INGREDIENTS

- 2 cups water
- 1 teaspoon chicken bouillon concentrate
- 2 large-sized sweet potatoes, diced and peeled
- 1 cup baby carrot, halved
- 1/2 cup leeks, chopped
- 3/4 teaspoon dried dill weed
- 1/2 teaspoon red pepper flakes, crushed
- 2 cups 2% reduced-fat milk, divided
- 1 ½ pounds skinless fish fillets of choice, sliced
- 1 cup cucumber, seeded and chopped
- 1 tablespoon lime juice
- Celery salt to taste
- Chopped chives, as garnish
- Hard-cooked egg slices, as garnish

DIRECTIONS

- Combine first seven ingredients in your crock pot; cook on low 6 to 8 hours.
- Add in milk during last 30 minutes. Stir in fish and cucumber during last
- minutes of cooking time.
- Add lime juice and celery salt and stir to combine.
- Garnish bowls of soup with chives and hard-cooked egg slices.

Spicy Sweet Potato Chili

(Ready in about 8 hours | Servings 6)

INGREDIENTS

- 1 pound chicken breast, boneless and skinless
- 2 cups chicken broth
- 1 tablespoon apple cider vinegar
- 2 cups canned beans, rinsed and drained
- 1 cup spring onions, chopped
- 2 cloves garlic, minced
- 1 cup button mushrooms, sliced
- 1 carrot, thinly sliced
- 2 medium-sized sweet potatoes, peeled and cubed
- 3/4 teaspoon jalapeño chilli
- 1 ½ teaspoon gingerroot
- 1 teaspoon, ground cumin
- 1/2 teaspoon ground coriander
- 1/2 teaspoon allspice
- Salt, to taste
- Ground black pepper, to taste
- Sour cream, as garnish

DIRECTIONS

- Combine all of the ingredients, except sour cream, in your crock pot.
- Cover with a lid and cook on low heat setting 6 to 8 hours.
- Serve with sour cream and enjoy.

Chili with Turkey and Roasted Pepper

(Ready in about 8 hours | Servings 6)

INGREDIENTS

- 1 pound ground turkey
- 1 ½ cup canned tomatoes, stewed
- 1 can (15 ounces) red beans, rinsed drained
- 1 small-sized jalapeño pepper, minced
- 1 cup red onion, chopped
- 1/2 cup roasted red pepper, coarsely chopped
- 1/2 tablespoon chili powder
- 1/4 teaspoon ground cinnamon
- Celery salt, to taste
- Black pepper, to taste
- Smoked paprika to taste

DIRECTIONS

- Heat a non-stick skillet over medium-high flame. Brown turkey for about
- 5 minutes, crumbling with a fork. Transfer browned ground beef to the crock pot.
- Add the rest of ingredients; cover with a lid and cook on low heat setting approximately 8 hours.
- Serve with corn chips, if desired.

Black Bean Chili with Squash

(Ready in about 8 hours | Servings 6)

INGREDIENTS

- 1 pound ground beef
- 2 cups tomato juice
- 1 cup chunky tomato sauce
- 1 cup water
- 1 tablespoon lime
- 1 ½ cups canned black beans, rinsed and drained

- 2 cups scallions, chopped
- 2 cloves garlic, minced
- 1/2 cup celery, cubed
- 2 cups butternut squash
- 1 cup zucchini
- 1 cup mushrooms
- 1 small-sized jalapeño chili, finely chopped
- 1 ½ teaspoons chili powder
- 1 sea salt
- 1/4 teaspoon ground black pepper
- 6 lime wedges

DIRECTIONS
- ✓ First of all, brown ground beef in non-stick skillet about 8 minutes, crumbling with a fork. Transfer to the crock pot.
- ✓ Stir in remaining ingredients, except lime wedges; set the crock pot to low and cook 6 to 8 hours.
- ✓ Serve garnished with lime wedges.

Turkey and Cannellini Bean Chili

⌀ **(Ready in about 8 hours | Servings 6)**

INGREDIENTS
- 1 pound lean ground beef
- 2 cups tomato sauce
- 2 cups cannellini beans
- 1 cup spring onions, chopped
- 1 clove garlic, minced
- 1 tablespoon chili powder
- 2 teaspoons brown sugar
- 1 teaspoon celery seeds
- 1 teaspoon ground cumin
- Salt, to taste
- Ground black pepper, to taste

DIRECTIONS
- ✓ Cook ground beef in a cast-iron skillet over medium heat 8 to 10 minutes or until browned.
- ✓ Add remaining ingredients and cook on low 6 to 8 hours.
- ✓ Divide prepared chili among six soup bowls and serve warm with your favorite salad.

Easy Beef and Pork Chili

⌀ **(Ready in about 8 hours | Servings 6)**

INGREDIENTS
- 1 tablespoon olive oil
- 1 pounds lean ground beef
- 1/2 pounds ground pork
- 2 cups pinto beans, rinsed and drained
- 2 cups stewed tomatoes
- 2 cups whole kernel corn
- 1 cup leeks, chopped
- 1/2 cup red bell pepper, chopped
- 2 tablespoons taco seasoning mix
- Salt to taste
- Black pepper to taste
- Paprika to taste
- Reduced-fat sour cream, as garnish
- Biscuits, as garnish

DIRECTIONS
- ✓ Heat the olive oil in a wide saucepan. Next, cook ground beef and pork about 10 minutes. Crumble with a fork.
- ✓ Add the rest of ingredients, except sour cream and biscuits; cover and cook on low for about 8 hours.
- ✓ Divide among serving bowls, serve with sour cream and biscuits.

Italian-Style Chili

⌀ **(Ready in about 8 hours | Servings 8)**

INGREDIENTS
- 12 ounces lean ground turkey
- 3 cups water
- 1 can (28-ounce) tomatoes, crushed
- 1 red bell pepper, sliced
- 1 yellow bell pepper, sliced
- 1/2 cup onion, chopped
- 3 cloves garlic, minced
- 1 teaspoon ground cumin
- 2 tablespoons chili powder
- 1 dried parsley
- 2 teaspoons dried oregano leaves
- 1 teaspoon allspice
- Salt, to taste
- 1/4 teaspoon black pepper
- 1 pound spaghetti, cooked
- Reduced-fat Cheddar cheese, shredded

DIRECTIONS
- ✓ In a large non-stick skillet, brown the ground turkey over medium heat, about 5 minutes.
- ✓ Combine turkey with remaining ingredients, except spaghetti and
- ✓ Cheddar cheese, in your crock pot; cook on low 8 hours.
- ✓ Serve with spaghetti and Cheddar cheese.

Family Favourite Chili

⌀ **(Ready in about 8 hours | Servings 8)**

INGREDIENTS
- 1 pound ground beef
- 1 cup onions, chopped
- 1 green bell pepper, chopped
- 1 red bell pepper, chopped
- 1 poblano pepper, minced
- 2 cloves garlic, minced
- 2 teaspoons ground cumin
- 1 teaspoon dried oregano leaves
- 1 teaspoon dried basil leaves
- 1/2 teaspoon grated ginger
- 1 tablespoon cilantro
- 2 cups tomatoes, undrained and diced

- 1 cup water
- 1 can (15 ounces) pinto beans, rinsed and drained
- 1/4 cup tomato ketchup
- 3/4 cup beer
- 1 tablespoon unsweetened cocoa
- Salt, to taste
- Black pepper, to taste
- Paprika, to taste
- Sour cream, as garnish

DIRECTIONS
- First of all, cook ground beef in lightly greased saucepan over medium heat. Cook until the beef is browned and cooked through or about 10 minutes.
- Add beef to the crock pot. Then, add remaining ingredients, except sour cream, to the crock pot; cover with a lid and cook on low about 8 hours.
- Garnish each bowl of chili with sour cream.

Easy Tenderloin Chili

(Ready in about 6 hours | Servings 4)

INGREDIENTS
- 1 pound pork tenderloin, cubed
- 1 can (15-ounces) reduced-sodium fat-free vegetable broth
- 1 can (15-ounces) beans, rinsed
- 1 pound plum tomatoes, sliced
- 1 large-sized jalapeño chili, minced
- 1 tablespoon chili powder
- 1 teaspoon toasted cumin seeds
- Salt, to taste
- Black pepper, to taste
- Cayenne pepper to taste
- Corn chips, as garnish

DIRECTIONS
- Combine all ingredients, except corn chips, in a crock pot.
- Cook covered on high about 6 hours.
- Serve with corn chips and enjoy!

Yummy Tomato Bean Soup

(Ready in about 7 hours | Servings 6)

INGREDIENTS
- 1 quart chicken stock
- 2 cans (15-ounce) navy beans, rinsed, drained
- 1 cup cooked bacon, chopped
- 1 pound lamb, cubed
- 1 cup scallions
- 1 rib celery, chopped
- 1 large-sized carrot, chopped
- 1 clove garlic, minced
- 1 teaspoon Italian seasoning mix
- 3 Roma tomatoes, chopped
- Salt, to taste
- Black pepper, to taste
- Cayenne pepper, to taste

- Biscuits, as garnish

DIRECTIONS
- Combine all ingredients, except biscuits, in a crock pot.
- Next, cover and cook on low for about 7 hours.
- Serve with biscuits and enjoy!

Lamb Chili with Ham

(Ready in about 8 hours | Servings 6)

INGREDIENTS
- 1 quart vegetable stock
- 2 cans (15-ounce) pinto beans, rinsed, drained
- 1 cup partially cooked ham, diced
- 1 pound lamb, cubed
- 1 large-sized red onion, finely chopped
- 2 cloves garlic, minced
- 1 large-sized carrot, chopped
- 1 rib celery, chopped
- 1 teaspoon Italian seasoning mix
- 1 cup tomato sauce
- Salt, to taste
- Black pepper, to taste
- Cayenne pepper, to taste
- Sour cream, as garnish

DIRECTIONS
- Place all ingredients, except sour cream, in a crock pot.
- Set the crock pot to low; cook your chili for 7 to 8 hours.
- Garnish with a sour cream and serve.

Creamy Vegetable Soup

(Ready in about 4 hours | Servings 4)

INGREDIENTS
- 2 cups vegetable stock
- 2-3 spring onions, chopped
- 3/4 cup mushrooms, thinly sliced
- 1 cup frozen artichoke hearts, thawed and finely chopped
- 1 cup light cream
- 2 tablespoons cornstarch
- Salt, to taste
- Black pepper, to taste
- Red pepper flakes, as garnish

DIRECTIONS
- Combine first four ingredients in your crock pot; cover and cook on high heat setting 4 hours.
- Combine light cream and cornstarch. Add this mixture to the crock pot, stirring 2 to 3 minutes.
- Season with salt and black pepper. Sprinkle each bowl of soup with red pepper flakes.

Fall Brussels sprouts Soup

(Ready in about 4 hours | Servings 4)

INGREDIENTS

- 1 pound Brussels sprouts, halved
- 1/2 cup sweet onion, chopped
- 1 clove garlic, minced
- 1 teaspoon onion powder
- 1 teaspoon celery seeds
- 1/2 teaspoon dried rosemary leaves
- 1 cup vegetable broth
- 1 cup 2% reduced-fat milk
- Salt, to taste
- Black pepper, to taste
- Ground nutmeg, as garnish

DIRECTIONS
✓ Add Brussels sprouts, sweet onion, garlic, onion powder, celery seeds, rosemary, and vegetable broth to the crock pot; cover and cook on high 3 to 4 hours.
✓ Pour the soup in a food processor or a blender. Add 2% reduced-fat milk. Blend until a smooth consistency is reached.
✓ Season with salt and black pepper. Divide among four soup bowls and sprinkle lightly with nutmeg; serve.

Vegetarian Creamed Corn Soup

(Ready in about 4 hours 30 minutes | Servings 4)

INGREDIENTS

- 3 ½ cups vegetable stock
- 1/2 cup scallions, chopped
- 1 large-sized carrot, chopped
- 2 medium-sized potatoes, peeled and cubed
- 1 clove garlic, minced
- 1 can (151/2 ounces) whole kernel corn, drained
- 1 cup reduced-fat milk
- 2 tablespoons cornstarch
- Celery salt, to taste
- White pepper, to taste
- Paprika, as garnish
- Sour cream, as garnish

DIRECTIONS
✓ Combine vegetable stock, scallions, carrot, potato, and garlic.
✓ Cover and cook on high 4 hours. Purée soup in your food processor until creamy and smooth; return to the crock pot.
✓ Add kernel corn and continue cooking on high 30 minutes longer. Then, add combined reduced-fat milk and cornstarch, stirring constantly 3 minutes. Sprinkle with celery salt and white pepper and stir again. Garnish with paprika and sour cream.

Rich Potato Pistou Soup

(Ready in about 4 hours 20 minutes | Servings 6)

INGREDIENTS

- 2 quarts water
- 1 envelope onion soup mix
- 2 cups onions, chopped
- 5 cloves garlic, halved
- 4 Yukon gold potatoes, peeled and diced
- 5 plum tomatoes, seeded and chopped
- 2 medium-sized zucchini, sliced
- 3/4 teaspoon celery seeds
- 1 teaspoon dried basil leaves
- 1/4 cup Parmesan cheese, grated
- Salt, to taste
- Black pepper, to taste
- Red pepper flakes, for garnish

DIRECTIONS
✓ In a crock pot, combine water, onion soup mix, onions, garlic, potatoes, tomatoes, zucchini, celery seeds, and basil leaves.
✓ Next, set your crock pot to high and cook 3 to 4 hours.
✓ Then, add soup to a food processor. Stir in the rest of ingredients, except red pepper flakes; blend until your desired consistency is reached.
✓ Return creamy soup to the crock pot; cover and cook on high 15 to 20
✓ minutes longer; sprinkle with red pepper flakes and serve warm.

Refreshing Roasted Red Pepper Soup

(Ready in about 3 hours | Servings 4)

INGREDIENTS

- 1 ½ cups vegetable stock
- 3/4 cup jarred roasted red peppers
- 1 tablespoon balsamic vinegar
- 1 cup water
- 1/2 cup onion, chopped
- 1 cucumber, chopped
- 1 cup potato, cubed
- 1 teaspoon ground allspice
- Salt, to taste
- White pepper, to taste
- Paprika, to taste
- 1 ½ cups plain yogurt
- 2 tablespoons cornstarch

DIRECTIONS
✓ In a crock pot, combine all ingredients, except yogurt and cornstarch; cover and cook on high about 3 hours.
✓ Add combined yogurt and cornstarch, stirring constantly, 2 to 3 minutes.
✓ Purée mixture in your food processor until smooth, creamy and uniform; set in a refrigerator and serve chilled.

Old-Fashioned Beef Stew

(Ready in about 8 hours | Servings 4)

INGREDIENTS

- 1 cup reduced-sodium fat-free beef stock
- 1 pound beef round steak, cut into strips
- 1/2 cup dry red wine
- 2 cups green beans
- 1 onion, finely chopped
- 2 medium-sized potatoes
- 1 celery stalk, chopped
- 3 carrots, thickly sliced

- 1 teaspoon dried marjoram leaves
- 1 teaspoon dried thyme leaves
- 1 teaspoon dried sage
- Salt and black pepper, to taste
- Cayenne pepper, to taste

DIRECTIONS
- ✓ In a crock pot, combine all ingredients.
- ✓ Cover with a lid and cook on low 8 hours.
- ✓ Serve hot over cooked noodles.

- Black pepper, to taste
- Paprika, to taste
- 2 tablespoons cornstarch
- 1/4 cup cold water

DIRECTIONS
- ✓ Place all ingredients, except cornstarch and cold water, in your crock pot; cover and cook on high 4 to 5 hours.
- ✓ Stir in combined cornstarch and cold water, stirring 2 to 3 minutes. Discard bay leaf and serve over rice, if desired.

Tangy Cucumber Soup

(Ready in about 3 hours | Servings 4)

INGREDIENTS
- 1 ½ cups chicken stock
- 2 tablespoons apple cider vinegar
- 1 cup water
- 1/2 cup spring onions, finely chopped
- 1 cucumber, chopped
- 1 teaspoon fresh dill weed
- 1 cup potato, diced
- 1 teaspoon ground cinnamon
- Salt, to taste
- Black pepper, to taste
- Red pepper flakes, to taste
- 1 ½ cups plain yogurt
- 2 tablespoons cornstarch

DIRECTIONS
- ✓ In your crock pot, place all ingredients, except yogurt and cornstarch.
- ✓ Cover with a lid and cook on high heat setting approximately 3 hours.
- ✓ In a measuring cup, whisk yogurt with cornstarch; add to the crock pot and cook, stirring often, 2 to 3 minutes.
- ✓ Pour this mixture into a food processor or a blender. Process until smooth and creamy; serve chilled.

Easy Yummy Beef Stew

(Ready in about 5 hours | Servings 6)

INGREDIENTS
- 2 pounds beef meat, cubed
- 1 cup beef broth
- 1 sweet red bell pepper
- 1 cup scallions, chopped
- 3 cloves garlic, minced
- 1 parsnip, cubed
- 1 celery, chopped
- 1/2 cup dry red wine or beef broth
- 2 medium-sized red potato
- 2 tablespoons tomato ketchup
- 1 tablespoon apple cider vinegar
- 1/2 teaspoon dried rosemary leaves
- 2 large bay leaves
- Salt, to taste

Hearty Chicken Stew

(Ready in about 6 hours | Servings 4)

INGREDIENTS
- 1 can (10 ¾ ounces) reduced-sodium condensed cream of chicken soup
- 1 ¼ cups 2% reduced-fat milk
- 1 cup water
- 1 red bell pepper, chopped
- 1 green bell pepper, chopped
- 1 poblano pepper, minced
- 1 pound chicken breasts, boneless, skinless and cubed
- 1 cup onion, sliced
- 1/2 cup turnip, diced
- 1/2 cup carrot, thinly sliced
- 1/2 teaspoon dried oregano
- 1/2 teaspoon dried rosemary
- 1/2 teaspoon celery salt
- 1/4 teaspoon red pepper flakes, crushed
- 1/4 teaspoon ground black pepper
- 2 tablespoons cornstarch
- 1/4 cup cold water

DIRECTIONS
- ✓ Combine cream of chicken soup, milk and water in a crock pot.
- ✓ Stir in remaining ingredients, except cornstarch and water; cover and
- ✓ cook on low 5 to 6 hours.
- ✓ Next, add combined cornstarch and cold water, stirring frequently 2 to 3 minutes. Serve over boiled potatoes, if desired.

Sausage and Turkey Stew

(Ready in about 5 hours | Servings 4)

INGREDIENTS
- 2 cups smoked turkey
- 2 cups sausage links, sliced
- 1 can (28-ounce) tomatoes, diced
- 2 cloves roasted garlic, undrained
- 2 tablespoons dry vermouth
- 1 cup onion, chopped
- 1 cup whole kernel corn
- 1 bell pepper, chopped
- 1/2 teaspoon dried basil leaves
- 1/2 teaspoon dried thyme leaves

- Salt, to taste
- Black pepper, to taste
- A few drops of Tabasco sauce

DIRECTIONS
- Combine all ingredients, except Tabasco sauce, in a crock pot.
- Cover and cook on high 5 hours.
- Drizzle with Tabasco sauce; serve.

Turkey and Kidney Bean Stew

(Ready in about 8 hours | Servings 4)

INGREDIENTS
- 1 pound turkey breast, cut into bite-sized pieces
- 2 cups kidney beans, rinsed and drained
- 1 can (14 ½ ounces) chicken stock
- 1 cup tomato juice
- 2 cups butternut squash, peeled and cubed
- 1 cup onion, chopped
- 1 cup sweet potato, cubed
- 1 jalapeño pepper, minced
- 1 teaspoon celery seeds, toasted
- Salt, to taste
- Black pepper, to taste
- 1/2 teaspoon dried basil
- 1/2 teaspoon dried oregano
- Fresh chives, as garnish
- 1/4 cup pine nuts, coarsely chopped

DIRECTIONS
- Put all ingredients, except fresh chives and pine nuts, into a crock pot.
- Cover with a lid and cook on low approximately 8 hours.
- Sprinkle each serving bowl with chives and chopped pine nuts.

Cod and Shrimp Stew

(Ready in about 4 hours | Servings 8)

INGREDIENTS
- 1 cup clam juice
- 1 can (28-ounces) stewed tomatoes
- 1/2 cup dry white wine
- 1/2 cup onion, finely chopped
- 3 cloves garlic, minced
- 1/2 teaspoon dried thyme
- 1 teaspoon dried basil
- 1 teaspoon dried oregano leaves
- 2 bay leaves
- Salt, to taste
- Black pepper, to taste
- 1 pound cod fillets, sliced
- 1 ½ cups shrimp, peeled and deveined

DIRECTIONS
- Place all of the ingredients, except cod fillets and shrimp, in a crock pot; cover with a lid.
- Set the crock pot to high and cook 3 to 4 hours, adding cod fillets and shrimp during last 15 minutes of cooking time. Discard bay leaves; serve with cornbread.

Summer Spiced Fish Stew

(Ready in about 5 hours 15 minutes | Servings 8)

INGREDIENTS
- 1 cup clam juice
- 1 cup dry white wine
- 2 cans (14 ½ ounces) tomatoes, undrained and diced
- 1 cup leeks, chopped
- 1 clove garlic, minced
- 1/2 cup fennel, thinly sliced
- 1/2 head broccoli, chopped
- 1/2 celery, chopped
- 1 bay leaf
- 1/2 teaspoon dried thyme
- 3/4 teaspoon dill weed
- 1 teaspoon lemon zest, grated
- 1/4 cup parsley, chopped
- 2 tablespoon cilantro
- Salt, to taste
- Black pepper, to taste
- Cayenne pepper, to taste
- 1 pound fish fillets, cubed
- 8 ounces shrimp, peeled and deveined
- 12 mussels, scrubbed

DIRECTIONS
- Place all of the ingredients, except seafood, in a crock pot; cover and cook on high 5 hours.
- Add fish fillets, shrimp and mussels to the crock pot and continue cooking
- more minutes.
- Discard bay leaf and serve warm with cooked rice.

Soft and Creamy Chicken Breasts

(Ready in about 5 hours | Servings 6)

INGREDIENTS
- 6 boneless chicken breasts
- 1/2 cup olive oil
- 1 package Italian dressing mix
- 1 can mushroom soup
- 4-ounce cream cheese
- 1/2 cup dry white wine
- 1 package pasta of choice
- Rosemary sprigs for garnish

DIRECTIONS
- Place chicken breasts in a crock pot.
- In a wide heavy skillet, heat the oil and add Italian dressing mix, mushroom soup, cream cheese and white wine. Pour this mixture over chicken.
- Set the crock pot on low and cook for 4 to 5 hours.

- Cook the pasta according to package DIRECTIONS. Place prepared chicken breasts over cooked pasta, garnish with rosemary and serve warm.

Spiced Chicken with Couscous

(Ready in about 8 hours | Servings 6)

INGREDIENTS

- 4 boneless chicken breasts, cut in halves
- 2 cups mushrooms, sliced
- 1 (14.5-ounce) can tomatoes
- 8-ounce frozen artichokes hearts, thawed
- 1 ¼ cup chicken broth
- 1 onion, finely chopped
- 3 cloves garlic, crushed
- 1/2 cup olives, pitted and sliced
- 3 tablespoons quick-cooking tapioca
- 2 teaspoon curry powder
- 1/2 teaspoon salt
- 1/4 teaspoon black pepper
- 4 cups cooked couscous
- Red pepper flakes for garnish

DIRECTIONS

- In a crock pot, place together mushrooms, tomatoes, artichoke hearts, chicken broth, onion, garlic and olives. Stir in tapioca, curry powder, salt, and black pepper.
- Add chicken breast to the crock pot.
- Cover the crock pot and cook your meal on low setting for 7 to 8 hours.
- Serve over hot cooked couscous and sprinkle red pepper flakes for garnish.

Artichokes with Herbs and Lemon

(Ready in about 5 hours | Servings 4)

INGREDIENTS

- 5 large artichokes
- 1 teaspoon fine sea salt
- 2 stalks celery, sliced
- 2 large carrots, cut into matchsticks
- Juice from 1/2 fresh lemon
- 1/4 teaspoon black pepper
- 1 teaspoon dried thyme
- 1 tablespoon dried rosemary
- Lemon wedges for garnish

DIRECTIONS

- Remove the stalks and tough leaves from artichokes. Place the artichokes in a crock pot and pour in 2 cups of boiling water.
- Add salt, celery, carrots, lemon juice, black pepper, thyme and rosemary.
- Set the crock pot on high and cook the artichokes for 4 to 5 hours. Serve warm with lemon wedges.

Pork Chops with Squash in Sauce

(Ready in about 6 hours | Servings 6)

INGREDIENTS

- 6 pork chops
- 2 medium acorn squash
- 1 teaspoon sea salt
- 2 tablespoons butter, melted
- 3/4 cup sugar
- 3/4 teaspoon brown bouquet sauce
- 1 tablespoon lemon juice
- 1 teaspoon lemon zest
- 1/4 teaspoon black pepper
- 5-6 peppercorns

DIRECTIONS

- Cut each squash into slices and discard the seeds.
- Lay 3 chops on bottom of a crock pot. Then lay the squash slices and then lay the remaining 3 chops.
- Mix salt, butter, sugar, bouquet sauce, lemon juice, lemon zest and black pepper. Pour this mixture over chop and squash. Sprinkle peppercorns.
- Cover the crock pot and set on low. Cook for 4 to 6 hours. Serve warm.

Smokey Ground Beef and Beans

(Ready in about 6 hours | Servings 4)

INGREDIENTS

- Vegetable oil to taste
- 1 lb. ground beef
- 3/4 lb. fried bacon
- 1 onion, chopped
- 2 cloves garlic, crushed
- 1 can pork & beans
- 2 (16-ounce) beans canned
- 1 cup tomato sauce
- 1/4 cup liquid smoke
- 1 teaspoon salt
- 1/2 teaspoon pepper
- 1 tablespoon dried rosemary
- Olives for garnish

DIRECTIONS

- Heat a large saucepan with a small amount of vegetable oil over medium-high heat. Sauté the onions and garlic until they are just tender and fragrant.
- Transfer sauteed vegetables to a crock pot. Add beef, bacon, pork & beans, canned beans, tomato sauce and liquid smoke.
- Season with salt, pepper, and rosemary and toss to combine all ingredients.
- Set the crock pot on low and cook 4 to 6 hours. Serve with olives.

Crockpot Style Barbecue

(Ready in about 5 hours | Servings 6)

INGREDIENTS

- 1 ½ lb. chuck steak, boneless
- 1 white onion, sliced
- 2 cloves garlic, crushed
- 1/4 cup wine
- 1 teaspoon cayenne pepper
- 2 tablespoons Worcestershire sauce
- 1/2 ketchup
- 1 teaspoon salt
- 1 teaspoon dry mustard
- 1/4 teaspoon black pepper
- 1/4 teaspoon white pepper

DIRECTIONS

✓ Cut the chuck steak on a diagonal. Place chuck steak in a crock pot.
✓ In a mixing bowl, combine onion, garlic, wine, cayenne, Worcestershire sauce, ketchup, salt, mustard, black pepper and white pepper. Stir to combine,
✓ Pour this mixture over the chuck steak and toss to combine.
✓ Cover the crock pot and cook the steak on low setting for 3 to 5 hours.

Two-Bean and Beef Chili

⌀ **(Ready in about 8 hours | Servings 6)**

INGREDIENTS

- 1 ½ lbs. beef
- 1 tablespoon dry mustard
- 1 teaspoon kosher salt
- 1/4 teaspoon freshly ground black pepper
- 1/2 teaspoon sweet paprika
- 2 cloves garlic, minced
- 1 Jalapeño, minced
- 1 (16-ounce) can tomatoes, undrained
- 1 onion, finely chopped
- 1 can brown beans, rinsed and drained
- 1 can chili beans
- 2 bay leaves

DIRECTIONS

✓ Combine together dry mustard, salt, pepper, paprika, garlic and jalapeño, and mix well to combine.
✓ Add beef and stir again. Place this mixture in a crock pot.
✓ Ad the remaining ingredients in the crock pot.
✓ Set the crock pot on low, and cook your dish, uncovered, for 6 to 8 hours.

Soft Beef with Bratwurst and Mushrooms

⌀ **(Ready in about 8 hours | Servings 4)**

INGREDIENTS

- 1 packet beef au ju powder
- 1 lb. beef
- 1 bratwurst
- 3 potatoes, peeled and diced
- 2-3 scallions
- 2 cloves garlic, crushed
- 1 teaspoon dry mustard
- 1/2 cup button mushrooms, sliced
- 1 red bell pepper, sliced
- Cooked rice for garnish

DIRECTIONS

✓ Pour 5 cups water and au ju powder in a crock pot and stir well to combine.
✓ Place beef, bratwurst, potatoes, scallions, garlic, mustard, mushrooms and red bell pepper.
✓ Set the crock pot on low and cook the beef for 6 to 8 hours. Serve over rice.

Easy Roast with Gravy

⌀ **(Ready in about 9 hours | Servings 6)**

INGREDIENTS

- 3 pounds roast beef cut into bite sized pieces
- 1 packet dry onion soup mix
- 2 cans cream of mushroom soup
- Pasta of choice

DIRECTIONS

✓ Cut the roast into small chunks and place them to a crock pot.
✓ Add onion soup mix and cream of mushroom soup.
✓ Set the crock pot on low. Cook for 9 hours.
✓ Serve over your favorite pasta.

Vegetarian Split Pea Soup

⌀ **(Ready in about 9 hours | Servings 6)**

INGREDIENTS

- 1 lb. Dry yellow split peas
- 2 celery stalks, finely chopped
- 1 carrot, grated
- 1 parsnip, grated
- 1 onion, chopped
- 2 tablespoon butter
- 1 tablespoon apple cider vinegar
- 1 teaspoon salt
- 1/4 teaspoon black pepper
- 1/2 teaspoon dried dill
- 2 vegetable bouillon cubes
- Croutons for garnish

DIRECTIONS

✓ In a crock pot, combine together peas, stalks, carrot, parsnip, onion, butter, and vinegar, and stir to combine.
✓ Add 2 qt water, salt, pepper, dill and your favorite vegetable bouillon cubes. Stir again to combine all ingredients well.
✓ Set the crock pot on low, cover and cook the soup for 7 to 9 hours.
✓ Garnish with croutons and serve hot.

Roast with Dill and Sour Cream

(Ready in about 8 hours | Servings 6)

INGREDIENTS

- 3 lb. roast
- 1 tablespoon balsamic vinegar
- 1 teaspoon salt
- 1/2 teaspoon freshly ground black pepper
- 3 tablespoons cornstarch
- 1 tablespoon dill
- 1 cup sour cream

DIRECTIONS

- In a crock pot, put the roast and pour in 1/4 cup of water and balsamic vinegar. Season with salt and pepper.
- Cover the crock pot and cook the roast for 8 hours on low setting.
- Stir in cornstarch and dill and continue cooking until the sauce is thickened.
- Mix in sour cream before serving.

Mushrooms with Sour Cream

(Ready in about 1 hour 30 minutes | Servings 4)

INGREDIENTS

- 2 (8-ounce) packages fresh mushrooms, sliced
- 1/2 cup butter, softened
- 1 package Italian dressing mix
- Sour cream for garnish

DIRECTIONS

- In a crock pot, put the mushrooms, butter, and Italian dressing mix, and stir to combine.
- Set the crock pot on high, and cook, stirring occasionally, until the mushrooms become very soft and fragrant.
- Reduce the heat to low setting and cook for 1 hours longer. Serve hot with sour cream.

Vegetable Stew with Beans

(Ready in about 8 hours | Servings 6)

INGREDIENTS

- 1 medium eggplant, peeled and cut into bite-sized chunks
- 2 cups tomato, chopped
- 2 large carrots, sliced
- 15 ounces canned brown beans, rinsed and drained
- 8 ounces canned black beans, rinsed and drained
- 1 large red onion, finely chopped
- 3 cloves garlic, minced
- 3 cups vegetable broth
- 1/2 cup tomato sauce
- 1/2 teaspoon dried basil
- 1 teaspoon salt
- 1/4 teaspoon pepper
- 1/4 teaspoon paprika
- 2 bay leaves

DIRECTIONS

- In a crock pot, combine together eggplant, tomatoes, carrots, beans, onion, and garlic.
- Stir in vegetable broth, tomato sauce, basil, salt, pepper, paprika and bay leaves. Stir to combine all ingredients.
- Cover, set the crock pot on low heat and cook for 7 to 8 hours. Serve
- warm.

Chip Beef Onion Soup

(Ready in about 8 hours | Servings 6)

INGREDIENTS

- 2 quarts Beef Stock
- 3 large red onions, finely chopped
- 1/4 cup canola oil
- 1 teaspoons garlic salt
- 1/4 teaspoon salt
- 1 tablespoon
- 1 balsamic vinegar
- 2 tablespoons flour
- Fresh parsley to taste
- Mozzarella cheese for garnish

DIRECTIONS

- Pour beef stock in a crock pot. Cover the crock pot and set on high.
- Heat canola oil in a wide saucepan and sauté the onions until very tender.
- Add salt, sugar and flour. Stir well to combine and add to the crock pot. Cook on low for 6 to 8 hours.
- Divide among serving bowls and sprinkle parsley. Garnish with mozzarella cheese and serve warm.

Pork Stew with Sweet Potatoes

(Ready in about 10 hours | Servings 6)

INGREDIENTS

- 3 ½ pound boneless pork loin roast
- 1 tablespoon extra-virgin olive oil
- 1 teaspoon salt
- 1/2 teaspoon black pepper
- 3 cups sweet potatoes, peeled and sliced
- 1 red onion, sliced
- 6 cloves garlic, peeled
- 1 cup pork broth
- Fresh parsley for garnish

DIRECTIONS

- Remove unwanted fat from the meat.
- Heat olive oil in a saucepan over medium heat. Season with salt and black pepper. Cook pork for 10 minutes, stirring occasionally.
- Place potatoes, onion and garlic in a slow cooker. Add the pork to the crock pot. Pour the broth over meat and vegetables.
- Cover and cook on low setting for 8 to 10 hours.

- ✓ Divide among serving bowls, sprinkle parsley and serve hot.

Beans with White Bacon

⌀ **(Ready in about 8 hours | Servings 6)**

INGREDIENTS

- 1 package dried beans
- 2 tablespoons sugar
- 1 teaspoon salt
- 1/2 teaspoon black pepper
- 1 teaspoon dried mustard
- 1/2 cup molasses
- 1 (3-ounce) piece white bacon
- 1 red onion, sliced

DIRECTIONS

- ✓ Place beans in a water and soak them overnight. Drain the beans.
- ✓ Parboil the beans for 10 to 15 minutes.
- ✓ In a crock pot, arrange the onions, then arrange the beans. Stir in sugar, salt, pepper, mustard, and molasses.
- ✓ Add hot water to coat the top of beans.
- ✓ Place salt pork on top of the crock pot. Set the crock pot on high, cover and cook for 6 to 8 hours. Liquid will evaporate during cooking, so add a certain amount of water every 3 hours.

Green Beans with Bacon

⌀ **(Ready in about 4 hours | Servings 4)**

INGREDIENTS

- 1/4 pound white bacon, slice into bite-sized cubes
- 2 pounds green beans
- 2 ripe tomatoes, peeled and diced
- 2 cups vegetable stock
- 1/2 teaspoon salt
- 1/4 teaspoon freshly ground black pepper
- 1/4 teaspoon ground white pepper
- 1 teaspoon cayenne pepper
- 1 bay leaf

DIRECTIONS

- ✓ Arrange bacon in the crock pot. Add green beans.
- ✓ Stir in tomatoes and season with salt, black pepper, white pepper, cayenne pepper and bay leaf. Cover the crock pot and cook on high setting for 3 to 4 hours.
- ✓ Remove bay leaf and serve hot.

Bean and Kale Soup with Ham

⌀ **(Ready in about 12 hours | Servings 4)**

INGREDIENTS

- 1 pound dried beans
- 1 jalapeño pepper, minced
- 1 parsnip, sliced
- 1 teaspoon salt
- 1/2 teaspoon black pepper
- 1 teaspoon paprika
- 4 cups water
- 1 ham butt
- 2 red onions, finely chopped
- 1 package frozen peas, thawed
- 3 cloves garlic, crushed
- 1/2 head kale, shredded

DIRECTIONS

- ✓ Soak the beans overnight. The next day, drain and rinse the beans.
- ✓ In a crock pot, arrange beans, jalapeño, parsnip, salt, peper, paprika, water, ham, onions and garlic. Cover the crock pot and cook vegetables on low setting for 10 to 12 hours.
- ✓ Set to high and remove ham. Add peas and kale. Cook on high for 1 to 2 hours longer.

Winter Beef Stew

⌀ **(Ready in about 12 hours | Servings 8)**

INGREDIENTS

- 2 pounds stew beef, cut into bite-sized cubes
- 4 medium carrots, sliced
- 1 parsnip, sliced
- 1 onion, chopped
- 2 stalks celery, sliced
- 1 (28-ounce) can tomatoes
- 1/2 cup quick-cooking tapioca
- 1 teaspoon salt
- 1/4 teaspoon black pepper
- 1 teaspoon cayenne pepper

DIRECTIONS

- ✓ Trim all excess fat from the beef.
- ✓ In a crock pot, place meat, carrots, parsnip, onion, celery, tomatoes and tapioca. Mix well to combine.
- ✓ Season with salt, pepper and cayenne and stir to combine all ingredients well.
- ✓ Cover and cook on low setting for 10 to 12 hours.

Thick Potato Soup

⌀ **(Ready in about 3 hours 30 minutes | Servings 8)**

INGREDIENTS

- 6 large potatoes, peeled and cut into 1/2" cubes
- 2 onions, sliced
- 2 carrots, thinly sliced
- 2 cans (14 ½-ounce) vegetable broth
- 1 teaspoon thyme
- 1/2 teaspoon dried dill
- 1 teaspoon salt
- 1/2 teaspoon black pepper
- 1/4 cup all-purpose flour
- 1 ½ cups half-and-half

DIRECTIONS

- ✓ Combine together potatoes, onions, carrots, broth, thyme, dill, salt, and black pepper in a crock pot.

- ✓ Cover and cook on high setting for 3 hours.
- ✓ Stir in flour and half-and-half.
- ✓ Continue cooking for 30 minutes more.

Old-Fashioned Vegetable Soup

(Ready in about 9 hours | Servings 6)

INGREDIENTS

- 1 (10-ounce) package frozen green beans
- 1 (10-ounce) package frozen corn
- 1 cup scallions, finely chopped
- 1 cup zucchini, chopped
- 2 cloves garlic, crushed
- 6 cups vegetable broth
- 1 (6-ounce) can tomato paste
- 1 teaspoon dried marjoram
- 1 teaspoon dried basil
- 1 ½ cups pasta of choice

DIRECTIONS

- ✓ In a crock pot, place beans, corn, scallions, zucchini, garlic, vegetable broth, tomato paste, marjoram and basil. Stir to combine.
- ✓ Cover the crock pot and cook on low setting for 7 to 9 hours.
- ✓ Add your favorite pasta and cook for 1 hour longer. Serve hot.

Vegetable Beef Soup

(Ready in about 10 hours | Servings 6)

INGREDIENTS

- 1 pound boneless beef chuck roast
- 2 medium carrots
- 1 parsnip, sliced
- 2 potatoes, peeled
- 1 onion, finely chopped
- 1 teaspoon salt
- 1/2 teaspoon black pepper
- 1/2 teaspoon dried marjoram
- 1 bay leaf
- 2 (14.5-ounce) cans tomatoes with juice
- 1 cup frozen chickpea

DIRECTIONS

- ✓ To prepare ingredients: Trimm unwanted fat from the beef and cut it into bite-size chunks. Slice the vegetables into very small pieces.
- ✓ In a crock pot, combine together beef, carrots, parsnip, potatoes, and onion.
- ✓ Season with salt, pepper and marjoram. Add bay leaf, tomatoes, and 1 cup of warm water. Stir to combine well.
- ✓ Set the crock pot on low and cook for 8 to 10 hours.
- ✓ Discard bay leaf. Stir in chickpeas and cook another 10 minutes until the
- ✓ chickpeas are heated through.

Chicken with Vegetables and Noodles

(Ready in about 8 hours | Servings 6)

INGREDIENTS

- 2 large boneless chicken breasts
- 1 onion, finely chopped
- 2 stalks celery, chopped
- 2 large carrots, shredded
- 12 cups noodles of choice
- 1 teaspoon sea salt
- 1/4 teaspoon black pepper
- 1 teaspoon basil

DIRECTIONS

- ✓ Place chicken, onions, celery, carrots and noodles in a crock pot. Pour in
- ✓ 6 cups of water and season with salt, black pepper and basil. Stir to combine.
- ✓ Set the crock pot to low and cook for 6 to 8 hours.
- ✓ When chicken breasts are cooked, chop them into bite-sized chunks. Add chicken chunks back to the crock pot and cook for another 15 minutes.

Beef and Rice Casserole

(Ready in about 9 hours | Servings 8)

INGREDIENTS

- 1 lb. lean ground beef
- 1 onion, finely chopped
- 1 red bell pepper, thinly sliced
- 1 (16-ounce) can kidney beans, rinsed and drained
- 2 (14.5-ounce) cans tomatoes with juice
- 1 (8-ounce) can tomato sauce
- 1 tablespoon chili powder
- 1/4 teaspoon black pepper
- 1 1/3 cups instant brown rice, uncooked
- 1 cup mozzarella cheese
- Fresh rosemary for garnish

DIRECTIONS

- ✓ Heat a wide saucepan and brown the beef and onion.
- ✓ Combine together red bell pepper, beans, tomatoes, chili powder and black pepper. Add at least 1/4 cup of water and cooked beef with onions. Stir to combine.
- ✓ Set the crock pot on low and cook the dish for 8 to 9 hours.
- ✓ After that, stir in brown rice, cover, and cook until the rice is soft. Finally, scatter the cheese. Continue cooking until Mozzarella cheese is melted.
- ✓ Divide among serving bowls, sprinkle with fresh rosemary and serve hot.

Chicken, Corn and Bean Chili

(Ready in about 8 hours | Servings 6)

INGREDIENTS

- 4 chicken breasts, boneless
- 1 (16-ounce) jar salsa
- 3 cloves garlic, minced
- 1 teaspoon chili powder
- 1 teaspoon salt

- 1/2 teaspoon freshly ground black pepper
- 1 (11-ounce) can Mexican-style corn
- 1 (15-ounce) can beans

DIRECTIONS
- Put chicken breasts and salsa into a crock pot. Add garlic, chili powder, salt, and black pepper.
- Cook, covered, for 6 to 8 hours on low setting.
- Transfer the chicken breasts on a cutting board, and shred them, for example, with 2 forks.
- Return the chicken to the crock pot and add the corn and the beans. Cook until the vegetables are just tender.

Soft Meat in Chili Sauce

(Ready in about 5 hours | Servings 6)

INGREDIENTS
- 3 lbs. beef, cut into bite-sized cubes
- 1 cup beef broth
- 1 large onion, finely chopped
- 1 teaspoon garlic powder
- 1 cup chili sauce
- 1 cup mild ketchup
- 3 tablespoon dry red wine
- 1 teaspoon salt
- 1/2 teaspoon black pepper
- 1/3 cup light brown sugar
- 1 teaspoon ground cumin

DIRECTIONS
- Place beef, broth and onions in a crock pot. Turn the crock pot on high and cook 4 to 5 hours. Shred beef with 2 forks.
- Add the remaining ingredients to the crock pot and stir well to combine. Cook for another 45 minutes.

Fluffy Vegetarian Pilaf

(Ready in about 2 hours 30 minutes | Servings 6)

INGREDIENTS
- 2 cups basmati rice
- 1 envelope dry onion soup mix
- 1 bunch scallions, chopped
- 8 ounce mushrooms, sliced
- 1/4 cup butter, softened
- Parsley for garnish

DIRECTIONS
- Place together rice, onion soup mix, scallions, mushrooms and butter in a crock pot.
- Pour in 4 cups of water. Cover and cook on high setting for 2 ½ hours.
- Divide the pilaf among serving plates and sprinkle the parsley on top.

Veggie Chili with Almonds

(Ready in about 10 hours | Servings 4)

INGREDIENTS
- 2 tablespoons olive oil
- 2 onions, finely chopped
- 2 cloves garlic, minced
- 1 red bell pepper, finely sliced
- 1 yellow bell pepper, finely sliced
- 2 (28-ounce) cans diced tomatoes
- 1 package frozen corn
- 2 cans black beans
- 1 cup salsa sauce
- 1 teaspoon paprika
- 1 teaspoon salt
- Chopped and toasted almonds for garnish
- Shredded hard cheese for garnish

DIRECTIONS
- Heat the olive oil in a large heavy skillet. Sauté onions and garlic until they are tender.
- Then add the peppers, sauté until they are tender.
- Transfer onion and peppers mixture to the crock pot. Add tomatoes, corn, beans and salsa sauce to the crock pot. Season with paprika and salt.
- Cook, covered, on low setting for 10 hours.
- Divide among serving bowls, scatter almonds and cheese and serve warm.

Stuffed Peppers in Red Sauce

(Ready in about 10 hours | Servings 4)

INGREDIENTS
- 2 yellow bell peppers
- 2 green bell peppers
- 1/2 cup white rice
- 1 (15.25-ounce) can whole kernel corn, drained
- 3 yellow onions, finely chopped
- 1/ teaspoon garlic salt
- 1/4 teaspoon pepper
- 1 ½ (14.5-ounce) can diced tomatoes with juice
- 3 tablespoons dry white wine

DIRECTIONS
- Cut off tops of peppers, remove stems and discard the seeds.
- Place the peppers upright in a crock pot.
- To make the filling: Combine rice, corn, onions, salt, pepper, and 1/4 cup tomatoes in another mixing bowl. Stir well to combine.
- Stuff the peppers with prepared filling.
- Mix remaining tomatoes, wine and 3 tablespoons of water. Pour this mixture over stuffed peppers.
- Cover the crock pot, set to low and cook the peppers 6 to 7 hours.

Turkey Breast with Bacon and Herbs

(Ready in about 8 hours | Servings 6)

INGREDIENTS
- 3 lb. turkey breast, boneless and skinless

- 2 cups chicken broth
- 1 bunch scallions, finely chopped
- 2 cloves garlic
- 4 strips bacon
- 1/2 teaspoon black pepper
- 1/2 teaspoon thyme
- 1/2 teaspoon marjoram
- 1 teaspoon dried mustard
- 1/2 cup honey

DIRECTIONS
- Place the meat in a crock pot and add broth. Add scallions in broth. Press garlic cloves in the meat.
- Place bacon over it and season with black pepper, thyme, and marjoram.
- Evenly spread mustard and honey. Cook on low setting for 8 hours. Serve over rice.

Thick Beef Stew with Kale

(Ready in about 8 hours | Servings 4)

INGREDIENTS
- 2 tablespoon canola oil, for frying
- 1 lb. beef
- 1 teaspoon garlic salt
- 1/4 teaspoon garlic pepper
- 1/2 cup flour
- 1 can (15-ounce) diced tomatoes
- 2 cloves garlic, minced
- 2 cups kale, chopped
- 1 can (15-ounce) peas, drained and rinsed
- 1 teaspoon cayenne pepper

DIRECTIONS
- Coat the beef with the garlic salt, pepper and flour. Heat oil in a heavy skillet and lightly brown the beef. Transfer the beef to the crock pot.
- Add diced tomatoes to the skillet and cook for about 6 minutes, stirring occasionally. Transfer cooked tomatoes to the crock pot.
- Then add garlic, kale and peas. Add cayenne pepper and stir to combine.
- Cover and cook on low setting for 6 to 8 hours. Serve warm.

Tortilla Vegetable Soup

(Ready in about 6 hours | Servings 4)

INGREDIENTS
- 2 tablespoons butter
- 1 onion, finely chopped
- 2 cloves garlic, minced
- 2 ribs celery, chopped
- 1 large red bell pepper, thinly sliced
- 1 zucchini, thinly sliced
- 1 yellow squash, thinly sliced
- 1 (16-ounce) bag frozen corn
- 2 cans vegetable broth
- 2 cans diced tomatoes
- 1/2 teaspoon chili powder
- shredded cheese cheddar to taste
- tortilla chips to taste

DIRECTIONS
- Melt the butter in a wide saucepan and cook the onion, garlic, celery and bell pepper.
- Transfer the vegetables to the crock pot and add the remaining ingredients. Stir to combine.
- Set the crock pot on low, cover and cook your meal for 6 hours.
- Divide among serving bowls, scatter the cheese and add tortilla chips on
- the top.

Tortilla Chili Pie

(Ready in about 7 hours | Servings 6)

INGREDIENTS
- 1 ½ lb. ground beef
- 1 onion, chopped
- 1 clove garlic, minced
- 1 teaspoon garlic salt
- 1/4 teaspoon pepper
- 1 teaspoon basil
- 3 cup hard cheese, shredded
- 1 (10-ounce) can enchilada sauce
- 1 (8-ounce) tomato paste
- 2 (16-ounce) cans chili beans
- 1 (16-ounce) can corn, drained
- 1 (6-ounce) can olives, pitted
- 6 corn tortillas

DIRECTIONS
- Heat a cast-iron skillet and cook beef, onion, and garlic. Season with salt, pepper and basil.
- Place 1 tortilla into the bottom of the crock pot. Then spoon the beef mixture, a little amount of enchilada sauce, tomato paste and shredded cheese. Top with another tortilla.
- Then place the beans, corn, and a few olives. Repeat this process until all
- ingredients are used. The cheese and olives should be on top.
- Cover and cook on low setting 5 to 7 hours. Serve with additional olives.

Tex-Mex Pork with Onions and Guacamole

(Ready in about 8 hours | Servings 6)

INGREDIENTS
- 3 pounds pork shoulder
- 2 ounces taco seasoning mix
- 1 teaspoon chili powder
- 1 tablespoon red pepper flakes
- Chopped onions for garnish
- Guacamole for garnish

DIRECTIONS
- ✓ Place pork in a crock pot and add taco seasoning mix.
- ✓ Toss the chilli and red pepper flakes. Stir in water to cover the meat.
- ✓ Cover the crock pot and cook the meat on low for 8 hours.
- ✓ Garnish with onions and guacamole and serve warm.

Family Goulash with Macaroni

(Ready in about 3 hours 30 minutes | Servings 4)

INGREDIENTS
- 2 lbs. lean ground beef
- 1 red onion, chopped
- 2 cloves garlic, minced
- 1 can tomatoes
- 1 can corn
- 2 cups uncooked macaroni
- 1 can beef bouillon
- 1/2 package chili mix
- 1 teaspoon fine sea salt
- 1/4 teaspoon black pepper
- 1 teaspoon sweet paprika
- 1/2 teaspoon dried oregano
- Rosemary for garnish

DIRECTIONS
- ✓ Heat a cast-iron skillet and brown the meat and onion. Transfer this mixture to the crock pot.
- ✓ Add the remaining ingredients and stir well to combine.
- ✓ Turn your crock pot on low setting. Cook for 3 to 3 ½ hours.
- ✓ Divide among serving dishes, sprinkle rosemary and serve warm.

Soft Teriyaki Chicken

(Ready in about 6 hours | Servings 4)

INGREDIENTS
- 4 chicken breast, boneless
- 1 teaspoon ginger, ground
- 1 tablespoon sugar
- 1/2 cup soy sauce
- 1 clove garlic, crushed
- 2 tablespoons sherry

DIRECTIONS
- ✓ Combine together all ingredients in the crock pot.
- ✓ Set the crock pot on low. Cook about 6 hours.

Teriyaki Pork Chops

(Ready in about 6 hours | Servings 4)

INGREDIENTS
- 4 pork chops, boneless
- 1 teaspoon salt
- 1/4 teaspoon black pepper
- 1 can pineapple slices with juice
- 1 bottle teriyaki sauce of choice
- 1/2 cup olives, pitted

DIRECTIONS
- ✓ Evenly coat the pork chops with salt and pepper.
- ✓ Place the meat in the crock pot. Pour in pineapple with juice and teriyaki sauce.
- ✓ Cover and cook on low setting for about 6 hours.
- ✓ Garnish with your favorite olives and serve warm.

Pork Chops and Squash with Rice

(Ready in about 8 hours | Servings 4)

INGREDIENTS
- 6 medium pork chops
- 2 medium acorn squash
- 1 teaspoon salt
- 1/4 teaspoon black pepper
- 1/2 teaspoon dried thyme
- 2 tablespoons extra-virgin olive oil
- 1/4 cup brown sugar
- 1 teaspoon browning sauce
- 1 tablespoon lime juice
- 1 teaspoon lime zest
- Cooked rice of choice for garnish

DIRECTION
- ✓ Trim unwanted fat from the meat. Cut the squash into 4 slices and discard the seeds.
- ✓ Arrange 3 chops on bottom of the crock pot. Then lay squash and then place the layer of 3 remaining pork chops.
- ✓ Im a small bowl, mix together the salt, pepper, thyme, oil, sugar, sauce, lime juice and lime zest.
- ✓ Pour this mixture over chops and squash in the crock pot.
- ✓ Cook, covered, on low setting 6 to 8 hours. Serve over your favorite rice.

Swiss Steak with Potatoes

(Ready in about 8 hours | Servings 8)

INGREDIENTS
- 2 pounds round steak
- 1/2 cup all-purpose flour
- 2 tablespoons canola oil
- 2 onions chopped
- 1 tablespoon Worcestershire sauce
- 2 celery stalks, chopped
- 1 teaspoon Dijon mustard
- 2 cups beef bouillon
- Boiled potatoes for garnish

DIRECTIONS
- ✓ Slice the steak into serving-size pieces. Dredge them in flour. Heat canola oil in a large saucepan and fry the meat until browned.
- ✓ Transfer the meat to the crock pot. Add onions, Worcestershire sauce, celery, mustard, and beef bouillon
- ✓ Cook for 6 to 8 hours on low setting.

✓ Serve with boiled potatoes.

Creamy Chicken with Swiss Cheese

⌀ **(Ready in about 10 hours | Servings 8)**

INGREDIENTS

- 6 chicken breasts, boneless and skinless
- 6 slices Swiss cheese
- 1 can chicken broth
- 1/4 cup milk
- Salt to taste
- Pepper to taste
- 2 cups stuffing mix
- 1/2 cup margarine, melted
- Fresh parsley for garnish

DIRECTIONS

✓ Arrange the chicken breasts in a crock pot. Then place Swiss cheese.
✓ Mix together chicken broth and milk and add this mixture to the crock pot. Adjust the seasonings and add salt and pepper to taste.
✓ Scatter the stuffing mix and drizzle melted margarine on top.
✓ Turn the crock pot on low setting and cook for 8 to 10. Divide among serving dishes, sprinkle with parsley and serve warm.

Old-Fashioned Roast

⌀ **(Ready in about 10 hours | Servings 6)**

INGREDIENTS

- 2 pounds roast, cut into serving pieces
- 3-4 cloves garlic
- 1 envelope onion soup mix
- 1 can (4-ounce) mushrooms, sliced and drained
- 1 red bell pepper, sliced
- 1 can (20-ounce) tomatoes
- 1 teaspoon salt
- 1/2 teaspoon freshly ground black pepper
- 1 teaspoon sweet paprika
- 1½ cups water

DIRECTIONS

✓ Place roast in a crock pot and add garlic and onion soup mix.
✓ Add mushrooms, red bell pepper and tomatoes. Season with salt, pepper and paprika. Pour in the water.
✓ Cover, turn on low setting and cook for 8 to 10 hours.

Pork in Sweet and Sour Sauce

⌀ **(Ready in about 10 hours | Servings 6)**

INGREDIENTS

- 6 pork shoulder steaks
- 1 tablespoon olive oil
- 1 can (15-ounce) pineapple, sliced
- 1/2 cup water
- 2 tablespoons brown sugar
- 1 tablespoon quick-cooking tapioca
- 2 tablespoons tamari sauce
- 1 teaspoon dry mustard
- 1 teaspoon kosher salt
- 1/2 teaspoon black pepper
- 1 teaspoon marjoram

DIRECTIONS

✓ Heat olive oil in a wide and deep saucepan. Cook the pork steaks until lightly browned. Transfer to a crock pot.
✓ Combine together pineapple, water, brown sugar, tapioca, tamari sauce and mustard. Add salt, pepper and marjoram and stir to combine all ingredients well. Pour this mixture over pork steaks in the crock pot.
✓ Cover and cook on low setting for 8 to 10 hours or on high setting for 4 to
✓ 5 hours. Serve with your favorite vegetables.

Holiday Turkey Stew

⌀ **(Ready in about 8 hours | Servings 4)**

INGREDIENTS

- 16-ounce turkey, cut into bite-sized cubes
- 3 cups potatoes, peeled and sliced
- 1 cup parsnip, chopped
- 2 cups carrots, sliced
- 1 cup scallions, finaly chopped
- 2 cloves garlic, crushed
- 1 cup green bell pepper
- 1 ¾ cups tomato paste
- 1 teaspoon dried rosemary
- 1 teaspoon dried oregano
- 1/2 teaspoon dried dill

DIRECTIONS

✓ Heat a non-stick saucepan and brown ground turkey.
✓ In a crock pot, place the potatoes, parsnip, carrots, scallions, garlic and bell pepper.
✓ Arrange the meat over vegetables.
✓ To make the sauce: In a mixing bowl, mix tomato paste, rosemary, oregano, and dill. Pour the sauce over meat.
✓ Cook, covered, on low setting for 6 to 8 hours.

Soup with Vegetables and Sausages

⌀ **(Ready in about 12 hours | Servings 6)**

INGREDIENTS

- 2 cups turkey sausage, sliced
- 1 cup dry split peas
- 1 cup onion, finely chopped
- 1 cup celery, chopped
- 1 cup zucchini, diced
- 1/2 teaspoon dried thyme, crushed
- Salt to taste
- Black pepper to taste
- 3 cups chicken bouillon
- 3 cups water
- 1 cup quick-cooking rice

DIRECTIONS
- ✓ In a crock pot, place together sausages, peas, onion, celery, zucchini, thyme, and pepper to taste. Add salt to taste.
- ✓ Pour chicken bouillon over the mixture in the crock pot.
- ✓ Cover, set the crock pot on low and cook for 10-12 hours.
- ✓ Stir in rice and serve warm.

Creamy Cheesy Spinach with Herbs

(Ready in about 1 hour | Servings 4)

INGREDIENTS
- 2 (10-ounce) boxes frozen chopped spinach, thawed
- 2 cups cottage cheese
- 1/4 cup olive oil
- 2 cloves garlic, crushed
- 1 1/2 cups cheddar cheese, shredded
- 3 eggs, beaten
- 1/4 cup flour
- 1 teaspoon salt
- 1/4 teaspoon freshly ground black pepper
- 1/4 teaspoon dried dill
- 1/2 teaspoon sage

DIRECTIONS
- ✓ In the crock pot, combine together spinach, cottage cheese, olive oil, garlic, and cheddar cheese.
- ✓ Mix the eggs with flour, salt, pepper and herbs and add to the crock pot.
- ✓ Turn the crock pot on high setting and cook for about 1 hour.

Smoky Baby Potatoes in Sauce

(Ready in about 7 hours | Servings 6)

INGREDIENTS
- 1 tablespoon olive oil
- l teaspoon salt
- 1/4 teaspoon red pepper
- 2 tablespoons cornstarch
- 2 lb. Beef
- 2 lb. bag of Baby potatoes
- 2 ripe tomatoes, chopped
- 2 tablespoons smoky tomato ketchup
- 1/2 cup red wine
- 3 cloves garlic, minced
- 1 teaspoon chili powder
- 1 teaspoon cumin
- 1/2 cup barbecue sauce
- 1/4 cup salsa
- 2 cups frozen corn

DIRECTIONS
- ✓ Heat olive oil in a heavy skillet. Add salt, red pepper, cornstarch and beef and cook until the meat is browned. Reserve.
- ✓ Arrange baby potatoes in the crock pot. Add tomatoes, ketchup, wine, garlic, chili powder, cumin, barbecue sauce and salsa to the crock pot.
- ✓ Cook on low heat for 6 hours. Add frozen corn and continue cooking for
- ✓ 1 hour more.

Quick and Easy Spaghetti

(Ready in about 4 hours 30 minutes | Servings 4)

INGREDIENTS
- 3 (15-ounce) cans tomato sauce
- 1 (12-ounce) can tomato paste
- 1 large red onion, finely chopped
- 1 teaspoon paprika
- 1 teaspoon garlic powder
- 1 teaspoon dried oregano
- 1 teaspoon dried basil
- 1 teaspoon dried rosemary

DIRECTIONS
- ✓ Place all ingredients in your crock pot.
- ✓ Turn the crock pot on low setting and cook for 4 to 4 ½ hrs.
- ✓ Prapare your favorite spaghetti according to package instructions.
- ✓ Pour the sauce over spaghetti and serve warm.

Spaghetti Bolognese Authentic Recipe

(Ready in about 8 hours | Servings 4)

INGREDIENTS
- 1 tablespoon extra-virgin olive oil
- 1 pound lean ground beef
- 1 onion, chopped
- 2 medium cans tomatoes
- 1 (8-ounce) can tomato sauce
- 1 (12-ounce) can tomato paste
- 1 teaspoon garlic, minced
- 1 cup beef bouillon
- 1 teaspoon dried oregano
- 1 teaspoon dried basil
- 1 teaspoon dried rosemary
- 1 teaspoon salt
- 1/4 teaspoon pepper
- 1/2 teaspoon paprika
- Cooked spaghetti of choice

DIRECTIONS
- ✓ Heat olive oil in a large saucepan and cook the meat and onion until browned and fragrant.
- ✓ Transfer prepared beef-onion mixture to the crock pot. Then add remaining ingredients.
- ✓ Cover and cook on low setting for 6 to 8 hours.
- ✓ Serve over your favorite spaghetti.

Easy Salsa Chicken

(Ready in about 8 hours | Servings 4)

INGREDIENTS
- Non-stick cooking spray
- 4 small chicken breast, skinless boneless

- 1 package taco seasoning mix
- 1 cup salsa
- 2 tablespoons cornstarch
- 1/4 cup sour cream

DIRECTIONS
- ✓ Lightly grease the crock pot with non-stick cooking spray. Add the chicken breasts to the crock pot. Sprinkle with taco seasoning mix. Add salsa on top.
- ✓ Cook on low setting for 6 to 8 hours. Remove the meat from the crock pot.
- ✓ Mix cornstarch with a small amount of water. Stir in the crock pot. Add sour cream and serve.

Beef and Bacon Gravy with Noodles

(Ready in about 10 hours | Servings 6)

INGREDIENTS
- 2 bacon slices
- 3 pound beef chuck roast
- 2 onions, chopped
- 1 zucchini, shredded
- 1 teaspoon salt
- 1/4 teaspoon black pepper
- 1/2 cup sour cream
- 3 tablespoon wheat flour
- cooked noodles

DIRECTIONS
- ✓ Heat a wide saucepan and fry bacon until crisp. Crumble fried bacon and refrigerate it.
- ✓ Remove excess fat from roast and cut it into serving size pieces. Cook meat in the same saucepan, in the bacon drippings.
- ✓ Transfer the roast to the crock pot. Stir in onion, zucchini, salt, pepper, and 1/4 cup water.
- ✓ Cook, uncovered, on low setting for 8 to 10 hours.
- ✓ Heat the liquid from the crock pot into the saucepan.
- ✓ To make the gravy: Mix together sour cream and flour and stir into the hot liquid. Cook until the sauce is thickened.
- ✓ Garnish with prepared bacon and serve over hot noodles.

Vegetarian Stew for All Seasons

(Ready in about 4 hours | Servings 4)

INGREDIENTS
- 1 ½ cups vegetable stock
- 1 cup green beans
- 1 cup new potatoes
- 1/2 cup carrots, chopped
- 1/2 turnips, chopped
- 2 medium-sized plum tomatoes, chopped
- 4 green onions, sliced
- 1/2 teaspoon dried marjoram leaves
- 4 slices vegetarian bacon, fried crisp, crumbled
- 1 cup Brussels sprouts
- 10 asparagus spears, cut into small chunks
- 2 tablespoons cornstarch
- 1/4 cup cold water
- 1/4 teaspoon ground black pepper
- Salt, to taste
- 1/4 teaspoon paprika
- 3 cups cooked brown rice, warm

DIRECTIONS
- ✓ In a crock pot, arrange vegetable stock, green beans, potatoes, carrots, turnips, tomatoes, onion and marjoram leaves.
- ✓ Cover and cook on high about 4 hours.
- ✓ Add remaining ingredients, except cooked rice, during last 30 minutes of cooking time.
- ✓ Serve over brown rice and enjoy!

Vegan Wheat Berry and Lentil Stew

(Ready in about 8 hours | Servings 8)

INGREDIENTS
- 3 cups vegetable broth
- 1/2 cup dried lentils
- 1 cup wheat berries
- 1 ½ pounds potatoes, cubed
- 1 cup leeks, chopped
- 1 carrot, chopped
- 1 stalk celery, chopped
- 3 cloves garlic, minced
- Celery salt, to taste
- Black pepper, to taste

DIRECTIONS
- ✓ Put all of the ingredients into your crock pot; cover the crock pot with a lid; cook approximately 8 hours.
- ✓ Serve with your favorite cornbread and enjoy!

DINNER RECIPES

Pork Shoulder with Noodles

(Ready in about 8 hours | Servings 6)

INGREDIENTS
- 1 pork shoulder roast, boneless
- 1 cup red onion, chopped
- 1 cup chicken broth
- 1/4 cup dry cherry
- 1 teaspoon garlic powder

- 1 teaspoon celery seeds
- 1/2 teaspoon cumin seeds
- Sea salt, to taste
- Ground black pepper, to taste
- 2 tablespoons cornstarch
- 1/3 cup cold water
- 6 cups cooked noodles, warm

DIRECTIONS
- Place first seven ingredients in a crock pot; cover and cook on low 8 hours.
- Remove pork shoulder and shred. Season with sea salt and black pepper.
- Turn the crock pot to high and cook 10 more minutes. Stir in combined cornstarch and cold water, stirring often 2 to 3 minutes.
- Return shredded pork to the crock pot and toss; serve over cooked noodles and enjoy.

Teriyaki Pork with Tortillas

(Ready in about 8 hours | Servings 6)

INGREDIENTS
- 1 cup vegetable stock
- 1/4 cup dry red wine
- 1 pork shoulder roast, boneless
- 1 package (1.06 ounces) teriyaki marinade mix
- 2 cloves garlic, minced
- 1 cup onion, chopped
- 1 teaspoon dried rosemary
- 1/2 teaspoon cumin seeds
- Sea salt, to taste
- Ground black pepper, to taste
- Red pepper flakes, crushed
- 6 flour tortillas

DIRECTIONS
- Add all of the ingredients, except tortillas, to the crock pot.
- Cook on low heat setting approximately 8 hours or until the pork is falling-apart tender.
- Next, cut cooked pork into shreds. Roll up in warm tortillas and enjoy!

Pork Chops with Creamy Sauce

(Ready in about 5 hours | Servings 4)

INGREDIENTS
- 4 loin pork chops, boneless
- Salt to taste
- Freshly ground black pepper, to taste
- 1/2 cup leeks, thinly sliced
- 1 small rib celery, sliced
- 1 can (10 ounces) cream of celery soup
- 1/2 cup 2% reduced fat milk
- Cornbread, as garnish

DIRECTIONS
- Sprinkle pork with salt and freshly ground black pepper; add to the crock pot.
- Place leeks and sliced celery on top.
- Combine cream of celery soup with milk; whisk to combine. Pour the mixture into the crock pot.
- Cover the crock pot with a lid and cook on low 4 to 5 hours. Serve with cornbread.

Pork Chops with Apricot and Hoisin Sauce

(Ready in about 3 hours | Servings 4)

INGREDIENTS
- 6 pork chops, boneless
- 1/2 teaspoon seasoned salt
- 1/2 teaspoon ground black pepper
- 1/2 teaspoon paprika
- 1/4 cup vegetable broth
- 1/2 cup apricot preserves
- 3 tablespoons hoisin sauce
- 1 tablespoon cornstarch

DIRECTIONS
- Sprinkle meat with salt, pepper and paprika; place in a crock pot; pour in vegetable broth.
- Cover and cook on low heat setting about 3 hours; reserve pork chops.
- To make the sauce, turn heat to high and cook 10 more minutes; add the rest of ingredients into the broth, stirring 2 to 3 minutes.
- Serve warm over steamed vegetables.

Pork Chops with Honey and Mustard

(Ready in about 4 hours | Servings 4)

INGREDIENTS
- 4 loin pork chops, boneless
- 1/4 cup leeks, chopped
- 1/2 cup chicken broth
- 1/2 cup dry white wine
- 1 tablespoon cornstarch
- 2 tablespoons honey
- 2 tablespoons mustard
- 1 teaspoon grated ginger
- Salt, to taste
- Black pepper, to taste

DIRECTIONS
- Combine pork chops, leeks, chicken broth and white wine in a crock pot.
- Cover and cook on low about 3 to 4 hours.
- Remove pork chops from the crock pot and keep warm.
- Add cornstarch, honey, mustard, ginger, salt and black pepper; continue cooking about 5 minutes. Serve warm.

Smoked Pork with Prunes

(Ready in about 8 hours | Servings 8)

INGREDIENTS

- 2 pounds pork loin, boneless and cubed
- 1 cup prunes, pitted
- 1 ½ cups vegetable broth
- 1/2 cup dry white wine
- 1 teaspoon lemon juice
- Salt, to taste
- Black pepper, to taste
- Smoked paprika, to taste
- 2 tablespoons corn starch
- 1/4 cup cold water
- Liquid smoke, to taste
- 4 cups cooked couscous, warm

DIRECTIONS
- Place all of the ingredients, except corn starch, water, liquid smoke and couscous, in a crock pot.
- Cover and cook on low approximately 8 hours. Next, turn heat to high; cook about 10 minutes.
- In a bowl, combine corn starch with cold water. Add this mixture and liquid smoke to the crock pot and stir constantly 2 to 3 minutes. Serve with couscous.

Sweet Orange Smoked Ham

(Ready in about 3 hours | Servings 10)

INGREDIENTS

- 3 pounds smoked ham, boneless
- 1/3 cup orange juice
- 1/4 cup honey
- 1 teaspoon allspice
- 1/2 teaspoon ground cinnamon
- 1 1/2 tablespoons corn starch
- 1/4 cup cold water
- 2 tablespoons dry sherry

DIRECTIONS
- Put all of the ingredients, except corn starch, water and sherry, into a crock pot.
- Cover and cook on low until ham is tender or about 3 hours. Transfer prepared ham to a serving platter.
- Measure 1 cup broth into skillet; heat to boiling; whisk in combined remaining ingredients about 1 minute.
- Serve ham with sauce and enjoy!

Sherry Chicken with Mashed Potatoes

(Ready in about 4 hours | Servings 4)

INGREDIENTS

For the Sherry Chicken:

- 1/4 cup dry sherry
- 1 cup raisins
- 4 medium-sized chicken breast
- 1 tart cooking apple, peeled and chopped
- 1 sweet onion, sliced
- 1 cup chicken broth
- Salt and pepper, to taste
- 2 pounds Idaho potatoes, peeled and cooked
- 1/4 sour cream
- 1/3 cup whole milk
- 2 tablespoons butter
- 1 teaspoon sea salt
- 1/4 teaspoon black pepper
- 1/4 teaspoon cayenne pepper

DIRECTIONS
- In a crock pot, place all of the ingredients for the sherry chicken; cover and cook on high until chicken breasts are tender or 3 to 4 hours.
- Meanwhile, beat potatoes, adding sour cream, milk, and butter; beat until
- smooth and uniform.
- Season with spices and serve on the side with sherry chicken.

Kicked Up Chicken with Zucchini

(Ready in about 4 hours | Servings 6)

INGREDIENTS

- 3 medium-sized chicken breasts, halved
- 1 cup almond milk
- 1/4 cup water
- 1/4 cup lemon juice
- 2 cloves garlic, minced
- 1 medium-sized onion, chopped
- Salt, to taste
- Red pepper, to taste
- 1 teaspoon ground ginger
- 1 teaspoon ground cumin
- 1 pound zucchini, sliced
- 1 tablespoon cornflour
- 2 tablespoons water
- 1/3 cup fresh parsley, chopped
- 4 cups rice, cooked

DIRECTIONS
- Place all ingredients, except zucchini, cornflour, water, parsley and rice, in your crock pot.
- Cover and cook on low heat setting about 4 hours, adding zucchini during last 30 minutes of cooking time. Reserve chicken breasts.
- Turn heat to high and continue cooking 10 minutes; stir in combined cornflour and water, stirring about 3 minutes.
- Sprinkle with parsley; serve over rice.

Festive Cornish Hens

(Ready in about 6 hours | Servings 4)

INGREDIENTS

- 2 frozen Cornish hens, thawed

- 1/2 teaspoon sea salt
- 1/4 teaspoon ground black pepper
- 1/2 teaspoon cayenne pepper
- 1 clove garlic, minced
- 1/3 cup chicken broth
- 2 tablespoons cornflour
- 1/4 cup water

DIRECTIONS
- Sprinkle Cornish hens with salt, black pepper and cayenne pepper; add minced garlic and place in a crock pot. Pour in chicken broth.
- Cover and cook on low 6 hours. Remove Cornish hens and reserve.
- Stir in combined cornflour and water, stirring 2 to 3 minutes; serve.

Salmon with Caper Sauce

(Ready in about 45 minutes | Servings 4)

INGREDIENTS
- 1/2 cup dry white wine
- 1/2 cup water
- 1 yellow onion, thin sliced
- 1/2 teaspoon salt
- 1/4 teaspoon black pepper
- 4 salmon steaks
- 2 tablespoons butter
- 3 tablespoons flour
- 1 cup chicken broth
- 2 teaspoons lemon juice
- 3 tablespoons capers

DIRECTIONS
- Combine wine, water, onion, salt and black pepper in a crock pot; cover and cook on high 20 minutes.
- Add salmon steaks; cover and cook on high until salmon is tender or about 20 minutes.
- To make the sauce, in a small skillet, melt butter over medium flame. Stir in flour and cook for 1 minute.
- Pour in chicken broth and lemon juice; whisk for 1 to 2 minutes. Add capers; serve the sauce with salmon.

Herbed Salmon Loaf with Sauce

(Ready in about 5 hours | Servings 4)

INGREDIENTS

For the Salmon Meatloaf:
- 1 cup fresh bread crumbs
- 1 can (7 ½ ounce) salmon, drained
- 1/4 cup scallions, chopped
- 1/3 cup whole milk
- 1 egg
- 1 tablespoon fresh lemon juice
- 1 teaspoon dried rosemary
- 1 teaspoon ground coriander
- 1/2 teaspoon fenugreek
- 1 teaspoon mustard seed
- 1/2 teaspoon salt
- 1/4 teaspoon white pepper
- 1/2 cup cucumber, chopped
- 1/2 cup reduced-fat plain yogurt
- 1/2 teaspoon dill weed
- Salt, to taste

DIRECTIONS
- Line your crock pot with a foil.
- Mix all ingredients for the salmon meatloaf until everything is well incorporated; form into loaf and place in the crock pot.
- Cover with a suitable lid and cook on low heat setting 5 hours.
- Combine all of the ingredients for the sauce; whisk to combine.
- Serve your meatloaf with prepared sauce.

Lazy Man Mac and Cheese

(Ready in about 4 hours | Servings 4)

INGREDIENTS
- Non-stick cooking spray-butter flavour
- 16 ounces macaroni of choice
- 1/2 cup butter, melted
- 1 (12-ounce) can evaporated milk
- 1 cup milk
- 4 cups Colby jack cheese, grated

DIRECTIONS
- Lightly grease a crock pot with cooking spray.
- First of all, cook your favourite macaroni according to package DIRECTIONS; rinse and drain; transfer to the crock pot.
- Add the rest of ingredients and stir well. Cook on low heat setting 3 to 4 hours. Enjoy!

Mediterranean Chicken with Zucchini

(Ready in about 8 hours | Servings 4)

INGREDIENTS
- 4 medium-sized chicken breasts, skinless
- 2 cups petite-diced tomatoes
- 1 stock cube
- 1/2 cup dry white wine
- 1/2 cup water
- 1 medium zucchini, sliced
- 1 large-sized onion, chopped
- 1/3 cup fennel bulb, chopped
- 1 teaspoon ground cumin
- 1 teaspoon dried basil leaves
- 1 bay leaf
- A pinch of black pepper
- 1/4 cup olives, pitted and sliced
- 1 teaspoon lemon juice
- 3 cups cooked rice

DIRECTIONS
- Place all ingredients, except olives, lemon juice and cooked rice, in a crock pot; cover and cook on low about 8 hours, adding pitted olives during last 30 minutes of cooking time.

- Add lemon juice; discard bay leaf. Serve over cooked rice and enjoy.

Mediterranean Stuffed Spaghetti Squash

(Ready in about 8 hours | Servings 4)

INGREDIENTS

- 1 medium-sized spaghetti squash, halved lengthwise and seeded
- 2 Roma tomatoes, diced
- 2 cans (6-ounces) tuna in water, drained and flaked
- 1 teaspoon dried basil leaves
- 1 teaspoon dried oregano leaves
- 1/2 teaspoon dried thyme
- Salt, to taste
- Black pepper, to taste
- Cayenne pepper, to taste
- 1/2 cup water
- 1/4 cup Pecorino Romano, grated

DIRECTIONS
- Place squash halves on a plate.
- In a measuring cup or a mixing bowl, combine all of the ingredients, except water and Pecorino Romano. Spoon this mixture into squash halves and place in the crock pot.
- Add water to the crock pot; cover and cook 6 to 8 hours on low.
- Sprinkle with Pecorino Romano and serve.

Everyday Tomato Casserole

(Ready in about 3 hours | Servings 6)

INGREDIENTS

- 8 ounces macaroni, cooked
- 1 can (16-ounce) petite-diced tomatoes, drained
- 1/2 cup leeks, chopped
- 1 cup whole milk
- 1 cup water
- 1 tablespoon cornflour
- 3 eggs, lightly beaten
- 1/2 cup sharp cheese, grated
- 1/2 teaspoon ground cinnamon
- Salt, to taste
- Paprika, as garnish

DIRECTIONS
- Combine macaroni, tomatoes and leeks in a crock pot.
- In a bowl, mix remaining ingredients, except paprika; pour over macaroni in the crock pot.
- Cook on low about 3 hours or until custard is set; divide among serving plates and sprinkle with paprika.

Four Cheese Macaroni Casserole

(Ready in about 3 hours | Servings 8)

INGREDIENTS

- Non-stick cooking spray-butter flavour
- 3 cups whole milk
- 1/3 cup all-purpose flour
- 1 cup Colby-Jack, crumbled
- 1 cup reduced-fat mozzarella, shredded
- 1 cup Cheddar cheese, shredded
- 1 pound macaroni, cooked al dente
- 1/2 cup Parmesan cheese

DIRECTIONS
- Treat a crock pot with cooking spray.
- In a large mixing bowl, combine milk and flour until smooth; add the rest of ingredients, except macaroni and Parmesan cheese.
- Stir in macaroni and sprinkle with Parmesan cheese.
- Cover and cook on low 3 hours.

Creamy Vegetable Noodle Casserole

(Ready in about 5 hours | Servings 6)

INGREDIENTS

- 1 cup 2% reduced-fat milk
- 1 ½ cups cream of mushroom soup
- 2 tablespoons mayonnaise, reduced-fat
- 1 cup processed cheese, shredded
- 1 green bell pepper
- 1 large-sized carrot, chopped
- 1/3 celery stalk, chopped
- 1/3 cup onion, chopped
- 1/4 teaspoon sea salt
- 1/4 teaspoon ground black pepper
- 6 ounces noodles, cooked al dente
- 1/2 cup chickpea
- 1 tablespoon butter
- 1/3 cup fresh bread crumbs
- 1/3 cup pine nuts, chopped

DIRECTIONS
- In a crock pot, combine first ten ingredients.
- Stir in cooked noodles; cover with a suitable lid and cook on low 5 hours. Add chickpeas during last 30 minutes of cooking time.
- In a cast-iron skillet, melt butter over medium heat; cook bread crumbs
- and pine nuts about 5 minutes. Sprinkle on prepared casserole and serve!

Old-Fashioned Pasta Bolognese

(Ready in about 7 hours | Servings 6)

INGREDIENTS

- 1/2 pound ground pork
- 1/2 pound ground beef
- 1/4 cup onion, chopped
- 3 cloves garlic, minced
- 1/4 cup carrot, chopped
- 1 1/2 teaspoons dried Italian seasoning
- 1 can (8-ounces) tomato sauce, undrained,

- 1 large-sized tomato, diced
- 1/4 cup dry red wine
- 1 teaspoon sea salt
- 1/4 teaspoon pepper
- 1/4 teaspoon cayenne pepper
- 12 ounces spaghetti, cooked

DIRECTIONS
- In a non-stick heavy skillet, brown ground meat over medium heat for 8 minutes; crumble with a fork.
- Add remaining ingredients, except spaghetti, to the crock pot. Cover and cook on low 6 to 7 hours.
- Ladle prepared sauce over spaghetti and serve warm.

Apple with Brats and Sauerkraut

(Ready in about 4 hours | Servings 4)

INGREDIENTS
- 1 lb. bratwursts, cut into fourths on a diagonal
- 4 apples (e.g. Granny Smith), cored
- 1 (27-ounce) can sauerkraut
- 1/4 cup sugar
- 1/4 cup water

DIRECTIONS
- Slice the apples into wedges and place them in a crock pot. Add bratwursts, sauerkraut, sugar and water.
- Stir gently to combine. Cover the crock pot, set on low and cook for 3 to
- 4 hours.

Tender Chicken with Vegetables

(Ready in about 4 hours | Servings 6)

INGREDIENTS
- 4 chicken breasts, skinless and boneless
- 12 ounces fresh mushrooms, sliced
- 2 cans Cream of Mushroom Soup
- 1 cup water
- 1 onion, sliced
- 1 large carrot, sliced
- 1 large potato, cubed

DIRECTIONS
- Slice the chicken into small pieces. Heat a wide saucepan and fry the chicken breast and onion until they are browned.
- Add mushrooms and sauté for 5 minutes longer, or until they are tender and fragrant.
- Place carrots and potatoes at the bottom of the crock pot. Then add the mixture from the saucepan.
- Pour soups and water into the saucepan and cook until they are heated through. Pour this mixture over the vegetables and meat in the crock pot.
- Cook on low setting for another 4 to 5 hours.

Spiced Glazed Ham

(Ready in about 7 hours | Servings 12)

INGREDIENTS
- 5 lb. cooked ham
- 8 peppercorns
- 2 bay leaves
- 1/2 cup brown sugar
- 1 tablespoon Dijon mustard
- 2 tablespoons wine vinegar
- 1 tablespoon cold water
- 1 tablespoon cornstarch
- Horseradish for garnish

DIRECTIONS
- Put ham into a crock pot together with the peppercorns and bay leaves.
- Combine together brown sugar, mustard and vinegar. Pour this mixture over ham, and set the crock pot on high. Cook, covered, for 1 hour.
- Reduce the temperature on low and cook for another 6 to 7 hours. Remove the ham from crock pot and set aside.
- To make the sauce: Mix together cold water and cornstarch. Gradually add cornstarch mixture to the crock pot, and cook, stirring frequently, until the sauce is thickened.
- Transfer the ham to a serving platter and spoon the sauce over it. Serve with horseradish.

Turkey Breasts with Pineapple

(Ready in about 8 hours | Servings 8)

INGREDIENTS
- 4 lb. turkey breast
- 1 can (8-ounce) pineapple, sliced
- 1 jar (10-ounce) cherry preserves
- 1 tablespoon lime juice
- 1 teaspoon salt
- 7-8 peppercorns

DIRECTIONS
- Place turkey breasts in a crock pot.
- In a medium bowl, mix together remaining ingredients. Pour this mixture over the meat.
- Cover the crock pot, turn on low setting and cook the meal for 7 to 8 hours. Serve over rice.

Pork Chops in Cherry Sauce

(Ready in about 5 hours | Servings 6)

INGREDIENTS
- 6 pork chops
- 1/2 teaspoon garlic salt
- 1/4 teaspoon freshly ground black pepper
- 1 tablespoon canola oil
- 1 cup cherry pie filling
- 1 tablespoon lime juice
- 1 tablespoon lime zest
- 1/2 cup chicken bouillon

DIRECTIONS

- Season pork with garlic salt and black pepper. Heat canola oil in a large saucepan and cook the meat until browned.
- In a crock pot, combine the cherry pie filling, lime juice, lime zest and chicken bouillon. Lay the pork chops on top.
- Cover the crock pot, set on low and cook for 4 to 5 hours.

Chicken in Sweet and Spiced Sauce

(Ready in about 4 hours | Servings 6)

INGREDIENTS

- 4 chicken breasts, boneless and skinless
- 1/2 cup honey
- 1 teaspoon dried mustard
- 1/2 cup soy sauce
- 1 large onion, finely chopped
- 1/4 cup tomato paste
- 2 tablespoons olive oil
- 2 cloves garlic, minced
- 1 teaspoon garlic salt
- 1/2 teaspoon freshly ground black pepper
- 1 teaspoon marjoram
- 5-6 peppercorns
- 2 tablespoons cornstarch
- Fresh parsley for garnish

DIRECTIONS

- In a crock pot, mix together the honey, mustard, soy sauce, onion, tomato paste, olive oil, garlic, salt, black pepper, and marjoram. Stir to combine well.
- Add the chicken and sprinkle peppercorns. Cook on low heat setting for 3 to 4 hours.
- Remove the meat from the crock pot.
- To make the sauce: Mix the cornstarch with 1/3 cup of water and pour this mixture into the crock pot. Turn the heat to high and cook the sauce until it is thickened.
- Sprinkle chicken with parsley and serve with sauce.

Marinated Pork Roast with Pineapple

(Ready in about 7 hours | Servings 8)

INGREDIENTS

- 3 lbs. pork roast, boneless
- 1/2 cup soy sauce
- 2 tablespoons brown sugar
- 1 can (8-ounce) pineapple, crushed
- 1 teaspoon salt
- 1/4 teaspoon black pepper
- 10-12 peppercorns
- 1/4 teaspoon red pepper flakes
- 1 teaspoon dried mustard
- Spring onion for garnish

DIRECTIONS

- Place the pork roast in a large bowl.
- To make the marinade: In another, medium bowl, mix together the remaining ingredients, and whisk well to combine.
- Then pour this mixture over pork roast, refrigerate and marinate overnight.
- Place pork roast in the crock pot, and pour marinade to cover the meat. Cover the crock pot, set on low heat and cook 6 to 7 hours.
- Garnish with chopped spring onions and serve.

Chicken Sandwiches with Mushrooms

(Ready in about 9 hours | Servings 8)

INGREDIENTS

- 3 lbs. chicken thighs, boneless and skinless
- 1 teaspoon salt
- 1/4 teaspoon pepper
- 1 tablespoon olive oil
- 1 cup mushrooms
- 1 cup dry white wine
- 1 teaspoon dried oregano
- 1 teaspoon dried basil
- 1 teaspoon dried rosemary
- 8 large sandwich buns

DIRECTIONS

- Season the meat with salt and pepper. Heat olive oil over medium-high heat in a large saucepan. Brown the chicken thighs and transfer them to the crock pot.
- In the same saucepan, sauté the mushrooms over medium heat until tender and fragrant. Add wine to the saucepan and cook 5 minutes more.
- Pour mushroom and wine mixture over chicken in the crock pot. Sprinkle oregano, basil and rosemary.
- Cover and cook on low heat setting for 8 to 9 hours.
- To make the sandwiches: Place the meat and spoon the mushroom sauce
- over it.

Pork Pockets Stuffed with Corn

(Ready in about 10 hours | Servings 4)

INGREDIENTS

- 4 double pork chops
- 1 teaspoon salt
- 1/4 teaspoon black pepper
- 1 teaspoon sweet paprika
- 1 bag (16-ounce) frozen whole kernel corn, thawed
- 1 cup stuffing mix
- 1 can (8-ounce) tomato sauce
- 1/2 cup tomato ketchup

DIRECTIONS

- Form the pockets from the pork chops. Season with salt, pepper and paprika.
- To make the filling: Combine together corn and stuffing mix. Stuff pork pockets with this filing and close stuffed pockets up with toothpicks.
- Pour tomato sauce and ketchup in a crock pot and place stuffed pork pockets.
- Cover and cook on low setting for 8 to 10 hours.

Lasagna with Vegetable and Cheese

(Ready in about 5 hours | Servings 4)

INGREDIENTS

- 4 cups spinach
- 2 cups fresh mushrooms, sliced
- 1/2 cup pesto
- 1 ½ cups mozzarella cheese, shredded
- 1 (15-ounces) ricotta cheese
- 1 egg, beaten
- 3/4 cup (3-ounces) Parmesan cheese, shredded
- 1 (25.5-ounces) tomato-basil pasta sauce
- 1 cup tomato paste
- 2 tablespoons olive oil
- 12 precooked lasagna noodles

DIRECTIONS

- Combine together spinach, mushrooms, and pesto and mix well to combine. Reserve.
- Mix together mozzarella, ricotta, and egg in a medium mixing bowl. Add 1/4 cup of Parmesan cheese.
- In another bowl, combine tomato-basil pasta sauce and the tomato paste.
- Grease the bottom of a crock pot with olive oil.
- To make lasagna: Place 1 cup pasta mixture in the crock pot and then lay
- 3 noodles over it. Top with 1 cup cheese mixture and 1 cup spinach-
- mushrooms mixture.
- Repeat the process, ending with Parmesan cheese.
- Turn your crock pot on low setting and cook 5 hours.

Ham Hocks with Kale

(Ready in about 8 hours | Servings 8)

INGREDIENTS

- 4 ham hock slices (about 8 ounces)
- 1 cup beef broth
- 12 cups torn kale leaves
- 2 tablespoons olive oil
- 1 onion, finely chopped
- 1/2 teaspoon sweet paprika
- 2 tablespoons apple cider vinegar
- 1 teaspoon sea salt
- 1/4 teaspoon black pepper

DIRECTIONS

- Microwave ham with broth and 1½ cups water on high for about 3 minutes.
- Discard stems from the kale leaves and place them in the crock pot.
- Heat olive oil in a wide cast-iron skillet. Sauté the onion until tender, or about 5 minutes. Add onions to the crock pot.
- Cover and cook on low setting for 6 to 8 hours.
- Add the paprika, vinegar, salt, and black pepper, and mix well to combine. Serve warm.

Chicken Drumsticks in Sweet and Sour Sauce

(Ready in about 5 hours | Servings 8)

INGREDIENTS

- 3 lbs. chicken drumstick
- 1 teaspoon garlic salt
- 1/4 teaspoon black pepper
- 2 cups honey
- 1 cup soy sauce
- 1/2 cup marinara sauce
- 1/4 cup canola oil
- 1 teaspoon cayenne pepper
- 1 tablespoon dried rosemary, for garnish

DIRECTIONS

- Place drumsticks on a broiler pan. Season with garlic salt and black pepper. Cook under the broiler about 15 minutes.
- Transfer the chicken to the crock pot.
- In a medium mixing bowl, combine together honey, soy sauce, marinara sauce, canola oil, and cayenne pepper. Pour this mixture over the chicken drumsticks.
- Cover the crock pot, set on low and cook for 4 to 5 hours.
- Sprinkle with rosemary and serve warm with your favorite vegetables.

Family Red Chili

(Ready in about 8 hours | Servings 4)

INGREDIENTS

- 8 ounces ground beef sirloin
- 1 can (28-ounces) tomatoes, crushed
- 1 can (15-ounces) red kidney beans, rinsed and drained
- 1 red bell peppers, chopped
- 1 yellow bell pepper, chopped
- 1/2 cup red onion, chopped
- 1 cup large red onion
- 2 tablespoons red wine vinegar
- 1 teaspoon chili powder
- 1⁄4 teaspoon ground cinnamon
- 2⁄3 cup mild picante sauce
- Salt, to taste
- Black pepper, to taste

DIRECTIONS

- In lightly greased large skillet, brown ground beef over medium flame. Cook about 5 minutes, crumbling with a fork.
- Transfer cooked beef to a crock pot, then, add remaining ingredients; cover and cook on low 6 to 8 hours. Serve warm with cornmeal crisps, if desired.

Turkey Chili with Kale

(Ready in about 8 hours | Servings 8)

INGREDIENTS

- 1 tablespoon olive oil
- 1 ½ pounds lean ground turkey
- 2 cans (15-ounce) cannellini beans, rinsed and drained
- 1 cup tomato paste
- 1/2 cup red onion, chopped
- 1 bay leaf
- 1/2 teaspoon dried rosemary
- 1 teaspoon ground cumin
- 1/2 teaspoon caraway seeds
- 1 ½ cup kale, coarsely chopped
- 1/4 teaspoon black pepper
- 1/4 teaspoon cayenne pepper
- Celery salt, to taste

DIRECTIONS
- Lightly grease a large skillet with olive oil. Cook ground turkey until browned or about 10 minutes.
- Place cooked meat and remaining ingredients, except kale, in a crock pot; cover and cook on low heat setting approximately 8 hours.
- Add kale during the last 20 minutes of cooking time.
- Taste, adjust the seasonings and serve warm.

Piquant Chicken Sausage Chili

(Ready in about 6 hours | Servings 4)

INGREDIENTS
- 4 ounces chicken sausage, sliced
- 2 Roma tomatoes, chopped
- 2 heaping tablespoons tomato ketchup
- 2 cups canned beans
- 1 large-sized red onion, finely chopped
- 1 green bell pepper, chopped
- 1 red bell pepper, chopped
- 1 teaspoon ground cumin
- 1 tablespoon cilantro, chopped
- 1 tablespoon chili powder
- Salt, to taste
- Sour cream, as garnish

DIRECTIONS
- In a non-stick skillet, cook sausage until browned or about 6 minutes. Replace to the crock pot.
- Stir in remaining ingredients, except sour cream; cover and cook on low heat setting about 6 hours.
- Serve with a dollop of sour cream.

Pepperoni Hot Chili

(Ready in about 8 hours | Servings 8)

INGREDIENTS
- 12 ounces turkey sausage
- 4 ounces pepperoni, sliced
- 1 can (14 1/2 ounces) diced tomatoes, undrained
- 1 ½ cup beef broth
- 1 ½ cup tomato sauce
- 1 teaspoon lemon zest
- 1 cup garbanzo beans
- 1/2 cup canned green chilies, chopped
- 1 large-sized red onion, chopped
- 1 ½ teaspoons dried Italian seasoning
- 2 tablespoons hot chili powder
- 1 tablespoon Worcestershire sauce
- Salt, to taste
- Paprika, to taste
- Hot pepper sauce, optional

DIRECTIONS
- Cook sausage and pepperoni in lightly greased saucepan over medium heat. Cook 10 to 12 minutes; transfer to a crock pot.
- Add the rest of ingredients; cover and cook on low about 8 hours.
- Divide among serving bowls and serve with cornbread.

Spaghetti with Beans and Asparagus

(Ready in about 3 hours | Servings 4)

INGREDIENTS
- 1 cup vegetable stock
- 1/2 cup green beans
- 1 can (15-ounces) Great Northern beans, rinsed and drained
- 2 medium-sized tomatoes, chopped
- 2 medium-sized carrots, chopped
- 3/4 teaspoon dried rosemary leaves
- 1 pound asparagus, cut into bite-sized pieces
- 1/2 teaspoon celery salt
- 1 teaspoon onion powder
- 1 teaspoon garlic powder
- 8 ounces spaghetti, cooked
- 1/4 cup Parmesan cheese, shredded

DIRECTIONS
- In a crock pot, place vegetable stock, green beans, Great Northern beans, tomatoes, carrots, and rosemary.
- Cook covered for 3 hours, adding asparagus pieces during last 30 minutes of cooking time.
- Season with celery salt, onion powder and garlic powder; toss with spaghetti and Parmesan cheese. Enjoy!

Easy Spicy Green Beans

(Ready in about 4 hours | Servings 4)

INGREDIENTS
- 1 pound green beans
- 1 can (28-ounce) petite-diced tomatoes
- 1 large-sized red onion, chopped
- 4 cloves garlic, minced
- 1 teaspoon celery seeds
- 1 teaspoon dried basil
- 1 teaspoon dried oregano
- 1 teaspoon sea salt
- 1/4 teaspoon freshly ground black pepper
- 1/4 teaspoon red pepper flakes, crushed

DIRECTIONS
- ✓ Combine all ingredients in a crock pot.
- ✓ Cook covered on high about 4 hours or until green beans are tender.
- ✓ Taste, adjust the seasonings and divide among serving bowls. Enjoy this easy and healthy dinner with boiled potatoes and favorite seasonal salad!

Favorite Creamy Green Beans

(Ready in about 6 hours | Servings 4)

INGREDIENTS
- 1/2 cup sour cream
- 1/4 cup 2 % reduced-fat milk
- 1 ½ cup canned fat-free cream of mushroom soup
- 1 package (10 ounces) green beans, thawed
- 2 cloves garlic, minced
- 1 carrot, chopped
- 1 celery stalk, chopped
- Salt, to taste
- Cayenne pepper, to taste
- Chopped cashews, as garnish

DIRECTIONS
- ✓ Mix all of the ingredients, except cashews, in your crock pot.
- ✓ Cover and cook on low heat setting about 6 hours.
- ✓ Scatter chopped cashews on top; serve over macaroni or cooked brown rice.

Steak Roll Ups with Mushrooms

(Ready in about 6 hours | Servings 4)

INGREDIENTS
- 1 pound beef steaks, cut into 4 serving-size portions
- 4 slices of smoked ham
- 1 cup Portobello mushrooms, chopped
- 1/4 cup dill pickle, finely chopped
- 1 large-sized sweet onion, chopped
- 1 teaspoon Dijon mustard
- 1/2 teaspoon dried tarragon
- 1 teaspoon dried basil
- 1/2 teaspoon dried oregano
- 1/2 cup beef broth
- Celery salt, to taste
- Black peppercorns, to taste
- Mayonnaise, as garnish

DIRECTIONS
- ✓ Top each portion of beef steak with ham slice.
- ✓ In a mixing bowl, combine mushrooms, dill pickle, onion, mustard, tarragon, basil and oregano. Spread this mixture over ham.
- ✓ Next, roll up steaks and secure them with toothpicks; place in the crock pot.
- ✓ Pour in broth, sprinkle with celery salt and peppercorns; cook on low 5 to
- ✓ 6 hours. Garnish with mayonnaise and serve.

Favorite Hot Rouladen

(Ready in about 6 hours | Servings 4)

INGREDIENTS
- 1 pound beef steaks, cut into 4 serving-size portions
- 4 slices of reduced-fat Provolone cheese
- 1 sweet red bell pepper, cut into thin strips
- 1 sweet green bell pepper, cut into thin strips
- 1/4 cup sun-dried, finely chopped
- 1 jalapeño pepper, minced
- 1/2 cup green onions, chopped
- 1 teaspoon mustard
- 1 teaspoon dried basil
- 1/2 teaspoon celery seeds
- Sea salt, to taste
- Ground black pepper, to taste
- 1/2 cup beef broth

DIRECTIONS
- ✓ Top each portion of beef steak with the slice of cheese. Then, place bell peppers on each slice of steak.
- ✓ In a bowl, combine the rest of ingredients, except beef broth. Spread this mixture over slices of cheese.
- ✓ Then, roll up steaks; secure with toothpicks; place in the bottom of your crock pot.
- ✓ Pour in beef broth; cook covered on low about 6 hours. Serve warm.

Juicy Beef Short Ribs

(Ready in about 8 hours | Servings 4)

INGREDIENTS
- 1/2 cup dry red wine
- 1/2 cup beef broth
- 1 teaspoon mustard
- 4 large-sized carrots, sliced
- 1 large-sized red onion, cut into wedges
- 1 heaping tablespoon cilantro
- 1/2 teaspoon dried tarragon
- 2 pounds beef short ribs

DIRECTIONS
- ✓ Arrange all ingredients in a crock pot, placing beef short ribs on the top.
- ✓ Cover and cook on low approximately 8 hours.
- ✓ Serve warm with some extra mustard.

Easy Italian-Style Meatloaf

(Ready in about 7 hours | Servings 4)

INGREDIENTS
- 1 ½ pounds lean ground beef
- 1 cup quick-cooking oats
- 1 teaspoon lemon zest
- 1/2 cup milk

- 1 medium-sized egg
- 1/4 cup tomato catsup
- 1/2 cup scallions, chopped
- 1 green bell pepper, chopped
- 1 teaspoon granulated garlic
- 1 teaspoon Italian seasoning
- 1 teaspoon sea salt
- 1/2 teaspoon ground black pepper

DIRECTIONS
- ✓ Mix all ingredients until everything is well incorporated; place your meatloaf on slow cooker liner in a crock pot.
- ✓ Cover and cook on low 6 to 7 hours.
- ✓ Serve over mashed potatoes and enjoy!

Cheesy Everyday Meatloaf

(Ready in about 6 hours | Servings 4)

INGREDIENTS
- 1/2 pound lean ground pork
- 1/2 pound lean ground beef
- 1/2 cup reduced-fat cream cheese
- 1 cup quick-cooking oats
- 2 tablespoons Worcestershire sauce
- 1 medium-sized egg
- 1/4 cup tomato ketchup
- 1/2 cup onion, chopped
- 1 green bell pepper, chopped
- 1/2 teaspoon ground ginger
- 1 clove garlic, minced
- 1 teaspoon sea salt
- 1/2 teaspoon ground black pepper
- 1/2 cup reduced-fat Cheddar cheese, grated

DIRECTIONS
- ✓ In a large-sized mixing bowl, combine all of the ingredients, except Cheddar cheese. Shape into a meatloaf.
- ✓ Place the meatloaf on slow cooker liner in a crock pot.
- ✓ Cook on low approximately 6 hours.
- ✓ Scatter grated Cheddar cheese on top and let stand until cheese is melted.
- ✓ Serve.

Curried Peanut Meat Loaf

(Ready in about 6 hours | Servings 4)

INGREDIENTS
- 1 cup quick-cooking oats
- 1 teaspoon grated ginger
- 1/2 cup milk
- 1 egg
- 1/4 cup chutney, chopped
- 1/2 cup onion, chopped
- 1 sweet red bell pepper, chopped
- 1 teaspoon granulated garlic
- 1 teaspoon dried basil
- 1/3 cup chopped peanuts

- 1 teaspoon curry powder
- 1 teaspoon sea salt
- 1/2 teaspoon ground black pepper
- 1 ½ pounds ground beef and pork, mixed

DIRECTIONS
- ✓ Line a crock pot with a wide strip of aluminium foil.
- ✓ In a large mixing bowl, combine oats, ginger, milk, egg, chutney, onion, bell pepper, garlic, basil, peanuts, curry powder, sea salt and black pepper. Mix well to combine.
- ✓ Stir in ground meat and mix again. Shape the mixture into a round loaf.
- ✓ Place in the crock pot; set crock pot to low and cook 6 hours. Serve warm or at room temperature.

Mom's Spiced Mashed Beans

(Ready in about 8 hours | Servings 10)

INGREDIENTS
- 9 cups water
- 3 cups canned pinto beans, rinsed
- 1 yellow onion, cut into wedges
- 1/2 poblano pepper, seeded and minced
- 2 cloves garlic, minced
- 1 tablespoon Cajun seasoning
- 1 teaspoon fine sea salt
- 1 teaspoon ground black pepper
- 1 teaspoon cayenne pepper

DIRECTIONS
- ✓ Arrange all of the ingredients in a crock pot.
- ✓ Cook on high heat setting for 8 hours.
- ✓ Strain and reserve the liquid. Mash the beans, adding the reserved liquid as needed. Serve with sausage and your favourite salad.

Kicked Up Cajun Jambalaya

(Ready in about 8 hours | Servings 12)

INGREDIENTS
- 1 (28-ounce) can tomatoes, diced
- 1 pound chicken breast, skinless, boneless and cut into bite-sized pieces
- 1 pound Andouille sausage, sliced
- 1 large-sized onion, chopped
- 1 celery stalk, chopped
- 1 bell pepper, chopped
- 1 cup chopped celery
- 1 cup chicken stock
- 1 teaspoon dried basil leaves
- 1 teaspoon dried oregano
- 1 teaspoon Cajun seasoning
- 1 teaspoon cayenne pepper
- 1 pound frozen cooked shrimp without tails
- 1 cup cooked rice

DIRECTIONS

- ✓ In a crock pot, place all of the ingredients, except shrimp and cooked rice.
- ✓ Cover and cook 8 hours on low.
- ✓ Stir in the shrimp and cooked rice during the last 30 minutes of cooking time. Enjoy!

Tangy Pork Roast

(Ready in about 8 hours | Servings 8)

INGREDIENTS

- 1 large red onion, sliced
- 2 cloves garlic, minced
- 2 pounds pork loin roast, boneless
- 1 cup water
- 2 tablespoons brown sugar
- 3 tablespoons dry red wine
- 2 tablespoons Worcestershire sauce
- 1/4 cup tomato juice
- 1/2 teaspoon salt
- 1/2 teaspoon black pepper

DIRECTIONS

- ✓ Arrange the slices of onion and minced garlic over the bottom of a crock pot; place the roast on top.
- ✓ In a measuring cup or a mixing bowl, mix together the rest of ingredients; pour over pork loin roast.
- ✓ Cover and cook on high for 3 to 4 hours or on low for 8 hours. Serve over mashed potatoes.

Hearty Stuffed Cabbage Leaves

(Ready in about 8 hours | Servings 4)

INGREDIENTS

- 8 large-sized cabbage leaves
- 1 pound lean ground beef
- 1/4 cup onion, finely chopped
- 1/4 cup water
- 1 red bell pepper
- 1/4 cup cooked rice
- 3/4 teaspoon salt
- 1/4 teaspoon ground black pepper
- 1 ½ cup tomato sauce
- 1 can (16-ounce) tomatoes, diced

DIRECTIONS

- ✓ Place cabbage leaves in boiling water and cook until softened; drain.
- ✓ Combine together ground beef and remaining ingredients, except tomato sauce and tomatoes. Stuff cabbage leaves, folding ends and sides over.
- ✓ Stir in tomato sauce and tomatoes; cover and cook on low approximately
- ✓ 8 hours.
- ✓ Serve with a dollop of sour cream.

Milk Braised Pork Loin

(Ready in about 4 hours | Servings 8)

INGREDIENTS

- Ground black pepper, to taste
- Fine cooking salt, to taste
- 1 pork loin roast, boneless
- 1 cup green onions, chopped
- 2 cloves garlic, minced
- 1/2 cup milk
- 1/4 cup dry red wine
- 1 teaspoon dried sage
- 1 teaspoon dried rosemary
- Chives for garnish

DIRECTIONS

- ✓ Rub black pepper and salt into pork loin roast. Place in a crock pot.
- ✓ Scatter chopped onions and minced garlic on top; then add combined milk and wine. Sprinkle with sage and rosemary.
- ✓ Cover and cook on low about 4 hours.
- ✓ Sprinkle with fresh chives and serve!

Mashed Potatoes with Carrots

(Ready in about 3 hours | Servings 8)

INGREDIENTS

- 5 pounds red potatoes, cut into chunks
- 2 cloves garlic, minced
- 2 carrots, thinly sliced
- 1 cube chicken bouillon
- 1 cup sour cream
- 1 cup cream cheese
- 1/2 cup butter
- 1/2 teaspoon salt
- 1/2 teaspoon ground black pepper

DIRECTIONS

- ✓ In a large stockpot of boiling water, cook the potatoes, garlic, carrots and chicken bouillon about 15 minutes. Reserve water.
- ✓ Next, mash boiled potatoes with sour cream and cream cheese.
- ✓ Transfer the mashed potato to the crock pot; cover the crock pot with a lid, cook on low for about 3 hours.
- ✓ Stir in butter; sprinkle with salt and black pepper; serve.

Holiday Cooked Ham

(Ready in about 8 hours | Servings 24)

INGREDIENTS

- 1 cured, bone-in picnic ham
- 2 cups packed brown sugar
- 1/4 teaspoon ground cloves
- 2 tablespoons balsamic vinegar

DIRECTIONS

- ✓ Spread brown sugar and ground cloves on the bottom of the crock pot.
- ✓ Place the ham in the crock pot and then add balsamic vinegar.
- ✓ Cover and cook on low approximately 8 hours.

Family Favourite Apple Butter

 (Ready in about 10 hours | Servings 24)

INGREDIENTS

- 5 pounds apples, peeled, cored and chopped
- 4 cups brown sugar
- 1/2 teaspoon grated nutmeg
- 1 tablespoon ground cinnamon
- 1/2 teaspoon ground cloves
- A pinch of salt

DIRECTIONS

- ✓ Place the chopped apples in your crock pot.
- ✓ In a medium-sized bowl, mix remaining ingredients until everything is well combined.
- ✓ Pour this mixture over the apples in the crock pot and stir to combine.
- ✓ Cover and cook on high for 1 hour. Turn heat to low and then cook about
- ✓ 9 hours. Stir with a whisk and refrigerate.

Italian-style Chicken with Broccoli

 (Ready in about 9 hours | Servings 6)

INGREDIENTS

- 3 chicken breasts, skinless and boneless
- 1 cup Italian-style salad dressing
- 1 ½ cups cream of chicken soup
- 1 cup chicken stock
- 1 cup cream cheese
- 1 teaspoon dried oregano
- 1/2 teaspoon dried basil
- Celery salt, to taste
- Ground black pepper, to taste
- Cayenne pepper, to taste

DIRECTIONS

- ✓ In a crock pot, combine the chicken breasts with Italian-style dressing.
- ✓ Cover, set the crock pot to low and cook for 8 hours.
- ✓ Shred the chicken meat and return to the crock pot. In a medium-sized mixing bowl, mix remaining ingredients.
- ✓ Pour over the shredded chicken in the crock pot; add broccoli. Turn the heat to low and continue cooking for about 1 hour.

Chicken and Ham in Cheese-Tomato Sauce

 (Ready in about 7 hours | Servings 6)

INGREDIENTS

- 1 tablespoon olive oil
- 1 1/2 lbs. chicken
- 1 cup cooked ham, sliced
- 1 can (10-ounces) cheese soup
- 1 can (14-ounces) tomatoes
- Fine sea salt to taste
- 10-12 peppercorns

DIRECTIONS

- ✓ Heat olive oil in a large saucepan and cook the chicken until browned.
- ✓ Place chicken in a crock pot and then place cooked ham.
- ✓ Whisk the soup, tomatoes, and 1/2 cup water, and add salt to taste. Pour this mixture over the meat and scatter the peppercorns
- ✓ Set the crock pot to low, cover and cook for 6 to 7 hours.
- ✓ Serve over boiled potatoes or your favorite cooked rice.

Chicken Thighs with Sweet Potatoes

 (Ready in about 8 hours | Servings 6)

INGREDIENTS

- 6 sweet potatoes, cleaned
- 1 teaspoon salt
- 1/4 teaspoon black pepper
- 1 teaspoon dried basil
- 1 cup mushrooms, sliced
- 1/2 cup yellow bell pepper
- 6 chicken thighs
- 1 cup orange marmalade
- 1/2 cup broth of choice

DIRECTIONS

- ✓ Place sweet potatoes in the crock pot. Season with salt, pepper and basil.
- ✓ Then lay the chicken thighs over the potatoes. Lay the mushrooms and yellow bell pepper over the chicken. Adjust the seasonings.
- ✓ Whisk together orange marmalade and broth. Pour this mixture over the chicken thighs.
- ✓ Set the crock pot to low and cook for 6 to 8 hours.

Korean Chicken with Potatoes

 (Ready in about 2 hours | Servings 6)

INGREDIENTS

- 2 tablespoons Korean chili paste
- 4 tablespoons tamari sauce
- 2 tablespoons corn syrup
- 1 tablespoon olive oil
- 4 cloves garlic, minced
- 1 tablespoon sesame seeds
- 2 lbs. chicken thighs and breasts
- 8 ounces potatoes
- 1 onion
- Fresh parsley

DIRECTIONS

- ✓ To make the sauce: Whisk together Korean chili paste, tamari sauce, corn syrup, olive oil, garlic and sesame seeds,
- ✓ Trim unwanted fat, skin and bones from the chicken pieces, and cut them into bite-sized chunks.

- Slice potatoes into the small cubes, and cut and separate onions into the rings,
- Place the meat and vegetables in the crock pot. Pour the sauce over meat and vegetables.
- Cover and cook on high heat setting for 2 hours. Transfer to a serving
- platter, sprinkle the parsley and serve warm.

Beef Roast and Potatoes in Creamy Sauce

(Ready in about 8 hours | Servings 12)

INGREDIENTS

- Cooking oil for frying
- 4 lbs. beef roast
- 3 cloves garlic, minced
- 1 can cream of mushroom soup
- 1/2 cup water
- 6 potatoes, peeled and halved
- 1 teaspoon sea salt
- 1/4 teaspoon ground black pepper

DIRECTIONS

- Place cooking oil in a heavy skillet, and brown the beef roast over medium heat. Add garlic and set aside.
- In the same skillet, place soup and water and cook, stirring occasionally.
- Pour liquid from the skillet into the crock pot, then place the roast. Place the potatoes around the roast. Season with salt and black pepper.
- Cover and cook on low setting for 6 to 8 hours.

Meat and Beans Casserole

(Ready in about 5 hours | Servings 8)

INGREDIENTS

- 2 large ham slices
- 2 onions, finely chopped
- 2 cloves garlic, crushed
- 1 teaspoon dried oregano
- 1 teaspoon dried rosemary
- 1 teaspoon salt
- 1/4 teaspoon black pepper
- 1/2 teaspoon paprika
- 2 (14.5-ounce) cans diced tomatoes, drained
- 2 (15-ounce) cans beans, drained
- 1 pound boneless pork roast, cut into bite-sized cubes
- 1/2 pound sausage, sliced
- 1/2 cup Parmesan cheese, shredded

DIRECTIONS

- Heat a wide saucepan and fry the ham until crisp. Crumble the ham and set aside.
- Add onion, garlic, oregano, and rosemary to the saucepan. Cook 5 minutes more. Return the crumbled ham to the saucepan. Season with salt, pepper and paprika, add tomatoes and cook for 5 minutes longer. Set aside.
- Mash half of beans. Add remaining half of beans, pork, and sausage. Mix
- well to combine.
- Place half of bean and meat mixture at the bottom of the crock pot. Then place tomato and spices mixture. Repeat this process again.
- Cover and cook on low heat setting for 5 hours. Divide among serving bowls, sprinkle Parmesan cheese and serve warm.

Spare Ribs in Spiced Sauce

(Ready in about 7 hours | Servings 8)

INGREDIENTS

- 1 tablespoon olive oil
- 3 lbs. pork spare ribs, cut into serving size pieces
- 1 teaspoon garlic salt
- 1/2 teaspoon black pepper
- 1 teaspoon dry mustard
- 2 cans (15-ounce) can tomatoes, diced
- 1 onion, finely chopped
- 2 large carrots, thinly sliced
- 2 tablespoons cornstarch

DIRECTIONS

- Heat olive oil in a cast-iron skillet and cook spare ribs until browned. Season with salt, pepper and transfer to the crock pot.
- Add mustard, tomatoes, onion, and carrots to the cast-iron skillet. Cook until the onion is fragrant, then transfer to the crock pot.
- Mix the cornstarch with 3 tablespoons of water, and cook in the skillet, stirring constantly, until heated through. Pour this mixture in the crock pot.
- Set your crock pot on low, cover, and cook for 6 to 7 hours.

Chicken Sandwiches with BBQ Sauce

(Ready in about 8 hours 15 minutes | Servings 6)

INGREDIENTS

- 2 lbs. chicken breast, boneless and skinless
- 1 white onion, sliced into rings
- 1 teaspoon dry mustard
- 1 cup barbecue sauce of choice
- 6 burger buns
- Lettuce for garnish

DIRECTIONS

- Place the chicken at the bottom of a crock pot. Then add the onion rings and mustard.
- Pour in the barbecue sauce.
- Set the crock pot on low and cook for 8 hours.
- Shred the chicken. Divide chicken and sauce among 6 burger buns, add lettuce leaves and serve warm.

Sandwiches with Ham and Pineapple Sauce

(Ready in about 4 hours | Servings 12)

INGREDIENTS

- 1 ½ cups cooked ham, cut into very small chunks
- 1/2 cup brown sugar, packed
- 1/2 cup mustard
- 1 red bell pepper, thinly sliced
- 1 onion, finely chopped
- 1 (20-ounce) can pineapple, crushed
- 12 hamburger buns
- 3 small tomatoes, sliced

DIRECTIONS
- In the crock pot, combine together ham, sugar, mustard, bell pepper, onion, and pineapple.
- Cover, turn to low setting and cook for 4 hours.
- Divide among buns, add tomatoes and serve warm or at room temperature.

Summer BBQ Pork Ribs

(Ready in about 10 hours | Servings 8)

INGREDIENTS

- 3 lbs. pork loin ribs, cut into serving size
- 1 teaspoon smoked paprika
- Liquid smoke to taste
- 1 teaspoon salt
- 1 teaspoon black pepper
- 1 ½ cup barbecue sauce of choice

DIRECTIONS
- Combine together the paprika, a few drops of liquid smoke, salt, and pepper in a medium mixing bowl. Mix well to combine.
- Rub the pork ribs with this mixture. Place ribs in the crock pot.
- Combine together barbecue sauce and 1/2 cup of water, and pour over the pork ribs.
- Cover and cook on low for 8 to 10 hours.

Chicken Sandwiches with Root Beer Sauce

(Ready in about 6 hours | Servings 6)

INGREDIENTS

- 1 ½ pounds chicken breasts
- 1 cup root beer of choice
- 1 cup barbecue sauce of choice
- 1 tablespoon corn starch
- Black pepper to taste
- Fresh rosemary to taste
- Sliced cucumber for garnish
- 6 sandwich buns

DIRECTIONS
- Place the chicken breasts in the crock pot.
- To make the sauce: Whisk the root beer with barbecue sauce.
- Pour this mixture over the chicken breasts. Set the crock pot on low and cook for 4 to 6 hours.
- Shred the chicken with two forks. Whisk the cornstarch into the sauce, and add pepper and rosemary.
- Return the chicken breasts to the crock pot and stir well to combine. Let the chicken soak in the sauce.
- To make the sandwiches: Divide the chicken breast and sauce among sandwich buns, and add cucumber slices for garnish.

Saucy Chicken in Pretzel Buns

(Ready in about 4 hours 15 minutes | Servings 6)

INGREDIENTS

- 1 tablespoon canola oil
- 2 pounds chicken breast, cut into bite-sized pieces
- Salt to taste
- Black pepper to taste
- 1 onion, diced
- 2 cloves garlic, minced
- 1 yellow bell pepper, thinly sliced
- 1 can (14.5-ounces) tomatoes
- 1/4 cup hot pepper sauce
- 2 tablespoons mustard
- 6 pretzel bun
- Sliced tomato for garnish

DIRECTIONS
- Heat canola oil in a wide saucepan over medium-high heat. Brown the chicken in hot oil for about 5 minutes. Season with salt and pepper and transfer the chicken to the crock pot.
- In the same saucepan, sauté onion, garlic and yellow bell pepper. Add 1 cup of water, stirring occasionally and cook about 10 minutes. Pour this mixture over chicken in the crock pot.
- In a medium bowl, combine together tomatoes, hot pepper sauce, and
- mustard. Pour in the crock pot. Stir well to combine.
- Cook on high setting, covered until chicken is very soft or for 4 hours.
- To make the sandwiches: Divide chicken among pretzel buns, spoon the sauce in each bun and garnish with slices of tomato.

Smokey Beef Tacos

(Ready in about 10 hours | Servings 10)

INGREDIENTS

- 4 pounds beef brisket, fat trimmed
- liquid smoke to taste
- 1 (12-ounce) beer
- 1 teaspoon salt
- 1 teaspoon black pepper
- 10 Corn tortillas
- 1 cup Cheddar cheese, cubed
- 1 large onion, sliced into rings

- Salsa for garnish

DIRECTIONS
- ✓ Place the first 5 ingredients into a deep and large bowl, cover and marinate overnight.
- ✓ Set the crock pot on low and cook for 8 to 10 hours.
- ✓ On a serving platter, arrange corn tortillas, beef brisket, Cheddar cheese, and onions. Serve alongside your favorite salsa.

Saucy Sausages with Vegetables

(Ready in about 9 hours | Servings 4)

INGREDIENTS
- 1 lb. sausage, sliced
- 3 cups frozen hash brown potatoes
- 1 onion, diced
- 1 can (15-ounce) corn
- 1 ¼ cup potato cream soup
- 1 teaspoon dry mustard
- 1 teaspoon basil
- 2 cups water
- Salt to taste
- Black pepper to taste

DIRECTIONS
- ✓ Place sausages and hash brown potatoes in the crock pot.
- ✓ In a medium mixing bowl, combine together the onion, corn, cream soup, mustard, basil, water, salt, and pepper. Pour this mixture into the crock pot.
- ✓ Cover and cook on low heat setting for 8 to 9 hours.

Saucy Chicken Thighs with Vegetables

(Ready in about 6 hours 15 minutes | Servings 8)

INGREDIENTS
- 2 ribs celery, chopped
- 1 large carrot, sliced
- 1 bulb fennel, cored and chopped
- 1 bunch scallions, chopped
- 4 cloves garlic, crushed
- 1/2 teaspoon dried oregano
- 1 teaspoon salt
- 1/4 teaspoon black pepper
- 12 chicken thighs, boneless and skinless
- 3/4 cup chicken broth
- 3/4 cup water
- 1/4 cup all-purpose flour
- 1 tablespoon lemon zest
- Rosemary for garnish

DIRECTIONS
- ✓ In the crock pot, combine together celery, carrot, fennel, scallions, garlic, oregano, salt and pepper.
- ✓ Place chicken over the vegetables in the crock pot. Add chicken broth and water.
- ✓ Cook, covered on low setting 5 to 6 hours.
- ✓ To make the sauce: Mix the flour with 1 cup of the liquid from the crock pot and lemon zest until smooth. Add this mixture to the crock pot and cook for another 15 minutes.
- ✓ Sprinkle rosemary and serve warm.

Bean and Quinoa Chili

(Ready in about 5 hours | Servings 8)

INGREDIENTS
- 3 can brown beans, rinsed
- 1 cup quinoa, uncooked
- 3 cups vegetable broth
- 2 cups water
- 1 can yellow sweet corn
- 1 can tomatoes, diced
- 1 tablespoon fresh cilantro, chopped
- 1 poblano pepper, finely diced
- 1 red bell pepper
- 2 cloves garlic, minced
- 1 red onion, finely chopped
- 2 tablespoons chili powder
- 1/2 teaspoon salt
- 1/2 teaspoon ground pepper

DIRECTIONS
- ✓ Place all ingredients in a crock pot.
- ✓ Turn heat to high setting. Cook, covered, for 4 to 5 hours.

Thai Chicken and Vegetables with Rice

(Ready in about 12 hours | Servings 8)

INGREDIENTS
- 2 onions, thinly sliced
- 1 teaspoon black pepper
- 2 large carrots, thinly sliced
- 1 green bell pepper, thinly sliced
- 2 pounds chicken breasts, boneless and skinless
- 3/4 cup chicken broth
- 3 tablespoons peanut butter
- 1 tablespoon orange zest
- 2 tablespoons apple cider vinegar
- 2 tablespoons tamari sauce
- 2 tablespoons cornstarch
- 3 teaspoons red curry paste
- 4 garlic cloves, minced
- 1/2 cup heavy cream
- 1 cup frozen chickpeas
- Cooked rice for garnish

DIRECTIONS
- ✓ Place onions, black pepper, carrots, bell pepper and chicken in a crock pot.
- ✓ Whisk together chicken broth with remaining ingredients (except heavy cream and chickpeas). Mix well to combine. Pour this mixture over chicken and vegetables in the crock pot.

- ✓ Cover the crock pot, turn on low heat setting and cook 12 hours. Stir in heavy cream and chickpeas.
- ✓ Serve chicken and vegetables over hot cooked rice.

Smoky Black Beans with Sausages

(Ready in about 12 hours | Servings 8)

INGREDIENTS

- 2 cans (15-ounce) black beans, drained and rinsed
- 2 pork sausages, cut into bite-sized pieces
- 1 teaspoon dry mustard
- A few drops of liquid smoke
- 1 can (15-ounce) diced tomatoes
- 4 cups chicken broth
- 1/2 teaspoon garlic salt
- 1/2 teaspoon garlic pepper

DIRECTIONS

- ✓ Combine all ingredients in the crock pot.
- ✓ Turn the crock pot on low heat setting and cook covered for 5 to 6 hours.
- ✓ Serve over hot cooked rice or with shredded sauerkraut.

Easy and Light Veggies with Noodles

(Ready in about 9 hours | Servings 4)

INGREDIENTS

- 2 cans (14-ounce) beef broth
- 1 can (14-ounce) diced tomatoes
- 16 ounces frozen mixed vegetables of choice
- Salt to taste
- Black pepper to taste
- 1 teaspoon sweet paprika
- 1 teaspoon basil
- 1 ½ cups noodles, uncooked

DIRECTIONS

- ✓ In a crock pot, combine together beef broth, tomatoes, mixed vegetables, paprika, and basil. Season with salt and black pepper to taste. Pour in 2 cups water.
- ✓ Cover the crock pot and cook on low heat setting for 8 to 9 hours.
- ✓ Add noodles and cook, covered, for another 30 minutes.

Saucy Beef with Mushrooms

(Ready in about 8 hours | Servings 4)

INGREDIENTS

- 1 lb. beef stew meat
- 1 can (10-ounce) golden cream of mushroom soup
- 4 ounces canned mushrooms, sliced
- 1 cup water
- 1/2 teaspoon garlic salt
- 7-8 peppercorns
- 1/2 teaspoon oregano
- 1 teaspoon dill
- 6 cups cooked noodles of choice

DIRECTIONS

- ✓ In the crockpot, combine together beef, soup, mushrooms, water, garlic salt, peppercorns, oregano, and dill.
- ✓ Turn the crock pot on low heat setting, cover and cook for 6 to 8 hours.
- ✓ Serve over your favorite hot cooked noodles.

Curried Pork with Apples and Onions

(Ready in about 9 hours | Servings 6)

INGREDIENTS

- 2 lbs. pork stew meat, cubed
- 2 teaspoons olive oil
- 1 teaspoon salt
- 1/4 teaspoon pepper
- 1 teaspoon grated ginger
- 1 cup water
- 3 tablespoons curry powder
- 1 apple, cut into wedges
- 1 sweet onion, cut into wedges
- Fresh parsley for garnish

DIRECTIONS

- ✓ Heat olive oil in a wide and deep saucepan, and cook the meat until browned. Season with salt and pepper and add ginger.
- ✓ Mix water and curry powder and add to the saucepan.
- ✓ Arrange apple and onion in the crock pot. Then place meat and sauce from the saucepan.
- ✓ Cover and cook on low heat setting for 7 to 9 hours.
- ✓ Sprinkle with parsley and serve warm.

Old-Fashioned Macaroni and Cheese

(Ready in about 6 hours | Servings 4)

INGREDIENTS

- Non-stick cooking spray
- 1 cup macaroni, cooked
- 3 cups Cheddar cheese, shredded
- 1 can evaporated milk
- 1 ½ cups milk
- 2 eggs
- 1 teaspoon salt
- 1/2 teaspoon black pepper
- 1 teaspoon oregano
- 1 cup Mozzarella cheese

DIRECTIONS

- ✓ Oil a crock pot with non-stick cooking spray. Drain and rinse macaroni. Arrange the cooked macaroni in the crock pot.
- ✓ Add the remaining ingredients to the crock pot and mix well to combine. Scatter Mozzarella cheese.
- ✓ Cover and cook on low heat setting for 5 to 6 hours.

Glazed Pork Roast

(Ready in about 12 hours | Servings 10)

INGREDIENTS

- Salt to taste
- Black pepper to taste
- 4 lb. pork loin roast
- 6 apples, cored
- 1/4 cup apple juice
- 2 tablespoons brown sugar
- 1 teaspoon ginger, ground
- Lemon, cut into wedges

DIRECTIONS

- Rub roast with salt and pepper. Cook pork roast under broiler until browned.
- Cut apples into thin slices. Arrange apples in the crock pot, then place the roast.
- Combine apple juice, brown sugar, and ginger. Pour over the roast.
- Cover and cook on low heat setting for 10 to 12 hours. Garnish with lemon wedges and serve warm.

Bread with Raisins and Almonds

(Ready in about 6 hours | Servings 6)

INGREDIENTS

- 3/4 cup raisins
- 1 cup all-purpose flour
- 1 teaspoon baking powder
- 1 teaspoon baking soda
- 1 teaspoon salt
- 1/2 cup sugar
- 2 tablespoons honey
- 3/4 cup milk
- 1 egg
- 1 tablespoon butter, melted
- 1/2 cup whole wheat flour
- 1 cup chopped almonds

DIRECTIONS

- Add raisins to a large mixing bowl. Sift the flour, baking powder, baking soda, salt, and sugar. Whisk together the honey, milk, slightly beaten egg, and melted butter.
- Add whole wheat flour and almonds.
- Transfer into greased and floured baking dish and put the lid. Place the baking dish on a rack in the crock pot.
- Cook on high heat setting for 4 to 6 hours.

Baked Ham with Wine

(Ready in about 7 hours | Servings 10)

INGREDIENTS

- 1/2 cup water
- 1/4 cup red wine
- 4 pound cooked ham
- 10-12 peppercorns
- 2 bay leaves

DIRECTIONS

- Pour water and wine in the crock pot. Add peppercorns and bay leaves.
- Wrap cooked ham in foil, and place in the crock pot.
- Cover, set on high and cook 1 hour. Reduce the heat to low and cook another 6 to 7 hours.

Banana Almond Bread

(Ready in about 3 hours | Servings 8)

INGREDIENTS

- 1/3 cup shortening
- 1/2 cup brown sugar
- 1 teaspoon vanilla extract
- 2 eggs
- 1 ¾ cup all-purpose flour
- 1 ½ teaspoon baking powder
- 1/2 tea salt
- 1 cup ripe bananas, mashed
- 1/2 cup almonds, chopped and toasted

DIRECTIONS

- Combine together shortening, brown sugar and vanilla. Add the eggs and beat well to combine. Sift the flour, baking powder, and salt.
- Add mashed bananas and almonds. Pour into greased and floured baking dish and cover with a foil.
- Pour 2 cups of hot water in the crock pot. Place baking dish on a rack in the crock pot. Put the lid and cook on high 2 to 3 hours.

Juicy BBQ Chicken

(Ready in about 4 hours | Servings 4)

INGREDIENTS

- 1 whole medium chicken
- 1 cup tomato paste
- 2 tablespoons ketchup
- 3/4 cup brown sugar
- 1 teaspoon garlic powder
- 1 teaspoon salt
- 1/2 teaspoon black pepper
- 3 tablespoons Worcestershire sauce

DIRECTIONS

- Place chicken in the crock pot.
- Combine together remaining ingredients and pour over chicken.
- Set the crock pot on high and cook for 4 hours.

Meatballs in Spiced Sauce

(Ready in about 6 hours | Servings 10)

INGREDIENTS

- 2 lbs. ground beef
- 1 tablespoon Dijon mustard
- 2 teaspoon Worcestershire sauce
- 2/3 cup evaporated milk
- 1 dry onion soup mix

- 1/2 teaspoon freshly ground black pepper
- 2 cup tomato paste
- 1 teaspoon garlic powder
- 1 cup brown sugar, packed
- 1 tablespoon Worcestershire sauce

DIRECTIONS
- Combine together beef, mustard, Worcestershire sauce, evaporated milk, soup mix and black pepper. Shape into meatballs.
- Cook under the broiler for 12 minutes.
- To make the sauce: Mix together tomato paste, garlic powder, sugar, and Worcestershire sauce.
- Pour the sauce over meatballs in the crock pot.
- Turn the crock pot on low heat setting and cook meatballs for 5 to 6 hours.

Barley with Mushrooms

(Ready in about 5 hours | Servings 4)

INGREDIENTS
- 1 cup barley
- 2 cups garlic chicken broth
- 3 green onions, finely chopped
- 6 ounces fresh mushrooms, sliced
- 1 teaspoon seasoned salt
- 1/4 teaspoon black pepper
- 1/2 teaspoon cayenne pepper
- 2 teaspoons butter

DIRECTIONS
- Combine all ingredients in the crock pot.
- Cover and cook on low heat setting for 4 to 5 hours.

Mexican Traditional Enchiladas

(Ready in about 1 hour 15 minutes | Servings 6)

INGREDIENTS
- 1 pound mixed ground beef and pork
- 3 slices of Canadian bacon, chopped
- 1 ¼ cups water
- 1 (1-ounce) package taco seasoning mix
- 1 cup chunky salsa
- 2 cups chicken stock
- Sea salt, to taste
- 4 cups Mexican cheese blend, shredded
- 10 corn tortillas, quartered

DIRECTIONS
- In a wide saucepan, cook ground meat and bacon over medium heat. Cook until they are browned or about 10 minutes.
- In a medium-sized mixing bowl, combine together water, taco seasoning mix, salsa, chicken stock, salt and 2 cups of cheese.
- Arrange a layer of tortillas on the bottom of a crock pot. Add a layer of the ground beef, and then spoon a layer of the salsa mixture over that.
- Repeat the layers one more time, ending with the layer of tortillas. Top with remaining 2 cups of cheese.

- Cover with a lid; cook on high for 1 hour.

Stuffed Chicken Breasts

(Ready in about 3 hours | Servings 4)

INGREDIENTS
- 1/2 cup sharp cheese, shredded
- 1 red bell pepper, chopped
- 1 green bell pepper, chopped
- 1 yellow bell pepper, chopped
- 2 heaping tablespoons fresh parsley, chopped
- 1/4 cup cilantro, minced
- 1/4 cup tomatoes, diced
- 1/2 teaspoon chili powder
- 1/2 teaspoon celery salt
- 4 small-sized chicken breast, boneless and pounded to 1/4 inch thickness

DIRECTIONS
- In a bowl, mix together all of the ingredients, except chicken.
- Spread this mixture on the chicken breast. Roll up chicken breasts tightly and secure them with toothpicks or the skewers.
- Arrange the chicken rolls in the crock pot. Cover and cook 3 hours on high.

Pasta with Tomato Sauce

(Ready in about 7 hours | Servings 6)

INGREDIENTS
- 4 large-sized tomatoes, chopped
- 1 large-sized yellow onion, finely chopped
- 2 cloves garlic, minced
- 1/2 cup dry red wine
- 2 tablespoons tomato ketchup
- 1 tablespoon brown sugar
- 1 teaspoon dried oregano leaves
- 1 teaspoon celery seeds
- 1 teaspoon dried thyme leaves
- 1/8 teaspoon paprika
- 1/4 teaspoon kosher salt
- 12 ounces pasta, cooked and warm

DIRECTIONS
- Combine all of the ingredients, except pasta, in your crock pot.
- Cover and cook 7 hours on low.
- Ladle sauce over pasta and enjoy.

Farfalle with Mushroom Sauce

(Ready in about 8 hours | Servings 6)

INGREDIENTS
- 1 onion, finely chopped
- 2 cloves garlic, minced
- 1 medium-sized plum tomatoes, chopped
- 1 ½ cups cream of mushroom soup
- 2 tablespoons tomato ketchup

- 1 tablespoon brown sugar
- 1 teaspoon dried oregano leaves
- 1 cup mushrooms, thinly sliced
- 1 teaspoon dried basil leaves
- 1/4 teaspoon kosher salt
- 1/4 teaspoon ground black pepper
- 12 ounces Farfalle, cooked and warm

DIRECTIONS
- In a crock pot, place all ingredients, except farfalle.
- Cover with a lid and cook about 8 hours on low.
- Ladle mushroom sauce over Farfalle and serve.

Northern Italian Risi Bisi

(Ready in about 1 hour 30 minutes | Servings 4)

INGREDIENTS
- 1 cup water
- 2 cups vegetable stock
- 1/2 cup green onions, finely chopped
- 2 cloves garlic, minced
- 1 ½ cups rice
- 1 teaspoon dried oregano leaves
- 1 tablespoon dried basil leaves
- Ground black pepper, to taste
- Cayenne pepper, to taste
- 8 ounces green peas, trimmed
- 1 teaspoon fresh lemon juice
- 1/2 cup Parmesan cheese, grated

DIRECTIONS
- In a crock pot, arrange all ingredients, except green peas, lemon juice and cheese.
- Cover and cook on high heat setting about 1 ¼ hours or until the liquid is almost absorbed. Add green peas in the last 15 minutes of cooking time.
- Stir in lemon juice and cheese; divide among serving plates and serve.

Pecorino and Green Pea Risotto

(Ready in about 1 hour 30 minutes | Servings 4)

INGREDIENTS
- 2 cups vegetable stock
- 1 cup tomato juice
- 1/2 cup shallots, finely chopped
- 2 cloves garlic, minced
- 1 ½ cups cooked chicken, cubed
- 1 ½ cups rice
- 1 teaspoon dried Italian seasoning
- Salt, to taste
- Ground black pepper, to taste
- Paprika, to taste
- 8 ounces green peas, trimmed
- 1/2 cup Pecorino cheese, grated

DIRECTIONS

- In your crock pot, place all ingredients, except green peas and Pecorino cheese.
- Cover; cook on high about 1 hour 30 minutes, adding green peas during last 15 minutes of cooking time.
- Add cheese and serve warm.

Risotto with Zucchini and Yellow Squash

(Ready in about 1 hour 25 minutes | Servings 4)

INGREDIENTS
- 3 cups vegetable broth
- 1 medium-sized onion, chopped
- 2 cloves garlic, minced
- 1 cup sliced cremini mushrooms
- 1 teaspoon dried rosemary
- 1 ½ cups short-grain rice
- 1 cup each zucchini, cubed
- 3/4 cup summer yellow squash, cubed
- 1 sweet potato, peeled cubed
- 1/4 cup Pecorino cheese, grated
- 1/2 teaspoon sea salt
- 1/2 teaspoon ground black pepper
- 1/2 teaspoon cayenne pepper

DIRECTIONS
- Combine all ingredients, except cheese, in your crock pot.
- Cover and cook on high about 1 ¼ hours or until rice is al dente.
- Stir in cheese; divide among four serving plates and enjoy.

Egg Pie with Mushrooms

(Ready in about 4 hours | Servings 4)

INGREDIENTS
- 4 large-sized eggs
- 1/4 cup all-purpose flour
- 1/2 teaspoon baking soda
- 1/4 teaspoon salt
- 1/8 teaspoon freshly ground black pepper
- 2 cups Colby Jack cheese, shredded
- 1 cup reduced-fat cottage cheese
- 1 Chipotle pepper, minced
- 1 cup mushrooms, sliced
- 1/2 teaspoon dried rosemary
- 1/2 teaspoon dried basil leaves

DIRECTIONS
- In a large bowl, beat the eggs until foamy; mix in flour, baking soda, salt, and ground black pepper. Stir in remaining ingredients.
- Pour the mixture into oiled crock pot; cover and cook about 4 hours on low.
- Divide among four serving plates and enjoy!

Aromatic Apple Risotto

(Ready in about 9 hours | Servings 6)

INGREDIENTS

- 1/4 cup butter, melted
- 1 ½ cups Arborio rice
- 3 apples, cored and sliced
- 1/4 teaspoon freshly ground nutmeg
- 1/4 teaspoon ground cloves
- 1 teaspoon ground cinnamon
- 1/3 cup brown sugar
- A pinch of salt
- 1 cup apple juice
- 2 cups whole milk
- 1 cup water

DIRECTIONS
- ✓ Add the butter and rice to the crock pot.
- ✓ Then, add the rest of ingredients; stir to combine.
- ✓ Cover and cook 9 hours on low. Serve with dried fruit, if desired.

Delicious Savory Soufflé

(Ready in about 3 hours | Servings 8)

INGREDIENTS

- 8 slices of bread
- 8 ounces Cheddar cheese, shredded
- 8 ounces mozzarella cheese, shredded
- Non-stick cooking spray
- 2 cups fat-free evaporated milk
- 4 eggs
- 1/4 teaspoon allspice

DIRECTIONS
- ✓ Tear the bread into pieces and reserve.
- ✓ Combine the cheeses and reserve.
- ✓ Grease your crock pot with non-stick cooking spray. Then, add bread and cheese. Stir to combine.
- ✓ In a measuring cup or a mixing bowl, whisk the milk, eggs, and allspice. Pour over the bread and cheese in the crock pot. Cook 2 to 3 hours on low.
- ✓ Serve sprinkled with pitted and chopped olives, if desired.

Spaghetti with Asparagus and Beans

(Ready in about 3 hours | Servings 8)

INGREDIENTS

- 1 can (15-ounce) Great Northern beans, rinsed and drained
- 3/4 cup vegetable stock
- 2 tomatoes, chopped plum
- 1 carrot, chopped
- 1 teaspoon dried basil leaves
- 1 teaspoon dried rosemary leaves
- Salt and pepper, to taste
- 1 pound asparagus, sliced
- 8 ounces spaghetti, cooked
- 1/2 cup Parmesan cheese, shredded

DIRECTIONS

- ✓ Combine all ingredients, except asparagus, spaghetti and cheese, in your crock pot.
- ✓ Cook on low about 3 hours, adding asparagus during last 30 minutes of cooking time.
- ✓ Adjust seasonings to your taste, then, add spaghetti and Parmesan cheese; serve.

Easy Yummy Green Beans

(Ready in about 4 hours | Servings 8)

INGREDIENTS

- 1 pound green beans
- 4 large-sized tomatoes, chopped
- 1/2 cup shallots, chopped
- 3 cloves garlic, minced
- 1 teaspoon dried basil leaves
- 1 teaspoon dried rosemary
- 1/2 teaspoon celery salt
- 1/4 teaspoon black pepper
- 1/4 teaspoon cayenne pepper

DIRECTIONS
- ✓ Combine all ingredients in your crock pot.
- ✓ Cover with a lid; then, cook on high about 4 hours or until beans are tender.
- ✓ Serve with poultry entrée.

Vegan Mediterranean Treat

(Ready in about 2 hours | Servings 8)

INGREDIENTS

- 2 cups green beans
- 1/4 cup onion, finely chopped
- 2 cloves garlic, minced
- 1 large-sized red bell pepper, chopped
- 1 large-sized carrot, chopped
- 1 teaspoon ginger root, ground
- 1/2 cup water
- 1 cup canned black beans, drained
- 1 tablespoon rice wine vinegar
- 2 teaspoons tamari sauce
- 1/2 teaspoon sea salt
- 1/4 teaspoon ground black pepper

DIRECTIONS
- ✓ In your crock pot, combine green beans, onion, garlic, bell pepper, carrot, ginger root, and water; cover with a lid and set the crock pot to high.
- ✓ Cook about 1 ½ hours; drain. Add remaining ingredients and cook 30 minutes longer. Taste, adjust the seasonings and serve.

Hot Baked Beans

(Ready in about 6 hours | Servings 8)

INGREDIENTS

- 1 cup chopped onion

- 2 cans (15-ounce) pinto beans, rinsed and drained
- 1 serrano pepper, chopped
- 1 jalapeño chili, finely chopped
- 1 cup whole kernel corn
- 1 cup cherry tomatoes, halved
- 2 tablespoons sugar
- 1/2 teaspoon dried thyme leaves
- 1 bay leaf
- 1/2 teaspoon sea salt
- 1/4 teaspoon white pepper
- 1/2 cup Pecorino cheese, grated
- 1/4 cup fresh parsley, finely chopped

DIRECTIONS
- ✓ Combine all ingredients, except cheese and parsley, in your crock pot.
- ✓ Cover and cook on low 5 to 6 hours.
- ✓ Sprinkle with cheese and parsley and serve!

Baked and Herbed Cannellini Beans

(Ready in about 6 hours | Servings 6)

INGREDIENTS
- 1 cup vegetable broth
- 3 cans (15-ounces) cannellini beans
- 1/2 cup leeks, chopped
- 2-3 cloves garlic, minced
- 1 celery stalk, chopped
- 1 sweet red bell pepper, chopped
- 1 teaspoon dried sage
- 2 bay leaves
- 6 sun-dried tomatoes, softened and sliced
- 1/2 teaspoon paprika
- 1/2 teaspoon sea salt
- 1/4 teaspoon freshly ground black pepper

DIRECTIONS
- ✓ Put all of the ingredients into your crock pot.
- ✓ Cover and cook 5 to 6 hours on low. Serve with sausage and your favorite salad, if desired.

Delicious Sweet-Spiced Beans

(Ready in about 6 hours | Servings 10)

INGREDIENTS
- 1 ½ cups leeks, chopped
- 4 cans (15-ounce) Great Northern beans, rinsed and drained
- 2 tablespoons gingerroot, finely chopped
- 3 cloves garlic, minced
- 1 tablespoon sugar
- 1 cup tomato paste
- 1 teaspoon mustard seeds
- 1 teaspoon dried thyme leaves
- 1 teaspoon dried sage leaves
- 1/4 teaspoon nutmeg, grated
- 2 bay leaves
- Black pepper, to taste
- 5-6 peppercorns
- 1/2 cup gingersnap crumbs, coarsely ground

DIRECTIONS
- ✓ Combine all ingredients, except gingersnap crumbs, in a crock pot.
- ✓ Cover the crock pot with a lid and cook 6 hours on low, adding gingersnap crumbs during last hour.
- ✓ Discard bay leaves and serve warm.

Easy Honey Beets with Raisins

(Ready in about 2 hours 30 minutes | Servings 6)

INGREDIENTS
- 2 cups hot water
- 1 ½ pounds medium beets
- 1 large-sized red onion, finely chopped
- 2 cloves garlic, minced
- 1/4 cup raisins
- 3 heaping tablespoons pine nuts, toasted
- 1/4 cup honey
- 3 tablespoons red wine vinegar
- 1 tablespoon olive oil
- Salt and pepper, to taste

DIRECTIONS
- ✓ In a crock pot, place hot water and beets; cover and cook on high approximately 2 hours; drain.
- ✓ Next, peel beets and cut into small pieces. Return to the crock pot; add remaining ingredients.
- ✓ Cook for 30 minutes longer. Serve with poultry entrée and enjoy!

Glazed Brussels Sprouts with Pearl Onions

(Ready in about 2 hours 10 minutes | Servings 6)

INGREDIENTS
- 8 ounces frozen pearl onions, thawed
- 8 ounces small Brussels sprouts
- 11/2 cups hot water
- 1/4 teaspoon ground black pepper
- 1/4 teaspoon cayenne pepper
- 1/2 teaspoon sea salt
- 1 tablespoon margarine
- 1/4 cup brown sugar

DIRECTIONS
- ✓ Combine pearl onions, Brussels sprouts and hot water in a crock pot.
- ✓ Cover with a lid and cook on high about 2 hours or until the vegetables are tender; drain. Season with black pepper, cayenne pepper, and sea salt.
- ✓ Add margarine and sugar and cook 10 more minutes. Serve warm and enjoy.

Herbed Potato-Carrot Purée

(Ready in about 3 hours 30 minutes | Servings 8)

INGREDIENTS

- 2 cups potato, peeled cubed
- 2 pounds carrots, sliced
- 1 cup water
- 2 tablespoons butter
- 1/4 cup milk, warm
- 1/2 teaspoon dried rosemary
- 1/2 teaspoon allspice
- 1/2 teaspoon celery seeds
- 1 teaspoon dried basil
- 1 teaspoon dried oregano
- 1/2 teaspoon salt
- 1/2 teaspoon red pepper flakes, crushed

DIRECTIONS
- Place potatoes, carrots and water in your crock pot; cover with a lid and cook 3 hours on high. Drain well.
- Purée cooked potato and carrots in a food processor until creamy and uniform; return to the crock pot. Uncover and cook on high about 30 minutes; stir occasionally.
- Beat butter and milk into mashed potatoes and carrots. Make a creamy consistency. Season with spices and serve.

Winter Cabbage with Bacon

(Ready in about 4 hours | Servings 6)

INGREDIENTS

- 1 head cabbage, thinly sliced
- 3/4 cup leeks, chopped
- 2 medium-sized carrots, chopped
- 1 sweet red bell pepper, thinly sliced
- 2 cloves garlic, minced
- 1/2 teaspoon anise seeds
- 1/4 cup canned beef broth
- 1/4 cup dry white wine
- Salt, to taste
- 1/2 teaspoon ground black pepper
- 2 slices of diced bacon, cooked crisp and drained

DIRECTIONS
- Combine all ingredients, except bacon, in your crock pot.
- Cover and cook on high about 4 hours or until cabbage is tender.
- Add bacon, adjust the seasonings to taste, and enjoy!

Vegetarian Creamed Cabbage

(Ready in about 4 hours 10 minutes | Servings 6)

INGREDIENTS

- 1 large-sized head cabbage, thinly sliced
- 3/4 cup red or yellow onion, chopped
- 2 medium-sized carrots, chopped
- 1 sweet bell pepper, thinly sliced
- 2 cloves garlic, minced
- 1/2 teaspoon caraway seeds
- 1/2 teaspoon celery seeds
- 1 cup canned vegetable stock
- Salt, to taste
- Ground black pepper, to taste
- Cayenne pepper, to taste
- 1/2 cup reduced-fat sour cream
- 1 tablespoon cornflour

DIRECTIONS
- In your crock pot, place all ingredients, except sour cream and cornflour.
- Cover with a lid and cook 4 hours on high.
- Stir in combined sour cream and cornflour and continue cooking 10 minutes longer. Serve warm.

Amazing Orange-Glazed Carrots

(Ready in about 3 hours 10 minutes | Servings 4)

INGREDIENTS

- 1 pound baby carrots
- 3/4 cup orange juice
- 1 tablespoon butter
- 1/2 cup brown sugar, packed light
- 1/2 teaspoon allspice
- 1/4 teaspoon ground mace
- 1/2 teaspoon sea salt
- 1/2 teaspoon white pepper
- 2 tablespoons cornflour
- 1/4 cup water

DIRECTIONS
- In a crock pot, place all ingredients, except cornflour and water; cover and cook on high about 3 hours or until carrots are crisp-tender.
- In a small mixing bowl, combine cornflour and water; add to the crock pot. Stir 2 to 3 minutes.
- Divide among four serving plates and serve with meat or fish entrée, if desired.

Mediterranean Creamy Cabbage

(Ready in about 4 hours 10 minutes | Servings 6)

INGREDIENTS

- 1 large-sized head Savoy cabbage, sliced
- 3/4 cup red or yellow onion, chopped
- 1 celery rib, chopped
- 1 green bell pepper, thinly sliced
- 1 yellow bell pepper, thinly sliced
- 2 cloves garlic, minced
- 1 teaspoon celery seeds
- 1 cup canned vegetable stock
- Salt, to taste
- Ground black pepper, to taste
- Paprika, to taste

- Grating of nutmeg
- 1 cup spinach, torn into pieces
- 1/2 cup plain Greek yogurt
- 1 tablespoon corn starch

DIRECTIONS
- In a crock pot, arrange all of the ingredients, except spinach, yogurt and corn starch.
- Cook covered for 4 hours, adding the spinach during last 30 minutes of cooking time and sprinkling with some extra spices, if desired.
- Add combined yogurt and corn starch, stirring about 10 minutes. Serve warm and enjoy!

Orange-Glazed Sweet Potatoes

(Ready in about 3 hours 5 minutes | Servings 4)

INGREDIENTS
- 1 pound sweet potatoes
- 3/4 cup orange juice
- 1 tablespoon margarine
- 1/2 cup brown sugar
- 1/2 teaspoon grated nutmeg
- 1/4 teaspoon ground mace
- 1/4 teaspoon ground cloves
- 1/2 teaspoon ground cinnamon
- 1/2 teaspoon kosher salt
- 1/2 teaspoon white pepper
- 2 tablespoons cornflour
- 1/4 cup water

DIRECTIONS
- Place all ingredients, except cornflour and water, in a crock pot.
- Cover and cook on high about 3 hours or until sweet potatoes are crisp-tender.
- Add combined cornflour and water, stirring constantly 3 to 4 minutes. Serve with your favorite meat entrée.

Delicious Family Corn Flan

(Ready in about 3 hours | Servings 6)

INGREDIENTS
- 1 teaspoon sugar
- 1 cup milk
- 3 eggs, lightly beaten
- 1 ½ cup creamed corn
- 1 cup kernel corn
- 1/2 teaspoon allspice
- 1/2 teaspoon salt
- 1/4 teaspoon white pepper

DIRECTIONS
- Mix all of the ingredients together. Place in a soufflé dish.
- Place this soufflé dish on a rack in the crock pot.
- Cover and cook on low about 3 hours.

Spicy Corn Pudding

(Ready in about 3 hours | Servings 6)

INGREDIENTS
- Non-stick cooking spray
- 3 medium-sized eggs
- 1 cup whole milk
- 1/2 cup frozen whole kernel corn, thawed
- 2 tablespoons all-purpose flour
- 1/2 teaspoon ground cumin
- 1 teaspoon fine sea salt
- 1/4 teaspoon red pepper flakes, crushed
- 1/4 teaspoon black pepper
- 1/2 cup creamed corn
- 2 cups reduced-fat sharp cheese, shredded
- 1 chipotle pepper, minced

DIRECTIONS
- Treat the inside of your crock pot with non-stick cooking spray.
- Purée eggs, milk, whole-kernel corn, all-purpose flour, cumin, salt, red pepper flakes and black pepper in your food processor or a blender until uniform and smooth.
- Pour the mixture into the oiled crock pot. Add the rest of the ingredients.
- Cover and cook about 3 hours on low.

Pork Shoulder with Hot Sauce

(Ready in about 12 hours | Servings 10)

INGREDIENTS
- 1 pork shoulder roast
- 1/2 teaspoon ground black pepper
- 1/2 teaspoon cayenne pepper
- 1 teaspoon fine sea salt
- 1 tablespoon fresh orange juice
- 1 cup balsamic vinegar
- 2 tablespoons brown sugar
- 1 tablespoon Tabasco sauce

DIRECTIONS
- On the bottom of your crock pot, place the pork. Season with black pepper, cayenne pepper, and sea salt. Pour in orange juice and balsamic vinegar.
- Cover and cook 12 hours on low.
- Remove the pork from the crock pot; discard any bones.
- To make the sauce, save 2 cups of liquid. Add sugar and tabasco sauce to the reserved liquid.
- Shred the pork and return to the crock pot. Pour the sauce over the pork.
- Keep warm before serving time.

Leek and Garlic Custard

(Ready in about 3 hours | Servings 6)

INGREDIENTS
- 2 tablespoons extra-virgin olive oil

- 4 leeks (white parts only), sliced
- 2 cloves garlic, minced
- 1/2 teaspoon allspice
- 2 eggs, lightly beaten
- 1 cup whole milk
- 1/8 teaspoon ground nutmeg
- 1/2 teaspoon sea salt
- 1/4 teaspoon ground black pepper
- 1/4 teaspoon red pepper flakes, crushed
- 1/2 cup Swiss cheese, shredded

DIRECTIONS
- In a small cast-iron skillet, heat olive oil over medium-high. Sauté leeks and garlic about 8 minutes.
- Add sautéed leeks and garlic to a suitable soufflé dish; add remaining ingredients; place on a rack in your crock pot.
- Cover and cook on low 3 to 3 ½ hours or until custard is set.
- Let stand for 10 minutes before slicing and serving. This custard can be a delicious dinner and it also will complement your favorite entrée.

Stuffed Vidalia Onions

(Ready in about 4 hours | Servings 6)

INGREDIENTS
- 4 medium-sized Vidalia onions, peeled
- 1/2 cup bread crumbs
- 1/2 cup Queso fresco cheese, Crumbled
- 4 sun-dried tomatoes, chopped
- 1/4 cup water chestnut
- 2 cloves garlic, minced
- 1/2 teaspoon dried basil leaves
- 1/4 teaspoon salt
- 1/4 teaspoon black pepper
- 1 egg white
- 1/2 cup warm chicken stock

DIRECTIONS
- Boil Vidalia onions in water about 10 minutes; drain.
- Cut Vidalia onions into halves and remove centres. You can reserve centres for another use.
- In a mixing bowl, mix together remaining ingredients, except chicken stock; fill onion halves with prepared mixture.
- Add stuffed onions to the crock pot; pour in chicken stock.
- Cook covered on high about 4 hours.

Fruit and Nut Candied Yams

(Ready in about 4 hours | Servings 8)

INGREDIENTS
- 2 pounds yams, peeled and thinly sliced
- 1/4 cup currants
- 1/4 cup toasted pecans, chopped
- 2/3 cup packed light brown sugar
- A pinch of salt
- 1/2 teaspoon allspice
- 1/4 teaspoon ground black pepper
- 2 tablespoons cold butter
- 1/2 cup water
- 2 tablespoons cornflour

DIRECTIONS
- Arrange yams in your crock pot, sprinkling with currants, pecans, brown sugar, salt, allspice and pepper and dotting with cold butter. Repeat the layers until you run out of ingredients.
- Combine water and cornflour; pour into a crock pot.
- Cover and cook on low 3 hours; then turn heat to high and cook 1 hour longer. Enjoy!

Maple Honey Ribs

(Ready in about 5 hours | Servings 6)

INGREDIENTS
- 3 pounds pork ribs
- 1 cup canned vegetable broth
- 1/2 cup water
- 1/4 cup honey
- 3 tablespoons mustard
- 1/4 cup barbeque sauce
- 1/4 cup tamari sauce
- 1/4 cup pure maple syrup

DIRECTIONS
- In the crock, mix together all ingredients, except pork ribs.
- Slice ribs apart; place the pork ribs in the crock pot.
- Cover and cook 5 hours on high or until the pork falls from the bones. Serve warm with hot tomato sauce and some extra mustard, if desired.

Yam Loaf for Winter Holidays

(Ready in about 3 hours | Servings 6)

INGREDIENTS
- 1 ¼ cups yams, peeled and coarsely grated
- 1/3 cup shallots, finely chopped
- 2 tart apples, shredded
- ¼ cup golden raisins
- 1/8 teaspoon ground nutmeg
- ¼ teaspoon ground cloves
- ¼ teaspoon ground cinnamon
- ¼ cup all-purpose flour
- ¼ cup fresh orange juice
- A pinch of salt
- 1/4 teaspoon white pepper
- 1 large-sized egg

DIRECTIONS
- Mix all ingredients, except egg; adjust the seasonings to taste. Mix in egg.
- Put the mixture into greased loaf pan; place the loaf pan on rack in your crock pot. Cover with aluminium foil.
- Pour 2 inches hot water into the crock pot; cover and cook on high about
- 3 hours.

- Let stand on wire rack at least 5 minutes; invert onto serving plates and serve.

Squash and Sweet Potato Pudding

(Ready in about 3 hours 30 minutes | Servings 6)

INGREDIENTS

- Canola oil
- 1 cup Hubbard squash
- 1 cup carrots, sliced
- 4 medium-sized sweet potatoes, peeled and cubed
- 1/4 cup orange juice
- 2 tablespoons butter
- 1/4 cup packed light brown sugar
- 1/4 teaspoon cloves
- A pinch of salt
- 3 eggs, lightly beaten
- 1 cup miniature marshmallows

DIRECTIONS

- Oil the inside of the crock pot with canola oil.
- Add squash, carrots, and sweet potatoes; cover and cook on high about 3 hours.
- Remove vegetables from the crock pot; mash with remaining ingredients, except marshmallows.
- Return mashed vegetables to the crock pot; cover and cook on high 30 minutes longer. Scatter the marshmallows on top and serve.

Rich and Creamy Potato Gratin

(Ready in about 3 hours 30 minutes | Servings 8)

INGREDIENTS

- 2 pounds potatoes, peeled and sliced
- 1/4 cup green onion, sliced
- 1/2 teaspoon salt
- 1/4 teaspoon ground black pepper
- 2 tablespoons butter
- 3 tablespoons shallots, finely chopped
- 3 tablespoons all-purpose flour
- 1 cup milk
- 2 ounces reduced-fat processed cheese, cubed
- 1 cup Cheddar cheese, shredded
- 1/2 teaspoon dried basil leaves
- 1/2 teaspoon dried oregano leaves
- 1/2 teaspoon paprika

DIRECTIONS

- Layer half of the sliced potatoes and green onions in the bottom of your crock pot; sprinkle with salt and ground black pepper.
- To make the sauce, melt butter in a small skillet; add shallots and flour and cook about 2 minutes. Gradually whisk in milk, stirring until thickened or 2 to 3 minutes.
- Then, turn the heat to low; add remaining ingredients. Stir until everything is well combined and melted.
- Pour half of this cheese sauce over layers in the crock pot. Repeat layers, ending with cheese sauce.

- Cover and cook on high about 3 ½ hours. Serve warm and enjoy!

Creamy Potatoes with Smoked Ham

(Ready in about 4 hours | Servings 8)

INGREDIENTS

- 2 pounds potatoes, sliced
- 12 ounces smoked ham, cubed
- 1 cup canned cream of mushroom soup
- 1 teaspoon dried basil leaves
- 1 cup milk
- 1 ½ cups Monterey Jack cheese
- Sea salt, to taste
- 1/4 teaspoon black pepper, freshly ground
- 1/4 teaspoon cayenne pepper
- Smoked paprika, to taste

DIRECTIONS

- Place potatoes and smoked ham in the bottom of the crock pot.
- In a large-sized mixing bowl, combine the rest of ingredients; pour into the crock pot.
- Cover and cook on high approximately 4 hours. Enjoy!

Creamed Root Vegetables

(Ready in about 5 hours | Servings 6)

INGREDIENTS

- 4 small potatoes, sliced
- 1 medium-sized fennel bulb, sliced
- 1 turnips, sliced
- 1 large-sized carrot, sliced
- 2 medium parsnips, sliced
- 3 small leeks (white parts only), sliced
- 2 cloves garlic, minced
- 1/2 teaspoon dried basil leaves
- Salt, to taste
- 1/4 teaspoon ground black pepper
- 1/4 teaspoon paprika
- 1 cup chicken broth
- 1/2 cup half-and-half
- 1 cup sour cream
- 2 tablespoons cornflour

DIRECTIONS

- Combine all ingredients, except sour cream and cornflour, in your crock pot.
- Cover and cook on high about 5 hours or until the vegetables are tender.
- Add combined sour cream and cornflour, and continue cooking, stirring 2 to 3 minutes. Serve.

Mushroom and Zucchini Soufflé

(Ready in about 4 hours | Servings 8)

INGREDIENTS

- 4 medium-sized eggs
- 3/4 cup whole milk
- 1/4 cup all-purpose flour
- 1 cup mushrooms, sliced
- 1 pound zucchini, chopped
- 2 tablespoons parsley, coarsely chopped
- 1 clove garlic, minced
- 1/2 teaspoon dried basil leaves
- 1/2 teaspoon dried oregano leaves
- 1/2 teaspoon dried rosemary
- 1 teaspoon salt
- 1/4 teaspoon ground black pepper
- 1/4 teaspoon cayenne pepper
- 1/2 cup Parmesan cheese, grated

DIRECTIONS

- In a mixing bowl, beat eggs, milk, and all-purpose flour until smooth.
- Next, add remaining ingredients, except 1/4 cup Parmesan cheese.
- Pour this mixture into casserole; sprinkle with remaining 1/4 cup of Parmesan cheese.
- Place casserole dish on a rack in the crock pot; cover and cook 4 hours on
- high. Serve warm.

Cheesy Spinach and Noodle Delight

(Ready in about 4 hours | Servings 8)

INGREDIENTS

- 1/2 cup reduced-fat cream cheese
- 1 cup cottage cheese
- 3 large eggs, lightly beaten
- 1 cup whole milk
- 1/2 cup currants
- 1/2 teaspoon allspice
- 2 cups spinach
- 1/2 cup egg noodles, cooked al dente
- 1/2 teaspoon salt
- 1/2 teaspoon ground black pepper
- 1/2 teaspoon red pepper flakes, crushed
- Parmesan cheese, as garnish

DIRECTIONS

- In a medium-sized bowl, combine cream cheese and cottage cheese; whisk eggs and add to the cheese mixture.
- Stir in remaining ingredients, except Parmesan cheese; spoon into a soufflé dish.
- Sprinkle with Parmesan cheese; place soufflé dish on a rack in the crock pot.
- Cover and cook on low about 4 hours or until set.

Savory Bread Pudding

(Ready in about 5 hours | Servings 8)

INGREDIENTS

- Non-stick cooking spray
- 8 ounces bread, cubed
- 1 teaspoon dried basil leaves
- 1/2 teaspoon mustard seeds
- 2 tablespoons butter, melted
- 1 celery rib, thinly sliced
- 1 large-sized carrots, sliced
- 8 ounces mushrooms, thinly sliced
- 1 cup shallots, finely chopped
- 1 clove garlic, minced
- 1 cup light cream
- 1 cup whole milk
- 4 eggs, lightly beaten
- 1/2 teaspoon salt
- 1/4 teaspoon ground black pepper
- 1/4 cup Provolone cheese, shredded

DIRECTIONS

- Spray bread cubes with non-stick cooking spray; sprinkle with basil and mustard seeds and toss.
- Bake on a cookie sheet at 375 degrees F about 15 minutes or until golden
- brown.
- Heat butter in a heavy skillet. Sauté celery, carrots, mushrooms, shallots and garlic about 8 minutes.
- In a large bowl, mix the rest of ingredients, except Provolone cheese; add greased bread cubes and sautéed vegetables.
- Spoon into greased crock pot; scatter shredded Provolone cheese on top and refrigerate overnight. Cook covered on high approximately 5 hours.

Corn and Potatoes with Shrimp

(Ready in about 2 hours | Servings 8)

INGREDIENTS

- 4 ears corn, halved
- 2 pounds red potatoes, peeled and quartered
- 1/4 cup shrimp boil seasoning
- 1 tablespoon celery seeds
- 1 teaspoon dried basil leaves
- 4 leeks, thinly sliced
- Water, as needed
- 1 ½ pounds medium shrimp

DIRECTIONS

- Place all ingredients, except shrimp, in a crock pot.
- Cook for 2 to 2 ½ hours on high.
- Add the shrimp; continue to cook for 20 minutes or until the shrimp is thoroughly cooked. Serve warm.

Rich and Healthy Summer Paella

(Ready in about 6 hours | Servings 12)

INGREDIENTS

- 1 tablespoon extra-virgin olive oil
- 2 medium-sized onions, sliced
- 3 cloves garlic, minced
- 1 pound spicy sausage

- 2 pounds tomatoes, chopped
- 2 cups chicken stock
- 2 cups clam juice
- 1 cup dry vermouth
- 2 ½ cups rice, uncooked
- 1/2 teaspoon ground cumin
- 1/2 teaspoon caraway seeds
- 1 teaspoon saffron
- Sea salt, to taste
- 1/4 teaspoon ground black pepper
- 2 tablespoons olive oil
- 1 pound fish, cubed
- 1 pound shrimp
- 1 pound fresh mussels
- 1 green pepper, minced
- 1 cup fresh green peas

DIRECTIONS
- Heat olive oil in a heavy skillet over medium heat; then, sauté the onions, garlic and sausage until sausage is browned and crumbled. Drain and transfer to the crock pot.
- Stir in tomatoes, chicken stock, clam juice, vermouth, rice, cumin, caraway seeds, saffron, salt and black pepper; cover and cook on low for 6 hours.
- In the same skillet, heat 2 tablespoons of oil; sauté the fish and shrimp. Transfer to the crock pot. Add remaining ingredients and cook until cooked through. Serve warm.

Rabbit in Coconut Sauce

(Ready in about 6 hours | Servings 8)

INGREDIENTS
- 1 cup coconut milk
- 1 cup water
- 3 medium-sized tomatoes, diced
- 2 leeks, chopped
- 1 teaspoon salt
- 1 bay leaf
- 1/2 teaspoon ground black pepper
- 1/2 teaspoon red pepper flakes, crushed
- 3 pounds rabbit meat, cut into serving-sized pieces

DIRECTIONS
- In a crock pot, combine all of the ingredients.
- Cover with a lid and heat on low for 5 to 6 hours.
- Serve over noodles or cooked rice.

Vegetarian Potato and Eggplant Moussaka

(Ready in about 7 hours | Servings 8)

INGREDIENTS
- 1 cup dry brown lentils, rinsed and drained
- 3 medium-sized potatoes, peeled and sliced
- 1 cup water
- 1 bouillon cube
- 1 celery rib, diced fine
- 1 medium-sized onion, sliced
- 3 cloves garlic, minced
- 1/2 teaspoon salt
- 1/4 teaspoon freshly ground black pepper
- 1/4 teaspoon ground cinnamon
- 1 teaspoon Italian seasonings
- 1 cup carrots, sliced
- 1 medium-sized eggplant, diced
- 1 cup tomatoes, diced
- 1 cup cream cheese, softened
- 2 large eggs

DIRECTIONS
- In your crock pot, layer ingredients as follows: lentils, potatoes, water, bouillon cube, celery, onions, garlic, salt, pepper, cinnamon, Italian seasonings, carrots and eggplant.
- Cover and heat on low for 6 hours.
- Stir in diced tomatoes, cream cheese and eggs. Cover and cook on low one more hour.

Curried Chicken Thighs with Potatoes

(Ready in about 8 hours | Servings 8)

INGREDIENTS
- 1 tablespoon curry powder
- 1 teaspoon ground cloves
- 1 teaspoon ground nutmeg
- 1 teaspoon ground ginger
- 2 pounds chicken thighs, boneless, skinless cubed
- 1 teaspoon olive oil
- 1 medium-sized yellow onion, chopped
- 2 cloves garlic, chopped
- 1 chili pepper, minced
- 1 ½ pounds red skin potatoes, cubed
- 1 cup coconut milk

DIRECTIONS
- In a medium-sized mixing bowl, whisk the curry powder, cloves, nutmeg, and ginger. Cut the chicken thighs into bite-sized pieces. Add the chicken to the bowl; toss to coat evenly.
- Heat olive oil in a skillet; sauté seasoned chicken pieces until they start to brown. Add to the crock pot.
- Add the rest of the ingredients. Stir to combine. Cook approximately 8 hours on low heat setting.

Yummy Evening Pear Clafoutis

(Ready in about 3 hours | Servings 4)

INGREDIENTS
- 2 pears, cored
- 1/2 cup rice flour
- 1/2 cup arrowroot starch
- 1 teaspoon baking soda
- 1 teaspoon baking powder
- 1/2 teaspoon xanthan gum
- A pinch of salt
- 1/4 cup sugar

- 1 teaspoon cloves
- 1/2 teaspoon grated nutmeg
- 1 teaspoon ground cinnamon
- 2 tablespoons vegetable shortening, melted
- 2 eggs
- 1 cup milk
- Maple syrup for garnish

DIRECTIONS
- Cut the pears into chunks and transfer them to the crock pot.
- In a large-sized mixing bowl, whisk together the rice flour, arrowroot starch, baking soda, baking powder, xanthan gum, salt, sugar, cloves, nutmeg and cinnamon.
- To make the batter, create a well in the centre of the dry ingredients; add shortening, eggs, and milk. Stir well to combine.
- Pour batter over pear chunks in the crock pot. Vent a lid of the crock pot with a chopstick.
- Cook on high for 3 hours. Serve with maple syrup.

Evening Risotto with Apples

(Ready in about 9 hours | Servings 6)

INGREDIENTS
- 1/4 cup butter, melted
- 1 ½ cups Carnaroli rice
- 3 apples, peeled, cored, and sliced
- 1/4 teaspoon ground cloves
- 1 teaspoon ground cinnamon
- 1/4 teaspoon kosher salt
- 1/3 cup brown sugar
- 1 cup water
- 2 cups whole milk
- 1 cup apple juice

DIRECTIONS
- Add the butter and rice to your crock pot; stir to coat.
- Add the rest of ingredients; stir well to combine.
- Cover with a lid and cook on low for 9 hours. Serve warm.

Cheese and Bread Casserole

(Ready in about 3 hours | Servings 8)

INGREDIENTS
- 1 tablespoon butter, melted
- 8 ounces Gruyère cheese, shredded
- 8 ounces cream cheese, shredded
- 8 slices bread
- 2 cups milk
- 4 eggs
- Salt, to taste
- 1/2 teaspoon dried basil
- 1/4 teaspoon paprika
- Chopped fresh chives, as garnish

DIRECTIONS
- Treat a crock pot with butter.
- In a mixing bowl, combine the cheeses; reserve.
- Tear the slices of bread into pieces; transfer to the crock pot. Place cheese mixture on the bread layer. Alternate layers, ending with the bread.
- In a small-sized mixing bowl, whisk remaining ingredients, except chives. Pour over the layers in the crock pot.
- Set the crock pot to low and cook for 3 hours. Serve garnished with fresh chives and enjoy!

French-Style Sandwiches

(Ready in about 2 hours | Servings 12)

INGREDIENTS
- 1 cup leeks, chopped
- 1 beef bottom round roast
- 1 cup water
- 1/2 cup dry red wine
- 1 envelope au jus gravy mix
- Salt, to taste
- 1/4 teaspoon freshly ground black pepper
- 1/4 teaspoon red pepper flakes, crushed
- French bread

DIRECTIONS
- Line bottom of the crock pot with the leeks.
- Add roast to the crock pot on top of the leeks.
- Next, add remaining ingredients, except bread; vent a lid and cook on low for 2 hours.
- Cut the roast into thin slices. Serve on French bread. Use the sauce for dipping.

Bratwurst and Sauerkraut Pitas

(Ready in about 2 hours 30 minutes | Servings 6)

INGREDIENTS
- 2 tablespoons olive oil
- 2 pounds sauerkraut, drained
- 1 large-sized apple, cored and chopped
- 1 teaspoon ground cumin
- 1 teaspoon celery seeds
- 6 bratwursts
- 1/2 cup dry white wine
- 2 bay leaves
- 5-6 black peppercorns
- 1 tablespoon mustard
- 6 pita loaves

DIRECTIONS
- Heat olive oil in a heavy skillet over medium heat. Sauté the sauerkraut and apple until the sauerkraut is soft and the liquids are reduced. Add cumin and celery seeds and gently stir to combine.
- In a separate non-stick skillet, brown the bratwurst on all sides over medium heat; drain. Pour in white wine; add bay leaves and peppercorns; cook an additional 10 minutes.
- To make the sandwiches: roll bratwursts and sauerkraut into the pita loaves. Add mustard and wrap the sandwiches in aluminium foil. Pour water to coat the bottom of the crock pot.

- Place the sandwiches in the crock pot. Heat on a high setting for about 2 hours.

Romantic Winter Dinner

(Ready in about 2 hours 20 minutes | Servings 6)

INGREDIENTS

- 6 spicy sausages
- 6 long sourdough rolls
- 2 tablespoons mustard
- 2 tablespoons tomato ketchup
- 6 pickles, sliced

DIRECTIONS
- Heat a non-stick skillet over medium flame. Then, sauté the sausages until thoroughly cooked and browned; drain.
- Next, cut off the tips of the sourdough rolls. Make sandwiches with sausage and mustard.
- Next, wrap the sandwiches in a foil; arrange on a trivet in the crock pot. Then, you need to pour lukewarm water around the base of the trivet.
- Cover with a lid and heat on a high setting for 2 hours. Serve with ketchup and pickles.

Hot Pita Sandwiches

(Ready in about 2 hours 15 minutes | Servings 6)

INGREDIENTS

- 1/2 pound roast beef
- 2 tablespoons canola oil
- 1/4 teaspoon black pepper
- 1/4 teaspoon paprika
- 1/2 teaspoon sea salt
- 1 teaspoon dried thyme
- 1 teaspoon granulated garlic
- 12 slices of pita bread
- 1/2 pound ham
- 1/2 pound mozzarella cheese

DIRECTIONS
- Slice the beef into thin strips. Heat canola oil in a skillet over medium heat. Sprinkle with spices. Sauté the beef strips until browned.
- To make the sandwiches; place browned meat, ham and mozzarella cheese on each pita bread.
- Wrap the pitas in foil; place the sandwiches on a trivet in the crock pot. Pour lukewarm water around the base of the trivet.
- Cover and heat on a high setting for 2 hours. Serve warm with your favorite salad.

Turkey and Bacon Sandwiches

(Ready in about 2 hours | Servings 6)

INGREDIENTS

- 12 slices bacon
- 12 slices bread
- 1/4 cup mayonnaise
- 1/2 pound turkey, sliced
- 2 tomatoes, sliced
- Sea salt to taste
- 1/4 teaspoon ground black pepper
- 1/4 teaspoon cayenne pepper
- 1/2 teaspoon garlic powder
- 1/4 pound Swiss cheese, sliced

DIRECTIONS
- In a heavy skillet, over medium heat, brown the bacon until crispy; drain.
- Toast the slices of bread.
- Make the sandwich layers in the following order: bread, mayonnaise, turkey, bacon, tomato, spices and cheese, ending with the bread slices.
- Wrap the sandwiches in foil and arrange on a trivet in your crock pot. Pour lukewarm water around the base of the trivet. Cover; set the crock pot on a high and cook 1 to 2 hours.

Kicked Up Pears with Cheese

(Ready in about 2 hours | Servings 4)

INGREDIENTS

- 2 ounces sharp cheese, thinly sliced
- 4 small sourdough buns
- 1/4 cup orange marmalade
- 1/2 medium-sized pear, thinly sliced
- 2 tablespoons blue cheese, crumbled

DIRECTIONS
- Place slices of cheese on bottoms of sourdough buns.
- Top with orange marmalade, pear, blue cheese; finally, place bun tops.
- Wrap each sandwich in foil and place in the crock pot.
- Cover and cook on low heat setting about 2 hours.

Oatmeal with Veggies and Cheese

(Ready in about 8 hours | Servings 4)

INGREDIENTS

- 1 cup steel cut oats
- 3 cups vegetable broth
- 1 cup dry white wine
- 3/4 cup mushrooms, thinly sliced
- 1 large-sized carrot, thinly sliced
- 1 celery rib, chopped
- 1 leek (white part only), thinly sliced
- 2 cloves garlic, minced
- 1 teaspoon dried thyme leaves
- 1 teaspoon dried basil,
- 1 teaspoon salt
- 1/2 teaspoon white pepper
- 3/4 cup Parmesan cheese, grated

DIRECTIONS
- Combine all ingredients, except Parmesan cheese, in the crock pot.

- ✓ Cover and cook on low 8 hours.
- ✓ Stir in cheese. Let stand until cheese is melted and serve warm.

Creamy Polenta with Roasted Pepper

(Ready in about 1 hour 30 minutes | Servings 6)

INGREDIENTS

- 1 cup yellow cornmeal
- 2 ½ cups water
- 2 tablespoons butter
- Salt, to taste
- 1/4 teaspoon ground black pepper
- 1/3 cup coarsely chopped roasted red pepper
- 1/2 cup Parmesan cheese, grated

DIRECTIONS

- ✓ Mix cornmeal and water in a crock pot; cover and cook on high heat setting for 1 ½ hours; you need to stir once after 45 minutes.
- ✓ Add remaining ingredients during last 15 minutes of cooking time.
- ✓ Serve with some extra butter and paprika if desired.

Garlicky Polenta with Yellow Onion

(Ready in about 1 hour 30 minutes | Servings 6)

INGREDIENTS

- 1 tablespoon olive oil
- 1/4 cup yellow onion, finely chopped
- 5 cloves garlic
- 3/4 cup yellow cornmeal
- 2 cups water
- 2 tablespoons margarine
- Salt, to taste
- 1 teaspoon dried basil leaves
- 1/4 teaspoon ground black pepper

DIRECTIONS

- ✓ In a small cast-iron skillet, heat olive oil over medium-low heat. Sauté the onion and garlic 2 to 3 minutes or until onion is just tender and garlic is lightly browned and fragrant.
- ✓ Combine together yellow cornmeal and water in a crock pot; cover and cook on high for about 1 ½ hours; stir once after 45 minutes.
- ✓ Add sautéed onion and garlic as well as the rest of ingredients during last
- ✓ minutes of cooking. Serve warm with goat cheese or blue cheese.

Rice Torta with Spinach and Cheese

(Ready in about 3 hours | Servings 6)

INGREDIENTS

- 1 cup Basmati rice, cooked until al dente
- 1 tablespoon butter
- 1 ½ cup frozen spinach, thawed and squeezed dry
- 2 large-sized eggs, lightly beaten
- 1/2 cup onion, each: finely chopped
- 2 plum tomatoes, diced
- 3/4 cup mozzarella cheese, shredded
- 1/2 teaspoon salt
- 1/8 teaspoon pepper
- Oil-cured black olives, as garnish

DIRECTIONS

- ✓ In a bowl, combine rice, butter, spinach, and eggs; mix well to combine. Spoon into a greased spring form pan.
- ✓ Add remaining ingredients, except olives. Place your spring form pan on rack in your crock pot.
- ✓ Cover and cook on low about 3 hours or until set.
- ✓ Cut into 6 wedges; serve with olives.

Saucy Spicy Vegetables

(Ready in about 3 hours | Servings 6)

INGREDIENTS

- 2 tablespoons olive oil
- 1 red bell peppers, sliced
- 1 green bell pepper, sliced
- 1 yellow bell pepper, sliced
- 2 medium-sized zucchini, sliced
- 1 large-sized potato, peeled and diced
- 1 yellow onion, sliced
- 5-6 garlic cloves, peeled
- 1 teaspoon sea salt
- 1 teaspoon dried basil leaves
- 1 teaspoon dried oregano olives
- 1/2 teaspoon dried thyme
- 1/2 teaspoon ground black pepper
- 1 cup vegetable broth

DIRECTIONS

- ✓ Grease your crock pot with olive oil. Add vegetables and sprinkle with spices. Pour in vegetable broth.
- ✓ Cook 3 hours on high, stirring every hour.
- ✓ Serve warm as a healthy and light dinner. You can also serve with your favorite meat entrée.

Healthy Artichokes with Lemon Sauce

(Ready in about 3 hours | Servings 8)

INGREDIENTS

- 8 artichokes
- 3 cups water
- 1 ½ teaspoon sea salt
- 1/2 teaspoon white pepper
- 1/4 cup fresh lemon juice
- Cream cheese as garnish

DIRECTIONS

- ✓ Trim artichokes by cutting off the stems; then, cut 1-inch off the tops. Transfer to the crock pot. Pour in 3 cups of water.
- ✓ In a mixing bowl, combine together salt, pepper and lemon. Pour into the crock pot.

- Cover with a lid and cook on high about 3 hours.
- Serve with cream cheese and enjoy!

FAST SNACKS RECIPES

Party-Pleasing Fondue

(Ready in about 4 hours | Servings 12)

INGREDIENTS

- 2 cloves garlic, cut into halves
- 2 cups milk
- 1 cup sparkling white grape juice
- A few drops Tabasco sauce
- 1/4 cup all-purpose flour
- 1 teaspoon onion powder
- 1 teaspoon mustard seeds
- 1/2 teaspoon paprika
- 4 cups sharp cheese, cubed
- 4 cups semi-soft cheese, cubed

DIRECTIONS

- Rub the inside of the crock pot with the garlic.
- Add the milk, sparkling grape juice, and Tabasco sauce to the crock pot.
- Add remaining ingredients to a large zip-closure bag. Then, shake to mix well. Transfer to the crock pot.
- Cover and cook on low until heated through or for 4 hours.
- Serve with roasted asparagus spears or pickle slices.

Red Currant Jelly Meatballs

(Ready in about 6 hours | Servings 8)

INGREDIENTS

- 2 tablespoons olive oil
- 2 pounds precooked meatballs, frozen
- 1 cup red currant jelly
- 1 (12-ounce) jar chili sauce

DIRECTIONS

- Add the olive oil to the bag of meatballs; toss to coat as good as you can. Transfer to the crock pot. Cover and cook for 4 hours on high.
- In a measuring cup or a mixing bowl, mix the chili sauce with the red currant jelly. Pour over the meatballs in the crock pot.
- Cover and cook on low for 2 hours.

Jalapeño Corn and Cheese Dip

(Ready in about 2 hours | Servings 6)

INGREDIENTS

- 4 slices bacon, diced
- 6 cups canned whole kernel corn, drained
- 2 jalapeños, seeded and diced
- 1 cup Swiss cheese, shredded
- 1/2 cup sour cream
- 1 cup cream cheese, cubed
- 1/4 cup grated Parmesan cheese
- 1/2 teaspoon ground black pepper
- Salt to taste
- 1 heaping tablespoon cilantro, chopped

DIRECTIONS

- Brown bacon in a cast-iron skillet about 8 minutes. Drain and set aside.
- Place kernel corn, jalapeños, Swiss cheese, sour cream, cream cheese and Parmesan into a crock pot.
- Season with black pepper and salt. Cover and cook on low heat setting for
- 2 hours. Sprinkle with chopped cilantro.
- Serve with bell pepper strips or celery sticks.

Picante Bean Dipping Sauce

(Ready in about 2 hours | Servings 12)

INGREDIENTS

- 1 cup picante sauce
- 4 cups of refried beans
- 2 cups Cheddar cheese, shredded
- 1/4 fresh parsley, chopped
- 1/2 cup shallots, chopped

DIRECTIONS

- Place all of the ingredients in your crock pot.
- Cook covered on low for 2 hours.
- Serve with pickle slices or baby carrots.

Saucy Tomato Meatballs

(Ready in about 4 hours | Servings 8)

INGREDIENTS

- 2 pounds veal, coarsely ground
- 1 clove garlic, crushed
- 1/4 pound Mozzarella cheese, grated
- 3 eggs, lightly beaten
- 1 tablespoon cayenne pepper
- 1/2 ground black pepper
- 1 teaspoon salt
- 1 teaspoon dried oregano leaves
- 1 cup bread crumbs
- 1/2 cup whole milk
- 2 tablespoons olive oil
- 2 tomatoes, diced

- 1 cup tomato juice

DIRECTIONS
- ✓ In a large-sized mixing bowl, combine all ingredients, except tomatoes and tomato juice.
- ✓ Shape the mixture into ¾-inch balls.
- ✓ Heat olive oil in a saucepan over medium-high heat. Sauté the meatballs for about 10 minutes.
- ✓ Arrange sautéed meatballs in the crock pot.
- ✓ Pour the tomatoes and tomato juice over the meatballs in the crock pot.
- ✓ Cover and slow cook for 3 to 4 hours. Transfer to a serving platter and serve with skewers!

Turkey Meatballs with Paprika Sauce

(Ready in about 6 hours | Servings 6)

INGREDIENTS
- 12 frozen turkey meatballs, defrosted
- 1 teaspoon olive oil
- 1/2 cup green onions, chopped
- 2-3 cloves garlic, minced
- 1 celery rib, chopped
- 1 carrot, diced
- 4 cups canned tomatoes, crushed
- 2 tablespoons tomato paste
- 1/2 teaspoon kosher salt
- 1/2 teaspoon ground black pepper
- 1 teaspoon dried oregano leaves
- 1 teaspoon dried thyme leaves
- 1 teaspoon paprika

DIRECTIONS
- ✓ Place the meatballs in the crock pot.
- ✓ To make the sauce: Heat olive oil in a large non-stick pan. Sauté the onions, garlic, celery and carrot until the vegetables start to soften.
- ✓ Add the rest of the ingredients and continue cooking over medium-low heat until most of the liquid has evaporated.
- ✓ Pour prepared sauce over the meatballs in the crock pot. Slow cook about
- ✓ 6 hours on low.
- ✓ Serve with mini pumpernickel.

Beer-Braised Meatballs

(Ready in about 7 hours | Servings 10)

INGREDIENTS
- 2 medium-sized yellow onions, finely chopped
- 1 (16-ounce) package frozen meatballs
- 1 (12-ounce) can nonalcoholic beer
- 1 cup tomato paste
- 1/2 cup chili sauce
- Salt, to taste
- Ground black pepper, to taste
- 1 teaspoon dried tarragon
- 1/4 cup pickle relish

DIRECTIONS
- ✓ Arrange onions in a crock pot; add meatballs.
- ✓ In a mixing bowl or a measuring cup, combine remaining ingredients; pour into the crock pot.
- ✓ Cover and cook on low for about 7 hours. Serve mini pumpernickel and mustard, if desired.

Saucy Cocktail Franks

(Ready in about 4 hours | Servings 8)

INGREDIENTS
- 1/4 cup tomato sauce
- 2 tablespoons apple juice
- 2/3 cup apricot preserves
- 2 tablespoons apple cider vinegar
- 3 cloves garlic, minced
- 1 shallot, chopped
- 1/3 cup chicken stock
- 2 tablespoons soy sauce
- 1/4 teaspoon cayenne pepper
- 1/4 teaspoon black pepper
- 2 pounds mini cocktail frankfurters

DIRECTIONS
- ✓ In a crock pot, combine all ingredients, except franks; mix well to combine. Then, add franks.
- ✓ Cover and cook on high for 3 to 4 hours.
- ✓ Serve with toothpicks, garnished with mustard.

Best Cocktail Sausages

(Ready in about 7 hours | Servings 8)

INGREDIENTS
- 1 cup sweet chilli sauce
- 2 tablespoons apple cider vinegar
- 3 cloves garlic, minced
- 1 shallot, chopped
- 1 cup vegetable stock
- 1/2 cup cranberry sauce
- 2 tablespoons tamari sauce
- 1/4 teaspoon cayenne pepper
- 1/4 teaspoon black pepper
- 1 ½ pounds mini cocktail sausages

DIRECTIONS
- ✓ In your crock pot, arrange all ingredients. Stir to combine.
- ✓ Cover and cook 7 hours on high.
- ✓ Serve with cocktail sticks and enjoy.

Yummy Cereal Snack Mix

(Ready in about 3 hours | Servings 20)

INGREDIENTS
- 2 tablespoons margarine, melted
- 1/2 teaspoon onion powder
- 1 teaspoon garlic powder

- 1 teaspoon paprika
- 1 teaspoon Italian seasoning mix
- 1 teaspoon chili powder
- 1 tablespoon soy sauce
- 2 cups corn cereal squares
- 2 cups crispy wheat cereal squares
- 1 cup pretzels
- 1/2 cup roasted almonds
- 1/2 cup roasted walnuts

DIRECTIONS
- ✓ Place all ingredients into your crock pot, Stir well to combine.
- ✓ Cook on low for 2 to 3 hours, stirring every 30 minutes.
- ✓ Spread onto a baking sheet and allow to cool. Then, store in an airtight container.

Easy Smoked Pecans

(Ready in about 6 hours | Servings 24)

INGREDIENTS
- 8 cups raw pecans
- 3 tablespoons butter, melted
- 1 tablespoon tamari sauce
- 2 tablespoons Worcestershire sauce
- 1 teaspoons garlic powder
- 1 teaspoon celery seeds
- 1 teaspoon smoked salt, to taste
- 1/2 teaspoon white pepper
- 1 teaspoon smoked paprika

DIRECTIONS
- ✓ Add all of the ingredients to your crock pot. Stir to coat the pecans evenly.
- ✓ Cover and cook for 6 hours on low, stirring occasionally.
- ✓ Please store smoked pecans in a covered container.

Easy Summer Snack

(Ready in about 2 hours | Servings 16)

INGREDIENTS
- 1 pound raw pistachios
- 2 tablespoons olive oil
- 1/2 teaspoon cayenne pepper
- 1/2 teaspoon ground black pepper
- 1 teaspoon seasoned salt
- 1 teaspoon sugar

DIRECTIONS
- ✓ Put all ingredients into your crock pot.
- ✓ Cover and slow cook for 2 hours, stirring after 1 hour.
- ✓ Store in an airtight container.

Cajun Nut Mix

(Ready in about 3 hours | Servings 16)

INGREDIENTS

- 2 pounds almonds
- 1 pound walnuts, halved
- 2 tablespoons olive oil
- 2 tablespoons Cajun seasoning blend

DIRECTIONS
- ✓ Add all of the ingredients to the crock pot. Stir to combine; then cover and cook on low for 1 hour, stirring occasionally. Adjust seasonings to taste.
- ✓ Slow cook for 2 hours longer, stirring after 1 hour.

Spiced Party Pecans

(Ready in about 2 hours 30 minutes | Servings 16)

INGREDIENTS
- 2 pounds pecans
- 2 tablespoons butter
- 2 tablespoons Cajun seasoning blend
- 1 teaspoon salt
- 1 teaspoon freshly ground black pepper
- 1 teaspoon paprika

DIRECTIONS
- ✓ Place all of the ingredients into the crock pot.
- ✓ Set the crock pot to low, cover with a lid and slow cook your mix for about 2 ½ hours.
- ✓ Let pecans cool completely. Serve and enjoy!

Cinnamon Vanilla Walnuts

(Ready in about 2 hours 15 minutes | Servings 16)

INGREDIENTS
- 1 stick butter, melted
- 1 pound walnut halves
- 1 teaspoon cinnamon
- 2/3 cup powdered sugar
- 1 teaspoon vanilla
- A pinch of salt

DIRECTIONS
- ✓ Combine all of the ingredients in your crock pot.
- ✓ Cover with a lid and cook for 15 minutes on high.
- ✓ Next, turn heat to low, remove the lid and cook for 2 hours, stirring occasionally.
- ✓ Let stand to cool completely before serving and storing.

Curried Mixed Nuts

(Ready in about 2 hours 15 minutes | Servings 16)

INGREDIENTS

- 3 tablespoons coconut oil
- 2 tablespoons curry powder
- 1 tablespoon chili powder
- 1 tablespoon dried basil leaves
- 1 teaspoon smoked salt
- 3 cups walnuts, halved

- 3 cups pecans
- 2 cups almonds
- 1/2 cups pumpkin seeds

DIRECTIONS
- ✓ Treat the inside of a crock pot with coconut oil.
- ✓ Place remaining ingredients in the crock pot.
- ✓ Slow cook about 2 hours on low heat setting.
- ✓ Let stand to cool completely before serving and storing. You can freeze leftovers.

Chili Honey Snack Mix

(Ready in about 4 hours | Servings 12)

INGREDIENTS
- 2 teaspoons butter, melted
- 1 cup pecans
- 1/2 cup peanuts
- 1/4 cup balsamic vinegar
- 1/2 cup brown sugar
- 2 teaspoons cinnamon
- 1 teaspoon chili powder
- 1 teaspoon salt
- 2 teaspoons honey

DIRECTIONS
- ✓ Grease the inside of a crock pot with melted butter.
- ✓ Add remaining ingredients and cook on low for 4 hours.
- ✓ Pour this nut mixture out onto a baking sheet. Allow to cool; then, store in a container with an airtight lid.

Easy Velveeta Dipping Sauce

(Ready in about 3 hours | Servings 12)

INGREDIENTS
- 1 (15-ounce) can chili
- 2 roated bell peppers, chopped
- 1 pound Velveeta cheese, cubed

DIRECTIONS
- ✓ Add all ingredients to the crock pot.
- ✓ Cover and cook on low for 3 hours, stirring every half hour.
- ✓ Serve with bread sticks or crackers.

Mexican-Style Appetizer

(Ready in about 6 hours | Servings 24)

INGREDIENTS
- 3 pounds lean ground beef, cooked and drained
- 1 medium-sized yellow onion, sliced
- 2-3 cloves garlic, minced
- 1 (15-ounce) can refried beans
- 1 cup tomato paste
- 1/2 cup tomato juice
- 1 teaspoon cayenne peppers
- Salt to taste
- 1 cup salsa
- 2 pounds cream cheese, cut into cubes

DIRECTIONS
- ✓ In a wide pan, brown ground beef over medium heat for about 10 minutes. Transfer to the crock pot.
- ✓ Add the rest of the ingredients and stir to combine.
- ✓ Cook covered on low for 4 to 6 hours, stirring every 30 minutes.
- ✓ Taste for seasoning and add more spices if needed.

Old-Fashion Chicken Liver Pâté

(Ready in about 3 hours | Servings 16)

INGREDIENTS
- 1 pound chicken livers
- 1/4 cup red onion, finely chopped
- 1 apple, peeled, cored and chopped
- 1/2 cup butter, room temperature
- 1/2 teaspoon paprika
- 1/2 teaspoon ground black pepper
- Salt, to taste

DIRECTIONS
- ✓ Cook all ingredients in a crock pot about 3 hours.
- ✓ Transfer to a food processor. Puree until creamy and uniform.
- ✓ Serve chilled with crackers.

Smoked Salmon Pâté

(Ready in about 3 hours | Servings 10)

INGREDIENTS
- 1 ½ cups smoked salmon
- 2 cups cream cheese
- 2 tablespoons milk
- 1 tablespoon fresh lemon juice
- 1 teaspoon soy sauce
- 1/2 teaspoon ground black pepper
- 1/2 teaspoon paprika
- Fresh parsley, for garnish

DIRECTIONS
- ✓ Place all of the ingredients, except fresh parsley, in your crock pot.
- ✓ Slow cook about 3 hours.
- ✓ Sprinkle with fresh parsley and serve chilled.

Vegetarian Lentil Pâté

(Ready in about 2 hours | Servings 8)

INGREDIENTS
- 1 cup dried lentils
- 2 cups vegetable stock
- 3 tablespoons butter
- 1 teaspoon celery seeds
- 1 tablespoon cilantro
- 1/2 teaspoon seasoned salt

- 1/2 teaspoon ground black pepper

DIRECTIONS
- ✓ Simply arrange all of the ingredients in your crock pot.
- ✓ Cook covered for 2 hours on high heat setting.
- ✓ Serve chilled with the pickles slices, celery sticks or tortilla chips.

Appetizer Meatballs with Barbecue Sauce

(Ready in about 4 hours | Servings 12)

INGREDIENTS
- 1/2 pound ground pork
- 1 pound lean ground beef
- 1 small-sized onion, finely chopped
- 2 cloves garlic, minced
- 1 large-sized egg
- 1/3 cup dry bread crumbs
- 1/2 teaspoon seasoned salt
- 1/2 teaspoon red pepper flakes, crushed
- 1/2 teaspoon pepper ground black pepper
- 2 cups barbecue sauce
- 1 cup orange marmalade

DIRECTIONS
- ✓ Mix pork, beef, onion, garlic, egg, bread crumbs, salt, red pepper and black pepper. Mix well to combine; shape this mixture into 24 meatballs.
- ✓ Add meatballs to the crock pot. Then, add barbecue sauce and orange marmalade.
- ✓ Cook covered about 4 hours. Serve warm with cocktail sticks!

Hot Pineapple Chutney

(Ready in about 4 hours | Servings 6)

INGREDIENTS
- 1 cups fresh mango, cubed
- 3 cups fresh pineapple, cubed
- 2 tablespoons shallots, minced
- 2 teaspoons garlic, minced
- 1/4 cup balsamic vinegar
- 3 tablespoons lemon juice
- 1/4 cup sugar
- 1 teaspoon honey
- 1 jalapeño, minced

DIRECTIONS
- ✓ Put all ingredients into your crock pot. Stir well to combine.
- ✓ Turn the crock pot to high and cook 3 hours.
- ✓ Then, uncover and continue cooking for 1 hour on high.

Black Bean Dipping Sauce

(Ready in about 2 hours | Servings 24)

INGREDIENTS
- 1 teaspoon extra-virgin olive oil
- 1 poblano pepper, minced
- 2-3 cloves garlic, minced
- 1 medium-sized onion, chopped
- 1/2 teaspoon cayenne pepper
- 1 teaspoon celery seeds
- 1/4 cup reduced-fat sour cream
- 2 tablespoons lemon juice
- 4 cups canned black beans, drained and rinsed

DIRECTIONS
- ✓ Heat olive oil in a non-stick saucepan. Sauté the poblano, garlic and onion for about 10 minutes until tender.
- ✓ Add remaining ingredients and stir to combine. Mash the mixture.
- ✓ Add to the crock pot and cook on low for 2 hours.

Hot Corn Bean Dip

(Ready in about 2 hours | Servings 16)

INGREDIENTS
- 1 teaspoon olive oil
- 1/2 cup shallots, minced
- 2 cloves garlic, minced
- 1 jalapeño pepper, minced
- A few drops of hot sauce
- 1/2 teaspoon paprika
- 1/2 teaspoon cumin
- 2 tablespoons fresh lemon juice
- 1/4 cup cream cheese
- 2 cups canned cannellini beans, drained and rinsed
- 1/2 cup corn kernels
- 2 tablespoons fresh cilantro, coarsely chopped

DIRECTIONS
- ✓ Heat olive oil in a heavy skillet. Sauté the shallots, garlic and jalapeño until soft and fragrant or about 3 minutes.
- ✓ Pour into a large-sized mixing bowl. Add remaining ingredients, except cilantro.
- ✓ Mash with a potato masher. Transfer to the crock pot.
- ✓ Cook on low for 2 hours. Sprinkle with fresh chopped cilantro and serve with tortilla chips or pita chips, if desired.

Vegetable-Rich Dipping Sauce

(Ready in about 1 hour | Servings 16)

INGREDIENTS
- 2 cups cauliflower florets, steamed
- 2 cups broccoli florets, steamed
- 1 medium-sized onion, chopped
- 1 large-sized carrot, chopped
- 1 cup fresh spinach
- 1 jalapeño, minced
- 1 tablespoon Worcestershire sauce
- 1 cup plain yogurt
- Sea salt, to taste
- 1/4 teaspoon ground black pepper

- 1 tablespoon lemon juice

DIRECTIONS
- ✓ Place the cauliflower florets, broccoli florets, onion, carrot, spinach, jalapeño and Worcestershire sauce in a food processor.
- ✓ Pulse until the mixture is creamy and smooth. Add the yogurt, salt, black pepper, and lemon juice. Pulse again.
- ✓ Pour this mixture into the crock pot. Cover and cook for 1 hour on low heat setting. Serve chilled with soft pretzels or sliced baguette.

Eggplant Dip with Tahini and Cheese

(Ready in about 2 hours | Servings 12)

INGREDIENTS
- 2 large-sized eggplants, sliced
- 2-3 cloves garlic, minced
- 1 tablespoon fresh parsley
- 1/2 teaspoon dried thyme
- 1 teaspoon dried basil leaves
- 1 teaspoon dired oregano leaves
- 1 teaspoon sea salt
- 1/2 teaspoon ground black pepper
- 2 tablespoons lime juice
- 2 tablespoons tahini
- 1 cup Swiss cheese, grated

DIRECTIONS
- ✓ Arrange eggplant, garlic, parsley, thyme, basil, oregano, salt and black pepper in a crock pot. Slow cook on high for about 2 hours.
- ✓ Allow to cool; then, add lime and tahini. Pulse in a food processor until your desired consistency is reached.
- ✓ Reheat the mixture in a crock pot; add Swiss cheese and allow to melt. Serve warm or at room temperature. Serve with pumpernickel pretzels, raw vegetables or mini pitas.

Seafood Artichoke Dip

(Ready in about 1 hour | Servings 20)

INGREDIENTS
- 2 cups sour cream
- 1 cup reduced-fat cream cheese
- 1 cup leeks, chopped
- 1 tablespoon soy sauce
- 12 ounces artichoke hearts
- 1 cup shrimp
- 1 cup crabmeat

DIRECTIONS
- ✓ In a food processor, place sour cream, cream cheese, leeks, soy sauce and artichoke hearts.
- ✓ Pulse until everything is well combined.
- ✓ Scrape into a crock pot. Add shrimp and crabmeat; stir well to combine.
- ✓ Cook 40 minutes on low. Garnish with lemon slices and serve with sesame pretzels or baked potato chips.

Delicious Cashew Snacks

(Ready in about 2 hours 30 minutes | Servings 24)

INGREDIENTS
- 6 cups cashews
- 3 tablespoons butter, melted
- 1 tablespoon brown sugar
- A pinch of salt
- 2 tablespoons dried thyme
- 3 tablespoons dried rosemary leaves
- 3/4 teaspoon paprika
- 1/2 teaspoon onion powder
- 1/2 teaspoon garlic powder

DIRECTIONS
- ✓ Heat your crock pot on high for 15 minutes; then add cashews. Drizzle melted butter over cashews.
- ✓ Sprinkle cashews with combined spices and toss.
- ✓ Cover with a lid and cook on low about 2 hours, stirring every hour.
- ✓ Next, uncover and cook 30 minutes longer, stirring occasionally.
- ✓ Serve cool or at room temperature.

Curried Honey Cashews

(Ready in about 2 hours 30 minutes | Servings 24)

INGREDIENTS
- 3 cups cashews, whole
- 1 tablespoon sea salt
- 1 tablespoon honey
- 1 teaspoon red pepper flakes, crushed
- 2 tablespoons curry powder
- 2 tablespoons water
- 1 teaspoon olive oil

DIRECTIONS
- ✓ Set a crock pot to high and add cashews.
- ✓ Add remaining ingredients and toss to combine.
- ✓ Cook on low heat setting about 2 hours, stirring every hour. Uncover and cook an additional 30 minutes, stirring occasionally. Serve.

Party Pepper Almonds

(Ready in about 2 hours 30 minutes | Servings 24)

INGREDIENTS
- 6 cups whole almonds
- 4 tablespoons margarine, melted
- 1/2 teaspoon turmeric
- 1 teaspoon garlic powder
- 1 teaspoon ground black or red peppercorns
- 1 teaspoon ground green peppercorns

DIRECTIONS
- ✓ Heat a crock pot on high for 15 minutes; then, add almonds.

- Drizzle melted margarine over almonds and toss to combine; sprinkle with turmeric, garlic powder, and peppercorns; toss again. Turn heat to low; cook covered 2 hours; stir every 30 minutes.
- Next, increase heat to high; uncover and cook 30 minutes longer, stirring every 15 minutes.
- You can store the snack in a sealed container for up to 3 weeks.

Curried Party Mix

(Ready in about 2 hours 30 minutes | Servings 24)

INGREDIENTS

- 1 cup walnuts
- 1 cup almonds
- 1 cup peanuts
- 1 cup hulled sunflower seeds
- 4 tablespoons margarine, melted
- 2 tablespoons sugar
- 1 tablespoon curry powder
- 1 teaspoon garlic powder
- 1 teaspoon ground allspice

DIRECTIONS
- Set the crock pot to high for 15 minutes; add nuts and seeds.
- Drizzle margarine and toss to coat;
- Add combined remaining ingredients. Cover and cook on low heat setting for about 2 hours; stir every 20 minutes.
- Turn heat to high; remove a lid and cook 30 minutes longer, stirring after
- minutes.
- You can store this snack in a sealed container for up to 3 weeks.

Spiced Soy Nuts and Pumpkin Seeds

(Ready in about 2 hours 30 minutes | Servings 24)

INGREDIENTS

- 4 tablespoons butter, melted
- 5 cups roasted soy nuts
- 1 cup hulled pumpkin seeds
- 2 tablespoons sugar
- 1 tablespoon turmeric powder
- 1 tablespoon basil
- 1 teaspoon red pepper flakes
- Sea salt, to taste

DIRECTIONS
- Heat a crock pot on high for 15 minutes.
- Drizzle butter over soy nuts and pumpkin seeds; toss to coat.
- Sprinkle with combined remaining ingredients, cover and cook on low 2 hours, stirring every 15 minutes.
- Next increase heat to high; uncover and cook 30 minutes, stirring after 15 minutes.

Crunchy Colourful Mix

(Ready in about 2 hours | Servings 10)

INGREDIENTS

- 1/2 cup roasted peanuts
- 1 cup sesame sticks
- 3 cups rice cereal squares
- 1/2 cup wasabi peas
- 2 tablespoons butter, melted
- 1 tablespoon soy sauce
- 1 teaspoon paprika
- 1 tablespoon curry powder
- Sugar, to taste
- Sea salt, to taste

DIRECTIONS
- Heat the crock pot on high for 15 minutes; add peanuts, sesame sticks, rice cereal, and wasabi peas.
- Drizzle mixture with combined butter and soy sauce and toss.
- Next, sprinkle the mixture with paprika, curry powder, sugar and salt; toss again.
- Cook on high 1 ½ hours, stirring every 30 minutes. Serve warm or at room temperature.

Indian-Style Dipping Sauce

(Ready in about 2 hours | Servings 10)

INGREDIENTS

- 1 pound cream cheese
- 2 cups sharp cheese, shredded
- 2-3 cloves garlic, minced
- 1/2 cup chopped mango chutney, divided
- 1/3 cup sweet onion, finely chopped
- 1/4 cup Sultanas
- 1–2 teaspoons curry powder
- Veggie stick, as garnish

DIRECTIONS
- Place cream cheese and sharp cheese in a crock pot; cover and cook about
- minutes.
- Then, add remaining ingredients, except veggie sticks; cover and cook 1 to 1 ½ hours.
- Serve with favorite veggie stick and enjoy!

Party Favorite Artichoke Dip

(Ready in about 1 hour 30 minutes | Servings 16)

INGREDIENTS

- 1/2 cup cream cheese, room temperature
- 1/2 cup sharp cheese, grated
- 2 cups canned artichoke hearts, drained and chopped
- 1/2 cup mayonnaise
- 1 teaspoon lemon juice
- 1-2 green onions, sliced
- 1/2 teaspoon sea salt
- 1 teaspoon cayenne pepper
- Dippers: bread sticks

DIRECTIONS
- Melt cheese in a crock pot about 30 minutes.

- ✓ Stir in remaining ingredients, except dippers; cover and cook 1 to 1 ½ hours.
- ✓ Serve with dippers such as bread sticks and enjoy!

Artichoke Spinach Dip

(Ready in about 1 hour 30 minutes | Servings 16)

INGREDIENTS

- 1/2 cup Pecorino Romano, grated
- 1/2 cup cream cheese, room temperature
- 1/2 cup shrimp, chopped
- 2 cups canned artichoke hearts, drained and chopped
- 1/4 cup roasted red pepper, chopped
- 1/2 cup sour cream
- 2 tablespoons mayonnaise
- 1 teaspoon lemon juice
- 1/2 cup scallions, sliced
- 1/2 teaspoon sea salt
- 1 teaspoon cayenne pepper
- Dippers: crackers

DIRECTIONS

- ✓ Place cheese in a crock pot and cook about 30 minutes.
- ✓ Then, add remaining ingredients, except crackers; cook approximately 1 hour.
- ✓ Serve with crackers.

Cheese Pepperoni Dip

(Ready in about 2 hours | Servings 10)

INGREDIENTS

- 1 cup cream cheese
- 1/2 cup scallions, chopped
- 1 ½ cups Swiss cheese, shredded
- 1/2 cup pepperoni, chopped
- 1 teaspoon mustard seeds
- 1/4 teaspoon paprika
- 3/4 cup whole milk
- Chopped fresh chives for garnish
- Dippers: bread sticks

DIRECTIONS

- ✓ Place cheeses in the crock pot and cook about 30 minutes.
- ✓ Stir in remaining ingredients, except chives and dippers.
- ✓ Cover and cook about 1 ½ hours. Sprinkle with chopped chives and serve with bread sticks.

Cereal Mix with Peanuts

(Ready in about 3 hours | Servings 12)

INGREDIENTS

- 5 cups corn cereal
- 4 cups rice cereal
- 2 cups pretzels
- 1 cup breakfast cereal of choice
- 1 cup peanuts
- 1/3 cup butter, melted
- A pinch of black pepper
- 1 teaspoon garlic powder
- 1/2 teaspoon allspice
- 1 tablespoon seasoned salt
- 1/4 cup Worcestershire sauce

DIRECTIONS

- ✓ In your crock pot, place corn cereal, rice cereal, pretzels, breakfast cereal and peanuts.
- ✓ To make the sauce: In a middle-sized mixing bowl or a measuring cup, combine remaining ingredients. Mix well to combine.
- ✓ Drizzle the sauce over the top of the cereal-nut mixture. Toss to combine.
- ✓ Cover with a lid; slow cook on low for 3 hours, stirring every 1 hour. You can store this amazing snack in a sealed container for up to 3 weeks.

Crispy Hot Chicken Taquitos

(Ready in about 8 hours 15 minutes | Servings 8)

INGREDIENTS

- 1 ½ cups cream cheese
- 1/2 cup water
- 4 medium-sized chicken breasts
- 3 jalapeños, roughly chopped
- 1/2 teaspoon onion powder
- 1/2 teaspoon garlic powder
- 1 teaspoon salt
- 16 taco-sized flour tortillas
- 1 ½ cups Monterey jack, shredded
- 1/2 cup Mexican blend cheese
- Green goddess dressing to taste

DIRECTIONS

- ✓ Add cream cheese, water, chicken, jalapeños, onion powder, garlic powder and salt to a crock pot. Cover and cook on low for 8 hours.
- ✓ Meanwhile, preheat the oven to 425 degrees F; oil a cookie sheet with non-stick cooking spray.
- ✓ Cut cooked chicken into shreds with shredder claws or two forks. Remove to the crock pot. Stir to combine.
- ✓ Next, heat flour tortillas in the microwave to soften them up.
- ✓ Place cheese on each tortilla. Top with 3 tablespoons of chicken mixture.
- ✓ Roll stuffed tortillas into log-shape taquitos. Bake taquitos in preheated oven for 15 minutes. Serve with green goddess dressing and enjoy!

Mom's Cocktail Party Mix

(Ready in about 3 hours | Servings 12)

INGREDIENTS

- 9 cups rice cereal
- 1 cup almonds
- 1 cup pine nuts
- 1 cup peanuts

- 1/3 cup margarine, melted
- Cayenne pepper, to taste
- Black pepper, to taste
- 1/2 teaspoon onion powder
- 1/2 teaspoon garlic powder
- 1/2 teaspoon grated nutmeg
- 1 tablespoon seasoned salt
- 1/4 cup Worcestershire sauce
- 2 tablespoons tamari sauce

DIRECTIONS
- ✓ In a crock pot, place rice cereal, almonds, pine nuts and peanuts.
- ✓ To make the sauce, in a mixing bowl, combine the rest of the ingredients. Whisk well to combine.
- ✓ Drizzle the sauce over the top of the mixture in the crock pot. Toss to coat well.
- ✓ Then, slow cook for 3 hours on low, stirring every 1 hour. Keep in a cool
- ✓ dry place for up to 3 weeks.

Candied Cashews and Walnuts

⌀ **(Ready in about 3 hours | Servings 10)**

INGREDIENTS

- 2 cups cashews
- 2 cups walnuts
- 1 ½ cup sugar
- 1 tablespoon ground cinnamon
- 1 egg white
- 1 teaspoon pure almond extract
- 1/4 cup water

DIRECTIONS
- ✓ Place cashews and walnuts into a crock pot prepared with non-stick cooking spray.
- ✓ In a bowl, mix together sugar and cinnamon. Sprinkle over nuts.
- ✓ In another mixing bowl, beat egg white with almond extract until they become frothy.
- ✓ Cook covered 3 hours on low, stirring every 15-20 minutes. Pour water into the crock pot during last 20 minutes.
- ✓ Spread candied nuts out on a parchment paper to cool for 20 minutes.

Sugar-Glazed Pine Nuts and Pecans

⌀ **(Ready in about 3 hours | Servings 10)**

INGREDIENTS

- Butter-flavored cooking spray
- 2 cups pine nuts
- 2 cups pecan halves
- 3/4 teaspoon five-spice powder
- 1 cup sugar
- 1/2 cup powdered sugar
- 1 teaspoon ground cinnamon
- 1 egg white
- 1 teaspoon vanilla
- 1/4 cup water

DIRECTIONS
- ✓ Place pine nuts and pecans into a crock pot prepared with non-stick cooking spray.
- ✓ In a bowl, mix five-spice powder, sugar, powdered sugar and cinnamon. Sprinkle this mixture over nuts in the crock pot.
- ✓ In a separate mixing bowl, beat egg white with vanilla until they become frothy.
- ✓ Cook 3 hours on low, stirring every 20 minutes. Pour water into the crock pot during last 20 minutes of cooking time.
- ✓ Spread pine nuts and pecans out on a cookie sheet to cool for 20 minutes.

Granola and Fruit Mix

⌀ **(Ready in about 1 hour 30 minutes | Servings 16)**

INGREDIENTS

- 3 cups granola
- 2 cups mini pretzel twists
- 1/2 cup sesame sticks, broken into halves
- 2 cups blueberries, coarsely chopped
- 1 cup cranberries, coarsely chopped
- Butter-flavored cooking spray
- 1/2 teaspoon ground nutmeg
- 1 teaspoon ground cinnamon
- 1 teaspoon brown sugar

DIRECTIONS
- ✓ Heat your crock pot on high 15 minutes; add granola, pretzel, sesame sticks, blueberries and cranberries.
- ✓ Spray mixture generously with butter-flavored cooking spray and toss; sprinkle with nutmeg, cinnamon and sugar, and toss to coat.
- ✓ Cook on high 1 ½ hours, stirring every 30 minutes.

Kicked-Up Hot Party Mix

⌀ **(Ready in about 1 hour 30 minutes | Servings 16)**

INGREDIENTS

- 2 cups crackers
- 4 cups baked pita chips
- 1/2 cup almonds
- 1 cup dried pineapple chunks
- Hot red pepper sauce, to taste
- Butter-flavored cooking spray
- 1 teaspoon chili powder
- 1 teaspoon smoked paprika
- 1 teaspoon dried oregano leaves
- 1 teaspoon dried sage leaves
- A pinch of ground black pepper

DIRECTIONS
- ✓ Set a crock pot to high for 15 minutes; add crackers, pita chips, almonds, dried pineapple chunks and red pepper sauce. Generously grease the mixture with the cooking spray; toss to coat
- ✓ Sprinkle with combined herbs and spices. Toss to coat evenly.
- ✓ Remove a lid from the crock pot; cook on high 1 ½ hours, stirring every

✓ minutes.

Cereal and Nut Snack Mix

(Ready in about 1 hour 30 minutes | Servings 16)

INGREDIENTS

- 2 cups oat cereal
- 3 cups rice cereal
- 1 cup sesame sticks
- 1 ½ cups pretzels goldfish
- 1 cup walnuts, halved
- 1 cup almonds
- 1 cup pecans
- 1/2 cup pumpkin seeds
- 1 teaspoon sea salt
- 1/2 teaspoon garlic powder
- 1/4 cup butter, melted
- 3 tablespoons Worcestershire sauce
- 1 teaspoon hot pepper sauce

DIRECTIONS

✓ Set a crock pot to high for about 15 minutes. Add oat cereal, rice cereal, sesame sticks, pretzels, walnuts, almonds, pecans and pumpkin seeds.
✓ Drizzle remaining ingredients over mixture in the crock pot.
✓ Cook on high 1 ½ hours, stirring every 30 minutes.

Summer Pizza Dipping Sauce

(Ready in about 1 hour 30 minutes | Servings 12)

INGREDIENTS

- 2 cups mozzarella cheese, shredded
- 1 pound processed cheese, cubed
- 1/3 cup ripe olives, sliced
- 1 ½ cups pizza sauce
- 1 tablespoon Italian seasoning mix
- 1 cup salami, chopped
- Dippers: tortilla chips

DIRECTIONS

✓ Place mozzarella cheese and processed cheese in a crock pot. Cover and cook for about 30 minutes or until cheese is melted.
✓ Stir in remaining ingredients, except tortilla chips.
✓ Cover with a lid and cook 1 ½ hours. Serve with tortilla chips.

Italian Style Cheese Dip

(Ready in about 1 hour 30 minutes | Servings 12)

INGREDIENTS

- 1 ½ cups cream cheese
- 2 cups mozzarella cheese, shredded
- 1/3 cup roasted pepper, chopped
- 1 cup pizza sauce
- 1/2 cup tomato juice
- 1 teaspoon dried oregano leaves
- 1 teaspoon dried basil leaves
- 1 cup pepperoni, chopped
- 1/3 cup cilantro, chopped
- Dippers: celery sticks

DIRECTIONS

✓ Place cheese in a crock pot. Cover with a lid and cook about 30 minutes.
✓ Stir in remaining ingredients, except celery sticks.
✓ Cover with a lid and cook 1 ½ hours. Serve with celery sticks.

Sauerkraut Beef Dip

(Ready in about 2 hours | Servings 24)

INGREDIENTS

- 1 cup reduced-fat sharp cheese, shredded
- 1 ½ cups cream cheese
- 1 ½ cups sauerkraut, rinsed and drained
- 1 cup lean corned beef, chopped
- 1/4 cup Thousand Island dressing
- 1 tablespoon caraway seeds
- Kosher salt, to taste
- Vegetable sticks, as garnish

DIRECTIONS

✓ Place sharp cheese and cream cheese in a crock pot.
✓ Cover and cook approximately 30 minutes.
✓ Mix in remaining ingredients, except vegetable sticks; cover and cook 1 ½ hours.
✓ Serve with vegetable sticks.

Warm Dried Beef Dip

(Ready in about 2 hours | Servings 24)

INGREDIENTS

- 1 ½ cup cream cheese
- 1 cup reduced-fat mayonnaise
- 1/2 cup green onions, chopped
- 2-3 cloves garlic, minced
- 4 ½ ounces dried beef, chopped
- 1 teaspoon seasoned salt

DIRECTIONS

✓ Put the cream cheese into a crock pot; cook covered until cream cheese is melted, about 30 minutes.
✓ Next, add remaining ingredients and cook 1 to 1 ½ hours or until heated through.
✓ Serve with bread sticks or garlic crackers.

Roasted Pepper and Garlic Dip

(Ready in about 1 hour 30 minutes | Servings 24)

INGREDIENTS

- 1/2 goat cheese
- 1 ½ pound reduced-fat cream cheese, room temperature
- 1/2 cup roasted pepper, chopped
- 3 tablespoons roasted garlic, minced

- 1/4 teaspoon ground black pepper
- 1 teaspoon smoked paprika
- 1/4 teaspoon sea salt
- 3/4 cup milk

DIRECTIONS
- Arrange all of the ingredients into your crock pot.
- Cover the crock pot with a lid; cook 1 to 1 ½ hours.
- Serve with your favorite dippers.

Hot Cheese Bean Dip

(Ready in about 2 hours 20 minutes | Servings 12)

INGREDIENTS
- 1 pound processed cheese food, cubed
- 1 (14-ounce) can diced tomatoes with green chile peppers, drained
- 2 medium-sized cooked chicken breast, shredded
- 1/3 cup sour cream
- 1/4 cup scallions, chopped
- 1 large-sized poblano pepper, minced
- A pinch of black pepper (optional)
- 1 cup canned beans, rinsed and drained

DIRECTIONS
- Place all of the ingredients, except beans, into a crock pot.
- Cook about 2 hours on high, stirring occasionally.
- Stir in the drained beans and cook 20 more minutes. Serve with corn tortilla chips.

Yummy Chili Dipping sauce

(Ready in about 2 hours | Servings 12)

INGREDIENTS
- 2 small-sized roasted jalapeño pepper, coarsely chopped
- 1 cup shredded reduced-fat sharp cheese
- 2 cups reduced-fat processed cheese, shredded
- 1/3 cup plum tomatoes, chopped
- 2-3 cloves garlic
- 1/2 cup green onions, chopped
- 1/2 teaspoon dried basil leaves
- 1/2 teaspoon dried oregano leaves
- 3 tablespoons milk

DIRECTIONS
- Place cheeses in your crock pot; cover and cook until cheeses are melted or about 30 minutes.
- Add the rest of the ingredients.
- Cover and cook until heated through or about 1 ½ hours.

Three-Cheese Bean Appetizer

(Ready in about 1 hour 30 minutes | Servings 16)

INGREDIENTS
- 1 cup Provolone cheese, cubed
- 1 cup cream cheese, room temperature

- 1/2 cup sharp blue cheese, grated
- 1/2 cup mayonnaise
- 1 cup canned kidney beans, drained and rinsed
- 1 can green chilies, diced
- 1 teaspoon Tabasco sauce
- 2-3 cloves garlic, minced

DIRECTIONS
- Mix all ingredients in your crock pot.
- Cover and cook 1 to 1 ½ hours on high.
- Serve with your favorite dippers and enjoy!

Mexican Queso Fundido

(Ready in about 2 hours | Servings 16)

INGREDIENTS
- 1 ½ cups sharp cheese shredded
- 1 cup reduced-fat processed cheese, cubed
- 1/2 roasted red pepper, chopped
- 2/3 cup milk
- 1 cup chorizo sausage, chopped
- 2 teaspoons pickled jalapeño chilies
- 16 corn tortillas, warm
- Chopped cilantro, as garnish
- Chopped chives, as garnish

DIRECTIONS
- Place cheeses in a crock pot; cook on high until cheeses are melted, about
- minutes.
- Add remaining ingredients, except tortillas, cilantro and chives; cover and cook about 1 ½ hours.
- Divide prepared mixture among tortillas. Sprinkle with chopped cilantro and chives and roll up. Enjoy!

Easy Seafood Dipping Sauce

(Ready in about 2 hours | Servings 8)

INGREDIENTS
- 1 cup sharp cheese, cubed
- 1 cup cream cheese
- 3/4 cup whole milk
- 1 cup cooked shrimp, chopped
- 1 cup cooked crab, chopped
- 1 teaspoon red pepper flakes
- 1/2 teaspoon ground black pepper

DIRECTIONS
- Place cheeses in a crock pot; cover with a lid; set the crock pot to low and cook about 30 minutes.
- Add the rest of the ingredients; cover and cook 1 ½ hours.
- Serve with bread sticks, crackers or veggie sticks.

Delicious Salmon Dipping Sauce

(Ready in about 2 hours | Servings 16)

INGREDIENTS

- 1 cup cream cheese, at room temperature
- 1 cup mayonnaise
- 1 teaspoon Dijon mustard
- 1 can (14-ounce) artichoke hearts, drained and chopped
- 1 ½ cups canned salmon
- 1 tablespoon lemon
- 1/2 cup Monterey Jack cheese, diced
- 4 dashes hot pepper sauce
- Lemon wedges, as garnish

DIRECTIONS
- ✓ Arrange all ingredients in your crock pot.
- ✓ Cover and slow cook 2 hours on high heat setting.
- ✓ Garnish with lemon wedges; serve with dippers such as sweet bell pepper strips or steamed asparagus spears.

Romantic Cheese Fondue

(Ready in about 1 hour | Servings 12)

INGREDIENTS
- 2 cups Swiss cheese, shredded
- 1 tablespoon all-purpose flour
- 1 cup cream cheese, room temperature
- 3 tablespoons milk
- 3/4 cup apple juice
- 1/2 teaspoon allspice
- 1/2 teaspoon paprika
- 1-2 cloves garlic, minced

DIRECTIONS
- ✓ Toss Swiss cheese with flour.
- ✓ Combine Swiss cheese, cream cheese, milk, apple juice, allspice, paprika and garlic in your crock pot.
- ✓ Cook covered 1 to 1 ½ hours. Serve with bread sticks or sweet bell pepper strips and enjoy.

Honey Party Wings

(Ready in about 7 hours | Servings 10)

INGREDIENTS
- 3 pounds chicken wings
- 1/4 cup tamari sauce
- 1/4 cup honey
- 1/2 teaspoon celery salt
- 1/2 teaspoon ground black pepper
- 2 tablespoons chili sauce
- 1/2 teaspoon onion powder
- 1/2 teaspoon garlic powder

DIRECTIONS
- ✓ Place the wings into a crock pot.
- ✓ In a small-sized bowl, whisk the rest of the ingredients. Pour this sauce over the wings; toss to coat well.
- ✓ Cook for 7 hours on low.

Pecans with Syrupy Coating

(Ready in about 4 hours | Servings 16)

INGREDIENTS
- 2 cups whole pecans
- 1/2 cup apple cider vinegar
- 1/2 cup brown sugar
- 1 teaspoon allspice
- 1 teaspoon paprika
- 1 teaspoon kosher salt

DIRECTIONS
- ✓ Arrange all your ingredients in a crock pot. Cook on high until all the liquid has evaporated or about 4 hours, stirring every 15 minutes.
- ✓ Place the pecans in a single layer on the baking sheets that are coated with parchment paper. Let them cool completely before storing. Keep this pecans for up to 2 weeks.

Grandma's Blackberry Compote

(Ready in about 7 hours | Servings 6)

INGREDIENTS
- 2 cups blackberries
- 1/4 cup brown sugar
- 1 vanilla bean
- 1 cinnamon stick
- 1/4 cup lukewarm water
- 6 English muffins or favorite waffles, as garnish

DIRECTIONS
- ✓ Put all ingredients into a crock pot.
- ✓ At the beginning, set your crock pot to low heat. Cook the compote covered for about 3 hours.
- ✓ Next, remove the lid; increase the heat to high and cook 4 hours longer.
- ✓ Serve warm with English muffins or your favorite waffles. Enjoy this great old-fashioned snack!

Favorite Pear Butter

(Ready in about 22 hours | Servings 12)

INGREDIENTS
- 8 Bartlett pears, cored and quartered
- 1 cup water
- 2 tablespoons fresh orange juice
- 1/2 cup sugar
- 1/4 teaspoon ground cloves
- 1 stick cinnamon
- 1/2 teaspoon mace

DIRECTIONS
- ✓ Arrange all of the ingredients in your crock pot. Cook covered on low heat setting approximately 10 hours.
- ✓ Then, uncover and cook an additional 10 to 12 hours or until the mixture is thickened.
- ✓ Cool completely and then transfer to a food processor. Purée until smooth and uniform.
- ✓ Keep in clean glass jars. Refrigerate and serve chilled with pancakes, waffles or English muffins.

Hummus with Carrot Sticks

(Ready in about 8 hours | Servings 20)

INGREDIENTS

- Water
- 1 lb. chickpeas, dried
- 3 tablespoons tahini (sesame seed paste)
- 2 tablespoons balsamic vinegar
- 2-3 cloves garlic
- 1/2 teaspoon salt
- 10 large-sized carrots, cut into snack-friendly sizes

DIRECTIONS

- Pour water into your crock pot. Add chickpeas and let soak overnight.
- The next morning, cook for 8 hours on low; drain, but reserve the liquid.
- Transfer the cooked chickpeas to a food processor; add tahini, balsamic vinegar, garlic, and salt. Pulse until creamy and smooth, adding the reserved liquid as needed.
- Serve with carrot sticks and enjoy!

Traditional Middle Eastern Spread

(Ready in about 8 hours | Servings 20)

INGREDIENTS

- 1 pound canned chickpeas
- Water
- 5 tablespoons extra-virgin olive oil
- 3 tablespoons tahini
- 3 tablespoons freshly squeezed lemon juice
- 3 cloves garlic
- 1 teaspoon onion powder
- 1 teaspoon cayenne pepper
- 1 tablespoon fresh coriander, chopped
- 1/4 teaspoon kosher salt
- Falafel, as garnish

DIRECTIONS

- First of all, soak the chickpeas in water at least 8 hours or overnight.
- Cook for 8 hours on low heat setting; replace to a food processor.
- Add the rest of the ingredients, except falafel. Process until the mixture is creamy.
- Serve with falafel and enjoy!

Cream Cheese Vegetable Spread

(Ready in about 2 hours | Servings 20)

INGREDIENTS

- 2 tablespoons low-fat mayonnaise
- 1 cup cream cheese, at room temperature
- 1/2 cup sour cream
- 1/2 teaspoon garlic powder
- 1/2 teaspoon celery seeds
- 1 teaspoon Worcestershire sauce
- 1 stalk celery, minced
- 3 tablespoons fresh baby kale, minced
- 1/2 head cauliflower broccoli, chopped

DIRECTIONS

- Combine all ingredients in your crock pot. Cook for 2 hours on low.
- Stir before serving; serve with your favorite crackers or croutons.

Strawberry Fruit Dipping Sauce

(Ready in about 1 hour | Servings 18)

INGREDIENTS

- 1 cup cream cheese
- 1/2 cup strawberry purée
- 1 tablespoon brown sugar
- A pinch of salt
- 3/4 cup sour cream, reduced-fat
- 1/4 teaspoon grated nutmeg
- 1 teaspoon vanilla extract

DIRECTIONS

- Whisk together all ingredients in a mixing bowl.
- Pour into a crock pot; cook on low for 1 hour. Stir before serving.
- Serve with your favorite fruit dippers such as star fruit, banana, etc.

Sun-Dried Tomato Dip

(Ready in about 1 hour | Servings 18)

INGREDIENTS

- 2 cloves garlic
- 2 tablespoons mayonnaise, reduced-fat
- 1 teaspoon onion powder
- 3/4 ounce fresh cilantro
- 2 tablespoons pecans, toasted
- 1/2 teaspoon paprika
- 1/2 teaspoon black pepper
- 1/4 cup sun-dried tomatoes, julienned
- 1 cup reduced-fat cream cheese

DIRECTIONS

- Put the garlic, mayonnaise, onion powder, cilantro, pecans, paprika, and black pepper into a food processor.
- Process until a smooth paste forms. Add the sun-dried tomatoes and cream cheese and pulse until smooth and creamy.
- Transfer the mixture to the crock pot. Cook on low for 1 hour; stir before serving and serve with baked potato chips and pita chips.

Squid and Scallop Dip

(Ready in about 1 hour | Servings 12)

INGREDIENTS

- 1/2 cup scallions, chopped
- 1/3 cup squid, chopped
- 2/3 cup scallops, chopped
- 1 teaspoon garlic powder
- 1 cup cream cheese, reduced-fat
- 1/2 cup sour cream, reduced-fat
- 1 tablespoon balsamic vinegar
- 1 roasted red bell pepper, chopped
- Sea salt, to taste
- Cayenne pepper, to taste
- 1 tablespoon fresh parsley
- 1/8 teaspoon mustard seed

DIRECTIONS

✓ In a mixing bowl, combine together all of the ingredients.
✓ Scrape into a crock pot. Cook until heated through or for 1 hour on low.
✓ Serve with croutons and bell pepper sticks.

Mediterranean Seafood Treat

(Ready in about 1 hour | Servings 12)

INGREDIENTS

- 1/2 cup red onions, chopped
- 1/3 cup clams, chopped
- 2/3 cup shrimp, chopped
- 1/2 teaspoon celery seed
- 1/2 teaspoon garlic powder
- 1 cup cream cheese, reduced-fat
- 2 tablespoons mayonnaise
- 1/2 cup sour cream, reduced-fat
- 1 tablespoon lemon juice
- 1 large-sized Roma tomato, chopped
- 1 tablespoon fresh cilantro
- 1/4 teaspoon sea salt
- 1/4 teaspoon ground black pepper

DIRECTIONS

✓ Mix together all of the ingredients in a medium-sized bowl. Transfer to the crock pot.
✓ Then, cook covered for 1 hour on low heat setting.
✓ Sprinkle with chopped chives; serve chilled with your favorite dippers.

Spiced Date Spread

(Ready in about 6 hours | Servings 24)

INGREDIENTS

- 2 lbs. fresh dates
- 1 tablespoon ground ginger
- 1/4 teaspoon ground cinnamon
- 2 tablespoons orange juice
- 1/2 cup water
- 1/3 cup brown sugar
- 1 tablespoon honey

DIRECTIONS

✓ Combine all ingredients in your crock pot. Stir to combine well.
✓ Cook covered on low 2 to 3 hours. Then, remove the lid; cook an additional 3 hours until the mixture is thickened.
✓ Place in an airtight container and refrigerate up to 6 weeks.

Amazing Autumn Spread

(Ready in about 22 hours | Servings 24)

INGREDIENTS

- 4 pears, cored and sliced
- 4 apples, cored and sliced
- 1/2 cup pear cider
- 1/2 cup water
- 2 tablespoons molasses
- 1/4 cup sugar
- 1/4 teaspoon ground cloves
- 1/2 teaspoon grated ginger
- 1/2 teaspoon ground cinnamon
- 1/2 teaspoon grated nutmeg

DIRECTIONS

✓ Place all ingredients in a crock pot. Cook for 10 to 12 hours on low.
✓ Remove the lid; cook an additional 10 to 12 hours or until your spread is thickened. Allow to cool.
✓ Pour into the food processor; purée until uniform and smooth.
✓ Refrigerate and keep in glass jars up to 6 weeks.

Nutty Beef Dipping Sauce

(Ready in about 3 hours | Servings 6)

INGREDIENTS

- 1/2 cup beef, shredded
- 2 tablespoons scallions, finely chopped
- 1/2 cup pine nuts, finely chopped
- 1 cup cream cheese
- 2 tablespoons mayonnaise
- 1/2 cup sour cream
- 2 tablespoons water
- 1/4 teaspoon white pepper

DIRECTIONS

✓ Combine all ingredients in the crock pot.
✓ Cover and heat on a low setting for 2 to 3 hours. Serve with croutons and enjoy!

Cheesy Crab Dipping Sauce

(Ready in about 3 hours | Servings 6)

INGREDIENTS

- 1 cup cream cheese, crumbled
- 1 cup crabmeat, shredded
- 1 tablespoon water
- 1/2 teaspoon salt
- 1/2 teaspoon ground black pepper

- 1/4 cup pecans, toasted

DIRECTIONS
- ✓ Put all ingredients, except pecans, into a crock pot.
- ✓ Cover with the lid; heat on a low setting approximately 3 hours.
- ✓ Sprinkle the dipping sauce with the pecans and serve with your favorite dippers.

Pepperoni Cheese Dip

(Ready in about 3 hours | Servings 16)

INGREDIENTS
- 1 pound Cheddar cheese, shredded
- 1 pound Mozzarella cheese, shredded
- 1 sweet red bell pepper, chopped
- 1 sweet green bell pepper, chopped
- 1 teaspoon Dijon mustard
- 1/2 pound pepperoni, sliced
- 1 cup cream cheese
- 1 cup mayonnaise

DIRECTIONS
- ✓ Combine all the ingredients in the crock pot. Cover with the lid.
- ✓ Heat on low setting for 2 to 3 hours, until all the cheese is melted.
- ✓ Serve with your favorite crackers or veggie sticks.

Rich-Tasting Prosciutto Spread

(Ready in about 3 hours | Servings 16)

INGREDIENTS
- 1/3 pound Prosciutto, chopped
- 2 pounds Cheddar cheese, shredded
- 1 poblano pepper, minced
- 1 teaspoon onion powder
- 1 teaspoon garlic powder
- 1 teaspoon mustard
- 1 cup sour cream
- 1 cup cream cheese
- 1 cup mayonnaise

DIRECTIONS
- ✓ Put all ingredients into the crock pot.
- ✓ Cover; heat 2 to 3 hours on a low setting.
- ✓ Serve with celery sticks or bread sticks.

Best Cocktail Meatballs

(Ready in about 4 hours | Servings 8)

INGREDIENTS
- 1 (16-ounce) can whole cranberry sauce
- 1 ½ cup chili sauce
- Salt to taste
- 2 bay leaves
- 27 ounces sauerkraut, undrained
- 1 cup water
- 1/2 cup brown sugar
- 1 (16-ounce) package meatballs

DIRECTIONS
- ✓ In a mixing bowl, combine cranberry sauce, chili sauce, salt, bay leaves, sauerkraut, water, and brown sugar. Mix well to combine.
- ✓ Then, pour sauce and meatballs into the crock pot; stir again.
- ✓ Cook covered for 4 hours. Serve with cocktail sticks.

Saucy Meat Appetizer

(Ready in about 40 minutes | Servings 8)

INGREDIENTS
- Non-stick cooking spray
- 2/3 cup milk
- 1 pound lean ground beef
- 2-3 cloves garlic, minced
- 1 tablespoon tamari sauce
- 1/4 cup Worcestershire sauce
- 1/2 teaspoon ground black pepper
- 1 teaspoon onion powder
- 1 cup tomato paste
- 1/2 cup brown sugar

DIRECTIONS
- ✓ Begin by preheating the oven to broil. Coat a roasting pan with non-stick cooking spray.
- ✓ In a mixing bowl, combine milk, ground beef, garlic, tamari sauce, Worcestershire sauce, black pepper, and onion powder. Roll the mixture into meatballs.
- ✓ Arrange meatballs on a roasting pan. Broil about 10 minutes, or until the meatballs are cooked through.
- ✓ In a mixing bowl, mix tomato paste and brown sugar. Transfer mixture to the crock pot. Add the broiled meatballs.
- ✓ Cook meatballs for about 30 minutes on high. Transfer to a serving
- ✓ platter.

Chicken Pita Bites

(Ready in about 7 hours | Servings 6)

INGREDIENTS
- 3 tablespoons olive oil
- 1 large-sized onion, chopped
- 2 cloves garlic, minced
- 1 teaspoon celery seeds
- 1 teaspoon allspice
- 1/2 teaspoon cinnamon
- 1 teaspoon paprika
- 1 pound chicken, cubed
- 1 ½ cups chicken stock
- 1 tablespoon apple cider vinegar
- Salt, to taste
- 6 pita bread

DIRECTIONS

- In a heavy skillet, heat the olive oil; sauté the onion and garlic until the onion is just tender.
- Add the celery seeds, allspice, cinnamon, and paprika. Cook a few minutes, stirring frequently.
- Mix well and cook a few minutes longer.
- Place chicken in the crock pot. Pour the spiced onion mixture over it.
- Pour in chicken stock; add vinegar and salt. Cover with the lid and let it
- slow cook 7 hours on low.
- Toast pitas about 10 minutes or until crispy. Cut your pitas into small wedges. Serve with cooked chicken.

Juicy Orange Chicken Wings

(Ready in about 7 hours | Servings 8)

INGREDIENTS

- 1/4 cup fruit vinegar
- 1/4 cup tamari sauce
- 3 tablespoons molasses
- 1 clove garlic, minced
- 1 teaspoon ground ginger
- 3 tablespoons orange juice
- 2 lbs. chicken wings
- 4 teaspoons cornflour
- 1 tablespoon water
- 2 tablespoons fresh parsley, chopped

DIRECTIONS

- In a measuring cup or a mixing bowl, whisk together fruit vinegar, tamari sauce, molasses, garlic, ginger, and orange juice.
- Place wings into a crock pot. Pour orange sauce over wings; stir gently to combine. Cook on low heat setting for 6 to 7 hours.
- In a small-sized bowl, whisk together cornflour and water. Stir in the crock pot.
- Cover and cook until your sauce has thickened. Sprinkle with fresh parsley and serve warm or at room temperature.

Zesty Chicken Drumettes

(Ready in about 7 hours | Servings 6)

INGREDIENTS

- 1 cup apples, cubed
- 1/2 teaspoon ground black pepper
- Salt, to taste
- 1 tablespoon lemon juice
- 1 teaspoon lemon rind
- 1/4 teaspoon grated ginger
- 1 garlic clove, minced
- 1/2 cup honey
- 1/2 cup soy sauce
- 1 teaspoon Creole mustard
- 10-12 chicken drumettes

DIRECTIONS

- To make the sauce: In a medium-sized mixing bowl, combine all ingredients, except chicken drumettes. Mix well to combine.
- Next, rinse chicken drumettes under cold running water and drain them.
- Arrange chicken drumettes in your crock pot; pour sauce over it.
- Cover and cook on low approximately 7 hours. Serve warm and enjoy!

Kielbasa Bites with Tomato-Mustard Sauce

(Ready in about 5 hours | Servings 6)

INGREDIENTS

- 2 cups tomato paste
- 2 tablespoons tomato ketchup
- 1/2 cup honey
- 1 tablespoon soy sauce
- 1 tablespoon orange juice
- 1 teaspoon mustard
- 1 chili pepper, minced
- 1 cup shallots, finely chopped
- 1/2 cup bourbon
- 2 pounds kielbasa, cut into 1/2 inch thick rounds

DIRECTIONS

- Arrange all of the ingredients in the crock pot.
- Cover with the lid and cook on low for about 5 hours.
- Serve warm with cocktail sticks and some extra mustard.

Amazing Country Bites

(Ready in about 3 hours | Servings 12)

INGREDIENTS

- 2 ½ cups miniature smoked sausages
- 1 pound Polish sausage, cut into 1/2-inch slices
- 2 cups BBQ sauce of choice
- 1 teaspoon dried tarragon
- 1 teaspoon dried basil leaves
- 1 teaspoon mustard
- 2/3 cup orange marmalade

DIRECTIONS

- Place smoked sausages and Polish sausage in a crock pot.
- In a medium-sized mixing bowl, or a measuring cup, whisk together the rest of the ingredients. Pour the sauce into the crock pot.
- Cover the crock pot and cook until heated through or about 3 hours.
- Serve with cocktail sticks or toothpicks.

Sweet Hot Bites

(Ready in about 4 hours | Servings 8)

INGREDIENTS

- 1 ½ pounds Mennonite sausage, cut into rounds
- 2 bay leaves

- 1 teaspoon mustard
- 2 teaspoons Sriracha Hot Sauce
- 1 cup apricot jam

DIRECTIONS
- Arrange the sausage in your crock pot. Then, add bay leaves.
- In a measuring cup, combine together remaining ingredients. Whisk until everything is well combined. Add to the prepared crock pot.
- Cover and cook on high for about 4 hours.
- Insert a toothpick into each of sausage rounds and transfer them to a serving platter.

Tangy Smoked Sausage

(Ready in about 6 hours | Servings 8)

INGREDIENTS
- 1 (15.25-ounce) can pineapple tidbits, drained and juice reserved
- 2 tablespoons apple cider vinegar
- 1/2 cup maple syrup
- 1/3 cup water
- 1 ½ teaspoon whole grain mustard
- 2 tablespoons cornflour
- 1 pound mini smoked sausages

DIRECTIONS
- Drain the pineapple tidbits, reserving the juice.
- In a medium-sized mixing bowl, blend reserved pineapple juice, apple cider vinegar, maple syrup, water, and mustard; stir in the cornflour.
- Pour the mixture into the crock pot.
- Add reserved pineapple tidbits and sausages; stir gently to combine.
- Cover and cook on low setting approximately 6 hours.

Cheesy Sausage Snack with Mini Pitas

(Ready in about 4 hours | Servings 10)

INGREDIENTS
- 2 ½ pounds smoked sausage, cut into small 1/4 inch pieces
- 2-3 cloves garlic, minced
- 2 pounds cream cheese, crumbled
- 1 ½ cups canned diced tomatoes, drained
- 1 tablespoon ground cumin
- 1 teaspoon smoked paprika
- 1 cup sour cream
- 2 tablespoons mayonnaise
- 1/2 cup fresh parsley, chopped
- Mini pitas, as garnish

DIRECTIONS
- In a medium-sized skillet, brown the sausages about 5 minutes. Add minced garlic and sauté an additional 3 minutes.
- Transfer to the crock pot. Add the rest of the ingredients and stir to coat sausages; cover with the lid.
- Slow cook for 4 hours on high. Serve with mini pitas and enjoy!

Tomato-Pepper Sausage Dip

(Ready in about 4 hours | Servings 12)

INGREDIENTS
- 1 pound bulk sausage
- 2-3 spring onions
- 1 cup cream cheese, crumbled
- 1 ½ cup canned tomatoes, diced
- 1 jalapeño, minced
- 1 teaspoon dried oregano leaves
- 1 teaspoon dried basil leaves
- 1 teaspoon dried rosemary
- 2-3 heaping tablespoons chopped chives, as garnish
- Potato chips, as garnish

DIRECTIONS
- Heat a large non-stick skillet; then, sauté the sausages and spring onions until the onions are tender and translucent.
- Transfer to the crock pot. Then, add the rest of the ingredients, except, chives and potato chips.
- Slow cook for 4 hours or until everything is heated through.
- Transfer to a nice serving bowl and sprinkle with fresh chopped chives; serve with potato chips.

Party Smoked Sausage Bites

(Ready in about 3 hours | Servings 16)

INGREDIENTS
- 16 ounces smoked sausage, sliced into bite-size rounds
- 1 ½ cups barbecue sauce
- 2 tablespoons apple cider vinegar
- 1 cup plum jam
- 1 teaspoon dry mustard
- 1 poblano pepper, minced
- Decorative toothpicks

DIRECTIONS
- In a large heavy skillet, cook the sausages until they are browned. Replace to the crock pot.
- In a mixing bowl, combine barbecue sauce, apple cider vinegar, plum jam, dry mustard and minced poblano pepper.
- Cook covered on high-heat setting for about 3 hours. Serve these delicious sausage bites with decorative toothpicks and enjoy!

Summer Zesty Party Bites

(Ready in about 2 hours | Servings 12)

INGREDIENTS
- 1/4 cup dry red wine
- 1 cup fresh pineapple juice
- 1 teaspoon cumin powder
- 1 teaspoon garlic powder
- 1 tablespoon dried onion flakes
- 2 tablespoons all-purpose flour

- 1 tablespoon dry mustard
- 1/2 cup maple syrup
- 2 pounds sausage of choice, cut into bite-sized rounds

DIRECTIONS
- ✓ Arrange all of the ingredients in your crock pot.
- ✓ Stir gently to combine.
- ✓ Cook covered on high at least 2 hours. Transfer to a serving platter and serve with cocktail sticks.

Appetizer Saucy Franks

(Ready in about 4 hours | Servings 20)

INGREDIENTS
- 1 cup barbecue sauce of choice
- 1 tablespoon spicy brown mustard
- 2 cups jellied cranberry sauce
- 1 teaspoon ground cumin
- 1 teaspoon chili powder
- 2 pounds cocktail frankfurts

DIRECTIONS
- ✓ In your crock pot, place all ingredients and stir gently to coat the sausages well.
- ✓ Set the crock pot to high and slow cook your sausages for 4 hours.
- ✓ Transfer to a serving platter, and serve with sour cream, ketchup or mustard.

Kielbasa Chipotle Dipping Sauce

(Ready in about 4 hours | Servings 6)

INGREDIENTS
- 2 tablespoons olive oil
- 2 Polish kielbasa, crumbled
- 1 medium-sized onion, chopped
- 2 chipotle peppers, minced
- Sea salt to taste
- 1/2 teaspoon ground black pepper
- 1 teaspoon cayenne pepper
- 2 tablespoons flour
- 1 ½ cups half and half
- 1 cup sharp cheese, grated
- 1/2 cup cream cheese

DIRECTIONS
- ✓ Start by heating the oil in a heavy skillet. Sauté kielbasa and onions over medium heat; cook for about 10 minutes until the onions are translucent and the kielbasa is browned.
- ✓ Transfer to the crock pot. Add the rest of the ingredients and set your crock pot to high.
- ✓ Slow cook about 4 hours or until the mixture is heated through. Serve with your favorite dippers such as crusty bread, crackers, bread sticks or croutons.

Hot and Tangy Appetizer Meatballs

(Ready in about 4 hours | Servings 16)

INGREDIENTS
- 1/2 cup apple cider vinegar
- 1/2 cup water
- 1 teaspoon fine sea salt
- 1 teaspoon ground black pepper
- 1 teaspoon dried tarragon
- 1 teaspoon dried rosemary
- 1 cup brown sugar
- 1 cup tomato ketchup
- 1 tablespoon soy sauce
- 2 tablespoons mustard
- A few drops of hot pepper sauce
- 18 ounces cherry preserves
- 32 ounces meatballs, frozen

DIRECTIONS
- ✓ In your crock pot, combine all of the ingredients; stir gently to combine well.
- ✓ Set the crock pot to high; cook uncovered for 3 to 4 hours.
- ✓ Serve with decorative toothpicks and enjoy!

Favorite Party Queso

(Ready in about 2 hours | Servings 16)

INGREDIENTS
- 4 cups cans refried beans
- 1/2 canned green chiles, chopped
- 1/2 cup white wine
- 1/2 cup water
- 1 teaspoon dried basil leaves
- 1 teaspoon dried onion flakes
- 1/2 teaspoon garlic powder
- 1 cup beer
- 2 cups homemade cheese sauce
- 1/2 cup fresh parsley, chopped

DIRECTIONS
- ✓ In a large-sized mixing bowl, combine all of the ingredients, except beer, cheese sauce, and parsley.
- ✓ Mix well until the mixture becomes creamy and smooth. Next, add beer and cheese sauce.
- ✓ Slow cook for 2 hours on low heat setting. Sprinkle with fresh parsley and serve with tortilla chips or crusty bread.

Yummy Super Bowl Dip

(Ready in about 8 hours | Servings 6)

INGREDIENTS
- 2 tablespoons butter, melted
- 2 red onions, finely chopped
- 1/2 teaspoon seasoned salt
- 1 cup sour cream
- 1 teaspoon celery seeds
- 1/2 teaspoon garlic powder
- 1 teaspoon ground cumin
- 1/2 cup mayonnaise

DIRECTIONS
- Arrange butter, onions and seasoned salt in your crock pot.
- Slow cook for 8 hours on high, until onions are tender and browned.
- Drain any liquid. Stir in remaining ingredients; stir until everything is well blended; enjoy the Super Bowl!

Mom's Crowd-Pleasing Dip

(Ready in about 2 hours | Servings 6)

INGREDIENTS
- 1/2 cup mayonnaise
- 1 cup cream cheese, crumbled
- 1/4 cup prepared horseradish
- 2 tablespoons milk
- 1 teaspoon fine sea salt
- 1/2 teaspoon ground black pepper
- Toasted sesame seeds, as garnish

DIRECTIONS
- In a medium-sized mixing bowl, combine together mayonnaise, cream cheese, horseradish, and milk. Mix until everything is well incorporated.
- Season with salt and ground black pepper.
- Next, dump the mixture into your crock pot, cook covered 2 hours on low heat setting until cheese is melted and heated through.
- Sprinkle with sesame seeds and serve with your favorite dippers such as bread sticks or potato chips.

Yummy Game-Day Dip

(Ready in about 4 hours | Servings 8)

INGREDIENTS
- 1 cup cream cheese
- 10 ounces chunk chicken, drained
- 1/2 cup dry white wine
- 3/4 cup hot sauce
- 3/4 cups cheddar cheese, shredded
- Sea salt, to taste

DIRECTIONS
- Add all ingredients to your crock pot.
- Turn on crock pot and cook on low heat setting for 4 hours. Serve with crusty bread or veggie sticks and enjoy!

Cheesy Artichoke Dip and Crackers

(Ready in about 1 hour and 30 minutes | Servings 8)

INGREDIENTS
- 1 lb. shredded Mozzarella
- 1 c. grated Parmesan
- 1 cup mayonnaise of choice
- 1 cup artichoke hearts, chopped
- 2-3 scallions minced

DIRECTIONS
- Combine together all ingredients and place in a baking dish. Preheat oven to 350 degrees F. Bake for 20-30 minutes. Transfer the meal into greased crock pot.
- Set the crock pot on high and cook for 1 hour. Serve with your favorite crackers.

Spiced Bacon Dip

(Ready in about 1 hour and 15 minutes | Servings 8)

INGREDIENTS
- 16 slices bacon, fried, drained and crushed
- 2 (8-ounce) packages cream cheese, softened and cubed
- 4 cups cheddar cheese, shredded
- 1 cup half-and-half
- 1/2 teaspoon dry mustard
- 1/2 teaspoon salt
- 1 teaspoon paprika
- 16 slices toasted bread
- Spring onions for garnish, chopped

DIRECTIONS
- Place all ingredients in the crock pot and turn on low heat setting.
- Cook about 1 hour. Add bacon and cook another 15 minutes.
- Serve at room temperature or warm, with toasted bread and spring onions.

Apple Brown Betty

(Ready in about 4 hours | Servings 8)

INGREDIENTS
- 3 lbs. cooking apples, peeled and cored
- 4 cups bread of choice, cubed
- 1/2 teaspoon Allspice
- 1/4 teaspoon fine kosher salt
- 3/4 cup brown sugar
- 1 teaspoon vanilla extract
- 1/2 cup butter, melted

DIRECTIONS
- Cut the apples into wedges and arrange them in the bottom of the crock pot.
- Combine bread, Allspice, salt, sugar, butter and vanilla extract. Mix well to combine.
- Place this mixture over the apples in the crock pot.
- Place crock pot into outer shell. Cover and cook on low heat setting 3 to 4 hours.

Spiced Baked Apples

(Ready in about 3 hours 30 minutes | Servings 6)

INGREDIENTS
- 6 large apples, cored
- 3/4 cup mixed orange and lemon juice
- 1 teaspoon orange zest

- 3/4 cup rose wine
- 1 teaspoon vanilla extract
- 1/4 teaspoon cinnamon
- 1/4 teaspoon nutmeg
- 1/2 cup sugar
- Whipped cream, for garnish
- Chopped and toasted walnuts, for garnish

DIRECTIONS
- Arrange apples in the crock pot.
- Mix together ingredients except the ingredients for garnish. Pour this mixture over apples.
- Cover the crock pot, set on low heat and cook for about 3 hours 30 minutes.
- Let it cool and garnish with whipped cream. Sprinkle walnuts on top and serve.

Saucy Cocktail Meatballs

(Ready in about 4 hours | Servings 12)

INGREDIENTS
- 2 lbs. lean ground beef
- 1 1/3 cup ketchup
- 3 tablespoons dry bread crumbs
- 1 egg, slightly beaten
- 2-3 spring onions, finely sliced
- 3/4 teaspoon garlic salt
- 1/2 teaspoon black pepper
- 1 teaspoon paprika
- 6 ounces tomato paste
- 1/4 cup soy sauce
- 2 tablespoons apple cider vinegar

DIRECTIONS
- Preheat oven to 350 degrees F.
- Combine together beef, 1/3 cup ketchup, bread crumbs, egg, onions, salt, black pepper and paprika in a mixing bowl.
- Shape this mixture into small meatballs. Place meatballs in a baking pan and bake 20 minutes. Transfer meatballs to the crock pot.
- Mix 1 cup ketchup, tomato paste, soy sauce, and vinegar in a medium bowl. Pour this mixture over meatballs.
- Cover and cook on low heat setting for 4 hours. Arrange the meatballs on
- a serving platter with cocktail picks.

Party Barbecued Meatballs

(Ready in about 6 hours | Servings 12)

INGREDIENTS
- 2 lbs. ground beef
- 1 tablespoon Worcestershire sauce
- 2/3 cup evaporated milk
- 1 dry onion soup mix
- Black pepper to taste
- Marjoram to taste
- 1 tablespoon olive oil
- 2 cup tomato sauce
- 1 cup brown sugar, packed
- 1 teaspoon garlic powder

DIRECTIONS
- Mix together beef, Worcestershire sauce, milk, soup mix, black and marjoram.
- Shape the mixture into meatballs the size of walnuts. Heat olive oil in a wide saucepan and brown the meatballs.
- To make the sauce: Whisk together tomato sauce, sugar and garlic powder. Pour the sauce over meatballs in the crock pot. Set the crock pot on low and cook for 5 to 6 hours.

Cheesy Party Dip

(Ready in about 2 hours | Servings 16)

INGREDIENTS
- 1 pound package Velveeta cheese
- 1 can Chili
- 1 pound spicy sausage, browned and crumbled

DIRECTIONS
- Combine together all ingredients in the crock pot.
- Set the crock pot on low, and keep it warm until party time. Serve with chips, crackers or mini toasted bread.

Easy Peanuts Snacks

(Ready in about 7 hours | Servings 16)

INGREDIENTS
- 1 ½ quarts green uncooked peanuts
- 1/2 cup salt
- 2 tablespoons paprika
- 2 ½ quarts water

DIRECTIONS
- Thoroughly wash the green peanuts.
- Place the peanuts in the crock pot. Then add salt, paprika and water and stir well to combine.
- Cover and cook on high heat setting for 5 to 7 hours. Add additional water during cooking if necessary.

Chex Mix Snacks

(Ready in about 3 hours 10 minutes | Servings 12)

INGREDIENTS
- 9 cups Chex cereal
- 2 cups pretzels
- 1 cup Cheerios
- 1 cup peanuts
- 6 tablespoons butter, melted
- 1 tablespoon salt
- 1/4 cup Worcestershire sauce

DIRECTIONS
- Combine together cereal, pretzels, cheerios and peanuts in the bowl of a crock pot.

- To make the sauce: In another bowl, whisk together butter and salt. Add the Worcestershire sauce and stir until all ingredients are well combined.
- Drizzle the sauce evenly over the cereal mixture. Toss to combine ingredients.
- Cover, set the crock pot on low and cook for 3 hours, stirring occasionaly.
- Place prepared mixture onto the large baking trays and allow it to cool.

Candied Cashews

(Ready in about 3 hours | Servings 12)

INGREDIENTS

- Non-stick cooking spray
- 1 cup confectioners' sugar
- 1/2 cup brown sugar
- 1 tablespoon cinnamon
- 1 egg white
- 1 tablespoon almond extract
- 4 cups cashews
- 1/4 cup water

DIRECTIONS

- Grease a crock pot with non-stick cooking spray.
- In a large mixing bowl, combine together confectioners' sugar, brown sugar and cinnamon. Reserve.
- In another bowl, beat the egg white and almond extract until it is frothy.
- Place cashews in the crock pot. Pour in egg mixture and toss to combine.
- Cover and cook on low heat setting for 3 hours, stirring every 20 minutes. Add water in the first half of cooking time.
- Spread prepared snacks onto parchment paper and let it cool before serving.

Chicken Spread with Pita Bread

(Ready in about 7 hours | Servings 6)

INGREDIENTS

- 3 tablespoons olive oil
- 1 large onion, sliced
- 1 tablespoon ginger, minced
- 1 clove garlic, minced
- 1 tablespoon ground cumin
- 1 tablespoon cayenne pepper
- 1 lb. chicken thighs, boneless
- 1 ½ cups chicken stock
- 1 tablespoon balsamic vinegar
- 1 teaspoon salt
- 1/4 teaspoon black pepper
- 5-6 pita bread
- hummus
- rosemary for garnish

DIRECTIONS

- In a wide saucepan, heat the oil and sauté the onions. Add the ginger, garlic, cumin and cayenne pepper, and cook for a few minutes.
- In the crock pot, arrange the chicken thighs. Add chicken stock, vinegar, salt and pepper.
- Cover the crock pot, set on low heat and cook for 6 to 7 hours.
- Shred the chicken with two forks.
- Preheat the oven to 350 degrees F. Slice the pitas into triangles, arrange them on a baking sheet and bake for about 10 minutes.
- Divide hummus and chicken spread among pitas. Sprinkle the rosemary and serve warm.

Peanut Clusters

(Ready in about 1 hour | Servings 16)

INGREDIENTS

- 1 (20-ounce) package almond bark (vanilla flavored candy coating)
- 1 (12-ounce) package chocolate chips
- 3/4 cup roasted peanuts

DIRECTIONS

- In a crock pot, combine together almond bark and chocolate chips.
- Cover and cook on high setting for 1 hour. Stir well to combine ingredients. Stir in peanuts.
- Evenly spread the mixture onto wax paper and let it cool.

Veggie Sticks with Cheesy Bean Dip

(Ready in about 2 hours | Servings 12)

INGREDIENTS

- 2 (16-ounce) cans refried beans
- 1 (4.5-ounce) can chopped green chiles
- 1 cup salsa
- 1 teaspoon oregano
- 1 teaspoon cayenne pepper
- 1/2 teaspoon ground cumin
- 1 cup beer
- 2 cans (18-ounce) creamy three cheese cooking sauce
- 1/3 cup coriander, chopped
- Veggie sticks of choice

DIRECTIONS

- Combine together beans, chiles, salsa, oregano, cayenne pepper and ground cumin in a crock pot. Mix to combine ingredients.
- Stir in beer and cheese cooking sauce.
- Turn the crock pot to low setting and cook for 2 hours. Add coriander and serve with your favorite veggie sticks.

Golden Stuffed Apples

(Ready in about 5 hours | Servings 6)

INGREDIENTS

- 6 medium apples, cored

- 1 cup brown sugar
- 1 teaspoon cardamom
- 1/4 teaspoon grated nutmeg
- 1/4 cup golden raisins
- 1/4 cup butter, softened
- 1 tablespoon orange zest
- 2 cups very hot water
- 3 tablespoons orange juice

DIRECTIONS
- Grease a baking mold.
- Stuff the apples with brown sugar, cardamom, nutmeg, and raisins.
- Place the butter on tops and sprinkle the orange zest. Drizzle the orange juice over the apples.
- Pour hot water into the crock pot. Place the mold in the crock pot. Cover and cook on low heat setting for 3 to 5 hours.

Sweet and Sour Tofu Cubes

(Ready in about 2 hours | Servings 8)

INGREDIENTS
- 1 lb. Tofu, cut into bite-sized cubes
- 1/4 cup lemon juice
- 1/4 cup soy sauce
- 6 tablespoons water
- 1/4 cup tomato paste
- 2 tablespoon honey
- 1 teaspoon grated ginger
- 2 tablespoons olive oil
- 4 cloves garlic, minced
- 1 large onion, finely chopped
- 2 red bell peppers, thinly sliced
- 1 lb. mushrooms
- 1 cup toasted almonds, chopped

DIRECTIONS
- To make the marinade: Mix together lemon juice, soy sauce, water, tomato paste, honey, ginger, and garlic. Mix well to combine and let it marinate overnight.
- In the crock pot, combine together the onions, red bell peppers, and mushrooms until soft. Add the tofu with the marinade.
- Cover and cook on low setting for 1 to 2 hours.
- Scatter with almonds and arrange on a serving platter with cocktail picks.

Easy Mini English Muffins

(Ready in about 8 hours | Servings 10)

INGREDIENTS
- 3 lbs. roast meat
- 1 jar spaghetti sauce of choice
- 1 (8-ounce) jar Picante sauce
- 20 toasted Mini English Muffins

DIRECTIONS
- Place all ingredients in the crock pot. Set the crock pot on high heat.
- Cook 6 hours until the meat is falling-apart tender.
- Divide among 10 English muffins and serve.

Onion Dip with Potato Chips

(Ready in about 8 hours | Servings 10)

INGREDIENTS
- 2 onions, finely chopped
- 2 tablespoons extra-virgin olive oil
- 1 tablespoon butter, melted
- Salt to taste
- Black pepper to taste
- 1 teaspoon thyme
- 1 teaspoon paprika
- 1 cup sour cream
- 1/2 cup mayonnaise

DIRECTIONS
- Place onions, olive oil, butter, salt, black pepper, thyme and paprika into the crock pot. Stir well to combine.
- Cook on high setting for 8 hours.
- Combine this mixture with sour cream and mayonnaise. Mix well to combine.
- Serve with potato chips.

Tortilla Chips with Chili Cheese Dip

(Ready in about 1 hour 30 minutes | Servings 10)

INGREDIENTS
- 8 ounces cream cheese
- 2 (15-ounces) cans of chili
- 2 cups cheddar cheese, shredded
- 1 teaspoon sweet paprika
- 1 teaspoon seasoned salt
- 1/2 teaspoon ground black pepper
- Tortilla chips of choice

DIRECTIONS
- Place cream cheese and chili in a crock pot.
- Turn on low heat setting.
- Simmer for 1 to 1 ½ hours, stirring occasionally.
- Add cheddar cheese, stir, and simmer until it is warmed thoroughly. Add paprika, salt and pepper. Taste and adjust the seasonings
- Serve with tortilla chips.

Chicken and Cheese Dip

(Ready in about 1 hour | Servings 10)

INGREDIENTS
- 1 can chunk chicken, drained
- 1 (8-ounces) package cream cheese
- 1/2 cup ranch dressing
- 3/4 cup red hot sauce
- 3/4 cups cheddar cheese, shredded
- Chopped spring onions for garnish

DIRECTIONS
- ✓ Add all ingredients to a crock pot.
- ✓ Turn the crock pot on low setting and cook about 1 hour, stirring every 10 minutes.
- ✓ Garnish with spring onions and serve with your favorite crackers or tortilla chips.

Cheesy Spinach and Artichoke Dip

(Ready in about 2 hours | Servings 16)

INGREDIENTS

- 1/3 cup sun-dried tomatoes
- 1 cup boiling water
- 1 (10-ounce) package frozen chopped spinach, thawed
- 1 (14-ounce) can artichoke hearts, drained
- 8 ounces cream cheese
- 8 ounces sour cream
- 3/4 cup Parmesan cheese, shredded
- 3/4 cup fat-free milk
- 1/2 cup feta cheese, crumbled
- 1/2 cup mayonnaise
- 1 teaspoon garlic powder
- 1/2 teaspoon red pepper flakes
- Pita bread of choice

DIRECTIONS
- ✓ Combine together tomatoes and boiling water in a large mixing bowl. Let sit for 1 hour.
- ✓ Arrange remaining ingredients in the crock pot. Cover and cook on low heat setting for 1 hour.
- ✓ Stir in drained tomatoes and continue cooking for 1 additional hour.
- ✓ Serve chilled with pitas.

Beef and Bean Salsa Dip

(Ready in about 3 hours | Servings 32)

INGREDIENTS

- 1 pound ground beef
- 1 jalapeño, chopped
- 1 onion, finely chopped
- 1 (16-ounces) can kidney beans
- 1 (16-ounces) can mild salsa
- 1 cup mozzarella cheese, shredded
- 2 cups cheddar cheese, shredded
- Olives
- Tortilla chips of choice

DIRECTIONS
- ✓ In a wide and deep saucepan, cook the beef, jalapeño and onion until meat is lightly browned.
- ✓ Oil the crock pot with non-stick cooking spray.
- ✓ Transfer the meat to the crock pot, then add the beans, salsa, mozzarella and cheddar cheese. Add olives to taste.
- ✓ Cover and cook on low heat setting for 3 to 4 hours. Serve with your favorite tortilla chips.

Mushrooms Go-To Appetizer

(Ready in about 6 hours | Servings 16)

INGREDIENTS

- 1/2 cup hoisin sauce
- 1/4 cup water
- 2 tablespoons garlic, minced
- 3/4 teaspoon red pepper, minced
- 24 ounces mushrooms
- Fresh parsley for garnish

DIRECTIONS
- ✓ In a crock pot, combine together hoisin sauce, water, garlic, and red pepper. Add mushrooms and stir to combine all ingredients.
- ✓ Cover your crock pot and cook on low heat for 5 to 6 hours.
- ✓ Garnish the mushrooms with fresh parsley and arrange them on a serving platter.

Party Chicken and Yogurt Dip

(Ready in about 2 hours | Servings 32)

INGREDIENTS

- 8 ounces cream cheese
- 1/2 cup Franks Wing Sauce
- 1/2 cup Mozzarella cheese, shredded
- 1/4 cup Ranch Dressing
- 1/4 cup plain yogurt
- 2 (12.5 ounces) cans White Chunk Chicken, drained
- Veggie Sticks of choice
- Crackers of choice

DIRECTIONS
- ✓ In the crock pot, place cream cheese, Franks Wing Sauce, Mozzarella cheese and Ranch Dressing.
- ✓ Turn the crock pot to low and cook for 2 hours.
- ✓ Add yogurt and Chunk Chicken and mix well to combine all ingredients.
- ✓ Serve with your favorite veggie sticks and crackers.

Spiced Sweet Potatoes

(Ready in about 7 hours | Servings 4)

INGREDIENTS

- 2 lbs. sweet potatoes, cubed
- 1/4 cup brown sugar
- 1 teaspoon ground cinnamon
- 1/2 teaspoon ground nutmeg
- Sea salt to taste
- 2 tablespoons butter

DIRECTIONS
- ✓ In the crock pot, combine together all ingredients except the butter. Mix well to combine.
- ✓ Cover and cook on low setting about 7 hours.
- ✓ Add the butter and serve warm.

Cereals and Nuts Mix

(Ready in about 7 hours | Servings 20)

INGREDIENTS

- 7 cups cereals (oat, rice, wheat)
- 1 cup mixed nuts
- 1 cup mini pretzel sticks
- 1/2 cup butter, melted
- 1/4 cup Worcestershire sauce
- 1/2 teaspoon seasoned salt
- 1 teaspoon garlic salt
- 1 teaspoon cayenne pepper

DIRECTIONS

- In the crock pot, combine together cereals, nuts and pretzels.
- Then stir in melted butter and add Worcestershire sauce, salt and cayenne pepper. Pour this mixture over the mixture in the crock pot.
- Set the crock pot on high and cook for 2 hours. Stir every 30 minutes. Then turn the crock pot to low and cook another 4 to 5 hours.

Bacon Wrapped Hot Dogs

(Ready in about 3 hours | Servings 8)

INGREDIENTS

- 2 lbs. hot dogs of choice
- 1 lb. bacon, sliced
- 1 teaspoon dry mustard
- 2 tablespoons sugar

DIRECTIONS

- Slice hot dogs crosswise in halves and then cut them into smaller pieces. Wrap them with a bacon strips. Use the toothpicks to hold the wraps.
- Place the wraps in the crock pot. Sprinkle the mustard and sugar.
- Repeat this process until all ingredients run out.
- Set the crock pot on low and cook for 2 to 3 hours. Stir every 20 minutes. Serve warm with mustard and fat-free sour cream.

Barbecued Pork Appetizer

(Ready in about 6 hours | Servings 15)

INGREDIENTS

- 3 pounds lean pork
- 1/2 cup tamari sauce
- 1/4 cup dry white wine
- 1/2 cup brown sugar
- 2 cloves garlic, crushed
- 1 teaspoon garlic salt
- 1/8 teaspoon garlic pepper
- 1/2 cup barbecue sauce of choice
- 1 (8-ounce) can pineapple chunks, with juice

DIRECTIONS

- Trim unwanted fat from the pork, then slice the pork into strips. In a wide saucepan brown pork, stirring frequently.
- In the crock pot, combine together remaining ingredients. Add pork strips and stir to combine.
- Turn the heat to low and cook, covered, for 6 to 9 hours. Serve warm.

Spiced Pecans for Movie Night

(Ready in about 2 hours 15 minutes | Servings 8)

INGREDIENTS

- 1 pound pecans
- 1/4 cup butter, softened
- 1 tablespoon chili powder
- 1 teaspoon onion salt
- 1 teaspoon garlic salt
- 1 teaspoon dried basil
- 1 teaspoon dried thyme
- 1 teaspoon garlic powder
- 1/4 teaspoon ground cumin

DIRECTIONS

- Combine all ingredients in the crock pot. Toss to combine. Cover and set the crock pot on high and cook for 15 minutes.
- Reduce the heat to low and cook, stirring occasionally, for another 2 hours.
- Let it cool before serving.

Easy Meatballs Appetizer

(Ready in about 4 hours | Servings 8)

INGREDIENTS

- 1 bag prepared meatballs, frozen
- 14 ounces ketchup
- 12 ounces chili sauce
- 10 ounces grape jelly
- Chopped spring onions

DIRECTIONS

- Place the meatballs in the crock pot.
- Pour ketchup, chili sauce and grape jelly over the meatballs.
- Turn to low setting and cook for 4 hours. Sprinkle with chopped spring onions and serve with cocktail picks.

Crockpot Fondue with Bread Sticks

(Ready in about 2 hours | Servings 32)

INGREDIENTS

- 1 can (10 ½ ounces) Cheddar cheese soup
- 1 pound Velveeta cheese cut in cubes
- 16 ounces Swiss cheese, shredded
- 1 ½ cups apple cider
- 1/2 teaspoon freshly ground black pepper
- 1/2 teaspoon paprika

DIRECTIONS

- ✓ Place all ingredients in the crock pot. Stir to combine.
- ✓ Cover, set the heat on low, and cook about 2 hours.

Cocktail Sausages in Mustard Sauce

(Ready in about 2 hours | Servings 8)

INGREDIENTS

- 2 pounds Kielbasa (Polish sausage), sliced
- 1 jar apple jelly
- 9 ounces jar prepared mustard

DIRECTIONS

- ✓ Combine together jelly and mustard in the crock pot. Add Kielbasa and mix well to combine ingredients.
- ✓ Turn the crock pot to low heat setting and cook for 2 hours, stirring every
- ✓ minutes.

Mini Chicken Sandwiches with Spicy Sauce

(Ready in about 4 hours | Servings 15)

INGREDIENTS

- 4 tablespoons olive oil
- 3 chicken breasts, boneless and skinless
- 1 teaspoon salt
- 1/4 teaspoon black pepper
- 1 ½ cups beer
- 1/2 cup chicken broth
- 3 cloves garlic, minced
- 1 cup hoisin sauce
- 1 teaspoon chili powder
- 1/4 cup tamari sauce
- 15 mini bread rolls

DIRECTIONS

- ✓ Heat olive oil in a wide saucepan. Fry the chicken breasts until browned.
- ✓ Season the chicken with salt and black pepper. Place the chicken in a crock pot and pour in the beer and chicken broth. Add garlic, hoisin sauce, chili powder, and tamari sauce. Cook 3 to 4 hours.
- ✓ When chicken is cooked, remove it from the crock pot. Shred chicken by using the forks. Split bread rolls into halves and stuff with the chicken.

Pepper and Cheese Fondue

(Ready in about 4 hours | Servings 36)

INGREDIENTS

- 1 can diced tomatoes, undrained
- 2/3 cup onion, chopped
- 1/2 cup roasted sweet pepper, minced
- 1 jalapeño
- 1 4 ounce can diced green chile peppers
- 3 cups Monterey Jack cheese, cubed
- 3 cups semi-soft cheese, crumbled

DIRECTIONS

- ✓ In a crock pot, combine together tomatoes, onion, roasted sweet pepper, jalapeño, and green chile peppers. Add cheeses and toss to combine.
- ✓ Cover and cook on low setting for 3 to 4 hours.

Italian Mushrooms Fondue

(Ready in about 3 hours | Servings 10)

INGREDIENTS

- 4 ounces Italian sausage
- 1 onion, finely chopped
- 1 clove garlic, minced
- 1 jar spaghetti sauce
- 1 cup mushrooms, sliced
- 2/3 cup pepperoni, chopped
- 1 teaspoon dried basil
- 1 teaspoon thyme
- Bread cubes

DIRECTIONS

- ✓ In a wide and deep saucepan, cook the sausage, onion, and garlic until tender and fragrant.
- ✓ In a crock pot, combine spaghetti sauce, mushrooms, pepperoni, basil, and thyme. Add sausage and onion mixture. Cover, cook on low setting for 3 hours. Serve with bread cubes.

Orange Glazed Meatballs

(Ready in about 5 hours | Servings 8)

INGREDIENTS

- 28 ounces frozen meatballs
- 1 ½ cup orange marmalade
- 1/2 jalapeño, minced
- 1/4 cup orange juice
- 1/4 cup vegetable broth
- 4 scallions, finely chopped
- 1/2 teaspoon seasoned salt
- 1/4 teaspoon garlic pepper
- 1 teaspoon basil

DIRECTIONS

- ✓ In the crock pot, combine together marmalade, jalapeño, orange juice, vegetable broth, scallions, salt, pepper, and basil. Stir well to combine all ingredients.
- ✓ Add meatballs and stir gently to combine.
- ✓ Turn your crock pot to low setting and cook for 4 to 5 hours. Sprinkle additional scallions and serve with cocktail picks.

Family Pork Sliders

(Ready in about 10 hours | Servings 12)

INGREDIENTS

- 5 pound pork roast
- 3 cans root beer
- 2 bottles barbecue sauce
- 1/2 teaspoon black pepper
- 24 slider buns
- Shredded cabbage for garnish

DIRECTIONS
- Place pork roast in a crock pot, then pour in the root beer.
- Cook on low setting for 8 hours. Remove the pork roast from the crock pot and shred them with two forks.
- Add barbecue sauce and black pepper to the crock pot.
- Turn the crock pot to low setting and cook for 1 to 2 hours. To make the sandwiches: Arrange pork on each slider bun and spoon shredded cabbage.

BBQ Chicken Wings

(Ready in about 5 hours | Servings 6)

INGREDIENTS
- 3 pounds chicken wings
- 1 cup barbecue sauce
- 1 (18-ounce) jar apricot preserve
- 1 teaspoon dry mustard
- 1 teaspoon garlic powder
- 1 tablespoon Tabasco sauce

DIRECTIONS
- Preheat oven to 400 degrees F. Arrange the chicken wings on a baking sheet and bake for about 10 minutes.
- Place the chicken wings in the crock pot.
- In a medium mixing bowl, mix together the barbecue sauce, apricot, mustard, garlic powder and Tabasco sauce. Cover, set on low heat and cook for 5 hours.

Party Sticky Wings

(Ready in about 4 hours | Servings 8)

INGREDIENTS
- 4 pounds of chicken wings
- 1 teaspoon kosher salt
- 1/2 teaspoon black pepper
- 1 teaspoon paprika
- 1 teaspoon ground cumin
- 1 teaspoon garlic powder
- 1 teaspoon onion powder
- juice from 1 large lemon
- 1 handful fresh cilantro
- 2 tablespoons olive oil

DIRECTIONS
- Heat a non-stick pan and brown the chicken wings.
- Rub the chicken with spices. Add lemon juice, cilantro and olive oil. Marinate the chicken wings overnight.
- Cook on low heat setting for 4 hours. Serve with your favorite beer.

Sausage Bites with Onion Sauce

(Ready in about 7 hours | Servings 8)

INGREDIENTS
- 2 pounds chicken sausage
- 1 onion, sliced
- 1 jalapeño, minced
- 4 tablespoons grainy mustard
- 4 tablespoons lime juice
- 4 tablespoons maple syrup
- 3 tablespoons honey

DIRECTIONS
- Slice the chicken sausages into bite-sized pieces.
- Place sliced onion in the crock pot, then place the sliced sausages.
- Mix together jalapeño, mustard, lime juice, maple syrup and honey. Pour in the crock pot.
- Cover and cook on low heat setting for 6 to 7 hours. Serve with pretzel sticks.

Spiced Little Smokies

(Ready in about 4 hours | Servings 16)

INGREDIENTS
- 2 pounds little smokies
- 1 ½ cups tomato paste
- 1/2 teaspoon salt
- 1/4 teaspoon ground pepper
- 1 teaspoon ground cumin
- 1 teaspoon onion powder
- 1 teaspoon garlic powder
- 12 ounces apricot preserves
- 2 tablespoons molasses
- 2 tablespoons balsamic vinegar

DIRECTIONS
- In the crock pot, combine together tomato paste, spices, apricot preserves, molasses, and vinegar. Add the little smokies and toss to combine.
- Cover and cook on low heat setting for 3 to 4 hours.
-

Sun-Dried Tomato Dip

(Ready in about 2 hours 30 minutes | Servings 18)

INGREDIENTS
- 1 cup boiling water
- 1/4 cup sun-dried tomatoes
- 1 ½ cups canned artichoke hearts, drained and chopped
- 1/2 cup milk
- 1 cup sour cream
- 1 ½ cups cream cheese, crumbled
- 3/4 cup sharp cheese, grated light
- 1/2 cup mayonnaise

- 1-2 garlic cloves, minced
- Seasoned salt, to taste
- 1/2 teaspoon ground black pepper

DIRECTIONS

- ✓ In a medium-sized bowl, pour boiling water; add sun-dried tomatoes and let soak until soft or for 1 hour. Drain and replace to your crock pot.
- ✓ Add the rest of the ingredients to the crock pot. Cover and cook on low heat setting approximately 1 ½ hour.
- ✓ Serve with dippers of choice and enjoy!

Ground Meat and Olive Queso Dip

(Ready in about 4 hours | Servings 32)

INGREDIENTS

- 1/2 pound ground beef
- 1/2 pound ground pork
- 1 medium-sized sweet bell pepper, chopped
- 2 to 3 spring onions, chopped
- 1 cup canned beans
- 2 cups mozzarella cheese, shredded
- 1 cup salsa
- 2 cups cheddar cheese, shredded
- 1/2 cup pitted olives in oil

DIRECTIONS

- ✓ In a large non-stick skillet, cook the beef, pork, bell pepper and onion over medium heat; cook until veggies are tender and ground meat is no longer pink; drain.
- ✓ Transfer to the crock pot.
- ✓ Add the rest of the ingredients. Cover and cook for 3 to 4 hours on low; serve with dippers of choice and enjoy!

Mushroom Appetizer with Beer Sauce

(Ready in about 3 hours | Servings 4)

INGREDIENTS

- 1 tablespoon canola oil
- 2 pounds mushrooms
- 2 cloves garlic, minced
- 1 teaspoon seasoned salt
- 1/2 teaspoon ground black pepper
- 1 teaspoon dried dill weed
- 1/4 cup non-alcoholic beer

DIRECTIONS

- ✓ Arrange all of the ingredients in your crock pot.
- ✓ Cover and cook 2 to 3 hours on high.
- ✓ Transfer to a serving platter, sprinkle with fresh parsley or cilantro and serve.

Herbed Saucy Mushroom Appetizer

(Ready in about 2 hours | Servings 10)

INGREDIENTS

- 3 pounds cremini mushrooms
- 1 pound butter
- 1 teaspoon seasoned salt
- 1 teaspoon dried rosemary
- 1 teaspoon dried basil leaves
- 1 teaspoon dried oregano leaves
- 1/2 teaspoon onion powder
- 1/2 teaspoon garlic powder

DIRECTIONS

- ✓ Clean cremini mushrooms and arrange them in your crock pot.
- ✓ Add the rest of the ingredients and cook approximately 2 hours on high.
- ✓ Serve with tortilla chips, mini pitas or veggie sticks.

APPETIZER RECIPES

Cajun Spiced Pecans

Serves: 5 Preparation Time: 5 minutes Cooking Time: 15 minutes

INGREDIENTS

- 1-pound pecan halves
- ¼ cup melted butter
- 1 packet Cajun seasoning mix
- Salt and pepper to taste
- ¼ teaspoon ground cayenne pepper

INSTRUCTIONS

- ✓ Place all ingredients in the crockpot. Give a good stir to combine everything.
- ✓ Close the lid and cook on high for 15 minutes or on low for 1 hour.

  Nutrition information: Calories per serving: 713; Carbohydrates: 13.6g; Protein: 8.5g; Fat: 74.7g; Fiber: 8.9g

Crockpot Asian Glazed Meatballs

Serves: 4 Preparation Time: 10 minutes Cooking Time: 7 hours

INGREDIENTS

- 1-pound frozen meatballs
- ½ cup hoisin sauce
- 2 tablespoons apricot jam
- 2 tablespoons soy sauce
- ½ teaspoon sesame oil

INSTRUCTIONS

- Heat the skillet over medium flame and sauté the meatballs until all sides become light brown. Transfer into the crockpot and pour over the rest of the ingredients.
- Close the lid and cook on low for 7 hours.
- Once cooked, sprinkle with toasted sesame seeds and chopped green onions if desired. Serve on toothpicks.
- **Nutrition information: Calories per serving:447; Carbohydrates: 31.7g; Protein: 18.1g; Fat: 28.4g; Fiber: 3.7g**

Teriyaki Chicken Wings

Serves: 9 Preparation Time: 5 minutes Cooking Time: 8 hours

INGREDIENTS

- 3 pounds chicken wings
- 1 onion, chopped
- 2 cups commercial teriyaki sauce
- 1 tablespoon chili garlic paste
- 2 teaspoons ginger paste

INSTRUCTIONS

- Place all ingredients in the crockpot. Season with salt and pepper to taste.
- Give a good stir to combine everything. Close the lid and cook on low for 8 hours.
- **Nutrition information: Calories per serving: 214; Carbohydrates: 5.4g; Protein: 34.3g; Fat: 5.4g; Fiber: 1.3g**

Chili Cheese Taco Dip

Serves: 8 Preparation Time: 10 minutes Cooking Time: 8 hours

INGREDIENTS

- 1-pound ground beef
- 1-pound mild Mexican cheese, grated
- 1 can tomato salsa
- 1 packet Mexican spice blend
- Salt and pepper to taste

INSTRUCTIONS

- Heat a skillet over medium heat and sauté the ground beef until lightly golden. Transfer to the crockpot and add the rest of the ingredients.
- Give a good stir.
- Close the lid and cook on low for 8 hours. Serve with tortilla chips.
- **Nutrition information: Calories per serving:320; Carbohydrates: 3.1g; Protein: 24.8g; Fat: 22.7g; Fiber: 0.5g**

Cocktail Kielbasa with Mustard Sauce

Serves: 8 Preparation Time: 5 minutes Cooking Time: 6 hours

INGREDIENTS

- 2 pounds kielbasa (Polish sausage)
- 1 jar apple jelly
- 1 jar prepared mustard
- 1 bay leaf
- Salt and pepper to taste

INSTRUCTIONS

- Place all ingredients in the crockpot. Give a good stir to combine everything.
- Close the lid and cook on low for 6 hours. Remove the bay leaf.
- Serve on toothpicks.
- **Nutrition information: Calories per serving: 270; Carbohydrates: 8.1g; Protein: 15.3g; Fat:20.7g; Fiber: 0.6g**

Chicken Enchilada Dip

Serves: 8 Preparation Time: 5 minutes Cooking Time: 4 hours

INGREDIENTS

- 2 pounds cooked rotisserie chicken, shredded
- 1 can enchilada sauce
- 2 packages cream cheese, softened
- Salt and pepper to taste
- 2 green onions, sliced

INSTRUCTIONS

- Place all ingredients in the crockpot except for the green onions. Give a good stir to combine everything.
- Close the lid and cook on low for 4 hours.
- Garnish with green onions and serve with tortilla chips.
- **Nutrition information: Calories per serving: 312; Carbohydrates: 4.1g; Protein: 33.4g; Fat: 18.3g; Fiber: 0.5g**

Sweet and Spicy Mushrooms

Serves: 8 Preparation Time: 5 minutes Cooking Time: 4 hours

INGREDIENTS

- ½ cup hoisin sauce
- ¼ cup water
- 2 tablespoons minced garlic
- ¾ teaspoon crushed red pepper
- 24 ounces fresh mushrooms

INSTRUCTIONS
- Place all ingredients in the crockpot. Give a good stir to combine everything.
- Close the lid and cook on low for 4 hours.
  - **Nutrition information: Calories per serving:290; Carbohydrates: 71.9g; Protein: 8.8g; Fat: 1.4g; Fiber: 10.3g**

Beer-Braised Chicken

Serves: 3 Preparation Time: 5 minutes Cooking Time: 8 hours

INGREDIENTS
- 1 cup beer
- 1 cup hoisin sauce
- 3 chicken breasts, skin and bones removed
- ¼ cup soy sauce
- 1 thumb-size ginger, grated

INSTRUCTIONS
- Place all ingredients in the crockpot. Give a good stir to combine everything.
- Close the lid and cook on low for 8 hours.
  - **Nutrition information: Calories per serving: 959; Carbohydrates: 48.1g; Protein: 117.3g; Fat: 33.6g; Fiber: 3.1g**

Apricot Barbecue Wings

Serves: 9 Preparation Time: 5 minutes Cooking Time: 8 hours

INGREDIENTS
- 3 pounds chicken wings
- 1 cup prepared BBQ sauce
- 1 jar apricot preserve
- 1 teaspoon dry mustard powder
- 1 tablespoon Tabasco powder

INSTRUCTIONS
- Place all ingredients in the crockpot. Give a good stir to combine everything.
- Close the lid and cook on low for 8 hours.
  - **Nutrition information: Calories per serving: 203; Carbohydrates: 2.9g; Protein: 33.7g; Fat: 5.4g; Fiber: 0.6g**

Sweet and Hot Nuts

Serves: 6 Preparation Time: 5 minutes Cooking Time: 4 hours

INGREDIENTS
- 1-pound assorted nuts, raw
- ½ cup sugar
- 1/3 cup butter, melted
- ¼ teaspoon cayenne pepper
- Salt to taste

INSTRUCTIONS
- Place all ingredients in the crockpot except for the green onions. Give a good stir to combine everything.
- Close the lid and cook on low for 4 hours.
- Garnish with green onions and serve with tortilla chips.
  - **Nutrition information: Calories per serving: 631; Carbohydrates: 18.3g; Protein: 10.4g; Fat: 61.9g; Fiber: 2.8g**

SOUP RECIPES

Tomato Hamburger Soup

Serves: 8 Preparation Time: 10 minutes Cooking Time: 8 hours

INGREDIENTS
- 1-pound ground beef
- 1 can V-8 juice
- 2 packages frozen vegetable mix
- 1 can condensed mushroom soup
- 2 teaspoon dried onion powder

INSTRUCTIONS
- In a skillet over medium flame, sauté the ground beef until lightly brown. Transfer to a crockpot.
- Place all ingredients in the crockpot. Season with salt and pepper to taste. Give a good stir to combine everything. Close the lid and cook on low for 8 hours.

Nutrition information: Calories per serving: 227; Carbohydrates: 14.8g; Protein: 18.1g; Fat: 10.2g; Fiber: 3.2g

Home-Style Stew

Serves: 7 Preparation Time: 10 minutes Cooking Time: 8 hours

INGREDIENTS

- 1 ½ pounds beef stew meat, cut into chunks
- 2 packages frozen vegetables
- 1 can condensed cream of mushroom soup
- 1 can condensed tomato soup
- A sprig of basil leaves

INSTRUCTIONS

- In a skillet over medium flame, sauté the beef until lightly brown. Transfer to a crockpot.
- Place the vegetables, mushroom soup, and tomato soup in the crockpot. Season with salt and pepper to taste.
- Give a good stir to combine everything. Close the lid and cook on low for 8 hours. Garnish with basil leaves.
- **Nutrition information: Calories per serving: 415; Carbohydrates: 41g; Protein: 30g; Fat: 13g; Fiber: 2g**

Green Lentil Curry Stew

Serves: 8 Preparation Time: 5 minutes Cooking Time: 4 hours

INGREDIENTS

- 2 cans green lentils, drained
- 3 cups vegetable broth
- 1 tablespoon garam masala or curry powder
- 1 can coconut milk
- 1 onion, quartered

INSTRUCTIONS

- Place all ingredients in the crockpot. Season with salt and pepper to taste.
- Give a good stir to combine everything.
- Close the lid and cook on low for 4 hours. Garnish with chopped cilantro leaves.
- **Nutrition information: Calories per serving: 196; Carbohydrates: 13.8g; Protein: 4.4g; Fat: 15.4g; Fiber: 2g**

Creamy Cauliflower Soup

Serves: 4 Preparation Time: 5 minutes Cooking Time: 6 hours

INGREDIENTS

- 1 cauliflower head, chopped
- ½ cup onions, chopped
- 4 cups chicken broth
- 1 tablespoon butter
- 1 cup heavy cream

INSTRUCTIONS

- Place all ingredients in the crockpot. Season with salt and pepper to taste.
- Give a good stir to combine everything.
- Close the lid and cook on low for 4 hours. Use a hand blender to pulse until smooth.
- **Nutrition information: Calories per serving: 531; Carbohydrates: 7.3g; Protein: 53.9g; Fat: 30.8g; Fiber: 1.6g**

Crockpot Lazy Posole

Serves: 8 Preparation Time: 10 minutes Cooking Time: 4 hours

INGREDIENTS

- 1-pound pork tenderloin, cut into chunks
- 1 can white hominy, drained
- 1 can crushed tomatoes
- 1 packet Mexican seasoning mix
- Fresh cilantro, chopped

INSTRUCTIONS

- Place all ingredients in the crockpot except for the cilantro. Season with salt and pepper to taste.
- Give a good stir to combine everything. Close the lid and cook on low for 4 hours. Garnish with chopped cilantro leaves.
- **Nutrition information: Calories per serving: 115; Carbohydrates: 6.7g; Protein: 15.6g; Fat: 2.4g; Fiber: 1.5g**

Spicy Poblano And Corn Soup

Serves: 6 Preparation Time: 5 minutes Cooking Time: 4 hours

INGREDIENTS

- 1 package baby gold and white corn kernels
- 1 cup full-fat milk
- 4 poblano chilies, chopped
- 1 onion, chopped
- ½ cup cheddar cheese, grated

INSTRUCTIONS

- Place all ingredients in the crockpot. Season with salt and pepper to taste.
- Give a good stir to combine everything. Adjust the liquid by adding more water. Close the lid and cook on low for 4 hours.

Nutrition information: **Calories per serving: 276; Carbohydrates: 26.5g; Protein: 19.2g; Fat: 11.5g; Fiber: 3g**

Corn and Bacon Chowder

Serves: 4 Preparation Time: 2 minutes Cooking Time: 4 hours

INGREDIENTS

- ½ cup bacon, fried and crumbled
- 1 package celery, onion, and bell pepper mix
- 2 cups full-fat milk
- 2 packages frozen baby gold corn kernels
- ½ cup sharp cheddar cheese, grated

INSTRUCTIONS
- Place all ingredients in the crockpot. Season with salt and pepper to taste.
- Give a good stir to combine everything. Close the lid and cook on low for 4 hours.
- Nutrition information: **Calories per serving: 529; Carbohydrates: 52.1g; Protein: 33.3g; Fat: 23.1g; Fiber: 13g**

Sweet Potato, Leek, And Ham Soup

Serves: 6 Preparation Time: 2 hours Cooking Time: 4 hours

INGREDIENTS

- 1 cup cooked ham, diced
- 1 chopped leek, white and green parts separated
- 1 big potatoes, peeled and chopped
- 3 cups chicken broth
- 1 can evaporated milk

INSTRUCTIONS
- Place all ingredients in the crockpot. Season with salt and pepper to taste.
- Give a good stir to combine everything. Close the lid and cook on low for 4 hours.
- Nutrition information: **Calories per serving: 313; Carbohydrates: 17.8g; Protein: 32.8g; Fat: 11.6g; Fiber: 1.6g**

Southwest Chicken with White Bean Soup

Serves: 6 Preparation Time: 5 minutes Cooking Time: 4 hours

INGREDIENTS

- 1 cup cooked chicken breasts, chopped
- 1 packet taco seasoning
- 3 cups chicken broth
- 1 can cannellini beans, drained and rinsed
- 1 can green salsa

INSTRUCTIONS
- Place all ingredients in the crockpot. Season with salt and pepper to taste.
- Give a good stir to combine everything. Close the lid and cook on low for 4 hours.
- Serve with chopped cilantro on top.
- Nutrition information: **Calories per serving: 296; Carbohydrates: 12.5g; Protein: 36.6g; Fat: 10.4g; Fiber: 3.5g**

Chicken Cabbage Soup

Serves: 6 Preparation Time: 5 minutes Cooking Time: 3 hours

INGREDIENTS

- 1 can Italian-style tomatoes
- 3 cups chicken broth
- 1 cup cooked chicken breast, shredded
- ½ head of cabbage, shredded
- 1 packet Italian seasoning mix

INSTRUCTIONS
- Place all ingredients in the crockpot. Season with salt and pepper to taste.
- Give a good stir to combine everything. Close the lid and cook on low for 3 hours.
- Nutrition information: **Calories per serving: 248; Carbohydrates: 5.6g; Protein: 34.1g; Fat: 9.3g; Fiber: 1.4g**

PASTA AND RICE RECIPES

Crockpot Cheddar Spirals

⌖ Serves: 6 Preparation Time: 5 minutes Cooking Time: 2 hours

INGREDIENTS

- 1 package spiral pasta, cooked according to package
- 2 cups half and half cream
- 1 can condensed cheddar cheese sauce
- ½ cup butter, melted
- 4 cups cheddar cheese, grated

INSTRUCTIONS

✓ Place the pasta, cream, cheese sauce, and butter in the crockpot. Season with salt and pepper to taste.
✓ Give a good stir to combine everything. Top with grated cheddar cheese.
✓ Close the lid and cook on low for 2 hours.
  ⏱ **Nutrition information: Calories per serving: 260; Carbohydrates: 12g; Protein: 10g; Fat: 19g; Fiber: 1g**

Easy Crockpot Two-Cheese Lasagna

⌖ Serves: 8 Preparation Time: 6 minutes Cooking Time: 4 hours

INGREDIENTS

- 3 cups mozzarella cheese, grated
- 1 cup cheddar cheese, grated
- 1 jar spaghetti sauce
- 1 package lasagna noodles, cooked according to package
- 1 sprig fresh basil leaves, chopped

INSTRUCTIONS

✓ In a mixing bowl, combine the two types of cheeses. Set aside.
✓ Layer spaghetti sauce, lasagna noodles, and cheese in the Crockpot. Sprinkle with fresh basil leaves on top.
✓ Close the lid and cook on low for 4 hours.
  ⏱ **Nutrition information: Calories per serving: 291; Carbohydrates: 31g; Protein: 14; Fat: 11g; Fiber: 4g**

One Pot Pasta with Chicken and Cheese

⌖ Serves: 6 Preparation Time: 5 minutes Cooking Time: 3 hours

INGREDIENTS

- 1-pound Italian chicken sausage
- 1 bell pepper, chopped
- 1 package whole wheat penne pasta, cooked according to package
- 1 jar marinara sauce
- 1 cup mozzarella cheese, grated

INSTRUCTIONS

✓ Heat a skillet over medium heat and sauté the chicken sausages. Season with salt and pepper to taste. Cook until the sausages have turned slightly brown.
✓ Stir in the bell pepper, pasta, and marinara sauce. Mix to combine.
✓ Sprinkle with cheese on top.
✓ Close the lid and cook on low for 3 hours.
  ⏱ **Nutrition information: Calories per serving: 402; Carbohydrates: 63.9g; Protein: 33.9g; Fat: 3.4g; Fiber: 6.7g**

Chicken Alfredo Pasta

⌖ Serves: 4 Preparation Time: 5 minutes Cooking Time: 2 hours

INGREDIENTS

- 1-pound cooked chicken breasts, chopped
- 2 cups rigatoni pasta, cooked according to package instruction
- 1 jar Prego Alfredo Sauce
- ¼ cup mozzarella cheese
- ½ cup bacon bits, fried and crumbled

INSTRUCTIONS

✓ Place the chicken breasts, pasta, and Alfredo sauce in the crockpot. Give a good stir to combine everything.
✓ Sprinkle with mozzarella cheese on top. Close the lid and cook on low for 2 hours. Once cooked, sprinkle with bacon bits on top.
  ⏱ **Nutrition information: Calories per serving: 899; Carbohydrates: 26.5g; Protein: 53.4g; Fat: 64.5g; Fiber: 4.9g**

Chicken Spinach Pasta

⌖ Serves: 8 Preparation Time: 5 minutes Cooking Time: 3 hours

INGREDIENTS

- 1-pound cooked chicken breasts, chopped
- 1-pound bow tie pasta, cooked according to package
- 2 jars commercial pasta sauce
- 2 cups baby spinach
- ¼ cup parmesan cheese

INSTRUCTIONS

✓ Place the chicken, pasta, and sauce in the crockpot. Season with salt and pepper as well as other herbs of your choice.
✓ Mix to combine everything. Stir in the baby spinach.
✓ Top with parmesan cheese.
✓ Close the lid and cook on low for 3 hours.
  ⏱ **Nutrition information: Calories per serving: 216; Carbohydrates: 20.8g; Protein: 21.2g; Fat: 3.4g; Fiber: 4.1g**

Crockpot Cheesy Pesto Pasta

⌛ Serves: 9 Preparation Time: 5 minutes Cooking Time: 3 hours

INGREDIENTS

- 1 jar commercial pesto sauce
- 1 package elbow macaroni, cooked according to package
- 1 cup cottage cheese
- 1 cup parmesan cheese
- 1 cup mozzarella cheese

INSTRUCTIONS
- ✓ Place all ingredients in the crockpot. Give a good stir to combine everything.
- ✓ Close the lid and cook on low for 3 hours.
  - **Nutrition information: Calories per serving: 406; Carbohydrates: 9.7g; Protein: 16.1g; Fat: 34.8g; Fiber: 1g**

Chicken Parm Pasta

⌛ Serves: 8 Preparation Time: 6 minutes Cooking Time: 4 hours

INGREDIENTS

- 4 cooked chicken breasts, shredded
- 2 cans crushed tomatoes
- 1-pound penne pasta, cooked according to package
- 1 teaspoon herb seasoning mix of your choice
- ¼ cup parmesan cheese, grated

INSTRUCTIONS
- ✓ Place all ingredients in the crockpot. Season with salt and pepper to taste.
- ✓ Give a good stir to combine everything. Close the lid and cook on low for 4 hours.
  - **Nutrition information: Calories per serving:235; Carbohydrates: 18.5g; Protein: 29.5g; Fat: 4.6g; Fiber: 3.7g**

Butternut Squash and Chickpea Pasta

⌛ Serves: 6 Preparation Time: 5 minutes Cooking Time: 6 hours

INGREDIENTS

- 1 can chickpeas, rinsed
- 3 cups butternut squash, cubed
- 2 ½ cups vegetable broth
- 12-ounce pasta noodles, uncooked
- 1 cup heavy cream

INSTRUCTIONS
- ✓ Place all ingredients in the crockpot. Season with salt and pepper to taste.
- ✓ Give a good stir to combine everything. Close the lid and cook on low for 6 hours. Serve with cheese on top.
  - **Nutrition information: Calories per serving: 235; Carbohydrates: 35.3g; Protein: 9.2g; Fat: 5.5g; Fiber: 6.8g**

Butter Chicken Pasta

⌛ Serves: 8 Preparation Time: 5 minutes Cooking Time: 8 hours

INGREDIENTS

- 1-pound chicken thighs, bones, and skin removed
- ½ cup butter
- 1 packet Italian herb seasoning mix
- 1 cup frozen peas
- 1-pound rotini pasta, cooked according to package instruction

INSTRUCTIONS
- ✓ In the crockpot, mix together the chicken, butter, herb seasoning mix, and peas. Season with salt and pepper to taste.
- ✓ Close the lid and cook on low for 8 hours.
- ✓ Open the lid and shred the chicken using two forks. Serve with sauce on top on cooked pasta.
  - **Nutrition information: Calories per serving: 306; Carbohydrates: 17.3g; Protein: 11.5g; Fat: 21.5g; Fiber: 3.3g**

Cheesy Chicken Spaghetti

⌛ Serves: 4 Preparation Time: 5 minutes Cooking Time: 3 hours

INGREDIENTS

- 3 pounds spaghetti noodles, cooked according to package
- 1 can cream of mushroom soup
- 3 cups cheddar cheese, grated
- 1 cup cooked chicken, shredded
- ½ teaspoon garlic powder

INSTRUCTIONS
- ✓ Place all ingredients in the crockpot. Season with salt and pepper to taste.
- ✓ Give a good stir to combine everything. Close the lid and cook on low for 3 hours.
  - **Nutrition information: Calories per serving: 699; Carbohydrates: 62.4g; Protein: 33.8g; Fat: 33.5g; Fiber: 8.4g**

DESSERTS RECIPES

Slow Cooker Fruit Cobbler

Serves: 6 Preparation Time: 10 minutes Cooking Time: 4 hours

INGREDIENTS

- 4 cups frozen fruit slices
- ½ cup brown sugar
- ½ teaspoon ground cinnamon
- 1 package white cake mix
- ½ cup melted butter

INSTRUCTIONS
- ✓ Lightly coat the inside of the crockpot with cooking oil.
- ✓ Mix together the fruit slices with the sugar. Add in the cinnamon. Pour over the white cake mix and drizzle with melted butter on top. Close the lid and cook on low for 4 hours.
  - **Nutrition information: Calories per serving:738; Carbohydrates: 132.9g; Protein: 4.5g; Fat: 23.8g; Fiber: 4g**

Crockpot Banana Foster

Serves: 4 Preparation Time: 10 minutes Cooking Time: 4 hours

INGREDIENTS

- 4 bananas, peeled and sliced
- 4 tablespoons butter, melted
- 1 cup packed brown sugar
- ¼ cup rum
- ¼ cup walnuts, chopped

INSTRUCTIONS
- ✓ Place in the crockpot the bananas, butter, and sugar. Mix gently to combine.
- ✓ Drizzle in the rum and top with walnuts. Close the lid and cook on low for 4 hours.
  - **Nutrition information: Calories per serving:481; Carbohydrates: 82.5g; Protein:2.2g; Fat: 15.7g; Fiber: 3.4g**

Crockpot Rice Pudding

Serves: 8 Preparation Time: 5 minutes Cooking Time: 7 hours

INGREDIENTS

- 1 cup glutinous white rice, rinsed
- 1 cup white sugar
- 2 cans evaporated milk
- 1-ounce cinnamon stick
- 1 teaspoon vanilla extract

INSTRUCTIONS
- ✓ Place in the crockpot all the ingredients. Mix gently to combine.
- ✓ Close the lid and cook on low for 7 hours. Remove the cinnamon stick before serving.
  - **Nutrition information: Calories per serving: 226; Carbohydrates: 30.8g; Protein:6.3g; Fat: 8.9g; Fiber: 3.2g**

Warm Berry Compote

Serves: 6 Preparation Time: 5 minutes Cooking Time: 5 hours

INGREDIENTS

- 6 cups frozen mixed berries
- ½ cup white sugar
- 1 ½ teaspoons orange zest, grated
- ¼ cup orange juice
- 2 tablespoons cornstarch

INSTRUCTIONS
- ✓ Place in the crockpot all the ingredients. Mix gently to combine.
- ✓ Close the lid and cook on low for 7 hours.
  - **Nutrition information: Calories per serving: 132; Carbohydrates: 21.4g; Protein: 1.2g; Fat: 4.2g; Fiber: 4.7g**

Crockpot Custard Dulce De Leche

Serves: 8 Preparation Time: 10 minutes Cooking Time: 12 hours

INGREDIENTS

- 2 cans unsweetened condensed milk
- 1 cup sugar
- 4 egg yolks, beaten
- A pinch of salt
- 1 teaspoon vanilla extract

INSTRUCTIONS
- ✓ Mix all ingredients in a mixing bowl. Pour into mason jars and close the lid.

✓ Place the mason jars in the crockpot and pour water around the jars. Close the lid and cook on low for 12 hours.
  ⏱ **Nutrition information: Calories per serving: 152; Carbohydrates: 18.6g; Protein: 5.9g; Fat: 6.4; Fiber: 0g**

Crockpot Peach Cobbler

⏲ Serves: 6 Preparation Time: 10 minutes Cooking Time: 5 hours

INGREDIENTS

- 4 cups sliced peaches, canned
- ½ cup peach juice
- ½ cup brown sugar
- 1 teaspoon cinnamon
- 1/3 cup buttermilk baking mix

INSTRUCTIONS

✓ Place the peaches, peach juice, brown sugar, and cinnamon in the crockpot. Mix gently to combine.
✓ Sprinkle with buttermilk baking mix on top. Close the lid and cook on low for 5 hours.
  ⏱ **Nutrition information: Calories per serving: 215; Carbohydrates: 56.4g; Protein: 1.1g; Fat: 0.4g; Fiber: 2.8g**

Crockpot Applesauce

⏲ Serves: 10 Preparation Time: 5 minutes Cooking Time: 8 hours

INGREDIENTS

- 5 cored Gala apples, peeled and quartered
- 5 cored Golden Yellow Delicious apples, peeled and quartered
- ¼ cup sugar
- 1 teaspoon cinnamon powder
- ¼ cup apple juice

INSTRUCTIONS

✓ Place in the crockpot all the ingredients. Mix gently to combine.
✓ Close the lid and cook on low for 8 hours. Use a hand mixer and pulse until smooth.
  ⏱ **Nutrition information: Calories per serving:304; Carbohydrates: 77g; Protein: 1g; Fat: 1g; Fiber: 11g**

Crockpot Crème Brulee

⏲ Serves: 3 Preparation Time: 15 minutes Cooking Time: 3 hours

INGREDIENTS

- 3 egg yolks
- ½ cup heavy whipping cream
- ¼ cup sugar
- ¼ cup vanilla bean, scraped
- A pinch of salt

INSTRUCTIONS

✓ Get a long piece of the aluminum foil and create a ring that a ramekin with fit inside. Seal the edges. Make three rings. Set aside.
✓ In a mixing bowl, combine everything until frothy.
✓ Pour the custard mixture into the ramekins wrapped in foil rings. Place inside the crockpot.
✓ Pour boiling water in the slow cooker. Be careful not to splash water into the custard. Close the lid and cook on low for 3 hours.
✓ Chill for at least 6 hours.
✓ Before serving, sprinkle with sugar and blow a torch to burn the sugar.
  ⏱ **Nutrition information: Calories per serving: 159; Carbohydrates: 10.1g; Protein: 3.2g; Fat: 11.9g; Fiber: 0.2g**

Savory Sausages and Brussels Sprout Breakfast

⏲ Servings: 4 Cooking Times: Total Time: 5 hours and 10 minutes

INGREDIENTS

- 1/2 lb Brussels sprouts, chopped
- 8 eggs
- 2 turkey or chicken sausages, sliced 2 cloves garlic, finely chopped
- 1 cup Cheddar cheese, shredded
- Salt and pepper to taste, lard

DIRECTIONS

✓ Grease the bottom of the Crock Pot with lard.
✓ Place chopped and halved Brussels sprouts, half of the sausages, garlic and half of Cheddar into Crock Pot.
✓ Repeat this process with the remaining Brussels sprout, sausages, and cheese. In a bowl, whisk eggs with the salt and pepper.
✓ Pour the egg mixture over Brussels sprouts.
✓ Cover and cook on LOW for 4 to 5 hours. Serve hot.

Tropicana Coconut Cake

⏲ Servings: 10 Cooking Times: 1 hour and 55 minutes

INGREDIENTS

- 1 cup of coconut oil melted
- 3 large eggs beaten
- 1 cup stevia granulated sweetener (or to taste)
- 2 1/4 cup of coconut flour + baking powder
- 1/2 cup coconut milk canned

DIRECTIONS
- Line the bottom of your Crock Pot with parchment paper; set aside. Beat the melted coconut oil and stevia sweetener with an electric mixer. Add the eggs one by one and stir well after each egg.
- In a separate bowl, combine the coconut flour, and one teaspoon of baking powder.
- Add the coconut milk to the coconut oil mixture along with the coconut flour mix and stir until the flour is well mixed in.
- Spread dough evenly on baking paper.
- Cover and cook on HIGH about 1 - 1 1/2 hours.
- When ready, remove from the cooker and let cool for 10 - 15 minutes on the room temperature. Slice and serve.

Super Keto Lemon Bars

Servings: 8 Cooking Times: 3 hours and 10 minutes

INGREDIENTS

- 1/2 cup almond butter, melted
- 1 3/4 cups almond flour
- 1 cup powdered stevia sweetener
- 3 medium lemons
- 3 eggs from free-range chickens

DIRECTIONS
- Line your Crock Pot with parchment paper.
- Stir the almond flour, stevia and a pinch of salt together (optional). Add the almond mixture in your prepared Crock Pot.
- In a bowl, whisk the lemon juice from 3 lemons, lemon zest from the three lemons, eggs, and some stevia sweetener.
- Pour the lemon mixture over the almond mixture in your Crock Pot. Cover and cook on LOW setting for 3 hours.
- Open and check your cake; if too gooey and like a pudding cake, cover again and cook on HIGH for further 30 minutes.
- Let cool completely, cut in bars and serve.

Chocolate Coated Nut Candies

Servings: 36 Cooking Times

Preparation Time: 2 hours Inactive Time: 2 hours

INGREDIENTS

- 1 1/4 lbs Keto chocolate candy coating
- 8 oz dry roasted peanuts, unsalted
- 8 oz almonds finely chopped
- 8 oz hazelnuts (or any other nuts)
- 1 tsp pure vanilla extract

DIRECTIONS
- Dump all ingredients into your Crock Pot.
- Cover and cook on LOW setting for 1 hour without stirring. After one hour stir well.
- Cover, and cook for further 1 hour, stirring every 15 minutes. Line a platter with the wax paper.
- Drop spoonfuls of chocolate/nuts mixture onto a prepared platter and let cool. Place in refrigerator for 2 hours.
- Serve once cooled and store in the fridge.

Almond Fudge Brownies

Servings: 10 Cooking Times Preparation Time: 3 hours and 20 minutes Inactive Time: 15 minutes

INGREDIENTS

- 4 1/2 oz dark baking chocolate, melted
- 3/4 cup almond butter
- 2 cups stevia or Splenda granulated sweetener
- 4 large eggs
- 1 cup almond flour

DIRECTIONS
- Melt the chocolate in your microwave oven for one minute; stir. Line the inner pot of your Crock Pot with parchment paper.
- Beat (with an electric mixer) the almond butter with sweetener until the mixture stiffens. Add the eggs and continue to beat for one minute.
- Add the melted chocolate and beat again.
- Finally, add the almond flour and beat for another 1 to 2 minutes until smooth. Pour the batter in prepared Crock Pot.
- Cook on LOW setting 2 1/2 to 3 hours.
- When finished, let it rest for 15 minutes. Cut in cubes and serve.

Warm Collard greens and Kalamata Olive Salad

Servings: 4 Cooking Times: 6 hours and 10 minutes

INGREDIENTS

- 1 lb of Collard greens, trimmed
- 1 cup Kalamata olives, pitted and sliced
- 1/4 cup garlic-infused olive oil
- Lemon juice from 2 lemons, freshly squeezed
- Salt to taste
- 1 cup water

DIRECTIONS
- Clean the collard greens well; wash them in a sink, changing water until you don't see any grit in the water.
- Place the collard greens in the greased Crockpot along with all other ingredients from the list (except olives). Pour water into Crock Pot and cover.
- Cook on LOW setting for 6 hours or on HIGH setting for 3 hours. Remove the collard greens onto a serving plate.
- Add chopped olives and stir lightly.
- Dress salad with the salt, lemon juice, and olive oil before serving.

Mediterranean Egg Muffins

Servings: 12 Cooking Times: 7 hours

INGREDIENTS

- 12 eggs, separated from free-range chickens

- 2 bell peppers (any color), diced
- 1 green onion, finely sliced
- 2 cloves garlic minced
- 1 tomato grated
- Salt and pepper to taste

DIRECTIONS
- Grease a muffin tin with olive oil.
- Whisk the egg whites (with a whisker or electric mixer) in a copper or metal or glass bowl until they are stiff.
- Add egg yolks and the salt and pepper and continue to whisk until foamy.
- Add all remaining ingredients and continue to whisk until all ingredients combined well. Pour the batter into muffin cavities (3/4 of the cavity).
- Place filled muffin cups on the bottom of a large Crock Pot. Cook on LOW setting for 6 - 7 hours or until golden brown.
- Allow cooling slightly before removing from the muffin tin with a butter knife. Nutrition Facts

Crunchy Green Beans and Carrots Strips

Servings: 4 Cooking Times: 5 hours and 15 minutes

INGREDIENTS
- 1 lb green beans
- 2 carrots cut into strips
- 2 cloves of garlic minced
- 1/2 tsp cumin seed, ground
- Salt and black pepper, freshly ground
- 1/4 cup bone broth (or water)

DIRECTIONS
- Clean the green beans and rinse and slice carrots into strips. Place green beans and carrots into your Crock Pot.
- Add the garlic and sprinkle with cumin and the salt and pepper. Pour the bone broth or water and stir well.
- Cover and cook on LOW setting for 4 to 5 hours. Serve hot or cold.

Creamed Spinach Puree with Parmesan

Servings: 4 Cooking Times: 6 hours

INGREDIENTS
- 2 lbs fresh spinach tender leaves
- 1 bunch of dill finely chopped
- 1 cup of cream
- 1 cup grated Parmesan cheese
- Salt and ground black pepper

DIRECTIONS
- Grease your Crock Pot with oil or butter.
- Place all ingredients from the list above in the Crock Pot; stir well. Cover and cook on HIGH setting for one hour.
- Reduce heat to LOW and continue to cook for 4 to 5 hours.
- Transfer the spinach mixture to your high-speed blender and blend until creamy. Taste and adjust salt and pepper.
- Serve immediately.

"Kapamas" Cauliflower

Servings: 6 Cooking Times: 4 hours and 10 minutes

INGREDIENTS
- 2 lbs cauliflower florets
- 1 large onion finely chopped
- 2 carrots, grated
- 1 cup of grated tomatoes
- Garlic-infused olive oil, water, salt, and ground red pepper to taste

DIRECTIONS
- Rinse the cauliflower, clean and divide into florets.
- Grease the bottom of your Crock Pot with olive oil; add the cauliflower florets. Add the onion over cauliflower along with the grated carrots and tomatoes.
- Season with salt and ground red pepper; stir well. Pour half cup of water and stir again.
- Cover and cook for 4 hours or until tender.
- Open and taste; adjust the salt and red pepper; stir. Serve hot.

Savory Spinach and Bacon Chowder

Servings: 8 Cooking Times: 4 hours

INGREDIENTS
- 2 lbs of spinach cleaned, rinsed and chopped
- 2 spring onions finely chopped
- 1 cup bacon cut in cubes
- 4 cups bone broth or water
- 1 Tbsp fresh dill, finely chopped

DIRECTIONS
- Grease a 4 1/2 quart or larger Crock Pot.
- Place all ingredients in your Crock Pot; stir well. Cover and cook on LOW setting for 4 hours.
- Transfer soup into a blender and blend until smooth. Serve hot

Rabbit with Chorizo and Cinnamon

Servings: 4 Cooking Times: 8 hours

INGREDIENTS
- 3 Tbsp garlic-infused olive oil
- Salt and cayenne pepper, ground cinnamon
- 1 rabbit, cut into pieces
- 5 1/2 oz of chorizo sausages
- 2 onions, sliced

DIRECTIONS
- ✓ Pour the olive oil in your Crock Pot.
- ✓ Season the rabbit meat generously with the salt. Place the rabbit in the Crock Pot.
- ✓ Add the onions, chopped chorizo sausage, and cayenne pepper. Cover and cook on LOW setting for 6- 8 hours.
- ✓ Serve hot with a pinch of cinnamon.

Creamy Lamb with Artichokes

Servings: 8 Cooking Times: 6 hours and 5 minutes

INGREDIENTS

- 2 ¼ lbs of lamb chunks
- 12 artichokes hearts, cleaned and brushed with lemon
- 2 large onions grated
- 2 cups yogurt drained
- 1 cup fresh dill chopped Salt and ground pepper

DIRECTIONS
- ✓ Season the lamb generously with salt and pepper. Place the seasoned lamb in your Crock Pot.
- ✓ Place the artichokes brushed with lemon over the meat. Sprinkle grated onion over the artichokes.
- ✓ Stir yogurt with chopped dill and spread over lamb and artichokes. Cook on LOW setting for 5 to 6 hours.
- ✓ Serve hot.

Crockpot Cinnamon Almonds

Serves: 6 Preparation Time: 5 minutes Cooking Time: 4 hours

INGREDIENTS

- 1 cup brown sugar
- 3 tablespoons cinnamon powder
- 1 egg white, beaten
- 3 cups almond
- 1/3 cup water

INSTRUCTIONS
- ✓ Place in the crockpot all the ingredients. Mix gently to combine.
- ✓ Close the lid and cook on low for 4 hours.
- **Nutrition information: Calories per serving: 155; Carbohydrates: 39.3g; Protein: 0.9g; Fat: 0.4g; Fiber: 2.1g**

Bread Pudding with Figs and Cherries

(Ready in about 2 hours | Servings 4)

INGREDIENTS

- 2 cups whole milk
- 2 large-sized eggs
- 1 teaspoon vanilla extract
- 1/2 teaspoon allspice
- 1/2 teaspoon ground cloves
- 1/2 teaspoon cinnamon
- A pinch of sea salt
- 1/2 cup sugar
- 1/2 cup figs, chopped
- 1/2 cup dried cherries
- 2 cups bread cubes
- 1/2 cup hot water

DIRECTIONS
- ✓ In a measuring cup, beat together the milk, eggs, vanilla extract, allspice, cloves, cinnamon, sea salt, and sugar.
- ✓ Fold in the figs, cherries, and bread cubes.
- ✓ Pour the mixture into a suitable baking dish that will fit on the cooking rack inside of the crock pot.
- ✓ Pour the hot water into the crock pot.
- ✓ Cover and cook 2 hours on high. Turn off the crock pot and serve; you
- ✓ can top it with caramel sauce if desired.

Bread Pudding with Pecans and Fruits

(Ready in about 2 hours | Servings 4)

INGREDIENTS

- 2 eggs, lightly beaten
- 2 cups whole milk
- A pinch of sea salt
- 1 teaspoon pure almond extract
- 1/4 teaspoon ground anise seed
- 1/2 cardamom
- 1/2 teaspoon grated nutmeg
- 1/2 teaspoon cinnamon
- 1/2 cup brown sugar
- 1/2 cup toasted pecans, chopped
- 1/2 cup golden raisins
- 1/2 cup dried cranberries
- 2 ½ cups bread cubes
- 1/2 cup water

DIRECTIONS
- ✓ In a medium-sized mixing bowl, combine together eggs, milk, salt, almond extract, anise seed, cardamom, nutmeg, cinnamon, and brown sugar. Mix well until everything is well incorporated.
- ✓ Fold in the pecans, golden raisins, dried cranberries, and bread cubes.
- ✓ Transfer the batter to a baking dish. Place the baking dish on the cooking
- ✓ rack inside of the crock pot; then, pour in the water to cover the bottom of the crock pot.
- ✓ Cook covered 2 hours on high. Serve at room temperature and enjoy.

Summer Peach Treat

(Ready in about 3 hours | Servings 8)

INGREDIENTS

- 1 tablespoon canola oil
- 2 cups peaches, sliced

- 1 tablespoon cornflour
- 1/4 cup sugar
- 1 teaspoon vanilla extract
- 1 tablespoon molasses
- 1/2 teaspoon grated ginger
- 1/2 teaspoon cinnamon
- 9 ounces cake mix
- 4 tablespoons margarine, melted

DIRECTIONS

- Lightly grease the inside of your crock pot with 1 tablespoon of canola oil; then arrange the slices of the peaches in the bottom.
- Sprinkle with cornflour; then, toss to coat.
- Sprinkle with sugar, vanilla, molasses, grated ginger, and cinnamon. Fold in cake mix and drizzle melted margarine evenly over it.
- Cover and cook on high about 3 hours. Turn off the crock pot; serve and enjoy!

Banana Butter Cake with Coconut and Almonds

(Ready in about 4 hours | Servings 8)

INGREDIENTS

- 1 stick butter
- 1 cup cream cheese, softened
- 1 cup granulated white sugar
- 1 tablespoon molasses
- 3 medium-sized eggs
- 1/2 cup half-and-half
- 1 tablespoon orange juice
- 2 ripe bananas, sliced
- 1 1/3 cup cake flour
- 1 teaspoon baking soda
- 1/2 teaspoon baking powder
- A pinch of salt
- A dash of cinnamon
- A dash of cardamom
- 1/2 cup almonds, chopped
- 1/2 cup grated coconut, unsweetened

DIRECTIONS

- Add butter, cheese, sugar, molasses, eggs, half-and-half, orange juice and bananas to a food processor. Process until everything is well combined.
- Then, in a separate mixing bowl, combine together the cake flour, baking
- soda, baking powder, salt, cinnamon and cardamom. Stir to mix well.
- Scrape in the creamy banana mixture. Stir again. Fold in the almonds and coconut.
- Line the bottom of the crock pot with a parchment paper; pour in the prepared batter.
- Cover and cook on low for 4 hours.

Country Apple Cake with Walnuts

(Ready in about 4 hours | Servings 8)

INGREDIENTS

- 1 cup cream cheese, softened
- 1 stick butter
- 1 cup granulated white sugar
- 3 eggs, lightly beaten
- 1/2 cup buttermilk
- 2 tart apples, sliced
- 1 1/3 cup fine pastry flour
- 1 teaspoon baking powder
- Sea salt, taste
- 1/4 teaspoon ground mace
- 1/4 teaspoon allspice
- 1 cup walnuts, chopped

DIRECTIONS

- Combine cream cheese, butter, sugar, eggs, buttermilk and apples in your food processor. Blend until the mixture is well mixed.
- Next step, in another mixing bowl, combine together your fine pastry flour, baking powder, sea salt, mace and allspice. Stir to combine.
- Scrape in the apple mixture. Stir to combine. Fold in the walnuts.
- Coat the bottom of the crock pot with a parchment paper; pour the batter into the crock pot.
- Cook covered about 4 hours on low.

Date Pudding Cake

(Ready in about 4 hours | Servings 8)

INGREDIENTS

- 2 ½ cups dates, pitted and snipped
- 1 teaspoon baking soda
- 1 2/3 cups boiling water
- 2 cups packed brown sugar
- 1/2 cup butter, softened
- 1 teaspoon vanilla
- 1/4 teaspoon grated nutmeg
- 1/2 teaspoon cinnamon
- 3 large-sized eggs
- 3 ½ cups cake flour
- 1 tablespoon baking powder
- 1/4 teaspoon salt
- Non-stick spray (butter flavour)

DIRECTIONS

- In a mixing bowl, place dates together with baking soda and water. Set aside.
- In a food processor, place brown sugar and butter; process until creamy and uniform; then, continue to process adding vanilla, nutmeg, cinnamon and eggs.
- Scrape the mixture into the bowl and stir to mix.
- Add the cake flour, baking powder, and salt to the mixing bowl; stir to mix.
- Treat the crock pot with non-stick spray. Next, pour the batter into the crock pot.
- Cover and cook on low for 4 hours or until the center of the cake is set. Serve with a dollop of whipped cream.

Grandma's Orange Coffee Cake

⌀ **(Ready in about 2 hours 30 minutes | Servings 6)**

INGREDIENTS

- 4 eggs, separated
- 1/4 cup fresh orange juice
- 1 teaspoon grated ginger
- 1 teaspoon allspice
- 1 teaspoon vanilla extract
- 3 tablespoons butter
- 1 ½ cups whole milk
- 1 cup cake flour
- 1/2 cup powdered sugar
- 1/2 cup granulated white sugar
- A pinch salt
- A dash of cinnamon

DIRECTIONS

- In a food processor, combine egg yolks, orange juice, ginger, allspice, vanilla extract, and butter; process in order to cream all ingredients together.
- Continue to process and slowly add the milk.
- Stir in the rest of the ingredients; stir to mix. Add the egg yolk mixture to the bowl.
- In a separate bowl, whip the egg whites until stiff peaks form. Fold into the prepared batter.
- Transfer the batter to the crock pot. Cover and cook on low for 2 ½ hours. Enjoy!

Old-Fashioned Cheese Cake

⌀ **(Ready in about 3 hours | Servings 8)**

INGREDIENTS

- Non-stick cooking spray (butter flavour)
- 1 cup cream cheese, softened
- 1 stick butter, softened
- 1 (5.1-ounce) package instant vanilla pudding
- 3 large-sized eggs
- 1/2 cup fat-free half-and-half
- 1 teaspoon pure almond extract
- 1/2 teaspoon grated nutmeg
- 1 (18-ounce) package butter cake mix
- Toasted almonds, as garnish

DIRECTIONS

- Treat the inside of the crock pot with non-stick cooking spray.
- Whip the cream cheese with butter in a medium-sized mixing bowl. Beat in the vanilla pudding, eggs, half-and-half, almond extract, and grated nutmeg.
- Next step, fold in the butter cake mix.
- Drop prepared batter into the crock pot; lightly pat it down.
- Cover with the lid; cook on high for 3 hours or until a fork or a wooden skewer inserted in the center comes out clean.
- Invert the cake onto a plate, scatter almonds on top and serve.

Favorite Winter Compote

⌀ **(Ready in about 6 hours | Servings 10)**

INGREDIENTS

- 2 medium-sized apples, peeled, cored and sliced
- 1 medium-sized pear, peeled, cored and sliced
- 2/3 cup dried cherries
- 1 vanilla bean
- 1 cinnamon stick
- 1/2 cup dried prunes
- 1/2 cup dried apricots, halved
- 1 cup canned pineapple tidbits with juice, unsweetened
- 1/4 cup brown sugar
- 1/2 cup apple juice
- 2 tablespoons orange juice
- 1 (21-oz.) can peach pie filling

DIRECTIONS

- Simply place all of the ingredients in your crock pot.
- Cover and slow cook on low heat setting for about 6 hours.
- Divide among ten serving bowls and serve warm or at room temperature.

Everyday Dried Fruit Compote

⌀ **(Ready in about 5 hours | Servings 10)**

INGREDIENTS

- 4 cups dried apricots
- 6 ounces dried prunes
- 1 ½ cups golden raisins
- 1/2 cups dried dates
- 1/2 cup dried cranberries
- 1/3 cup dried figs
- 1 teaspoon lemon zest
- 2 cups pineapple juice
- 2 cups orange juice
- 1 cup white zinfandel
- 1 vanilla bean
- 1 cinnamon bean
- 1/4 teaspoon anise seed

DIRECTIONS

- Put all ingredients into your crock pot.
- Next, cover with the lid and cook for 4 to 5 hours on high.
- Turn off the crock pot. Divide among ten serving bowls; serve with a scoop of vanilla ice cream if desired.

Carrot Cake with Hazelnuts and Golden Raisins

⌀ **(Ready in about 3 hours 30 minutes | Servings 12)**

INGREDIENTS

- 3/4 cup light brown sugar
- 12 tablespoons butter, room temperature
- 3 medium-sized eggs

- 1 tablespoon fresh lemon juice
- 2 cups carrots, shredded
- 1/3 cup hazelnuts, coarsely chopped
- 1/3 cup golden raisins
- 1 ½ cups self-rising flour
- 1 teaspoon baking powder
- A pinch of salt
- 1/3 cup cream cheese, room temperature
- 1 tablespoon butter, room temperature
- 1 teaspoon almond extract
- 1 ½ cups powdered sugar
- Milk

DIRECTIONS

✓ Begin by making the batter. In a large-sized bowl, beat brown sugar and butter until fluffy; stir in eggs one at a time, beating well.
✓ Stir in lemon juice, carrots, hazelnuts, and golden raisins. Fold in flour,
✓ baking powder, and salt.
✓ Pour batter into greased and floured springform pan; place on a rack in your crock pot. Set your crock pot on high and cook your cake about 3 ½ hours.
✓ Meanwhile, make cream cheese glaze. In a medium-sized mixing bowl, beat cream cheese, butter and almond extract until smooth; add powdered sugar and milk in order to make a thick glaze consistency.
✓ Drizzle carrot cake with cream cheese glaze.

Ginger and Walnut Sponge Cake

(Ready in about 2 hours | Servings 6)

INGREDIENTS

- 1/2 cup packed light brown sugar
- 1/4 cup molasses
- 1/2 cup canned pumpkin
- 1/4 cup margarine, room temperature
- 1 large-sized egg
- 1/2 cup ground walnuts
- 1/2 teaspoon grated ginger
- 1/2 teaspoon ground mace
- 1 ½ cups fine cake flour
- 1/2 teaspoon baking powder
- 1 teaspoon baking soda

DIRECTIONS

✓ Combine brown sugar, molasses, pumpkin, margarine and egg in a large mixer bowl; mix at medium speed until everything is well blended.
✓ Stir in walnuts, ginger, mace, fine cake flour, baking powder and baking soda; blending at low speed until the mixture is moistened.
✓ Pour your batter into two greased and floured cans. Place cans in the crock pot; cover and cook on high until wooden skewer inserted in cake comes out clean or about 2 hours.
✓ Allow to cool 10 minutes before cutting and serving.

Winter Gingerbread Cake

(Ready in about 5 hours | Servings 12)

INGREDIENTS

- 1 ½ cups cake flour
- 1/2 cup all-purpose flour
- 1/2 teaspoon baking soda
- 1/2 teaspoon baking powder
- 1 teaspoon lemon juice
- 1/2 teaspoon ground cinnamon
- 1/4 teaspoon kosher salt
- 1/4 teaspoon allspice
- 8 tablespoons margarine, room temperature
- 3/4 cup brown sugar
- 2/3 cup molasses
- 1/2 cup whole milk
- 1 large-sized egg, lightly beaten

DIRECTIONS

✓ Combine cake flour, all-purpose flour, baking soda and baking powder in a large-sized bowl.
✓ Combine lemon juice, cinnamon, salt, allspice, margarine, sugar and molasses; microwave on high until margarine is completely melted, about 1 to 2 minutes.
✓ Add the margarine mixture to the flour mixture, whisk in milk and egg; mix to combine.
✓ Pour prepared batter into greased and floured baking pan; place on a rack in your crock pot. Cover and cook on high about 5 hours or until wooden skewer inserted in center of cake comes out clean.
✓ Drizzle with cream cheese glaze and serve.

Applesauce Genoise with Buttery Glaze

(Ready in about 3 hours | Servings 12)

INGREDIENTS

For the Cake:

- 1/2 cup butter, room temperature
- 1 tablespoon molasses
- 1 tablespoon orange juice
- 3/4 cup granulated white sugar
- 1 egg
- 3/4 cup applesauce
- 1 cup pastry flour
- 1/2 cup whole-wheat flour
- 1 tablespoon baking powder
- 1/2 teaspoon grated nutmeg
- 1/4 teaspoon ground cloves
- 1/2 teaspoon ground cinnamon
- 1/2 teaspoon salt
- 1/2 teaspoon baking soda

For Buttery Glaze:

- 1/2 teaspoon butter extract

- 1 cup powdered sugar
- Milk

DIRECTIONS
- Beat butter, molasses, orange juice and white sugar in a large-sized mixing bowl until the mixture is well blended; stir in egg and applesauce.
- Combine the rest of the ingredients for the cake. Add to the bowl.
- Pour batter into greased and floured 6-cup cake pan; place pan on a rack in the crock pot.
- Cover and cook on high about 3 hours, until wooden skewer inserted in center of cake comes out clean.
- In the meantime, combine all of the ingredients for buttery glaze. Mix in order to make a glaze consistency.
- Invert onto a rack and let cool completely before serving.

Easy Chocolate Peanut Butter Cake

(Ready in about 2 hours | Servings 12)

INGREDIENTS
- 1/3 cup margarine
- 1/3 cup light brown sugar
- 2 medium-sized eggs
- 1/2 cup peanut butter
- 1/2 cup sour cream
- 1 2/3 cups self-rising flour
- A pinch of sea salt
- 1/2 cup chocolate morsels

DIRECTIONS
- Beat margarine and light brown sugar in a mixing bowl until fluffy; add eggs and blend well to combine. Stir in peanut butter and sour cream.
- Add self-rising flour, sea salt, and chocolate morsels.
- Pour batter into greased and floured 6-cup cake pan; place on a rack in a crock pot.
- Slow cook on high 2 to 2 ½ hours.
- Serve with chocolate sauce if desired. Enjoy!

Delicious Apple Streusel Dessert

(Ready in about 8 hours | Servings 8)

INGREDIENTS

For the Cake:
- 6 cups tart apples, cored, peeled and sliced
- 1 teaspoon grated nutmeg
- 1/2 teaspoon ground mace
- 1 teaspoon ground cinnamon
- 1 tablespoon fresh lemon juice
- 3/4 cup milk
- 2 tablespoons canola oil
- 3/4 cup powdered sugar
- 2 eggs, beaten
- 1 teaspoon pure vanilla
- 1/2 cup baking mix
- 1 cup baking mix

- 1/3 cup sugar
- 1 tablespoon honey
- 3 tablespoons margarine, cold
- 1/2 cup walnuts, coarsely chopped

DIRECTIONS
- In a large-sized mixing bowl, toss sliced apples with nutmeg, mace and
- cinnamon, Drizzle with lemon juice and place in a greased crock pot.
- In a separate small-sized bowl, combine the milk, oil, powdered sugar, beaten eggs, vanilla and baking mix. Spoon this mixture over the apples in the crock pot.
- Combine all of the ingredients for the topping in a bowl.
- Slow cook on low about 8 hours. Serve with whipped cream if desired.

Holiday Pumpkin Pie Pudding

(Ready in about 7 hours | Servings 8)

INGREDIENTS
- Non-stick cooking spray
- 2 cups canned pumpkin
- 1 ½ cups whole milk
- 3/4 cup brown sugar
- 1/2 cup biscuit mix
- 2 medium-sized eggs, beaten
- 2 tablespoons margarine, melted
- 1 teaspoon grated ginger
- 2 teaspoons vanilla extract
- 2 ½ teaspoons pumpkin pie spice
- Whipped topping, as garnish

DIRECTIONS
- Coat the inside of a crock pot with non-stick cooking spray.
- In a large-sized mixing bowl, combine all ingredients, except whipped topping. Transfer to the crock pot. Slow cook on low for 7 hours. Serve with whipped topping.

Cocoa Cake with Vanilla Ice Cream

(Ready in about 3 hours | Servings 4)

INGREDIENTS
- 4 medium-sized eggs
- 1/2 cup butter, melted
- 1/2 teaspoon pure mint extract
- 2 teaspoons vanilla
- 1 ½ cups granulated white sugar
- 1 cup pastry flour
- 1/2 cup baking cocoa
- 1 tablespoon instant coffee granules
- A pinch of salt
- Vanilla ice cream, as garnish

DIRECTIONS
- In a large-sized mixing bowl, combine eggs, butter, mint extract, vanilla and white sugar until the mixture is blended.

- In a separate bowl, whisk pastry flour, cocoa, coffee granules, and salt.
- Transfer to a greased crock pot. Cook covered on low heat setting for 3 hours.
- If desired, serve warm cake with vanilla ice cream.

Easy Everyday Cherry Pie

(Ready in about 3 hours | Servings 12)

INGREDIENTS

- 1 (18-ounce) package yellow cake mix
- 1/2 cup butter
- 1 (21-ounce) can cherry pie filling
- A dash of cinnamon
- 1 teaspoon lemon rind

DIRECTIONS
- Combine cake mix with butter in a large-sized mixing bowl.
- Place cherry pie filling in your crock pot. Sprinkle the cake mixture over cherry pie filling. Sprinkle with cinnamon and lemon rind.
- Cover with the lid and slow cook on low for 3 hours. Sprinkle with granulated white sugar and serve.

Chocolate Candy with Almonds and Pecans

(Ready in about 3 hours | Servings 12)

INGREDIENTS

- 2 cups pecans, chopped
- 2 cups roasted almonds
- 1 (12-ounce) package semi-sweet chocolate morsels
- 1/2 cup chocolate bars
- 32 ounces white almond bark

DIRECTIONS
- Arrange pecans and almonds on the bottom of the crock pot.
- Layer the other ingredients over the nuts.
- Cook on low heat setting about 2 hours.
- Next, drop the candy into cupcake pan liners. Allow to cool completely before serving or storing.

Apple Sauce with Pecans

(Ready in about 6 hours | Servings 8)

INGREDIENTS

- 1 tablespoon unsalted butter
- 4 pounds apples, cored and sliced
- 1/2 cup brown sugar
- 1/2 teaspoon grated ginger
- 1/2 teaspoon cinnamon
- 1 cup water
- 1 tablespoon lemon juice
- 1 tablespoon finely chopped pecans

DIRECTIONS

- Put all of the ingredients into the crock pot.
- Cover and slow cook on low for 6 hours.
- Garnish with lightly sweetened whipped cream.

Family Apple Oatmeal Delight

(Ready in about 2 hours 30 minutes | Servings 8)

INGREDIENTS

- 1 cup oatmeal
- 1 cup sugar
- 1 tablespoon molasses
- 1/3 cup all-purpose flour
- 1 tablespoon fresh lemon juice
- 1 teaspoon allspice
- 1/2 teaspoon almond extract
- 1 teaspoon vanilla extract
- 1/2 cup butter, melted
- 1/2 cup almonds
- 6 apples, peeled, cored and sliced

DIRECTIONS
- In a medium-sized mixing bowl, combine oatmeal with sugar, molasses, flour, and lemon juice.
- Add allspice, almond extract, vanilla extract, butter and almonds to the oatmeal mixture.
- Put 1/2 of the apples into the crock pot; after that, spoon half of oatmeal mixture on top.
- Afterwards, place remaining 1/2 of apples and top with the rest of the oatmeal mixture.
- Slow cook on high 2 to 2 ½ hours. Serve with cool whip and enjoy!

Bananas Foster with Vanilla Ice Cream

(Ready in about 1 hour 10 minutes | Servings 4)

INGREDIENTS

- 1/2 cup butter
- 1/4 cup brown sugar
- 6 fresh bananas, sliced
- 1/4 cup rum
- Vanilla ice cream, as garnish

DIRECTIONS
- Melt margarine in the crock pot on low, about 10 minutes.
- Add brown sugar, banana slices, and rum.
- Cook on low for 1 hour.
- Spoon over vanilla ice cream and serve.

Spiced Apples with Currants

(Ready in about 2 hours | Servings 6)

INGREDIENTS

- 6 large-sized apples, cored, peeled and sliced
- 1 cup currants

- 1/4 cup light brown sugar
- 1 cup sugar
- 1/4 teaspoon nutmeg
- 1/2 teaspoon ground mace
- 1 cinnamon
- 3 tablespoons cornflour
- 4 tablespoons butter, sliced

DIRECTIONS
- ✓ Put all ingredients, except butter, into the crock pot; stir well; then, place slices of butter on top.
- ✓ Cook on high for 2 hours.
- ✓ Serve and enjoy!

Apple Walnut Cobbler

⌀ (Ready in about 3 hours | Servings 6)

INGREDIENTS
- 1 (21-ounce) can apple pie filling
- 1 (18 ounce) package yellow cake mix
- 1/2 cup ground walnuts
- 1 teaspoon ground mace
- 1/2 cup melted margarine

DIRECTIONS
- ✓ Place apple pie filling into the crock pot.
- ✓ Mix remaining ingredients.
- ✓ Place the mixture over apple pie filling in the crock pot.
- ✓ Cook on low for 3 hours.

Cherry Cobbler with Custard

⌀ (Ready in about 2 hours | Servings 6)

INGREDIENTS
- Non-stick cooking spray
- 1 (21-ounce) can cherry pie filling
- 1 cup all-purpose flour
- 1/4 cup sugar
- 1/4 cup margarine, melted
- 1/2 cup milk
- 1 teaspoon baking soda
- 1/2 teaspoon baking powder
- Salt, to taste
- 1 teaspoon cherry flavored liqueur
- 1 cup toasted pine nuts, chopped
- Custard for garnish

DIRECTIONS
- ✓ Lightly grease the inside of a crock pot with non-stick cooking spray.
- ✓ Place the cherry pie filling into the oiled crock pot. To make the batter, in a large-sized mixing bowl, combine the rest of the ingredients, except custard.
- ✓ Spread the batter over the cherry pie filling. Cover on high for 2 hours.
- ✓ Turn off the crock pot. Serve with custard and enjoy.

Summer Peach Cake

⌀ (Ready in about 8 hours | Servings 6)

INGREDIENTS
- 1/2 cup sugar
- 2 teaspoons butter, melted
- 2 medium-sized eggs
- 1 ½ cups evaporated milk
- 3/4 cup white baking mix
- 2 cups peaches, mashed
- 1 tablespoon fresh lemon juice
- 1/2 teaspoon ground mace
- 3/4 teaspoon allspice

DIRECTIONS
- ✓ Oil your crock pot with non-stick cooking spray.
- ✓ Combine the rest of the ingredients in a mixing bowl.
- ✓ Pour into the crock pot. Cook on low for 8 hours.
- ✓ Turn off your crock pot; serve and enjoy!

Country Honey-Sauced Pears

⌀ (Ready in about 2 hours 30 minutes | Servings 6)

INGREDIENTS
- 6 pears, peeled and cored
- 1/2 cup brown sugar
- 1/4 cup honey
- 1 tablespoon butter, melted
- 1 teaspoon lemon zest
- 1/2 teaspoon ground mace
- 1/4 teaspoon ground ginger
- 1 tablespoon cornflour
- 2 tablespoons lemon juice

DIRECTIONS
- ✓ Place pears upright in a crock pot.
- ✓ In a bowl, mix remaining ingredients, except cornflour and lemon juice; pour the mixture over pears.
- ✓ Cover with the lid and cook on high heat setting 2 ½ hours or until the pears are tender.
- ✓ Remove the pears from the crock pot and transfer to the dessert dishes.
- ✓ Combine together cornflour and lemon juice; mix to combine; pour into the crock pot. Cover and cook on high until sauce is thickened or approximately 10 minutes.
- ✓ Turn off your crock pot. Spoon sauce over pears and serve.

Apricot Cobbler with Ice Cream

⌀ (Ready in about 8 hours | Servings 6)

INGREDIENTS
- Non-stick cooking spray (butter flavour)
- 1 cup brown sugar
- 3/4 cup yellow baking mix
- 2 eggs
- 1/2 teaspoon allspice

- 1 tablespoon orange juice
- 1/2 teaspoon ground mace
- 1 teaspoon vanilla extract
- 1/2 cup whole milk
- 2 tablespoons margarine, melted
- 10 large-sized apricots, mashed
- Ice cream, as garnish

DIRECTIONS
- Treat the inside of your crock pot with non-stick cooking spray.
- In a large-sized mixing bowl, combine the rest of the ingredients, except apricots and ice cream. Mix well to combine all ingredients.
- Fold in mashed apricots; stir well to combine.
- Cover with the lid, set the crock pot to low and slow cook for 6 to 8 hours. Serve with your favorite ice cream.

Chocolate Raisin-Peanut Candy

(Ready in about 45 minutes | Servings 15)

INGREDIENTS
- 1 ½ cup milk chocolate
- 1/2 cup white chocolate
- 1 cup raisins
- 1 cup toasted peanuts, unsalted

DIRECTIONS
- Place all of the ingredients in your crock pot.
- Slow cook about 45 minutes on low heat setting.
- Turn off your crock pot. Drop the mixture into cupcake pan liners; allow to cool completely. Enjoy!

Coconut Chocolate Brownies

(Ready in about 2 hours 30 minutes | Servings 8)

INGREDIENTS
- 2 cups water
- 1 (21-ounce) package brownie mix
- 2 eggs
- 1/4 cup butter, melted
- 1⁄2 cup chocolate
- Non-stick cooking spray
- 1 cup sugar
- 1 teaspoon allspice
- 1/2 teaspoon anise seed
- 1/2 teaspoon grated nutmeg
- 1/2 cup shredded coconut
- 1/4 cup cocoa powder

DIRECTIONS
- Add 1⁄2 cup of the water, brownie mix, the eggs, butter and chocolate to a mixing bowl; stir to mix well.
- Treat the crock pot with non-stick cooking spray. Scrape the batter into the crock pot.
- Add the rest of the ingredients together with the remaining water to a medium-sized saucepan; cook over medium-high heat. Bring to a boil; next, pour over the batter in the crock pot.
- Cover and cook on high approximately 2 ½ hours. Let your brownie cool
- slightly before slicing and serving.

Kicked up Lemon Cake

(Ready in about 4 hours | Servings 8)

INGREDIENTS
- 1 (18-ounce) lemon cake mix
- 1 cup sour cream
- 4 eggs
- 3/4 cup butter
- 1 cup milk
- 1 (3-ounce) package instant lemon pudding mix
- 1/4 teaspoon lemon extract
- 1/2 teaspoon allspice
- 1/4 teaspoon ground cloves
- 1 tablespoon butter, melted
- 1/4 cup sugar

DIRECTIONS
- Add all ingredients, except 1 tablespoon of butter and sugar, to a mixing bowl. Stir by hand in order to combine.
- Use the remaining 1 tablespoon of butter to grease the inside of your crock pot. Sprinkle the sugar evenly over the butter.
- Afterwards, carefully pour the batter into the crock pot. Cover, set the crock pot to low, and cook for 4 hours.

Old-Fashioned Butterscotch Caramel Sauce

(Ready in about 4 hours | Servings 12)

INGREDIENTS
- 2 cups fat-free half-and-half
- 1 stick butter
- 2 tablespoons fresh lemon juice
- 4 cups sugar
- 1/2 teaspoon ground cinnamon
- 1/2 teaspoon grated nutmeg
- 1/2 teaspoon ground cloves
- A pinch of sea salt

DIRECTIONS
- Add the half-and-half, butter, lemon juice, sugar, cinnamon, nutmeg, cloves and sea salt to your crock pot.
- Cover with the lid and cook on high for 1 hour.
- Then, reduce the heat to low and cook for 2 hours, stirring occasionally.
- Remove the lid and cook on low for 1 more hour or until the sauce reaches your desired thickness.

Hot Chocolate Fondue

(Ready in about 2 hours | Servings 12)

INGREDIENTS

- 2 sticks butter
- 1 cup heavy cream
- 1/2 cup corn syrup
- Pinch of salt
- 1/2 teaspoon ground cinnamon
- 1/4 teaspoon grated nutmeg
- 2 cups semisweet chocolate chips
- 1 tablespoon vanilla

DIRECTIONS
- ✓ Add the butter, heavy cream, corn syrup, salt, cinnamon and nutmeg to the crock pot.
- ✓ Cover with the lid and cook on low for 1 hour. Then, stir with a heatproof spatula, cover, and cook for another 1 hour.
- ✓ Add the chocolate chips and vanilla. Whisk until the chocolate is completely melted.

Amazing Coconut Rice Pudding

⌀ **(Ready in about 5 hours | Servings 8)**

INGREDIENTS
- 1 cup long-grain rice
- 2/3 cup sugar
- 3 ½ cups milk
- 1/3 cup shredded coconut
- 1/2 teaspoon vanilla
- 1 teaspoon ground cinnamon
- 1/2 teaspoon grated nutmeg
- 1/2 teaspoon ground cloves
- A pinch of salt
- 1 teaspoon orange rind

DIRECTIONS
- ✓ Arrange all of the ingredients in your crock pot. Stir.
- ✓ Cook on low heat setting for 5 hours.
- ✓ Serve warm or at room temperature.

Rice Pudding with Whipped Cream

⌀ **(Ready in about 3 hours | Servings 6)**

INGREDIENTS
- Non-stick cooking spray (butter flavor)
- 3 cups milk
- 3/4 cup granulated sugar
- 3/4 cup Basmati rice
- 1 teaspoon allspice
- 1/2 teaspoon ground cinnamon
- A pinch of salt
- 1/3 cup butter, melted
- Whipped cream, as garnish

DIRECTIONS
- ✓ Grease your crock pot with non-stick cooking spray.
- ✓ Rinse rice thoroughly in a colander, under cold running water. Transfer to the crock pot; add remaining ingredients, except whipped cream; stir to combine.
- ✓ Set your crock pot to high for about 3 hours, and stir once or twice during cooking period; cook until your rice has absorbed the liquid.
- ✓ Spoon the pudding into dessert bowls and top with prepared whipped cream.

Pudding with Cranberries and Bananas

⌀ **(Ready in about 5 hours | Servings 8)**

INGREDIENTS
- 1 cup rice
- 2 cups water
- 2 cups evaporated milk
- 1/3 cup sugar
- 1/2 cup dried cranberries
- A pinch of salt
- 1 vanilla bean
- 1 cinnamon sticks
- 3 bananas, sliced

DIRECTIONS
- ✓ Combine all ingredients, except bananas, in your crock pot; stir well until everything is incorporated.
- ✓ Cover and cook on low heat setting for 4 to 5 hours.
- ✓ Divide among eight dessert bowls, garnish with banana slices and enjoy.

Rice Pudding with Candied Fruit

⌀ **(Ready in about 5 hours | Servings 8)**

INGREDIENTS
- Non-stick cooking spray
- 1 cup water
- 2 cups skim milk
- 3/4 cup white rice
- 3/4 cup sugar
- 1 stick cinnamon
- 1/3 cup butter, melted
- Candied fruit, as garnish

DIRECTIONS
- ✓ Place all ingredients, except candied fruit, in your crock pot; stir well.
- ✓ Cover and cook on low approximately 5 hours.
- ✓ Garnish with candied fruit and enjoy!

Aromatic Pears and Apples

⌀ **(Ready in about 2 hours | Servings 6)**

INGREDIENTS
- 3 large-sized pears, cored, peeled and sliced
- 3 large-sized apples, cored, peeled and sliced
- 1 tablespoon fresh orange juice
- 1 cup sugar

- 1 tablespoon maple syrup
- 1 cup raisins
- 1 cinnamon stick
- A few drops of anise flavor
- 1/8 teaspoon nutmeg
- 3 tablespoons corn flour
- 4 tablespoons butter, sliced

DIRECTIONS
- ✓ Put all of the ingredients, except butter, into your crock pot; stir well to coat pear and apple slices
- ✓ Next step, place the slices of butter on top.
- ✓ Cook on high for 2 hours, stirring once. Enjoy!

Berry Dump Cake with Ice Cream

(Ready in about 3 hours | Servings 8)

INGREDIENTS
- 1 (21-ounce) can blueberry pie filling
- 1 (18 ¼-ounce) package white cake mix
- 1/2 cup butter
- 1/2 teaspoon hazelnut extract
- 1/2 cup toasted almonds, chopped

DIRECTIONS
- ✓ First of all, place blueberry pie filling in the crock pot.
- ✓ In a large-sized bowl, combine dry cake mix with butter and hazelnut extract; spread over the pie filling in the crock pot.
- ✓ Sprinkle the chopped almonds on top. Cover and cook on low for 2 to 3 hours. Serve warm with your favorite ice cream.

Ooey Gooey Chocolate Cake

(Ready in about 3 hours | Servings 8)

INGREDIENTS
- 1 (18 ¼ ounces) package chocolate cake mix
- 1 (4-ounce) package instant chocolate pudding mix
- 1 cup sour cream
- 3 large eggs, beaten
- 1/3 cup butter, melted
- 1 teaspoon hazelnut extract
- 3 cups milk
- 3/4 teaspoon ground cinnamon
- 1/4 teaspoon grated nutmeg
- 1/2 teaspoon grated ginger
- 1/2 cup chocolate cook-and-serve pudding mix
- 1/2 cup toasted peanuts, chopped
- 1 ½ cups miniature marshmallows
- 1/2 cup chocolate morsel

DIRECTIONS
- ✓ Beat cake mix, chocolate pudding mix, sour cream, eggs, butter, hazelnut extract and 1 cup of milk with an electric mixer about 2 minutes, at medium speed.
- ✓ Pour prepared batter into a lightly greased crock pot.
- ✓ In a saucepan, over medium heat, cook remaining 2 cups of milk. Stir
- ✓ often and do not boil.
- ✓ Sprinkle cinnamon, nutmeg, ginger and cook-and-serve pudding mix over your batter. Pour hot milk over pudding. Cover and cook on low about 3 hours.
- ✓ Turn off your crock pot. Sprinkle cake with toasted peanuts, miniature marshmallows, and chocolate morsels. Let stand until marshmallows are slightly melted.
- ✓ Spoon into nice dessert dishes, serve warm and enjoy!

Halloween Caramel Apples

(Ready in about 1 hour 30 minutes | Servings 8)

INGREDIENTS
- 1/4 cup water
- 2 (14-ounce) packages caramel candies
- 8 Granny Smith apples

DIRECTIONS
- ✓ Place water and caramel candies in a crock pot.
- ✓ Cover and cook on high about 1 ½ hours on high, stirring often. Remove stems from the apples and insert stick into them.
- ✓ Set the crock pot to low; dip apples into the hot caramel sauce.
- ✓ Place the apples on a greased wax paper to cool completely.

Baker Days Zucchini Cake

(Ready in about 4 hours | Servings 8)

INGREDIENTS
- 1/4 cup applesauce
- 1/4 cup margarine
- 3/4 cup sugar
- 1 large-sized egg, lightly beaten
- 1/4 cup low-fat buttermilk
- 1 ¼ cups pastry flour
- 2 tablespoons cocoa powder
- 1 teaspoon baking powder
- 1/2 teaspoon anise seed
- 1 teaspoon ground cinnamon
- A pinch of salt
- 1 cup zucchini, peeled and shredded
- 1/4 cup semisweet chocolate, coarsely chopped
- Icing sugar, as garnish

DIRECTIONS
- ✓ Beat applesauce, margarine, and sugar in a large-sized bowl until uniform and smooth.
- ✓ Stir in egg and buttermilk; then, mix in combined flour, cocoa, baking powder, anise seed, cinnamon and salt.
- ✓ Stir in zucchini and chocolate.
- ✓ Pour prepared batter into greased and floured cake pan; place cake pan on a rack in the crock pot. Cover and slow cook 3 to 4 hours.
- ✓ Transfer to a wire rack for 10 minutes in order to cool.
- ✓ Sprinkle generously with icing sugar and cut into serving-sized pieces.

Cocoa Cake with Coffee Glaze

(Ready in about 4 hours 30 minutes | Servings 12)

INGREDIENTS

- 1 ¼ cups sugar
- 1 tablespoon molasses
- 6 tablespoons butter, room temperature
- 2 medium-sized eggs
- 1 pinch of salt
- 1 cup cake flour
- 1/3 cup cocoa powder
- 1/2 teaspoon baking soda
- 1/2 teaspoon baking powder
- 1/3 cup sour cream
- 1 tablespoon instant espresso powder
- 2 tablespoons strong brewed coffee
- 3/4 cup powdered sugar
- 1 tablespoon butter, melted

DIRECTIONS

✓ In a small-sized mixing bowl, beat sugar, molasses and butter until fluffy; add eggs one at a time, and continue to beat.
✓ Add salt and combined flour, cocoa powder, baking soda and baking powder. Stir to combine. Add sour cream and instant espresso.
✓ Then, pour prepared batter into greased and floured cake pan; place pan
✓ on a rack in the crock pot.
✓ Cover and cook on high until a wooden toothpick inserted in center of cake comes out clean, or about 4 ½ hours.
✓ In the meantime, make the coffee glaze by mixing coffee, powdered sugar and melted butter.
✓ Drizzle your cake with coffee glaze and serve.

Sinfully Delicious Mocha Mousse Cake

(Ready in about 3 hours | Servings 8)

INGREDIENTS

- 3/4 cup sugar
- 1/2 cup Dutch process cocoa
- 3 tablespoons fine pastry flour
- 2 teaspoons instant espresso powder
- A pinch of salt
- 3/4 cup milk
- 1 teaspoon hazelnuts extract
- 1/2 bittersweet chocolate, coarsely chopped
- 1 whole egg
- 3 egg whites
- 1/3 cup granulated sugar
- Powdered sugar, as garnish

DIRECTIONS

✓ In a saucepan, over medium-low heat, cook sugar, Dutch process cocoa, flour, espresso powder, and salt; gradually whisk in milk and cook until the mixture is hot.
✓ Remove saucepan from the heat and add hazelnuts extract and chocolate, stirring until it is melted. Add whole egg and cool to room temperature.
✓ Beat egg whites to stiff peaks, gradually adding granulated sugar. Add egg whites to the chocolate mixture.
✓ Pour batter into greased cake pan; place on a rack in your crock pot. Place
✓ 3 layers of paper towels under the lid and cover the crock pot; cook on high about 3 hours. The cake will look moist.
✓ Sprinkle top of the cake generously with powdered sugar. Serve chilled.

Orange-Glazed Chocolate Cake

(Ready in about 4 hours | Servings 8)

INGREDIENTS

- 3/4 cup low-fat buttermilk
- 1/2 teaspoon baking soda
- 1/2 teaspoon baking powder
- 6 tablespoons butter, room temperature
- 1 teaspoon orange extract
- 1 cup granulated sugar
- 1 egg
- 1 ½ cups cake flour
- A dash of ground cinnamon
- A dash of grated nutmeg
- A pinch of salt
- 1/4 cup semisweet chocolate, melted
- 3/4 cup powdered sugar
- 1/2 cup orange juice

DIRECTIONS

✓ Mix together buttermilk, baking soda and baking powder. In a large-sized bowl, beat butter with orange extract and granulated sugar until fluffy.
✓ Then add whole egg, blending well. Stir in flour, cinnamon, nutmeg, and salt. Add egg mixture to the buttermilk mixture.
✓ Reserve about 1 ½ cups of prepared batter; add melted chocolate to
✓ remaining batter.
✓ Next, spoon batters alternately into greased and floured cake pan; you can swirl gently with a knife.
✓ Place cake pan on rack in the crock pot; cover, set the crock pot to high and cook about 4 hours.
✓ Meanwhile, make orange syrup in the following way. In a small-sized pan, heat 3 powdered sugar and orange juice, stirring frequently. Cook until sugar is dissolved.
✓ Pour orange syrup over prepared cake and allow to stand in order to cool before serving time.

Chocolate Almond Pound Cake

(Ready in about 4 hours | Servings 8)

INGREDIENTS

- 3/4 cup low-fat buttermilk
- 1 teaspoon baking powder
- 6 tablespoons margarine, melted
- 1 cup sugar
- 1 teaspoon almond extract
- 2 medium-sized eggs, lightly beaten
- 1 ½ cups all-purpose flour
- 1/2 cup almonds, chopped

- 1 teaspoon allspice
- 1/2 teaspoon grated ginger
- A pinch of salt
- 1/4 cup bittersweet chocolate, melted
- 1/2 cup powdered sugar

DIRECTIONS
- In a medium-sized bowl, combine buttermilk and baking powder.
- In another bowl, beat margarine with sugar for about 10 minutes or until fluffy. Stir in almond extract and whole eggs. Add flour, almonds, allspice, ginger, and salt. Add this mixture to the buttermilk mixture in the bowl.
- Then, reserve about 1 ½ cups of your batter; add bittersweet chocolate to remaining batter.
- Alternate batters into greased and floured cake pan; you can swirl gently with a knife.
- Place your pan on a rack in the crock pot; cover and cook about 4 hours on high. Dust the cake with powdered sugar and enjoy.

Orange Rice Pudding with Raisins

(Ready in about 3 hours | Servings 6)

INGREDIENTS
- 1/2 cup sugar
- 4 cups low-fat milk
- 2 tablespoons orange juice
- 1/2 cup rice, uncooked
- 2/3 cup raisins
- 2 teaspoons orange rind
- 1/2 teaspoon ground cloves
- Chocolate curls for garnish

DIRECTIONS
- In your crock pot, combine all of the ingredients, except chocolate curls.
- Cook on high about 3 hours, stirring occasionally.
- Spoon into the serving bowls; before serving, scatter chocolate curls on top.

Peach Hazelnut Cobbler

(Ready in about 2 hours | Servings 8)

INGREDIENTS
- 2 (21-ounce) cans peach pie filling
- 1 stick butter, melted
- 1 (18-ounce) package yellow cake mix
- 1/3 cup hazelnuts
- Whipped cream, as garnish

DIRECTIONS
- Dump peach pie filling into the crock pot.
- Combine butter with cake mix until crumbly. Evenly spread over pie filling in the crock pot.
- Sprinkle with hazelnuts.
- Cook 2 hours on high heat setting. Serve warm with whipped cream. Enjoy!

Amazing Fudge Pudding Cake

(Ready in about 2 hours | Servings 6)

INGREDIENTS
- 1 cup fine cake flour
- 1/2 cup packed brown sugar
- 6 tablespoons unsweetened cocoa powder
- 1/2 teaspoon baking soda
- 1 teaspoon baking powder
- 1/2 cup milk
- 2 tablespoons canola oil
- 1/3 cup granulated sugar
- Light whipped topping, as garnish

DIRECTIONS
- Wrap bottom of the cake pan in aluminum foil.
- In a medium-sized bowl, combine cake flour, sugar, 3 tablespoons cocoa, baking soda, and baking powder.
- Add combined milk and canola oil to the flour mixture; mix well.
- Spoon batter into greased and floured cake pan. Combine together remaining 3 tablespoons of cocoa and granulated sugar; sprinkle over batter in the cake pan.
- Place cake pan on a rack in the crock pot. Cover and cook on high about 2 hours. Serve with light whipped topping.

Warm Pudding-Style Cake

(Ready in about 6 hours | Servings 12)

INGREDIENTS
- Cooking spray
- 1 package (1-ounce) instant butterscotch pudding
- 1 package (18.25-ounces) spice cake mix
- 1 cup water
- 1 cup sour cream
- 3/4 cup canola oil
- 1 egg
- 1 teaspoon allspice
- 1 cup pineapple, crushed

DIRECTIONS
- Lightly grease a bottom and side of your crock pot with cooking spray.
- Combine remaining ingredients, except pineapple, in a bowl of an electric mixer. Mix at medium speed until everything is combined, or about 2 minutes. Add pineapple and stir to combine.
- Pour into the crock pot; cover and cook on low about 6 hours.
- Spoon warm cake onto serving platter.

Pear and Apple Oatmeal Pudding

(Ready in about 4 hours | Servings 6)

INGREDIENTS
- Non-stick cooking spray
- 3 pears, cored, peeled and diced
- 3 apples, peeled and diced

- 3 eggs
- 1/2 cup fine pastry flour
- 3/4 cup oats
- 1/3 cup powdered milk
- 1 cup sugar
- 2 teaspoons baking powder
- 1/2 teaspoon ground cinnamon
- 1 teaspoon vanilla extract

DIRECTIONS
- Lightly oil your crock pot with non-stick cooking spray.
- Arrange pears and apples in your crock pot. Then, place the rest of the ingredients.
- Mix well to combine. Cover and cook for 4 hours on low.
- Serve chilled and enjoy.

Rice Pudding with Prunes and Pistachios

(Ready in about 3 hours | Servings 18)

INGREDIENTS
- 1 tablespoon canola oil
- 1/2 cup agave nectar
- 1 cup rice
- 1/2 teaspoon anise seed
- 1 teaspoon ground allspice
- 1/2 cup dried prunes, chopped
- 8 cups soy milk, unsweetened
- 2 tablespoons pistachios, chopped

DIRECTIONS
- Treat the bottom and sides of a crock pot with canola oil.
- Then, add remaining ingredients, except pistachios.
- Cook for 3 hours on high; stir once or twice.
- Sprinkle with chopped pistachios and serve warm.

Pudding with Dried Cherries and Walnuts

(Ready in about 3 hours | Servings 18)

INGREDIENTS
- Non-stick cooking spray (butter flavor)
- 1/3 cup sugar
- 1 tablespoon honey
- 1 cup rice
- 1/2 teaspoon ground mace
- 1 teaspoon ground allspice
- 1 vanilla bean
- 1 cinnamon stick
- 1/2 cup dried cherries, chopped
- 8 cups skim milk
- 2 tablespoons walnuts, chopped

DIRECTIONS
- Oil the inside of your crock pot with cooking spray.
- Then, add remaining ingredients, except walnuts.
- Cover and slow cook for 3 hours on high, stirring once or twice.
- Sprinkle with chopped walnuts and serve warm or at room temperature.

Easiest Tapioca Pudding

(Ready in about 2 hours | Servings 6)

INGREDIENTS
- 1/4 cup small pearl tapioca
- 2 cups milk
- 1 teaspoon green tea powder
- 1/4 cup agave nectar
- 1/4 cup brown sugar
- 1 large-sized egg

DIRECTIONS
- Add all of the ingredients, except eggs, to the crock pot; then cook about
- 1 ½ hours on low.
- Whisk in the egg. Cook an additional 1/2 hour; serve warm.

Spiced Challah Pudding

(Ready in about 5 hours | Servings 10)

INGREDIENTS
- Cooking spray
- 4 cups cubed challah bread
- 1/3 cup dried cranberries
- 2 ½ cups fat-free milk
- 2 medium-sized eggs
- 1/3 cup sugar
- 1/2 teaspoon pure banana extract
- 1 teaspoon allspice
- 1/2 teaspoon ground ginger
- 1/2 teaspoon ground cloves

DIRECTIONS
- Grease a crock pot with cooking spray. Add the cubed challah bread and dried cranberries. Then, stir to combine.
- In a medium-sized bowl, whisk the rest of the ingredients.
- Pour the mixture over the cubed challah and dried cranberries in the crock pot.
- Cook covered for 5 hours on low.

Luscious Chocolate Bread Pudding

(Ready in about 5 hours | Servings 10)

INGREDIENTS
- Cooking spray
- 4 cups bread, cubed
- 2 eggs
- 2 ¼ cups fat-free evaporated milk
- 1/3 cup light brown sugar
- 1/4 cup cocoa
- 1 teaspoon ground cinnamon
- 1 teaspoon almond extract

- 1/2 cup miniature marshmallows, as garnish

DIRECTIONS
- ✓ Spray a crock pot with non-stick cooking spray. Arrange the bread cubes in the crock pot.
- ✓ In a mixing bowl, or a measuring cup, combine the rest of the ingredients, except miniature marshmallows. Pour the egg mixture over the bread cubes.
- ✓ Cook for 5 hours on low, until the bread pudding is no longer liquid. Scatter miniature marshmallows on top and serve warm or at room temperature. Enjoy!

Pudding with Raisins and Walnuts

(Ready in about 5 hours | Servings 8)

INGREDIENTS
- 1 tablespoon butter, melted
- 3 ½ cups bread, cubed
- 1/4 cup sugar
- 1 tablespoon honey
- 2 medium-sized eggs
- 1/2 cup golden raisins
- 1/2 cup ground walnuts
- 2 ¼ cups soy milk
- 1/4 cup cocoa powder

DIRECTIONS
- ✓ Treat the inside of your crock pot with melted butter. Layer the bread cubes into your crock pot.
- ✓ In a measuring cup, combine the rest of the ingredients; pour the mixture over the bread cubes in the crock pot.
- ✓ Then, cover and cook for 5 hours on low heat setting. Serve warm or at room temperature.

Favourite Apple Brown Betty

(Ready in about 2 hours 20 minutes | Servings 6)

INGREDIENTS
- 1 tablespoon margarine, melted
- 6 apples, peeled, cored and cubed
- 1 tablespoon fresh orange juice
- 1 tablespoon maple syrup
- 1/2 teaspoon grated nutmeg
- 1/4 teaspoon allspice
- 1/4 teaspoon ground mace
- 1/2 teaspoon cinnamon
- 1 ¾ cups bread cubes

DIRECTIONS
- ✓ First of all, treat the inside of the crock pot with melted margarine.
- ✓ Add the apples, orange juice, maple syrup, and spices. Stir well to combine ingredients. Cook on high approximately 2 hours.
- ✓ Preheat your oven to 250 degrees F. Spread the bread cubes on a baking sheet and bake until browned, or about 10 minutes.
- ✓ Place the toasted bread cubes over the mixture in the crock pot. Cook on high heat setting for 10 minutes longer.

Easiest Orange-Vanilla Custard

(Ready in about 8 hours | Servings 8)

INGREDIENTS
- 1/2 teaspoon orange extract
- 1 teaspoon vanilla extract
- 2 cups fat-free milk
- 5 medium-sized eggs
- 1 tablespoon cornstarch
- 1/3 cup sugar
- A pinch of kosher salt

DIRECTIONS
- ✓ Combine all ingredients in a large-sized mixing bowl. Whisk until everything is well incorporated and blended.
- ✓ Pour into your crock pot.
- ✓ Cook for 8 hours on low, until the center of your custard looks set. Serve with vanilla ice cream if desired.

Apple-Carrot Pudding Cake

(Ready in about 6 hours | Servings 8)

INGREDIENTS
- Non-stick cooking spray
- 1 ounce instant butterscotch pudding
- 1 package (18.25-ounces) carrot cake mix
- 1 cup cold water
- 1 cup sour cream
- 3/4 cup margarine, melted
- 1 egg
- 1 cup apples, chopped

DIRECTIONS
- ✓ Lightly grease the bottom and side of your crock pot with non-stick cooking spray.
- ✓ In a large-sized mixing bowl, combine the rest of the ingredients; beat with your electric mixer at medium speed until everything is well blended, or about 2 minutes.
- ✓ Replace the mixture to the crock pot; cover and cook on low 6 hours. Spoon warm pudding cake onto plates and enjoy!

Triple-Chocolate Pudding Cake

(Ready in about 6 hours | Servings 8)

INGREDIENTS
- 1 tablespoon margarine, melted
- 1 ounce instant chocolate pudding
- 1 package (18.25-ounces) chocolate fudge cake mix
- 1 cup water
- 1 cup sour cream
- 3/4 cup vegetable oil
- 1 egg
- 1 cup pineapple, crushed
- Chocolate syrup, as garnish

DIRECTIONS

- Lightly grease the bottom and side of your crock pot with non-stick cooking spray.
- In a large-sized mixing bowl, combine the rest of the ingredients, except chocolate syrup; combine with an electric mixer, at medium speed, about two minutes or until everything is well mixed.
- Transfer the mixture to the crock pot; cover with the lid and cook 6 hours on low. Spoon warm pudding cake into serving bowls and serve with chocolate syrup!

New York-Style Latte Cheesecake

(Ready in about 3 hours + chilling time | Servings 8)

INGREDIENTS

- 4 tablespoons brown sugar
- 1 ¼ cups graham cracker crumbs
- 3 tablespoons butter, melted
- 1/2 cup sugar
- 1 lb. cream cheese, crumbled
- 2 large-sized whole eggs
- 2 egg yolks
- 1/3 cup double strength coffee
- 1 tablespoon corn flour
- A pinch of salt
- 3/4 cup sour cream
- 1 teaspoon vanilla
- Chocolate shavings, for garnish

DIRECTIONS

- To make the crust: combine brown sugar, graham crumbs and butter in a springform pan; pat mixture evenly on the bottom of springform pan.
- In a large-sized bowl, beat sugar with cream cheese until light and fluffy; then, beat in eggs, egg yolks, corn flour, and salt. Stir in sour cream and vanilla; pour into prepared crust in springform pan.
- Place pan on rack in a crock pot; place 3 layers of paper towels under the lid of the crock pot; cook on high 2 to 3 hours.
- Turn off heat and let stand, covered, in the crock pot for 1 more hour. Refrigerate overnight or for 8 hours. Sprinkle with chocolate shavings and serve chilled.

Chocolate Pecan Cheesecake

(Ready in about 3 hours + chilling time | Servings 8)

INGREDIENTS

- 1/4 cup toasted pecans, ground
- 3 tablespoons honey
- 1 cup vanilla wafer cookie crumbs
- 2 tablespoons butter, melted
- 1/2 cup sugar
- 1 lb. cream cheese, crumbled
- 2 large-sized whole eggs
- 1/2 cup toasted pecans, chopped
- 1/3 cup mini chocolate morsels
- 1 tablespoon corn flour
- A pinch of salt
- 3/4 cup sour cream
- 1 teaspoon almond extract
- Cocoa powder, for garnish

DIRECTIONS

- To make the crust: combine pecans, honey, vanilla wafer cookie crumbs and butter in a springform pan; pat mixture evenly on the bottom of your springform pan.
- In a mixing bowl, combine together sugar and cream cheese; beat until fluffy and uniform.
- Beat in eggs, pecans, mini chocolate morsels, corn flour, and salt. Add sour cream and pure almond extract; pour into prepared crust.
- Place pan on a rack in your crock pot; cover with the lid and cook on high approximately 3 hours.
- Refrigerate overnight. Dust with cocoa powder and serve chilled.

Cosy Winter Morning Apple Pudding

(Ready in about 4 hours | Servings 6)

INGREDIENTS

- 4-5 large-sized apples, cored, peeled and sliced
- 1/2 cup granulated sugar
- 1/2 teaspoon grated nutmeg
- 1/2 teaspoon allspice
- 1/2 teaspoon ground mace
- 1 teaspoon ground cinnamon
- 1/4 teaspoon kosher salt
- 1 ½ tablespoons pearl tapioca
- 1 cup boiling water
- 1 lemon, juiced
- 1/2 cup walnuts, chopped

DIRECTIONS

- In a large-sized mixing bowl, combine together apple slices, sugar, nutmeg, allspice, mace, cinnamon, salt, and pearl tapioca; toss to coat apples.
- Transfer the mixture to a crock pot. In a separate bowl, combine boiling water with lemon juice. Pour over the apples in the crock pot.
- Set the cooker to high and cook 3 to 4 hours. Sprinkle with chopped walnuts. Serve warm and enjoy your winter morning!

Orange Tapioca Pudding

(Ready in about 3 hours | Servings 8)

INGREDIENTS

- 1/2 cup sugar
- 4 cups milk
- 2 teaspoons orange extract
- A pinch of salt
- 1/2 teaspoon allspice
- 1/2 cup small tapioca pearls
- 3 egg yolks
- Oranges, sectioned

DIRECTIONS

- Place sugar, milk, orange extract, salt, allspice and tapioca pearls in a crock pot. Whisk thoroughly until the sugar has dissolved.
- Turn the crock pot to high, cover and cook for 2 hours.
- In a small-sized mixing bowl, whisk the egg yolks until frothy. Pour about 1 tablespoon of the hot tapioca pudding from the crock pot into the egg yolks; mix until combined.
- Then, gradually add hot pudding to the egg yolks until you get about 2 cups of the pudding-yolk mixture.
- Slowly pour this mixture into remaining tapioca pudding in the crock pot; mix until everything is well blended, or 4 to 5 minutes.
- Slow cook for 1 more hour on low. Serve warm with oranges and enjoy.

Peanut Butter Pudding Cake

(Ready in about 2 hours | Servings 12)

INGREDIENTS

- Non-stick cooking spray
- 1/2 cup sugar
- 1 ½ cups whole wheat pastry flour
- 1 teaspoon baking powder
- 1 cup peanut butter
- 3/4 cup fat-free sour cream
- 3 tablespoons margarine, melted
- 2 tablespoons boiling water
- 3/4 cup sugar
- 6 tablespoons cocoa powder
- 2 cups boiling water
- 2 tablespoons chocolate syrup

DIRECTIONS
- At the beginning, treat the inside of a crock pot with non-stick cooking spray.
- In a mixing bowl, combine together sugar, flour, and baking powder.
- In a separate bowl, combine peanut butter, sour cream, melted margarine, and 2 tablespoons of boiling water.
- To make the batter, stir dry sugar-flour mixture into wet and creamy peanut butter mixture. Dump the batter into the greased crock pot.
- In a mixing bowl, combine 3/4 cup of sugar, cocoa, and 2 cups of boiling water. Pour cocoa mixture over batter in the crock pot.
- Set the crock pot to high and cook covered about 1 ½ hours. Let your pudding cool for 20 minutes; then drizzle with chocolate syrup before serving.

Rum Bananas Foster with Pecans

(Ready in about 2 hours | Servings 4)

INGREDIENTS

- 4 ripe bananas, sliced
- 1 cup packed light brown sugar
- 4 tablespoons margarine, melted
- 1/4 cup rum
- 1 tablespoon orange juice
- 1 teaspoon vanilla extract
- 1/2 teaspoon allspice
- 1/4 cup pecans, chopped

DIRECTIONS
- Arrange the slices of banana at the bottom of your crock pot.
- In a medium-sized mixing bowl, combine sugar, margarine, rum, orange juice, vanilla and allspice; pour over banana slices.
- Cover and cook for 2 hours on low. Scatter chopped pecans on top and serve warm.

Coconut Bananas Foster

(Ready in about 2 hours | Servings 4)

INGREDIENTS

- Non-stick cooking spray (butter flavor)
- 4 ripe bananas, halved
- 1 tablespoon maple syrup
- 1 cup granulated sugar
- 3 tablespoons butter, melted
- 1/4 cup water
- 1 teaspoon almond extract
- 1/2 teaspoon ground cinnamon
- 1/4 teaspoon ground cloves
- 1/2 teaspoon grated ginger
- 1/4 cup coconut, shredded

DIRECTIONS
- Treat the inside of your crock pot with cooking spray.
- Place bananas in the bottom of your crock pot.
- In a mixing bowl, mix together the rest of the ingredients, except coconut; pour over banana slices. Cover with the lid and cook for 2 hours on low heat setting. Sprinkle with shredded coconut and serve warm.

Amazing Rice Pudding with Cherries

(Ready in about 1 hour 30 minutes | Servings 8)

INGREDIENTS

- 1 cup white granulated sugar
- 1 cup white rice, uncooked
- 1 ½ cups water
- 2 cups evaporated milk
- 1 teaspoon ground cloves
- 1/2 teaspoon anise seed
- 1 vanilla bean
- 1 cinnamon stick
- 1 teaspoon grated nutmeg
- Canned cherries, as garnish

DIRECTIONS
- Put the sugar, rice, water, evaporated milk, cloves, anise seed, vanilla bean, cinnamon stick and grated nutmeg into a crock pot.
- Then cover with the lid; set the crock pot to low and slow cook for 1 ½ hours, stirring occasionally.
- Discard vanilla bean and cinnamon stick; garnish with cherries and serve warm.

White Chocolate and Strawberry Pie

(Ready in about 3 hours | Servings 10)

INGREDIENTS

- 21 ounces strawberry pie filling
- 1 (18.25-ounce) package cake mix
- 1/2 cup margarine, melted
- 1/2 cup white chocolate, broken into small pieces

DIRECTIONS

- Layer strawberry pie filling on the bottom of a crock pot.
- In a large-sized mixing bowl, combine the rest of the ingredients. Spread the mixture over strawberry pie filling.
- Cover with the lid and cook on low for about 3 hours.
- Scatter chocolate pieces on top and serve warm.

Baked Stuffed Apples with Currants

(Ready in about 3 hours | Servings 4)

INGREDIENTS

- 4 Jonathan apples, cored
- 1/4 cup rolled oats
- 1/4 cup Zante currants
- 2 tablespoons brown sugar
- 1/4 teaspoon ground cloves
- 1/2 teaspoon ground cinnamon
- 1/2 teaspoon grated nutmeg
- 1 tablespoon margarine
- 1/2 cup orange juice

DIRECTIONS

- Line your crock pot with a slow cooker liner. Arrange apples in prepared crock pot.
- In a medium-sized mixing bowl, combine the rest of the ingredients, except orange juice.
- Spoon oat mixture into center of each apple with a metal spatula. Pour orange juice around apples in the crock pot.
- Cover and cook for 3 hours on low heat setting. Divide baked apples among nice serving bowls and enjoy.

Halloween Party Pie Pudding

(Ready in about 4 hours | Servings 8)

INGREDIENTS

- 1 tablespoon canola oil
- 3/4 cup biscuit baking mix
- 1 cup sugar
- 1 tablespoon fresh orange juice
- 1 teaspoon ground cloves
- 1 tablespoon ground cinnamon
- 2 teaspoons ground ginger
- 3 tablespoons butter, sliced
- 1 ½ cups whole milk
- 2 large-sized eggs
- 2 cups pumpkin puree
- 1/4 cup applesauce

DIRECTIONS

- Lightly grease a crock pot with 1 tablespoon canola oil.
- Place all of the ingredients in your food processor. Pulse until creamy, uniform and smooth.
- Pour this pumpkin mixture into the greased crock pot. Heat on low for about 4 hours.
- Serve warm and enjoy your Halloween party!

Hot Blackberry Peach Cobbler

(Ready in about 3 hours | Servings 8)

INGREDIENTS

- Non-stick cooking spray
- 2 cups blackberries
- 2 cups peach, sliced
- 2 tablespoons corn flour
- 1 tablespoon maple syrup
- 1/3 cup sugar
- 1/2 teaspoon allspice
- 1/4 teaspoon ground mace
- 1/2 teaspoon ground cinnamon
- 1/2 teaspoon anise seed
- 1 (18.25-ounce) package yellow cake mix
- 1/2 cup butter, melted

DIRECTIONS

- Lightly oil your crock pot with non-stick cooking spray. Then, place combined blackberries and peaches; sprinkle with corn flour and toss to coat evenly.
- Add remaining ingredients and gently stir to combine. Cook on high about 3 hours or until bubbling.

Vanilla Strawberry Cobbler

(Ready in about 2 hours | Servings 6)

INGREDIENTS

- Vegetable cooking spray
- 1 (21-ounce) can strawberry pie filling
- 1 cup whole wheat pastry flour
- 1/4 cup sugar
- 1 teaspoon baking powder
- 1/4 cup butter, melted
- 1/2 cup milk
- 1/2 teaspoon vanilla extract
- Mixed berries, for garnish

DIRECTIONS

- Treat the inside of your crock pot with vegetable cooking spray.
- Layer the strawberry pie filling on the bottom of the crock pot.
- In a medium-sized bowl, combine the rest of the ingredients, except mixed berries. Spread the mixture evenly over the strawberry pie filling.
- Cover, and cook on high for about 2 hours. Garnish with mixed berries and enjoy!

Winter Aromatic Fruit Compote

⌛ **(Ready in about 6 hours | Servings 10)**

INGREDIENTS

- 1/3 cup dried currants
- 1/2 cup dried cherries
- 1/4 cup dried prunes
- 1/4 cup dried apricots
- 1 vanilla bean
- 1 cinnamon stick
- 2 medium-sized apples, peeled and sliced
- 1 cup medium-sized pears, peeled, cored and sliced
- 1/4 cup brown sugar
- 3/4 cup orange juice
- 1 (21-oz.) can cherry pie filling

DIRECTIONS
- ✓ Arrange all of your ingredients in the crock pot. Cover and cook on low for about 6 hours.
- ✓ Divide among small dessert dishes and serve over ice cream.

Brownies with Hazelnut Ice Cream

⌛ **(Ready in about 3 hours | Servings 6)**

INGREDIENTS

- 1 stick butter, melted
- 1 ½ cups sugar
- 2/3 cup cocoa powder, unsweetened
- 1/3 cup cake flour
- 3 eggs, beaten
- 1 teaspoon pure hazelnut extract
- 1/2 teaspoon ground cinnamon
- 1/2 teaspoon grated nutmeg
- A pinch of kosher salt
- 1/2 cup chocolate chunks
- Hazelnut ice cream, as garnish

DIRECTIONS
- ✓ Line a crock pot with a large piece of foil; generously butter the foil.
- ✓ Whisk together the melted butter, sugar, cocoa, cake flour, eggs, and hazelnut extract. Sprinkle with cinnamon, nutmeg and salt. Finally, stir in the chocolate chunks.
- ✓ Scrape the batter out into the crock pot. Cover with the lid and cook for 3 hours on low, until the cake is gooey in the center.
- ✓ Serve the cake warm with hazelnut ice cream.

Easiest Banana Bread with Almonds

⌛ **(Ready in about 3 hours | Servings 8)**

INGREDIENTS

- 1/2 cup oat bran
- 1 cup all-purpose flour
- 1/2 cup whole wheat pastry flour
- 1/4 teaspoon ground cloves
- 1/4 teaspoon ground ginger
- 1/2 cup sugar
- 1 tablespoon molasses
- 1 teaspoon baking soda
- 1/4 teaspoon salt
- 3 ripe large-sized bananas, mashed
- 3/4 stick butter, melted
- 1/4 cup Greek yogurt
- 2 large-sized eggs, beaten
- 1 ¼ cups toasted almonds, chopped
- Icing sugar, for serving

DIRECTIONS
- ✓ Add the oat bran, flours, ground cloves, ginger, sugar, molasses, baking soda, and salt to a large-sized mixing bowl. Mix until everything is well combined.
- ✓ Add the rest of the ingredients, except icing sugar, to a food processor;
- ✓ pulse until a creamy consistency is reached.
- ✓ Grease the bottom of the crock pot with cooking spray. Cover and cook on high for 3 hours. Allow to rest uncovered before serving. Dust with icing sugar and enjoy.

Sinfully Delicious Cherry Pear Compote

⌛ **(Ready in about 6 hours | Servings 8)**

INGREDIENTS

- 1/2 cup sugar
- 1 tablespoon molasses
- 1 cup water
- 1/2 cup port wine
- 1/2 cup cherries
- 1 cup dried cranberries
- 4 large pears, peeled, cored and quartered
- 1 cinnamon stick
- 1 vanilla bean
- 4 cardamom pods, crushed

DIRECTIONS
- ✓ Place all of the ingredients in your crock pot.
- ✓ Cover with the lid; set the crock pot to low and cook for 6 hours.
- ✓ Discard the cinnamon stick and vanilla bean. Serve warm or at room temperature. You can serve this amazing compote over pound cake if desired. Enjoy!

Apple and Almond Sweet Delight

⌛ **(Ready in about 4 hours | Servings 8)**

INGREDIENTS

- Non-stick spray cooking spray
- 8 medium-sized apples, cored and sliced
- 1 tablespoon lemon juice
- 4 tablespoons water
- 1/2 cup almonds, chopped
- 1/3 cup sugar

- 1/4 cup butter, melted
- 1/2 teaspoon grated nutmeg
- 1/2 teaspoon cinnamon
- Whipped cream, for serving

DIRECTIONS
- Coat the crock pot with non-stick cooking spray. Arrange the apples over the bottom of the crock pot.
- Add the rest of the ingredients to the crock pot.
- Cover and cook for 4 hours on low heat setting. Serve chilled and topped with whipped cream.

Pear Homey Crumble

(Ready in about 3 hours 40 minutes | Servings 6)

INGREDIENTS
- Non-stick cooking spray
- 1 cup cherries
- 3 red pears, sliced
- 2 tablespoons brown sugar
- 1 tablespoon honey
- 2 tablespoons unsalted butter, melted
- 1/2 cup oats
- 1/8 cup all-purpose flour
- 1/4 teaspoon ground cloves
- 1/2 teaspoon grated ginger
- 1 teaspoon cinnamon

DIRECTIONS
- Grease your crock pot with non-stick spray. Add the cherries, pears, and brown sugar. Slow cook for 3 hours on high heat setting.
- In a medium-sized bowl, combine the honey, butter, oats, flour, cloves, ginger, and cinnamon.
- Sprinkle the mixture over the fruit in the crock pot; cook on high for 40 minutes.

Vanilla-Orange Poached Pears

(Ready in about 2 hours | Servings 4)

INGREDIENTS
- 1 cinnamon stick
- 1 vanilla bean
- 4 Bosc pears, peeled
- 1 tablespoon orange juice
- 1 teaspoon orange extract
- 1 tablespoon vanilla extract
- 1 teaspoon anise seed
- 2 cups water
- Whipped cream, for serving

DIRECTIONS
- Arrange all of the ingredients, except whipped cream, in the crock pot.
- Slow cook on low until the pears are tender or about 2 hours.
- Discard cinnamon stick and vanilla bean before serving. Serve warm or at room temperature, garnished with whipped cream. Enjoy!

Apricot-Peach Crisp with Walnuts

(Ready in about 2 hours | Servings 4)

INGREDIENTS
- 6 apricots, halved
- 6 peaches, pitted and sliced
- 1 teaspoon ground cloves
- 1/2 teaspoon grated ginger
- 1 teaspoon ground cinnamon
- 1/4 cup granulated sugar
- Non-stick spray
- 3/4 cup rolled oats
- 1/2 cup whole wheat pastry flour
- 1/2 cup light brown sugar, packed
- 6 tablespoons margarine, softened
- 1 cup walnuts

DIRECTIONS
- In a bowl, place apricots and peaches. Toss with the cloves, ginger, cinnamon, and sugar.
- Treat your crock pot with non-stick cooking spray. Arrange the apricots and peaches over the bottom of the crock pot.
- To make the topping, place remaining ingredients, except walnuts in a food processor. Pulse a couple of time until the mixture is uniform. Then, rough chop the walnuts; add to the prepared topping
- Spread the topping evenly over the apricots and peaches in the crock pot.
- Cover and cook on high for 2 hours. Serve warm or chilled with a dollop of whipped cream.

Old-Fashioned Apple Butter

(Ready in about 16 hours | Servings 24)

INGREDIENTS
- 5 pounds apples, peeled, cored, and sliced
- 1 cup maple syrup
- 1 teaspoon lemon rind
- 2 tablespoons apple cider vinegar
- 1/2 teaspoon ground cloves
- 1 teaspoons ground cinnamon
- 1/2 teaspoon ground mace
- 1 teaspoon vanilla extract

DIRECTIONS
- Layer apples in your crock pot.
- Add remaining ingredients and stir to coat apples.
- Cover and cook on low approximately 16 hours.
- Transfer to the pint jars and keep in the refrigerator for up to 6 weeks.

Ice Cream with Drunken Figs

(Ready in about 4 hours | Servings 10)

INGREDIENTS
- 2 pounds dried figs, halved

- 1 cinnamon stick
- 1 vanilla bean
- 2 cups sugar
- 1 tablespoon molasses
- 3 cups water
- 1 cup cognac
- Ice cream of choice

DIRECTIONS
- Combine all of the ingredients, except cognac and ice cream, in your crock pot.
- Cover and heat on a low setting about 4 hours, stirring once.
- Turn the crock pot off and add the cognac. Let stand approximately 1 hour, discard cinnamon stick and vanilla bean; serve over ice cream.

Cocktail Party Prunes in Brandy

(Ready in about 4 hours | Servings 12)

INGREDIENTS
- 2 pounds dried prunes
- 2 cups sugar
- 1 cinnamon stick
- 1/4 teaspoon grated nutmeg
- 1/2 teaspoon vanilla extract
- 3 cups water
- 1 cup brandy

DIRECTIONS
- Combine the prunes, sugar, cinnamon stick, grated nutmeg, vanilla and water in the crock pot.
- Cover with the lid and heat on a low setting for about 4 hours, stirring once.
- Add the brandy; allow to rest at least 1 hour. Serve on plain white cake if desired.

Vanilla Ice Cream with Steamy Fruit

(Ready in about 4 hours | Servings 12)

INGREDIENTS
- Rind of 1/2 lemon
- 1 ½ cups dried figs, halved
- 1 ½ cups dried apples, halved
- 1/2 cup dried prunes
- 1/2 cup dried cherries
- 2 cups grape juice
- 3 tablespoons maple syrup
- 1 teaspoon ground cinnamon
- 2 teaspoons ground anise seed

DIRECTIONS
- Arrange all of the ingredients in your crock pot.
- Cover and cook 3 to 4 hours on low heat setting.
- Serve over vanilla ice cream.

Delicious Father's Day Dessert

(Ready in about 3 hours | Servings 8)

INGREDIENTS
- 10 peaches, pitted and quartered
- 1 cup light brown sugar, packed
- 1/2 cup water
- 4 sprigs fresh mint
- 1 stick cinnamon
- 1 vanilla bean
- 1 cup brandy

DIRECTIONS
- Layer the peaches in the crock pot. Sprinkle with light brown sugar; pour in water. Add the rest of the ingredients, except the brandy.
- Cover with the lid; set the crock pot to low and cook about 3 hours.
- Add the brandy; allow to sit at least 1 hour. You can serve with a fluffy white cake.

Summer Fruit Treat

(Ready in about 4 hours | Servings 10)

INGREDIENTS
- 10 bananas, peeled and halved
- 1 cup dried apricots
- 1 cup fresh cranberries
- 1/4 cup light brown sugar
- 1/2 cup water

DIRECTIONS
- Arrange the bananas, apricots and cranberries in the crock pot.
- Sprinkle with the sugar and pour in the water.
- Cover with the lid and slow cook about 4 hours.

Bananas and Rhubarb in Aromatic Sauce

(Ready in about 4 hours | Servings 10)

INGREDIENTS
- 6 overripe bananas, halved
- 8 stalks rhubarb, cut into 2-inch pieces
- 1/2 teaspoon allspice
- 1 teaspoon fresh mint leaves, coarsely chopped
- 1/2 cup sugar
- 1/4 cup water
- 1/4 cup orange juice
- 1/4 cup butter, softened

DIRECTIONS
- Lightly coat the inside of the crock pot with melted butter.
- Arrange bananas and rhubarb on the bottom of the crock pot. Then, sprinkle with allspice, mint leaves and sugar.
- Pour in water and orange juice. Dot the bananas and rhubarb with the softened butter.
- Cover with the lid; heat on a low setting for about 4 hours. Enjoy with butter cookies if desired.

Spiced Caramel Popcorn

⌀ (Ready in about 1 hour | Servings 12)

INGREDIENTS

- 2 tablespoons butter, cubed
- 1 ½ cups sugar
- 1/8 teaspoon ground allspice
- 1 teaspoon garam masala
- 8 quarts air-popped popcorn

DIRECTIONS

✓ Combine butter, sugar, allspice, and garam masala.
✓ Slow cook for 1 hour on high, stirring occasionally.
✓ Drizzle over air-popped popcorn; toss to combine. Enjoy!

Chocolate and Sweet Potato Cake

⌀ (Ready in about 3 hours | Servings 16)

INGREDIENTS

- 1/2 cup butter
- 2 ¼ cups sugar
- 3 medium-sized eggs
- 1 cup sweet potatoes, mashed
- 1 ½ cups whole-wheat pastry flour
- 1 teaspoon baking soda
- 1 teaspoon baking powder
- A pinch of salt
- 1 teaspoon ground cinnamon
- 1/2 teaspoon ground nutmeg
- 1/2 teaspoon cream of tartar
- 1/2 cup milk
- 2 ounces bittersweet chocolate, grated

DIRECTIONS

✓ In a mixing bowl, beat the butter and sugar; then, add eggs and sweet potatoes; mix until everything is well blended.
✓ Next step, sift the whole-wheat pastry flour with the baking soda, baking powder, salt, cinnamon, nutmeg, and cream of tartar.
✓ Add the dry flour mixture to the potato mixture; gradually add milk and stir to combine. Add grated chocolate and stir again.
✓ Transfer the batter to 2 greased and floured loaf pans; loosely cover with a foil.
✓ Place on a trivet in the crock pot; then, you have to pour water around the base of the trivet.
✓ Cover with the lid and cook for about 3 hours.

Soft and Fudgy Chocolate-Coconut Cake

⌀ (Ready in about 3 hours | Servings 16)

INGREDIENTS

- 2 cups sugar
- 1/4 cup butter
- 1/4 cup coconut oil
- 2 large-sized eggs
- 1 cup potatoes, mashed
- 1/4 cup coconut flakes
- 1 ½ cups fine cake flour
- 2 teaspoons baking powder
- 1/2 teaspoon ground mace
- 1/4 teaspoon ground cinnamon
- 1/4 cup apple juice
- 1/4 cup milk
- 2 ounces semi sweet chocolate, grated

DIRECTIONS

✓ In a mixing bowl, vigorously mix sugar, butter and coconut oil; next, add eggs and mashed potatoes; mix to combine well.
✓ In another bowl, combine coconut flakes, cake flour, baking powder, ground mace, and ground cinnamon.
✓ Combine the dry coconut mixture and egg-potato mixture; gradually add apple juice and milk. Stir in chocolate and mix well to combine.
✓ Transfer prepared batter to a floured baking pan; loosely cover with a suitable lid.
✓ Then, place on a trivet in the crock pot; pour water around the base of the trivet.
✓ Cook for about 3 hours. Serve at room temperature and enjoy!

Avocado Cake with Dried Fruits

⌀ (Ready in about 3 hours | Servings 16)

INGREDIENTS

- 3/4 cup butter
- 1/2 cup honey
- 1 cup sugar
- 3 medium-sized eggs
- 2 avocados, pitted and diced
- 2 ¼ cups cake flour
- 3/4 teaspoon cinnamon
- 1 teaspoon allspice
- 1/2 teaspoon baking powder
- 1 teaspoons baking soda
- 3/4 cup buttermilk
- 1/4 cup figs
- 3/4 cup hazelnuts, chopped
- 3/4 cup dates
- Powdered sugar, for serving

DIRECTIONS

✓ In a mixing bowl, cream the butter, honey, and sugar. Beat in eggs and mix well to combine. Stir in avocado.
✓ Next, add cake flour, cinnamon, allspice, baking powder, baking soda, and buttermilk.
✓ Fold in the figs, hazelnuts, and dates. Transfer prepared batter to a floured baking pan; loosely cover with a suitable lid.
✓ Then, place on a trivet in the crock pot; pour water around the base of the trivet. Cook for 2 to 3 hours. Dust with powdered sugar and serve!

Apple-Lemon Pound Cake

⌀ (Ready in about 3 hours | Servings 18)

INGREDIENTS

- 1 cup light brown sugar
- 3/4 cup butter
- 1 cup milk
- 8 eggs, lightly beaten
- 3 cups whole-wheat pastry flour
- 1/2 teaspoon baking soda
- 1 tablespoon baking powder
- 4 apples
- 3/4 teaspoon ground cinnamon
- 1 teaspoon vanilla extract
- 1 tablespoon lemon zest
- 1 teaspoon fresh lemon juice

DIRECTIONS

- In a mixing bowl, cream the brown sugar and butter by hand; add milk and eggs.
- Sift the whole-wheat pastry flour with baking soda and baking powder; add to the butter mixture.
- Add the rest of the ingredients. Then, fill two greased loaf pans with the prepared batter. Loosely cover with the lid.
- Place on a rack in the crock pot. Cover, set the crock pot to high, and cook 2 to 3 hours.
- Serve with lemon sherbet if desired.

Favorite Lemony Cheesecake

(Ready in about 3 hours | Servings 12)

INGREDIENTS

- 2 eggs
- 1/4 cup sugar
- 1 package (9-ounce) yellow cake mix
- 2 tablespoons butter, room temperature
- 2 ounces cream cheese, room temperature
- 1/2 teaspoon ground mace
- 1/2 teaspoon allspice
- 1/2 teaspoon vanilla extract
- 2 tablespoons flour
- 1 tablespoon lemon rind
- A pinch of salt
- 1/2 cup powdered sugar
- 1 tablespoon lemon zest
- 3 teaspoons lemon juice

DIRECTIONS

- In a mixing bowl, combine eggs, sugar, yellow cake mix, egg, and butter; reserve 1 cup of the dough.
- Pat remaining dough in bottom of floured and greased springform pan. Bake at 350 degrees F in preheated oven for about 10 minutes.
- In a separate mixing bowl, mix together cream cheese, ground mace,
- allspice, vanilla extract, flour, lemon rind, and salt.
- Pour into springform pan; then, spread reserved dough over the top. Place pan on a rack in your crock pot. Cover and cook on high approximately 3 hours.
- In the meantime, make the lemon glaze by mixing together powdered sugar, lemon zest, and lemon juice.
- Drizzle the cake with the lemon glaze; enjoy!

Apple and Coconut Crisp

(Ready in about 3 hours | Servings 8)

INGREDIENTS

- 4 large Granny Smith apples, peeled, cored and sliced
- 1/2 cup coconut flakes
- 1/3 cup plus 1 tablespoon all-purpose flour
- 1/4 cup brown sugar
- 2 tablespoons maple syrup
- 1/2 cup ice cream topping
- 1/2 cup quick rolled oats
- 2 tablespoons butter

DIRECTIONS

- In a baking dish, combine apples, coconut flakes, 1 tablespoon flour, 1/3 cup brown sugar, and maple syrup. Add the ice cream topping.
- Combine together rolled oats and butter. Mix well to combine and add to the baking dish.
- Place the baking dish into the crock pot, cover and cook on high setting for 2 to 3 hours.

Apple Compote with Cranberries

(Ready in about 6 hours | Servings 6)

INGREDIENTS

- 6 apples such as pink lady, peeled, cored and sliced
- 1 cup fresh cranberries
- 1 teaspoon vanilla extract
- a dash of cinnamon
- 1 cup brown sugar
- 1 teaspoon orange zest
- 1/2 cups water
- 1/4 cups white wine

DIRECTIONS

- Place apple slices and cranberries in a crock pot. Add vanilla and cinnamon. Stir in brown sugar and orange zest.
- Pour in water and wine and stir to combine ingredients. Cover, cook on low-heat setting for 5 to 6 hours. Serve at room temperature.

Apple Pudding with Dates

(Ready in about 4 hours | Servings 6)

INGREDIENTS

- 5 apples, peeled, cored and diced
- 1/2 cup sugar
- 1/2 cup dates, chopped
- 1/2 cup toasted almonds, chopped
- 2 tablespoons flour
- 1 teaspoon baking powder
- 1 teaspoon salt
- 1/4 teaspoon nutmeg
- 2 tablespoons melted butter

- 1 egg, beaten

DIRECTIONS
- ✓ In the crock pot, place apples, sugar, dates and almonds. Stir well to combine ingredients.
- ✓ In a large mixing bowl, mix together flour, baking powder, salt and nutmeg and stir into the crock pot.
- ✓ Drizzle melted butter and beaten egg. Turn the crock pot on low setting and cook for 3 to 4 hours. Serve warm.

Fruit and Nuts Cheesecake

(Ready in about 3 hours | Servings 12)

INGREDIENTS
- 1 cup cracker crumbs
- 1/2 teaspoon Allspice
- 2 tablespoons brown sugar
- 3 tablespoons butter, melted
- 1/4 cup walnuts, finely chopped
- 16 ounces cream cheese
- 1/4 cup brown sugar
- 1/2 cup granulated white sugar
- 2 large eggs
- 3 tablespoons whipping cream
- 1 tablespoon cornstarch
- 1 teaspoon almond extract
- 1/4 teaspoon grated nutmeg
- 1 granny smith apple, thinly sliced
- 1 teaspoon Allspice
- 1/4 cup powdered sugar
- 1 tablespoon walnuts, finely chopped

DIRECTIONS
- ✓ To make the crust: Combine together cracker crumbs, Allspice, brown
- ✓ sugar, butter, and walnuts. Stir well to combine. Place the batter in a baking dish.
- ✓ To make the filling: Beat sugars with cream cheese until creamy, by using an electric mixer. Beat in eggs, whipping cream, cornstarch, almond extract, and nutmeg.
- ✓ Pour this mixture over the crust.
- ✓ To make topping: combine together apple slices with Allspice, sugar and walnuts. Spread topping evenly over the top of cheesecake.
- ✓ Place the cheesecake on a rack in the crock pot. Cover and cook on high for 2 to 3
- ✓ hours. Serve chilled.

Candied Bananas with Coconut

(Ready in about 2 hours | Servings 6)

INGREDIENTS
- 6 bananas, peeled
- 1/2 cup coconut flakes
- 1/2 teaspoon Allspice
- 1/2 cup dark corn syrup
- 1/4 cup butter, melted
- 1 tablespoon lemon zest
- 1/4 cup lemon juice

DIRECTIONS
- ✓ In the crock pot, place bananas and coconut flakes. Sprinkle the Allspice.
- ✓ In a medium mixing bowl, mix together corn syrup, butter, lemon zest, and lemon juice. Pour this mixture in the crock pot.
- ✓ Cover and cook on low-heat setting for 1 to 2 hours.

Caramel and Nuts Cake

(Ready in about 4 hours | Servings 10)

INGREDIENTS
- 16 ounces refrigerator biscuits
- 1/4 cup margarine, melted
- 1/2 cup sugar
- 1/4 cup mixed almonds and hazelnuts, chopped
- 1 teaspoon cinnamon

DIRECTIONS
- ✓ Combine together sugar, nuts and cinnamon. Mix well to combine. Dip biscuits in melted margarine, then dip in sugar and nuts mixture.
- ✓ Place in a cake pan.
- ✓ Cook on high setting for 3 to 4 hours.

Caramel Rum Fondue

(Ready in about 1 hour 30 minutes | Servings 12)

INGREDIENTS
- 7 ounces caramels
- 1/3 cup heavy whipping cream
- 1/4 cup miniature marshmallows
- 2 teaspoons rum

DIRECTIONS
- ✓ In the crock pot, combine caramels and whipping cream.
- ✓ Cover and cook on low setting for 1 hour. Stir in miniature marshmallows and rum.
- ✓ Cover and continue cooking 30 minutes more. Let the Fondue cool. Serve with pound cake and fresh fruits.

Old-fashioned Rice Pudding

(Ready in about 3 hours | Servings 6)

INGREDIENTS
- 3/4 cup white rice
- 3 cups milk
- 3/4 cup granulated sugar
- 1 teaspoon ground cinnamon
- 1/4 teaspoon grated nutmeg
- 1/4 teaspoon salt
- 1 teaspoon vanilla extract
- 1/3 cup butter, melted

DIRECTIONS

- Rinse rice under running water. Lightly grease the crock pot with melted butter.
- Add remaining ingredients and stir to combine well.
- Cover and cook on high setting for 2 to 3 hours. Serve with heavy whipped cream.

Caramel Apples

(Ready in about 3 hours | Servings 6)

INGREDIENTS

- 2 packages (14-ounces) bags caramels
- 1/4 cup water
- 8 apples such as 'pink lady'

DIRECTIONS

- In the crock pot, combine caramels and water. Cover and cook on high for
- 1 hour, stirring constantly.
- Insert stick into stem end of each apple. Reduce the crock pot to low.
- Dip apples into prepared caramel sauce. Serve chilled.

Apple Dessert with Ice Cream

(Ready in about 5 hours | Servings 10)

INGREDIENTS

- 10 apples, peeled and cored
- 1 cup sugar
- 1/2 cup water
- 1 tablespoon cinnamon
- 1 teaspoon vanilla extract

DIRECTIONS

- Slice the apples into very small chunks. Place them in a crock pot.
- In a mixing bowl mix sugar, water, cinnamon and vanilla extract.
- Pour this mixture over apples. Set the crock pot on low and cook for 4 to
- 5 hours.
- Serve warm with Ice Cream.

Homemade Apple Butter

(Ready in about 9 hours | Servings 32)

INGREDIENTS

- 4 lbs. apples, cored, sliced and unpeeled
- 1 1/3 cups packed sugar
- 1 cup sweet cider
- juice of one fresh lemon
- 1 tablespoon lemon zest
- 1 tablespoon grated ginger
- 1 teaspoon cinnamon
- 1 teaspoon vanilla extract

DIRECTIONS

- Place apples, sugar, sweet cider, lemon juice and lemon zest in the crock pot. Cover and cook on low-heat setting 9 to 10 hours or overnight. Cook until the apples are very tender.
- Add ginger, cinnamon, and vanilla extract. If apple butter has too much liquid, increase heat to high, uncover and cook until the butter is thickened. Put the mash through a purée sieve.
- Transfer to an airtight container and refrigerate. Serve with pancakes, waffles, oatmeal, biscuits and so on.

Bread Pudding with Dates

(Ready in about 2 hours | Servings 6)

INGREDIENTS

- 2 eggs, slightly beaten
- 2 ¼ cup milk
- 1/2 teaspoon Allspice
- 1/2 teaspoon salt
- 2 cups bread cubes
- 1/2 cup brown sugar
- 1/2 cup chopped dates

DIRECTIONS

- In medium bowl, combine eggs, milk, Allspice, salt, bread cubes, sugar, and dates. Pour into a baking dish.
- Place metal rack in bottom of your crock pot. Add 1/2 cup hot water in the crock pot. Place the baking dish on the metal rack. Cover, cook on high for about 2 hours.
- Serve chilled or warm.

Caramel Apples with Ice Cream

(Ready in about 6 hours | Servings 7)

INGREDIENTS

- 2 apples
- 1/2 cup apple juice
- 7 ounces unwrapped caramel candy squares
- 1/4 teaspoon ground cardamom
- 1/2 teaspoon ground cinnamon
- 1/3 cup cream-style peanut butter
- 1 qt vanilla ice cream

DIRECTIONS

- Peel, core, and slice each apple into wedges. Reserve.
- In the crock pot, combine apple juice, caramel candies, cardamom and cinnamon. Gradually add the peanut butter. Stir to combine ingredients.
- Add apples to the crock pot, cover and cook on low about 6 hours.
- Serve over vanilla ice cream.

Easy Strawberry Cobbler

(Ready in about 3 hours | Servings 12)

INGREDIENTS

- 1 (16-ounces) can strawberry pie filling
- 1 package cake mix for 1 layer cake

- 1 egg
- 3 tablespoons evaporated milk
- 1/2 teaspoon Allspice
- 1/2 cup almonds, chopped

DIRECTIONS
- Lightly grease the inside of the crock pot. Place the strawberry pie filling in the crock pot and cook on high setting for 30 minutes.
- Combine together the remaining ingredients and stir to combine well. Spoon this mixture onto the hot pie filling.
- Cover, decrease the heat to low and cook for 2 to 3 hours.

Creamy Lemon Cake

(Ready in about 3 hours | Servings 16)

INGREDIENTS
- 1 package Lemon-Poppy seed Bread Mix
- 1 egg
- 8 ounces light sour cream
- 1/2 cup water
- 1 tablespoon butter
- 3/4 cup water
- 1/2 cup sugar
- juice from 1 fresh lemon

DIRECTIONS
- Combine together Lemon-Poppy seed Bread Mix, lightly beaten egg, sour cream and water.
- Spread batter in the greased crock pot.
- Heat a medium saucepan and cook butter, water, sugar, and lemon juice. Bring to a boil.
- Pour this hot mixture over the batter in the crock pot. Cover and cook on high for 2 to 2 ½ hours. Let it stand for 30 minutes and cool enough to handle.

Tea Time Peach Butter

(Ready in about 4 hours | Servings 16)

INGREDIENTS
- 6 cup unsweetened peaches
- 3 cup white sugar
- 1 ½ cup apricot nectar
- 2 teaspoons orange juice
- 1 teaspoon vanilla extract
- Pancakes or waffles for serving

DIRECTIONS
- Blend all ingredients in an electric blender or a food processor. Transfer this blended mixture to the crock pot.
- Set the crock pot on high and cook for 4 hours. Serve over pancakes or waffles.

Cocoa Pudding Cake with Cream

(Ready in about 4 hours | Servings 16)

INGREDIENTS
- 1 cup flour
- 1/2 cup sugar
- 1/2 cup pecans, chopped
- 1/4 cup cocoa, unsweetened
- 1 teaspoon baking powder
- 1 teaspoon baking soda
- 1/2 teaspoon salt
- 1/2 cup whole milk
- 1/4 teaspoon cardamom
- 1 teaspoon almond extract
- 1/4 cup oil
- 1 cup boiling water
- 1/2 cup chocolate syrup
- Whipped cream for garnish

DIRECTIONS
- Sift first 7 ingredients and place this mixture in a lightly buttered cup mold.
- Stir in milk, cardamom, almond extract, and oil. Then add boiling water and chocolate syrup. Pour this wet mixture over dry mixture.
- Add 2 cups warm water to the crock pot.
- Place cup mold in the crock pot and cover it with 4 layers of paper towels.
- Cover and cook on high setting for 3 to 4 hours.
- Serve warm with whipped cream.

Pumpkin Pie Pudding

(Ready in about 7 hours | Servings 16)

INGREDIENTS
- 1 can (15-ounces) solid pack pumpkin
- 1 can (12-ounces) evaporated milk
- 3/4 cup Splenda
- 1/2 cup Bisquick baking mix
- 2 eggs, beaten
- 2 tablespoons butter, melted
- 1 tablespoon pumpkin pie spice
- 1 tablespoon vanilla extract

DIRECTIONS
- In a large mixing bowl, combine together all ingredients. Butter the inside of your crock pot.
- Replace this mixture to the crock pot. Put the lid and cook on low for 6 to
- 7 hours.
- Top with whipped cream (optional) and serve at room temperature.

Crock Pot Chocolate Treats

(Ready in about 8 hours | Servings 4)

INGREDIENTS
- 1 package chocolate cake mix
- 1 pint sour cream
- 1 package instant chocolate pudding
- 6 ounces chocolate chips
- 1 teaspoon grated ginger

- 1 teaspoon cardamom
- 3/4 cup oil
- 4 eggs
- 1 cup water
- Chopped and toasted almonds for garnish

DIRECTIONS
- Grease your crock pot with butter.
- Combine together all ingredients and pour into the crock pot.
- Cook on low for 7 to 8 hours. Scatter the almonds on top and serve.

Crock Pot Peach Treats

(Ready in about 3 hours | Servings 8)

INGREDIENTS
- 2 cups frozen peaches, with juice
- 1 tablespoon cornstarch
- 1 teaspoon almond extract
- 1/4 cup brown sugar
- 1 teaspoon Allspice
- 9 ounce Jiffy white cake mix
- 4 tablespoons margarine, melted
- Ice Cream for garnish.

DIRECTIONS
- Slice the peaches. Lightly butter the inside of your crock pot.
- Place sliced peaches in the bottom of the crock pot.
- Add cornstarch, almond extract, sugar Allspice, cake mix, and margarine. Put a lid and cook on high about 3 hours.
- Serve with Ice Cream on top.

Triple Chocolate Dessert

(Ready in about 3 hours | Servings 8)

INGREDIENTS
- 1 (18 ½ ounces) package chocolate cake mix
- 1 (4 ounce) package instant chocolate pudding mix
- 3/4 cup oil
- 1 cup water
- 4 eggs
- 1 (6-ounce) bag chocolate chips
- 1 pint sour cream
- Vanilla Ice Cream (optional)

DIRECTIONS
- Oil the crock pot with non-stick cooking spray.
- Combine together all ingredients and transfer them to the crock pot.
- Set the crock pot on low, cover and cook dessert for 5 to 6 hours. Serve with vanilla ice cream.

Cinnamon Raisin Biscuit

(Ready in about 3 hours | Servings 10)

INGREDIENTS

- 10 slices cinnamon-raisin bread
- 1 (14-ounce) can sweetened condensed milk
- 1/2 cup sugar
- 1 cup water
- 1 teaspoon almond extract
- 1/2 cup almonds, chopped
- 4 eggs, beaten

DIRECTIONS
- Grease the crock pot with butter. Arrange the slices of cinnamon-raisin bread in the crock pot.
- Combine together milk, sugar, water, almond extract, almonds, and eggs and mix to combine. Pour this mixture over bread cubes.
- Put a lid and cook on low for 2 to 3 hours.

Mashed Peach Dessert

(Ready in about 6 hours | Servings 6)

INGREDIENTS
- 1 cup sugar
- 1 tablespoon butter
- 12 ounces can evaporated milk
- 3/4 cup Bisquick baking mix
- 2 eggs
- 2 cups peaches, mashed
- 1 tablespoon almond extract
- 3/4 teaspoon cardamom

DIRECTIONS
- Lightly grease a crock pot. Combine together sugar, butter, milk, Bisquick, eggs, peaches, almond extract, and cardamom.
- Replace this mixture in the crock pot.
- Cook on low for 6 to 8 hours.

Blueberry Dump Cake

(Ready in about 3 hours | Servings 4)

INGREDIENTS
- 1 (21-ounce) can blueberry pie filling
- 1 (18 ¼ ounce) package yellow cake mix
- 1/2 cup butter
- 1 teaspoon Allspice
- 1/2 cup walnuts, chopped
- Ice Cream

DIRECTIONS
- Put pie blueberry filling in the crock pot.
- Combine together yellow cake mix, butter, and Allspice. Spread this mixture over the pie blueberry filling.
- Sprinkle the walnuts on top.
- Cover, set on low and cook for 2 to 3 hours. Serve warm in bowls. Top with your favorite ice cream.

Creamy Caramel Pie

(Ready in about 7 hours | Servings 12)

INGREDIENTS

- 1 graham cracker crust
- 2 (14-ounces) cans sweetened condensed milk
- 8 ounces whipped topping
- 1 (1 ½ ounce) caramel candies, chopped

DIRECTIONS

- ✓ Pour condensed milk in the crock pot.
- ✓ Set the crock pot on low, put the lid and cook 6 to 7 hours.
- ✓ Pour cooked milk over the graham cracker crust. Let it cool.
- ✓ Top with whipped topping and sprinkle chopped caramel candies. Serve chilled.

Rice Pudding With Coconut

(Ready in about 2 hours | Servings 6)

INGREDIENTS

- 5 cups basmati rice, cooked
- 1/2 cup dates, chopped
- 1/4 cup unbleached white sugar
- 1/4 cup brown sugar
- 1/4 teaspoon ground cardamom
- 1/4 teaspoon ground cinnamon
- 1 (15-ounce) can coconut milk
- 1 1/3 cups milk
- 1 egg
- 1 teaspoon vanilla extract
- Coconut flakes for garnish

DIRECTIONS

- ✓ Butter the crock pot.
- ✓ Combine together the rice, the dried fruit, sugars, cardamom, and cinnamon in the crock pot.
- ✓ Heat a wide saucepan and cook together the coconut milk, milk, and egg. Add vanilla extract and stir well to combine. Pour in the crock pot.
- ✓ Cook on low about 2 hours. Sprinkle coconut flakes and serve at room temperature.

Chocolate Cookies with Almonds

(Ready in about 4 hours | Servings 8)

INGREDIENTS

- 1 cup margarine, softened
- 2 eggs
- 1/2 cup brown sugar
- 1/2 cup granulated sugar
- 1 tablespoon vanilla extract
- 2 cups all-purpose flour
- 1/2 teaspoon baking powder
- 1/4 teaspoon salt
- 1 cup chocolate chips
- 1 cup almonds, coarsely chopped

DIRECTIONS

- ✓ Lightly grease the crock pot and line with a wax paper.
- ✓ In a medium mixing bowl, mix together margarine, eggs, sugars and vanilla. In another bowl, mix flour, baking powder and salt.
- ✓ Combine both mixtures together.
- ✓ Stir in chocolate chips and almonds.
- ✓ Spread the batter evenly in the crock pot. Cover and cook on low setting about 4 hours.

Rhubarb with Ginger and Orange

(Ready in about 6 hours | Servings 8)

INGREDIENTS

- 2 lbs rhubarb
- 1/2 cup water
- 1/4 cup dessert wine
- 8 tablespoons caster sugar
- 1 teaspoon Allspice
- 2 oranges, shredded
- 2 tablespoons grated ginger
- Ice Cream for serving

DIRECTIONS

- ✓ Combine together all ingredients in the crock pot.
- ✓ Set the crock pot on low heat and cook for 4 to 6 hours.
- ✓ Serve chilled with your favorite Ice Cream.

Chocolate Cake with Dried Fruits

(Ready in about 7 hours | Servings 10)

INGREDIENTS

- 1 (18-ounces) package chocolate cake mix
- 4 ounces instant chocolate pudding mix
- 2 cups sour cream
- 4 eggs
- 1 cup water
- 3/4 cup butter, melted
- 1 cup dark chocolate chips
- Whipped cream for decorating
- Dried fruits for decorating

DIRECTIONS

- ✓ In a large bowl, combine together chocolate cake mix, chocolate pudding mix, sour cream, eggs, water nad butter. Mix to combine all ingredients.
- ✓ Stir in dark chocolate chips.
- ✓ Slightly grease the crock pot. Pour this mixture into your crock pot.
- ✓ Cover and cook on low for 6 to 7 hours.
- ✓ Divide among serving bowls and serve with whipped cream and dried fruits.

Spiced Pears in Wine

(Ready in about 8 hours | Servings 8)

INGREDIENTS

- 8 medium pears, peeled and cored
- 2 cups red wine

- 1/2 cup sugar
- 1 teaspoon grated ginger
- 1 cinnamon stick, broken in half
- 1 star anise pod, broken in half
- 4-5 cloves
- 1 tablespoon orange zest

DIRECTIONS
- Slice the pears in halves lengthwise. Place them in the crock pot.
- Add the wine, the sugar, ginger, cinnamon stick, anise pod, cloves, and orange zest.
- Cover, turn the crock pot to low and cook for 6 to 8 hours.
- Serve chilled.

Chocolate and Peach Bread Pudding

(Ready in about 4 hours | Servings 8)

INGREDIENTS
- Non-stick cooking spray (butter flavor)
- 5 ½ cups whole-wheat bread, cubed
- 1 ½ cups canned peaches, drained
- 1 ½ cups reduced-fat evaporated milk
- 1/4 cups honey
- 1 cup brown sugar
- 1 cup cocoa
- 2 eggs
- A pinch of salt
- 1/4 teaspoon allspice
- 1/2 teaspoon grated ginger

DIRECTIONS
- Oil the inside of a crock pot with cooking spray. Toss bread cubes and peaches in the crock pot.
- In a wide and deep saucepan, heat the milk, honey, sugar, and cocoa over medium heat, stirring frequently, or about 5 minutes.
- Whisk 1/2 of the mixture into the eggs; sprinkle with salt, allspice, and grated ginger; add egg mixture back to saucepan. Pour this mixture over bread and peaches in the crock pot.
- Cover and cook on high about 4 hours or until pudding is set. Serve warm and enjoy!

Rice Pudding with Raspberries

(Ready in about 2 hours | Servings 6)

INGREDIENTS
- 1/2 cup sugar
- 2 cups milk
- 3/4 cup converted long-grain rice, cooked
- 2 cups water
- Salt, to taste
- 1 teaspoon ground cinnamon
- 1/2 teaspoon grated nutmeg
- 1/2 teaspoon ground cloves
- 2 tablespoons cornstarch
- 1 cup raspberries, for serving

DIRECTIONS
- In a deep saucepan, heat sugar and milk over medium-high heat; add to the crock pot.
- Add remaining ingredients, except raspberries; cook about 2 hours on high.
- Serve garnished with raspberries; sprinkle with granulated sugar if desired. Enjoy this refreshing slow cooker treat!

Rice Pudding with Blueberries and Almonds

(Ready in about 2 hours | Servings 6)

INGREDIENTS
- 2 cups water
- 1 cup milk
- 1 cup buttermilk
- 1/2 cup sugar
- 1 tablespoon molasses
- 3/4 cup brown rice, cooked
- 1/2 teaspoon ground cinnamon
- 1/2 teaspoon ground cloves
- 1/2 cup slivered almonds
- 1 cup blueberries, for serving

DIRECTIONS
- Put all of the ingredients, except almonds and raspberries, into your crock pot.
- Slow cook 1 ½ to 2 hours on high heat setting.
- Serve garnished with slivered almonds and blueberries. Enjoy!

Pears with Bittersweet Chocolate Syrup

(Ready in about 2 hours | Servings 4)

INGREDIENTS
- 4 pears, peeled
- 1/4 cup brown sugar
- 1 cup water
- 1 ½ cups apple juice
- 1/4 cup sugar
- 1/2 cup cocoa powder
- 1/3 cup milk
- 2 tablespoons butter
- 1/2 teaspoon ground cinnamon
- 1 teaspoon vanilla extract
- 1 ½ cups frozen vanilla yogurt

DIRECTIONS
- Place pears upright in the crock pot.
- In a saucepan, heat brown sugar, water and apple juice over medium-high heat; bring to a boil and then pour over pears in the crock pot.
- Cover and slow cook on high about 2 hours; drain.
- Meanwhile, prepare the chocolate sauce. Combine together sugar and cocoa in a small-sized saucepan; gradually pour in the milk.

- ✓ Add butter and cook over medium heat until boiling; then, turn down the heat and cook 3 to 4 minutes or until the sauce is slightly thickened. Add cinnamon and vanilla extract.
- ✓ Serve chilled with a scoop of frozen vanilla yogurt. Drizzle with prepared chocolate syrup and enjoy!

Printed in Great Britain
by Amazon